T0396018

LOVE, DESIRE AND TRANSCENDENCE
IN FRENCH LITERATURE

*Pour
ma Cindy
qui sait tout*

Love, Desire and Transcendence in French Literature

Deciphering Eros

PAUL GIFFORD
University of St Andrews, UK

ASHGATE

Published by
Ashgate Publishing Limited
Gower House
Croft Road
Aldershot
Hampshire GU11 3HR
England

Ashgate Publishing Company
Suite 420
101 Cherry Street
Burlington, VT 05401-4405
USA

Ashgate website: http://www.ashgate.com

British Library Cataloguing in Publication Data
Gifford, Paul
    Love, desire and transcendence in French literature : deciphering Eros
    1. French literature – 20th century – History and criticism 2. Erotic literature, French 3.
    Love in literature 4. Desire in literature 5. Sex in literature 6. Transcendence
    (Philosophy) in literature
    I. Title
    840.9'353'009045

Library of Congress Cataloging-in-Publication Data
Gifford, Paul.
  Love, desire and transcendence in French literature : deciphering Eros / Paul Gifford.
      p. cm.
  Includes bibliographical references and index.
   ISBN 0-7546-5269-6 (alk. paper)
  1. French literature—History and criticism. 2. Love in literature. I. Title.

  PQ145.1.L6G54 2006
  840.9'3543—dc22

2005010843

ISBN-10: 0 7546 5269 6

Printed and bound in Great Britain by MPG Books Ltd, Bodmin, Cornwall

Contents

Acknowledgements

I am grateful to the Arts and Humanities Research Board (UK), which granted me a Research Award indispensable in the preparation of this book, and to the Carnegie Trust (Scotland), which subsidised the cost of its production.

My lively thanks go to colleagues and friends who were kind enough to read, and offer valuable advice on, various chapters or parts of this book: Dr Kirsteen Anderson, Dr Gavin Bowd, abbé Yves Denis, Prof. Maurice Montabrut, Prof. Judith Robinson-Valéry and Dr Marion Schmid. My special thanks are due to Dr Toby Garfitt, who was brave enough to read and advise on the entirety of the manuscript. Remaining deficiencies are of course entirely mine.

My daughter Fiona designed the splendidly symbolic jacket cover.

Author's Note on
Translation of Quoted Material

Ideally, all French material quoted would have been presented in the French original along with English translations. The extent of such material in this text-based study, together with the large number of authors studied, would, however, have made for an impossibly lengthy book. The original French has therefore been retained only in the case of poetry. For the benefit of French specialists, all source references refer to editions of the original French text. For usable English translations of the French works studied, please see the Bibliography. All English translations of quoted material are the author's own.

Introduction

Qui déchiffrera l'énigme de cette folie?

'Who will decipher the enigma of this madness? Such frenzy was not necessary to the propagation of a species.'[1] Thus Paul Valéry, musing in 1921 on the extraordinary power of erotico-romantic passion, as experienced seismically within himself, to remind the rational intellect that, for all its dreams of mastery, it has yet to come to terms with the deeper places of human subjectivity – or to understand 'life'.

This book follows just this sense of a confounding enigma felt to lie at the very heart of what it is to be human. Valéry is by no means an isolated case: at the centre of many of the most creative writers of twentieth-century France has been the same insistently highlighted and irradiating question mark. Many refer to the agent of confusion, as Freud himself came to do, by the Greek word 'Eros'. Inherited from Plato, this ancient term signals the mysterious dynamic of deficit, appetite and aspiration which engages our vital energies in both sexual love and in the higher,'spiritual' forms of amorous realisation (such as artistic creation or the philosopher's love of wisdom and truth). More ordinarily, it is what we call – with the illusion of knowledgeable familiarity – 'Desire'.

In many ways, Desire, together with its reflective decipherments and its creative reconfigurings, can be seen as the mastermotif of a vast range of twentieth-century thought and writing. It is the one anthropological category which indubitably survives the modern rejection of metaphysics (including, most notably, Plato's) and the massive retreat of Western culture (particularly within Western Europe and specifically France) from traditional religious belief. Desire is posited and required by all the leading twentieth-century paradigms of secular self-understanding: by Nietzsche's message of an immanent human self-transcendence predicated on 'the death of God', but equally by Darwinian evolutionary theory and by Marx's analysis of capitalist alienation and class struggle. Most fundamentally, of course, it is the single hidden explicator of the individual and social psyche designated by Freud and the post-Freudians under the name of *libido*: that is, the capital of psychosomatic energy derived out of sexuality, subterraneously suffusing and dynamising all the acts and products of the mind. (The memory of the term 'eros' in our own times rarely goes back beyond Freud, so that contemporary usage – quite misleadingly, as we shall see – tends to make 'eros' a dignifying, pseudo-poetic synonym for Freudian *libido*.)

'Desire' thus bids fair to become the ultimate referent, tracked in its seemingly infinite metamorphoses by all the human sciences. It answers the twentieth century's larger negativities: cosmic loneliness, moral horror, ethical uncertainty, mortality and war (so Freud rediscovers 'Eros' during the First World War, as a life-principle answering 'Thanatos'). It is the value invoked and affirmed by all the 'revolutions' felt to mark twentieth-century progress: the social revolution, the media revolution, the consumer revolution, the bio-technological revolution and, of course, the sexual revolution. What other principle of value is available around which to re-invent a human cultural space? From the Surrealists to the theorists of libidinal economies such as Marcuse, championed by the Paris students of May 1968, movements of 'libido liberation' have identified in this word the magic cipher of individual and collective rebeginnings.

This status as defining anthropological principle, omnicompetent explicator and ultimate value has been seen by many sensitive observers of our culture to be increasingly problematic and unsatisfactory. It means that we inhabit in confusion an obsessively eroticised, single-chamber cultural mindsphere:

> Desire is now described as the cosmological principle of our secular age. Our *natura naturans*: it moves the stars in their courses, plumps the hazel shells, causes tumescence in mammalian organs and, thanks to its inexhaustible capacity for displacement and sublimation, it is the vitalising agent in art, science, religion, business, economics, international relations. Under earlier metaphysical dispensations, desire had many names; it was love, lust, appetite, gluttony, cupidity, concupiscence, covetousness, ambition; it was need, urge, impulse; it was hankering, longing, yearning, yen. The names of desire changed as its objects changed, and desires directed towards objects of a supra-terrestrial kind were distinguished by a special nomenclature from mere instinctual agitations. Nowadays, this untidy multitude of forces is often perceived as a single force, and the welter of names is often casually condensed into a single name.[2]

The best short definition of desire as construed by the late twentieth century might well be: omni-valent libidinal pleasure principle, explaining all, itself inexplicable; prime mover, god – or at least Godot ...

Nor is semantic inflation and confusion the most problematic feature of the 'age of Desire'. Together with this over-estimate of accredited effects, and this blurred vision of unitary meaning, has frequently gone a *diminished and reductive* perception of the phenomenon to be observed. It is as if we see less and less clearly what Eros actually is and does as our mental perceiving becomes more and more subject to the persuasion of 'eros-fever'. As the French proverb has it, 'By night, all cats are grey.' Academic critical discourse itself often illustrates the problem:

> Historically, erotic literature has been dominated by male writers. Feminist critics have argued its central motifs of voyeurism, sadomasochism, incest and violence to women's bodies are governed by the unconscious fantasies and prejudices of a patriarchal sociocultural order. The focus throughout this book is on how these [female French] writers deal with erotic language and rhetoric, their treatment of traditional themes of eroticism, and their vision of the female body and women's sexual pleasure.[3]

Here are reproduced many of the axioms generating a vast part of what has been thought, said and written at the latter end of the twentieth century on the subjects of love and desire. 'The erotic' is specified as synonymous, purely and simply, with whatever excites sexual arousal. Its metadiscourse of reference is that of Freudian *libido*, complete with disguises and complications; and *libido* is seen to begin and end in pleasure or *jouissance*. The drama of desire so defined is to have suffered alienation at the hands of a repressive sociocultural regulation. This has occluded its psychological roots and deformed its expression (here, its expression within what we have been conditioned to regard as a specifically male genre of 'erotic writing'). The academic critic is called on to denounce and correct these aberrations; there is an agenda of sexual politics to be pursued.

Lifting the veil, righting the record, liberating and empowering, ensuring that 'eros' speaks correctly, with the voice of the century: this is the essential thrust of nine out of ten of the proliferating studies, whether in French or in English, devoted in the last twenty or thirty years to the obsessively pursued themes of 'love and desire' (usually, in fact, *desire*: the status and meaning of the other term remaining entirely problematic). No quarrel is pursued here with these objectives (and I have nothing against 'women's erotic writing'). When the cultural history of love and desire in the Western tradition is viewed as a whole, it seems clear enough that the pursuit of them will have provided, reactively, a natural and necessary moment. Yet to restore the frame of reference provided by the larger historico-cultural picture is also to perceive in the approach just outlined the severest disabilities.

There is a failure to do justice to the real diversity, subtlety and complexity of the treatment offered in the greatest creative literature and thought of the century. With the honourable exception of a few of its very ablest exponents, 'desire-theory' roller-presses into its own likeness authentic literary voices which aspire to escape the gravity of approximate and common speech; it knows in advance what they should be saying, or else it finds its own image by interrogating minor writers and genres. We are given at best a philosophically restricted and thoroughly predictable hermeneutics, operating within a triangle of intellectual influences demarcated, broadly speaking, by Nietzsche, Freudo-Lacanian theory and Marxism (or at least Hegelianism), often further specified in reference and in tenor by the particular agendas of this or that form of sexual politics. Valéry's sense of significant enigma, existential mystery and anthropological challenge is simply evacuated; there is no poetry, no deepening of thought, no enhancement of reflection or of life. Taken in its collective affirmation, the late-twentieth-century moment of 'liberated', agenda-driven, pan-sexual theory may well come to be seen as having brought a formidable *diminishment* of a perennial and crucially important human theme.

The present study seeks to stand back and to contribute something to a new and more strategic recognition: a recognition acknowledging contemporary desire-theory and profiting on occasion from it, but unbound from its generic limitations. It proposes a series of free-standing, but interlinked and progressive, readings which trace the attempts at 'deciphering Eros' made by ten French writers of the twentieth century. These textual and author-based studies are preceded and introduced by five literary-historical essays, designed to open up once more the 'perennial problematics' of the themes treated and to display the deeper logic of twentieth-century decipherments.

All these chapters refer to the connection between the experienced enigma of
Eros and the narrativising, self-modelling, inventive-expressive act of the creative
writer; and all are 'readings'. I have sought, that is, to group together some of the
most significant texts of the century on love and desire, drawn from all types of
literary and theoretical writing, and to be maximally attentive to singular textual
voices, particular adventures, personally deciphered spiritual itineraries. In point of
interpretation, the term 'readings' implies a willingness to treat the topic in the form
of a supple-jointed, open enquiry, as a 'universe of relativity', centring on a
significantly highlighted question mark: what are we to make of the confounding
enigma of Eros, steadily questioned and envisaged as a whole? The reward for
consenting to be 'mere' readers, and of listening carefully, is, in the best hypothesis,
that we come to hear something of the deeper or stranger notes and to apprehend the
larger patterns that come to self-cognisance through the writing of them. It is hoped
that the book conceived in this form will be able to capture something of the
consequent, substantial and far-reaching reflection on the themes of love, desire and
transcendence that runs through French literature of the last century.

My study proceeds genetically. It follows, that is, the way in which Eros comes
to be recognised and modelled within the intellectual and literary tradition of France
and of Western culture generally. Of the fifteen chapters, no fewer than five relate to
cultural sources and origins, and to modern recognitions of antecedence (the fifteenth
shows this same perspective exactly replicated in Julia Kristeva's original exegesis
of love in the West). There is no better way of unlearning our modern confusion of
Platonic 'Eros' with Freudian libido – or, for that matter, with the cute Cupid on
Valentine cards – than actually reading Plato; no better way of seeing what might be
meant by 'love' than reading the Song of Songs; no more central an introduction to
the problematics of 'transcendence' than comparing *The Symposium* with the Book
of Genesis.

Careful attention to cultural inheritance allows the ten twentieth-century French
writers studied to be seen as variations on a series of common themes, each within
their own acknowledged field of reference, thus mapping out a recognisable cultural
landscape and disengaging the larger issues of a twentieth-century cultural crisis.
The grouping of texts and writers in six 'series' is designed to facilitate just such a
perception of larger patterns. The brief preliminary 'mappings' offered by way of
introducing each series of my chosen 'readings' offer a helpful basic guide to a more
local context of insertion (literary-historical, socio-political or hermeneutical).

A second, related, aim of this book is to recover a *holistic* approach to the
phenomenon of Eros itself. In Plato, and for almost all centuries save the one just
closed, Eros is emphatically *not* a mere synonym for *mobilised and irradiating
sexuality*, nor even for *erotico-romantic passion projected out of sexuality*. It implies
inseparably the triad of themes specified in my title: 'love, desire and transcendence'.

To put matters in an excessively simple preliminary form: *desire* is an appetitive
and unitive energy, realised at various levels of body, mind and spirit; *love* is the
complex or 'enriched' relational form which this energy can assume in human beings;

and *transcendence* is the carrying intentionality (or 'movement' or 'pull') that is felt to *reach out beyond* the subject of love and of desire, determining all sublimations and metamorphoses and seeking a larger wholeness of being. It connotes a 'vertical' dimension and refers to what all previous centuries would, without embarrassment, have called 'the life of the spirit'. (It is, of course, this latter function – rather than sexuality – that has become suspect in modern usage, in consequence of our own reaction against philosophic dualism, idealism, spiritualism and moralism.) The significance of the word 'Eros', however, is that it holds these distinct and distinguishable threads together in a single, complex human reality; it is, in this sense, an inhibitor of unilateral, partial or simplistic readings.

The second term of my triad is even more notoriously elusive. 'Love' is continuous with, but distinguishable from, 'desire'. Desire of itself is indeterminate and produces successive and multiple 'object cathexes' (to borrow Freudian terminology).[4] By contrast, desire fixated in love produces a qualitative change, and a transformation of extreme human significance, since it can unite durably and profoundly, at all levels of personality, two human subjects; this produces a new micro-community; which in turn has the double potential both to cause the relation to evolve and deepen and to generate new biological life. The relationship between desire and love is thus, broadly speaking, the difference between a dynamic energy and the relational application which, transforming that principle, gives it a richer developmental realisation.

What has my third term 'transcendence' to do with love and desire? If this word is interpreted metaphysically (as in the expression 'whatever is outside and beyond the world') or as a factor extraneous to the other two terms (as in the 'transcendent function' of algebra), the answer is: not very much – at least, not much that is proximate to most twentieth-century minds. But etymology and usage perfectly well allow (and the usage of French writers positively imposes) a somewhat weaker meaning which is directly pertinent. *Transcendere* (Lat.) is to rise (as in the cognate 'ascend'), passing over and beyond (*trans*). To 'transcend' is, etymologically, to exceed, excel or outstrip; thus, to be lifted beyond a given or average state, condition or level of being. This is indeed the heart of the matter: exactly what the 'exaltation' of love ('love-glory', 'the sublimity of this state', to borrow two further expressions from Valéry) actually feels like. And, as we have already noted, the relational community of self and other thus formed also opens onto higher developmental forms and effects.

We can therefore say of *desire* that it is 'transcending' (it wants more than it has; it reaches out beyond itself). We can also say that desire is a *principle of transcendence* in human beings (we exceed or excel because we desire, and reach out for some 'greater thing'). We can equally say: 'love *transcends* desire' – that is, there is more to it; it represents an added value in respect of some human potential, a 'more and other' in some obscure scale of being.

The major sense of this slippery term will be clear enough to anyone who follows the notion of *sublimation* as developed by Freud: that is, the notion of an – in principle – unconscious transposition of instinctual drives onto a higher plane of realisation.

Freud's 'aetiology' (causal logic) of this process (involving repression, displacement and compensatory re-emergence of the sex-drive) may or may not prove to be a reductive decipherment philosophically. Yet what the concept of sublimation points us towards in a more elementary way, and what is usually retained by the common mind of the century (including writers and theorists) is a *superabundant energy* clearing from below (hence 'exceeding' and 'excelling') its utilitarian – i.e. sexual and genital – function. Libido, in Freud, raises the column of personal psychic development and ultimately, at the level of the social collective, the whole flowering-and-fruiting tree of culture and civilisation.[5] Freud appears to be describing under this name an operative *dynamic of transcendence* within the 'normal' psyche, which he is ultimately obliged to describe as a 'life-force' – and which – following Plato (albeit problematically) – he does indeed come to call 'Eros'.

Though the most difficult to observe and the most theoretically elusive of the three points of the triangle, the function of 'transcendence' is in many ways the key to the decipherment of the other two. The twentieth century, as we shall see, is very fundamentally the century of the *crisis of transcendence*; that is, of the loss of the spiritualist-idealist 'other world' in which, for Plato – and all centuries after him, save only the one just closed – the intentionality of Desire itself had found its *telos*, its referent and its principle of explanation. In our century, Eros 'collapses' into a unidimensional figure: it reintegrates the horizontal plane and the 'single horizon' (Valéry's term) of a 'here-and-now' devoid of any immanent Depth or transcendent Elsewhere. The unidimensional modern sense of 'the erotic' comes into being at this point; with important consequential effects also for 'love'. Yet it does so under the sign of enigma: of something now devoid of any acknowledged, extrinsic key – a jigsaw-puzzle without a pattern-picture, an 'Other' without a pattern-face.

What is the meaning of this *power of excess*, of this dynamic and ever-unsatisfied *deficit* or *aspiration* or *relational potential* called 'desire' which indubitably traverses the mental and spiritual flesh of the observable human subject – and which has no very adequate explanation in biological or evolutionary or psychoanalytical or any other rationally intelligible system? Can it be – but then *how* is it? – transformed into love, re-projected as love? Do we in fact *know* what we mean by 'love'? This is the exposed nerve of so much of twentieth-century sensibility and thought: in function of the *culture-crisis* of that century, by reason of its *essentially reflexive bent and vocation*; by virtue of its attempted rebeginnings out of the brute fact of metaphysically bracketed *instinctually-based, biological desire-drives*. The exposed nerve has long echoes in the imaginative writers of the century; and it is the question which explains the sub-title of my book.

Just how love, desire and transcendence may still hold together, in which patterns, and with what overall decipherment of Sense, is the object of fascinated and problematising concern to modern writers. Love and desire represent, as we shall see, a stubborn 'remainder' (or *reminder*?) of transcendence, less easily to be evacuated from the mind that creates than from the mind of third-person science and of critical theory.

Deprived of conceptual form, of ontological grounding and *a priori* of any religious significance, Eros nevertheless remains the only trace left of the 'lost object of desire' (Lacan's term). It is the – enigmatic, obsessively grasped and gropingly followed – leading thread of human subject identity.

Notes

1 P. Valéry, *Cahiers* (Paris: CNRS, 1957–61), Vol. VII, p. 36.
2 M. Bowie, *Proust, Freud, Lacan* (Cambridge: CUP, 1987), p. 2.
3 Publisher's presentation of Alex Hughes & Kate Ince (eds.), *French Erotic Fiction: Women's Desiring Writing, 1880–1990* (New York: Berg, 1996).
4 Cathexis is defined as an accumulation of mental energy on some particular idea, memory, line of thought or action. It effects the 'hook-up' of libido to mental object.
5 See S. Freud, *Civilisation and its Discontents*: 'Sublimation of instinct is an especially conspicuous feature of cultural development; it is what makes it possible for higher psychical activities, scientific, artistic or ideological, to play such an important part in civilised life ... sublimation is a vicissitude which has been forced upon the instincts entirely by civilisation' (*The Standard Edition of the Complete Psychological Works of Sigmund Freud*, London: Hogarth Press and the Institute of Psycho-Analysis, 1953–66), Vol. 21 (1957), p. 97.

Origins, Recognitions

Chapter 1

Plato's *Symposium:*
The Transcending Enigma of Eros

'I know that I need a teacher. So tell me the cause of this and all other phenomena connected with love.'[1] Socrates' invitation to Diotima sounds thoroughly contemporary; and so, in important respects, it is. The *Symposium* is the first philosophic and literary text to take the full measure of its theme. To this day, Western culture has never ceased to explore it in an indefinite series of fugal variations; and the figure of erotic love it sketches is, in many ways, co-natural to the reflective mind in any age. It is a good place to start, both as a locus of cultural beginnings and as the reference point of modern self-recognitions.

The conversational drinking party imagined in Plato's text mingles alcohol and ideas in a way not unknown in modern cafés or campus bars. If the conversation is purposeful and searching, the atmosphere is convivial and frequently burlesque. The play of ideas is open, tolerant and relativistic, the participants turning around their agreed theme, each offering in turn his particular *ad hoc* insights before Socrates, modestly, and in part at second hand, attempts what ancient Greeks and modern intellectuals alike mean by 'critical theory' or *theoreia*: that is, a view from the One (or 'overview') integrating the best insights arrived at separately from within different discourses (we hear from a lover of boys, a lover of moral excellence, a physician, a comic dramatist and a poet). Socrates' attempt does not pass, then or now, without a secret absolutism of the rational mind, which has its sociologically conditioned power-relations; but here at least, the relativistic play of ideas returns reassuringly to play, as the assembly dissolves at length into drunkenness, only Socrates remaining awake and upright.

There are no taboos. The ambiance is, comfortably, that of homoerotic relationships; questions of the socio-cultural regulation of sexual preference and of personal morality are, indeed, raised, but lightly so, and without contention. One speaker invokes the 'principles of love which in human life issue in virtuous and god-fearing behaviour' (188e); but in this domain, as in others, the Greek gods have no concern or title to be scrupulous. The single ethical imperative, one fully consistent moreover with the natural tendency of desire in refined beings, will be the mastery of the highest potential for love innate in the erotic impulse itself. For the rest, diverse sexual orientations find justifying expression in the myth of the Androgyne.

* * *

In this semi-humorous fantasy, attributed by Plato to the comic poet Aristophanes, human beings are presented as separated halves of original wholes which were once doubly endowed with organs of generation facing in either direction (rather like paired individuals joined cylindrically, back-to-back). Of these, there were 'in the beginning' three prototypes, sexually differentiated as male, female and hermaphrodite (190b–191c). Sexual appetite and attraction are thereby accounted for in three morally equivalent forms which we might today gloss as gay, lesbian and heterosexual. Aristophanes' classification explicates the primordially bi-sexual prototype (ancestor of heterosexuals) rather more pejoratively than the two forms of homosexuality distinguished, since it is seen to explain male lovers-of-women, adulterers and licentious females.

Drawing out the logic of his myth, Aristophanes envisages a pre-sexual Golden Age, and an original 'fall' in which Zeus bisected the original, spherical bi-individuals, in order to neutralise their excess of erotic vigour and punish their presumption. Sexuality intervenes later. It begins, somewhat as an afterthought, when Zeus, out of compassion for the now mutilated creatures, shifts around the genital apparatus of the severed halves, thus permitting frontal embraces. It appears, on this account, less fundamental in the scheme of things than the yearning for the 'other half', viewed as the essence of love. (Freud misses this key point: he sees in the myth an attempt by Plato to 'trace the origin of an instinct to a need to restore an earlier state of things'.[2] In fact, it is not sexual instinct as such, but 'love', of which *sex is a derived and subsequent reality*, that in Plato demands this restoration.) Erotic love, has suffered a primordial prejudice; which neatly, if mythically, explains its present (re)-unitive tension. In this sense, love is 'simply the name for the desire and the pursuit of the whole' (192e).

The long echoes this myth has had in Western culture (and in the authors of the present study) indicate that Plato has here hit on a perennially recognisable paradigm. Our loves are diversely determined by gender and sexual orientation; what we desire and seek in loving is to transcend our singular, individual identities; the compulsion to transcend them implies some enigmatic woundedness, and some obscure reminiscence of wholeness. Inspired by a profounder sense of significant enigma, and with greater expenditure of intellectual means, Socrates will agree that what love actually seeks, in and through the contingent beloved, is an *integrity of being, allusively apprehended*: this myth already pre-sketches the philosopher's theory to come. In doing so, it suggests how immediate to common experience and how co-natural to the mind of the self-aware subject of desire is Plato's thinking. His genius, we observe, lies in formulating in the picture-language of myth, but then in explicating as rational dialectic, whatever is implied in a *natural psychopoetics of love and desire*.

What is most immediately 'given' about erotic love is that it constitutes a practical, universally available experience of *transcendence*. To love is to be carried outside, above and beyond the self. It is a life-enhancing exaltation, capable of producing fruits of courage, self-sacrifice (179c) and creativity: 'Anyone love touches becomes a poet. Love excels in any kind of artistic creation' (196b). In this same vein, the lover is spoken of as inspired or possessed; in which respect, he comes nearer than does the beloved to being 'divine'; and loving rather than being loved is blessed (180e). Agathon even extols the benevolent disposition and beneficent effects of human loves in tones that appear to prefigure from afar St Paul's celebrated hymn to charity in the First Letter to the Corinthians (1 Cor. 13: 1–13):

> It is love who empties us of the spirit of estrangement and fills us with the spirit of kinship; whose gift is the gift of good-will and never of ill-will. He is easily entreated and of great kindness; loveliest and best of all leaders of song, whom it behoves every man to follow singing his praise, and bearing his part in that melody wherewith he casts a spell over the minds of all gods and all men. (197d)

On the other hand, Pausanias recognises the ravages of the 'inordinate love' which French writers will come to know as *amour-passion*; this is comparable, he says, to epidemics and cosmic disorders (187c–188e). Generator of the highest aesthetic and moral virtues, but carrying also the greatest attendant risks, love is thus a hugely significant human phenomenon. Plato's business will be to account for its complexity and range, and to assume its 'transcendent' potential ethically, as a 'good' pursued in the name of enlightened, rationally discerning self-interest.

Clearly, not all loves are of equal status and value. Beside the common Aphrodite of carnal appetite, Pausanias evokes a nobler goddess, an Aphrodite tutelary to the spiritual and 'divine' longings in man (180e). The presence in us of higher and lower forms of Eros, manifesting an anthropological duality of spirit and flesh, will be the insistent leitmotif of all the opinions contributed and a major axis of Plato's theory.

All speakers recognise that desire seeks more than sensual gratification; and that love is more than a purely animal appetite. Even its intense delight is beyond mere physical enjoyment. 'It is clear that the soul of each has some other longing which it cannot express, but can only surmise and obscurely hint at' (192e). This longing is an ever-present energy, questing and fusional: the hope that the lover should 'melt into his beloved, that henceforth they should be one being instead of two' (192e). Hephaestus has 'welded together the lovers so that, instead of two, you shall be one flesh; as long as you live you shall live a common life, and when you die, you shall suffer a common death, and be still one not two, even in the next world'. Love, indeed, 'gives us a sure hope that if we conduct ourselves well in the sight of heaven, he will hereafter make us blessed and happy by restoring us to our former state and healing our wounds' (193e). In the common perception of the interlocutors of the *Symposium*, in short, the transcendent dynamic of Eros contains what all Romantic lovers ever declare: namely, intimations of immortality.

For Plato, clearly, 'this thing is bigger than both of us'. Pausanias declares it to be a cosmic principle, energising and all-pervasive, a *natura naturans* before and beyond man. It 'has many other spheres of action, the bodies of all animals for example, and plants which grow in the earth; in fact love is a great and wonderful god and embraces the worlds of gods and men alike' (186a). Is erotic love not a tendency imprinted in the nature of everything that exists? Nobody in the dialogue objects to this view; and the specific epistemological and ontological formulation Socrates will bring to it constitutes the crux of Plato's legacy. We in turn may note the intrinsic tendency of Plato's natural psychopoetics of love and desire, moulding itself to common experience, to posit a *metaphysical* transcendence in its own immanently experienced image and likeness.

* * *

Opinions and viewpoints having been offered, it belongs to Socrates, master dialectician and abstractor of essences, to offer a unitary account. The immensely influential theory he sketches in the second half of the *Symposium* is preferential and prescriptive, as much as it is descriptive, since it is presented as pointing to a way of life to be followed by the noblest love of all, the love of wisdom, or 'philosophy'. (This may give many moderns pause: not only is erotic love, when fully itself, *not* reducible to sex; it is disciplined, morally sighted and ushers in the quest for truth.)

Socrates' intervention takes the curious presentational form of a reported debate, rehearsing a series of insights supposedly revealed to him by the hierophant or prophetess Diotima of Mantinea. (The staging of ideas in the form of Chinese boxes is already heralded in the framing of the entire dialogue as a witness report.) Significantly, Diotima expresses herself in the language of the mystery religions, particularly in describing the ascent of the soul from the sensible to the eternal world. Commentators have speculated on the recourse to this *other*, authorising, viewpoint. Is it a dramatically appropriate device for confessing ideas which are Plato's own, having become so precisely in dialogue with the mystery religions, rather than those of his master and declared spokesman, the historical Socrates? Or does it represent on Plato's part a manner of intellectual distancing, given that he is here dealing with subjects such as love, the fate of the soul and the ordering of reality itself, about which no dialectically established certainty is possible? Should contemporary feminism rejoice, as Luce Irigaray forcefully argues,[3] at this 'veiled', but decisive, incursion of a feminine viewpoint into the otherwise masculinist and homoerotic world of the *Symposium*? The only – ambiguous – indication in the dialogue itself lies in Socrates' relationship to Diotima, who speaks as sage to pupil, doubting if the philosopher will be able to follow her all the way in the mystical reaches of her revelation to him. At all events, the inner enigma or mystery of Eros is highlighted as something 'other', known to reason only as a form of 'transcendental' insight mediated from outside the sphere of dialectical reason, through a feminine voice.

Yet feminine intuition is also resolved into discursive reason. Socrates, for his part, declares himself interested in 'what love invariably is' (205e). He recognises, that is, the inadequacy of isolating one particular kind of love and appropriating to it a name which properly belongs to the entire set of its very diverse manifestations (204d). He addresses, in fact, the question of the essential nature of love-and-desire, and will accept as an account of the generic concept (or 'universal') nothing less. The answer, as he shows in dialogue with those who have previously spoken, is not to be found in the *subjective experience of loving*, which exhibits only a common form: that of negativity or lack, a need for the possession of something which is experienced in the mode of privation, as – in both senses of the word –'wanting'.

Nor can it be found in the infinite variety of *proximate objects* on which, in practice, human loves and desires become fixed, but only in the *common aim or relational movement* which traverses them all like a permanently allusive reference to an ultimate Object. This common relational *telos* is reflected and expressed obliquely in all proximate objects of desire, but itself transcends them all.

It is this allusively transcending *Other-relatedness* which, ultimately – yet also, as we shall see, very problematically – makes the *Symposium* a theory of *love* as well as of *desire*. Plato, like Freud and many other thinkers, envisages humankind as basically desire-driven and acquisitive: appetitively in search of whatever will satisfy the entire set of needs, aspirations and yearnings whose satisfaction will procure 'happiness'. Today we might perhaps be inclined to reserve the word 'desire' for the dynamic deficit which drives the needy subject, and 'love' for the appreciative and benevolent tendency aroused by, and responding to, the object of desire. The distinguishing feature of *love*, in relation to *desire*, is perhaps, in elementary terms, that it adjusts the former perception relationally to the latter, acknowledging an Other not simply as the complement adjectival to desire, the thing necessary and required to satisfy its self-related appetitive or acquisitive tendency, but as having *prior reality* and *independent value*. We do – or at least, as a legacy of Judaeo-Christian culture, can – understand that loving something is, in this sense, not the same as desiring it, whatever ground, support or accompaniment love may find in desire, and whatever actual desires (for the company of the beloved, for sexual intimacy, for her/his welfare, etc.) are generated by love. It is, however, noteworthy that the Greek word ἔρωζ as used in the *Symposium* most often does duty for both aspects of the subject – object relationship. Plato is not concerned to distinguish between them – the Symposium is *about* 'erotic love'; even if the doublet 'love and desire' (φιλια και ἔρωζ) or 'desire and love' (ἔρωζ και φιλια) insistently recurs in his text, intuitively opening the logical space of just such a distinction.

Something does indeed call for the apparent 'doublet', implicitly pointing us to the specific nature of love. What erotic love always seeks is 'the good'. Whatever its object elect – wine, the beloved or Beauty – the constant motive is that we think it will conduce, directly or indirectly, to our greater well-being: nobody loves sour wine, an ugly beloved or discordant music! The 'good' was so obvious a value category to the Greek sensibility, and the abstract 'universal' so readily arrived at by the Greek intelligence, that the dialogue does not break its stride. Partly, too, we may suspect, the reason why Plato does not press the distinction is that the role of Eros, as Socrates presents it, is precisely to *mediate between* subject and object, mind and reality, hence also between this world and the 'eternal world': it exalts the lover, *both* in the sense of making him *feel godlike* in progressively fulfilled desire, and, reciprocally, in the sense of promoting him to *closer acquaintance and likeness* with the ultimate 'Good' he comes to appreciate. In the personalised (and anthropomorphic) language of yet another of the myths liberally scattered throughout the *Symposium*, Eros is said to be a *daimon*: that is, a spirit intermediate in nature between gods and men. We might be tempted to say, in a modernised terminology (and Plato may himself have thought) that he (more exactly, *it*) is a principle of transcendence immanent in man, bonding the human subject (its mind, language and conduct) to the reality of things.

Diotima herself explains carefully how the *daimon* was conceived in the mystery cults: 'being of an intermediate nature' between gods and men, the daimon 'bridges the gap between them, and prevents the universe from falling into two separate halves. [...] God does not deal directly with man'. Plato the philosopher would have agreed that this is, at least, an adequate metaphor. The allegorical interpretation given by Socrates of the parentage of Eros establishes his fitness for this capital and mysterious intermediary function. Eros is the son of Poverty, which is why he lives in want, but also of Contrivance, which makes him enterprising and resourceful in assuming the ascensional vocation which answers both the true goal of our desire and the ultimately real 'Other' of our loves (203b).

Erotic love always participates in a finality which transcends itself; it is a trans-rational and trans-human mediation, a way towards wholeness, truth and being. Within this perspective of transcendence, itself enigmatic, Plato succeeds in creating a 'unified field': comprehending all extant loves and susceptible of consistent elucidation. The search for truth and beauty pursued by individuals of the same sex emerges as the self-same impulse as that which prompts all love between individuals and the entire procreative drive in animals. All human activity, indeed, is seen as 'erotic'; all men are in some sense erotic 'lovers' – and erotic love is indeed that which 'makes the world go round'. Eros is simply particularised in different ways (concrete or abstract) at different levels of realisation (carnal and/or spiritual): it is 'the desire of generation in the beautiful, both with relation to the body and the soul' (205e). Anticipating Freud, Socrates' unitary theory supposes – and his dialectic of ascent towards the higher object of love will amply confirm – a sublimation of physical desire; albeit a fully conscious ethico-religious sublimation, deriving from the immediate given of sexual impulse a characterised intellectual and artistic spirituality.

The absent 'Good' which invariably constitutes the goal and 'other' of Eros, considered in its own innate intentionality, is said by Socrates to be eternal Beauty. The word 'eternal' is crucial. Desiring to possess the good, Socrates shows, includes desiring its perpetual possession: 'love is desire for the perpetual possession of the good' (205e). In turn, this implies the consequence which Socrates brings triumphantly to light in discussing animal reproduction and its relation to the loves of the human world. In both, it is true that 'mortal nature seeks, as far as may be, to perpetuate itself and become immortal' (207b); in animals, this implies the quest for biological perpetuity; in man, the quest to overcome contingency and death. 'It is in order to secure immortality that each individual is haunted by this eager desire and love' (208c). In the Beauty which Eros loves must also reside the virtue of stilling the needy soul's longing for immortality. Here Plato not only looks to explain Eros essentially; he contrives to do this by invoking its originating impulse and ultimate finality. His theory of love and desire, we recognise, is essentialist and teleological; in which respect, it is significantly *unmodern*.

The epistemological matrix for this account of the enigma and the transcendence of Eros lies, of course, in Plato's doctrine of Forms. Elementarily, this asserts that for every class of material or abstract thing which can be expressed under a common name, there exists a Form in the eternal world. At the apex of the hierarchy of Forms stands the trinity of the Good, the True and the Beautiful, which are not to be distinguished, being aspects of each other. The task of the philosopher is to pass by degrees out of the shadows of the sensible world towards the Forms which the soul saw (so the *Meno* suggests) before its embodiment in the phenomenal world. The manifold and ever-changing phenomena of the world of sense are thus seen as contingent imitations or copies of eternal and absolute archetypes which alone have true (i.e. non-contingent) being. The objects of our common or earthly loves likewise owe such partial reality as they possesses to their participation in this ultimate reality; they always implicate the higher term – and they are always, in this sense –'triangular'. The essential nature of Eros itself is the longing to regain the lost happiness of contact with the ultimately real: this is what is implied in the vision or contemplation of absolute Beauty.

Plato's mature theory, only hinted at in the *Symposium*, is of course an ontology (a theory of being) as well as a theory of knowledge. The suspicion which the modern – reflexive, critical, post-Kantian – mind will come to harbour about it is that it hypostasises the categories, structures and processes of the mind of the philosopher; and, consequently, that it is to be treated as no more than a symbolic psychology. This modern dismissal is, however, subject to caution. Some objections made against the theory of Forms may be a bad quarrel, based on an over-literal interpretation of the highly figurative and mythical language Plato habitually uses. Spatial metaphors ('elsewhere', 'behind', 'separate', and even the 'other' world, as implying the above) may be ways of speaking metaphorically of that about which it is impossible to speak at all except in terms borrowed from our familiar experience of extended time and space – a mysteriously significant depth of *this* world. Sympathetically understood, Plato's intention may simply be to assert that absolute Beauty is real and subsistent, *not* that it exists in a 'world' of its own, furnished with a ghostly lumber of abstract entities, spatially separate from the world of things and of states of affairs known to us: beauty is not merely a subjective illusion, 'in the eye of the beholder'; it does not come into to being with us, perishing through our agency or as we die. Eros may be 'separated' from its homeland; but it is not groundless or futile in its up-reaching.

It is also clear that, for Plato, the knowing mind moved by erotic love 'participates' in that which it knows; and that it knows it only in so far as it 'copies' or replicates within itself the Object of knowledge. If this is so, it cannot be a decisive objection against Plato's ontology to say that the theory simply maps out in projective reflection the operations of the knowing mind of the philosopher. Our suspicion would, in that case, amount to dismissing the possibility of the existence of the real Object *on the grounds that* we observe in the mirror of the mind a suggestive likeness to it. This observed correspondence might be held, on the contrary, to support Plato's view: it is what we would expect to find if it were true.

* * *

These all-too-rapid epistemological and hermeneutic remarks on the doctrine of Forms have considerable pertinence to a vast part of the subsequent – and modern – debates about love and desire. They are also of immediate help to us here; for they open up to understanding the two key doctrines at the heart of the *Symposium*: the doctrine of ascent and the related doctrine of higher and lower loves.

By 'ascent' is meant the conscious dialectic which learns to use the lesser forms of beauty as stepping stones towards the discernment and love of the higher, thus espousing consciously the innate tendency of Eros in its allusive upward flight to the realm of the ultimately real, the world of Forms. Diotima recapitulates this dialectic in a famous passage of the *Symposium*:

> When a man, starting from this sensible world and making his way upwards by a right use of his feeling of love for boys, begins to catch sight of that beauty, he is very near his goal. This is the right way of approaching or being initiated into the mysteries of love, to begin with examples of beauty in the world, using them as steps to ascend continually with that absolute beauty as one's aim, from one instance of physical beauty to two and from two to all, then from physical beauty to moral beauty, and from moral beauty to the beauty of knowledge, until, from knowledge of various kinds one arrives at the supreme knowledge whose sole object is that absolute beauty, and knows at last what absolute beauty is. [...] Do you not see that in that region alone where he sees beauty with the faculty capable of seeing it, will he be able to bring forth not mere reflected images of goodness, because he will be in contact not with a reflection but with the truth? And having brought forth and nurtured true goodness he will have the privilege of being beloved of God, and becoming, if ever a man can, immortal himself. (211a)

The Christian resonance of the expression 'beloved of God' should not be overstressed; despite the language of divine love, it can only refer to an impersonal ontological principle.[4] Nevertheless, we glimpse here the logic of attraction which has produced at many points in Western cultural tradition a near symbiosis of Christianity and Platonism; a cultural inflection so powerful that we shall observe modern anti-Platonists (including Nietzsche) failing almost entirely to distinguish one from the other. Yet what this expression actually confirms is that for Plato, erotic love, while primed by sexual desire, and drawing on its energies, is at bottom a 'godlike' or 'divine' principle of transcendence immanent in the human psyche. Far from being 'reducible' in the modern manner to its lower forms of realisation and, causally, to its humble psychosexual and biological origins, it irrepressibly engages consciousness, will, aesthetic sense and all higher aspects of personality in what is at bottom a teleologically oriented quest for the absolute.

The doctrine of higher and lower loves makes the individual and physical expressions of Eros the steppingstones for the higher (moral and aesthetic) ones; as post-Freudian thought might say, it provides the sublimatory springboard of ascent. This process in Plato is, however, largely rational and morally discriminating. Erotic love in its physical forms is what compels us to be critical and moves us forward.

Not however, without turbulence and struggle. The doctrine of higher and lower souls and their loves is existentially dramatic, as dualist systems tend to be. The *Phaedrus* gives us the myth of human nature as a pair of winged horses and a charioteer. The black horse, belonging to the world of sense, attempts to pull the charioteer towards the earth-bound gratification of plunging sensual appetite; the white horse tends to soar upwards towards the world of ideals from which the soul originated. Carnality and spirituality are unstably yoked together in the human composite, the violent or passionate carnal excess of the one playing against the 'divine madness' of the other.

The achievement of serenity by the sage who loves beauty, truth and goodness can only be a *purified and harmonious 'possession'* of and by ultimate realities: an achieved stillness above the storm. Thus the sage of the *Republic*, echoing the *Symposium* (and Plato's relation to Socrates):

> He contemplates a world of unchanging and harmonious order, where reason governs and nothing can do or suffer wrong; and like one who imitates an admired companion, he cannot fail to fashion himself in its likeness. So the philosopher, in constant companionship with the divine, will reproduce that order in his soul, and, as far as a man may, become godlike.[5]

* * *

The modern reader may well feel some incredulity at Plato's preferential specialisation. 'Starting with a vision of everything being in love, Plato ends up with the incredible suggestion that only the (Platonic) philosopher really is.'[6] Even if we admit the transcending enigma of Eros, is it to be so exclusively explained as a yearning for ultimate wisdom and so specifically fulfilled by the exercise of rationality and the aesthetic sense? Does the philosopher not ignore or downgrade in the process a great deal of what the modern mind rightly considers central to both love and desire? What of emotion? Of kinship or communion of feeling; of sexual blood-fever, but also of tenderness, warmth and caring? Can we countenance, in respect of 'desire', the relative marginalisation and downgrading of sexuality; or, in relation to 'love', Plato's tendency to ignore or misrepresent the love of persons, seen as occasions, merely, of a self-related dialectic which passes through them towards abstract universals situated beyond and elsewhere? Is not this misrecognition – together with the quest for a perfection not given to finite human beings – a formula for serial loves, perpetual infidelity and frustration?

More fundamentally: is not the transcendentalist and teleological framing of the whole theory a way of despising the world we have; a door opened to precisely the bloodless, ethereal 'transcendental idealism' that later Platonists and Neo-platonists, not to mention nineteenth-century 'spiritualists', 'idealists' and 'Symbolists' various, were to make out of it?

Precisely because Plato is such a brilliant reader of the very central and perennial enigma of Eros, he has generated infinite resonances, and hence also multiple recognitions and filiations; not all that is 'platonique' is 'platonicien' (to adopt a French distinction). Modern recognitions of origin, in respect of Plato, necessarily traverse this intermediate cultural space, and react to it in function of the dominant conditions and mindforms of their own time: we shall glimpse something of this process of selective development and appropriation in subsequent chapters. Where, as is predominantly the twentieth-century case, such recognitions obey some logic of reflexive, criticist or deconstructionist *anti-transcendentalism*, they react to Plato's posterity as much as to Plato himself; and this standpoint frequently obscures the ways in which their reaction is still determined by, and indeed perpetuates in variant or mutant forms, the tradition of Platonic Eros.

Freud himself is a case in point. Attuned to the Freudian 'revelation' or 'revolution', contemporary minds rarely stop to notice that Freud's psychic archaeology of love and desire is profoundly characterised, not so much as anti-platonician, but as a dissident reflexive variation on Plato. This is indeed confirmed by Freud in the very term 'Eros' which, overflowing the strictly individual and sexually-referred definition of 'libido', resurfaces irrepressibly in his writings at the time of the Great War, alongside its stable-mate 'Thanatos', as organising concept of the later unitary field 'metapsychology'. Explicating psychoanalytically the mechanisms of sublimation, Freud the cultural theorist follows Plato in seeing Eros as the great taproot of civilisation and, particularly, of its discontents. The general logic of his variation may be said to be that of a *specular inversion* of Plato's figure of erotic love conceived as universal enigma and immanent transcendence.

True to the reflexive and criticist mind-form of modern theory, the father of psychonalysis reads Plato's figure of Eros upside-down and backwards: no longer in function of the ontologically prior *telos* it finds in the world of Forms, but now as a localised and potentially solvable *rebus* relocated in the energies and ruses of the libidinal Unconscious; no longer as a dialectic of ascent towards truth, but now as a deconstructive descent into the psychic underworld of mind-generated phantasms, neuroses and delusory idealisations; no longer as an ethic of self-therapy, healing amorous privation, but now in 'scientific' and positive exorcism of a henceforth irremediable negativity: that of a perverse, knotted and mirror-bound sexual libido. In Freud, Plato's charioteer has wagered on the genealogy – or in his own more rationalistically confident language, on a psychoanalytical 'aetiology' – of the black horse and its death-bound shadow; to which the fortunes of the aspiring white stablemate, are, at the individual and societal levels, deterministically – and, we may think, precariously – in thrall.

Is the same debt of continuity and inverse variation not also clear in Lacan? The latter's perfected and mathematically schematised deconstructive model of the psyche invokes a *libido* which is indefinitely refracted throughout the mind-generated and culturally transmitted orders of the imaginary and the symbolic. It is set even more firmly than is the Freudian 'erotosphere' under the determining sign of specularity (the so-called 'stade du miroir'). Lacan's *béance* of incompletion thus aggravates the woundedness implied in Plato's account of desire as dynamic deficit. The allusive flight towards the 'lost Object' remembers the Platonic ascent, but now absurdly.

Plato's great amorous vector of ethico-human transcendence survives as a ghostly and impotent shadow, 'separated' from reality.

Late-twentieth-century critical theory more generally, with its 'libidinal economies' (Lyotard's term), perpetually rehearses Plato. Eros, ever more insistently re-immanentalised and re-configured in the logic of all the human sciences, provides indeed the only anthropological 'universal' left with which it can deal. Yet its ever-fascinated and ever-closer scrutiny explains away Plato's transcendent enigma, only to neglect its challenges. Imaginative artists, as we shall see, do rather better.

* * *

These filiations of twentieth-century theory are merely some of the latest avatars of Plato's vaster posterity. In pertinence, profundity and unified coherence, the theory of love, desire and transcendence offered in the *Symposium* is a remarkable beginning. At a stroke, Plato integrates these themes under the name of Eros and lifts them to a level of significance that has commanded the attention of Western thinkers for more than two thousand years. In all respects, perhaps, except one; yet one which is so urgently fundamental as to make the theory, when reviewed in the light of its original blind-spot, something perillously close to an anomaly, an unstable paradox.

What, after all, do we currently understand by the term 'love'? In our own day, the statistically probable response of most Westerners, if canvassed, would be a variation on some formula of Romantic antecedence such as: 'tender and passionate relationship with partner of the opposite sex'. The notion that love-and-desire, before being about homoerotic relations and their sublimated higher figures, refer *primarily to sexually-involved relationalities between men and women* would be overwhelming and unshakeable; and it would persist whatever was subsequently thought and said about homosexual loves and their socio-cultural regulation. At this point, the *Symposium* confounds the most central expectation we have as to what 'love' is about.

We approach here the crucial question of the homoerotic and masculinist context of reference of the *Symposium*. The practice of ascent commended to and by Socrates invokes 'the right use of a man's love for boys'. And the exemplification of love and desire envisaged throughout the dialogue is that of the common search for truth and beauty pursued by master philosopher, or other mature man of the world, and youthful male pupil: a case prevalent, indeed institutionalised, in the Athens of the fourth century BC.

It would certainly be open to a Freudian reading of the *Symposium* to explore whether, at an *unconscious* level, Platonic idealism can be significantly and properly described as 'a homosexual theory' in the sense of projecting an incompletely developed, maternally fixated, Oedipal resolution. The insistent devaluation of flesh in relation to spirit, with its accompanying language of 'noble' and 'base' loves, might indeed appear to lend some credence *a priori* to this hypothesis. It is a suggestive fact, too, in a Freudian perspective, that, in speaking of love, Plato expresses his thought in terms of a series of maternal figures: Diotima, who is the maternal figure initiating the philosopher into the secret of Being; the Heavenly Aphrodite, who is 'older and consequently free from wantonness' (182b); and even, in abstract and supra-sexual projection, Beauty itself, conceived as ideal matrix of the contingent beauties of the world.

In his essay 'The most prevalent form of degradation in Erotic Life', Freud points suggestively to the danger of a splitting of the self in cases where, as a result of the frustration and repression of tender, maternally-directed feelings, the sex-drive breaks away from feeling and concentrates on a purely sexual object. In extreme states: 'The erotic life of such people remains dissociated, divided between two channels, the same two that are personified in art as heavenly and earthly (or animal) love. In order to keep their sensuality out of contact with the objects they love, they seek out objects whom they need not love.'[7] There is something in ancient Greece, in Plato, and even more in Plato's posterity, which recalls this danger insistently. It is noticeable, too, that where Freud analyses civilisation as a masculine creation, he uses the language of aim-inhibited desire to characterise the erotic forces at work. His aim-inhibition, as we have stressed, is not Plato's: for Freud, all sublimation is causally reducible to sexuality, whereas Plato's principle of causal reference is the desire of the Good; yet both attribute to quasi-homosexual relations a unique function in the development of the noblest ideals.

If we are to look beyond this pertinent but partial Freudian explanation, we need to make a jump of historical imagination. The author of the *Symposium* wrote within an entirely male-dominated culture in which citizens were still warriors, revering the masculine virtue of *arete* (hardy uprightness and virile self-respect) above all others. Homosexuality was, in this socio-cultural order, extensively 'naturalised', even norm-setting among the leisured intelligentsia; and so was, to an even greater degree, the near-universal 'depreciation' of women.

If we set aside the maternal initiatrix Diotima, Plato's text contains only one female character, a servant-girl flautist, who appears fleetingly at the beginning, and is dismissed to play to the women of the household. Insistently, love for women is decried as a base and inferior expression of Eros. It is the maternal iniatrix Diotima who points out the continuity of this lower, carnal eros with animality; she herself being devoted, not to intercourse with men, but to intimacy with cosmic mysteries (in ancient Greece, temple prostitutes often fulfilled *both* roles). All agree that love of men for women has only one finality worthy of attention: the biological necessity of perpetuating the species. According to Aristophanes, Zeus, in re-arranging the genital organs of the sexes, intended that reproductive sexuality would be the humble labour of male-female unions:

His object in making this change was twofold; if male couples with female, children might be begotten and the race thus continued, but if male coupled with male, at any rate the desire for intercourse would be satisfied, and man set free to turn to other activities and to attend to the rest of the business of life. (191e)

Non-reproductive, homosexual relationships, exempt from the labour of reproduction, benefit from the entire bonus of liberated sexual pleasure, culture and sublime spirituality. Plato, we observe, is developing the logic of the 'afterthought' of Zeus.

This Hellenic reading of sexuality in fact implicates the whole socio-cultural regulation of loves and gender roles, which we merely glimpse from Plato's text. Women belong overwhelmingly to the domestic sphere; female slaves are for menial labour and casual sexual pleasure; *heirati* and common prostitutes are professionals specialising in this much-required role. Women do not otherwise frequent public places or walk the streets alone; male-female encounters are limited and regulated. Wives (to whom nothing is owed by way of fidelity) are for ordering households, procuring heirs and raising the youngest children; female infants could be and were – in democratic, cultured Athens at the apex of its civilised flowering – frequently 'exposed' on the hills to die.

In his time, Plato was a 'humane' man, 'advanced' in his social thinking: the *Republic* recommends education and citizenship for women. But still, he expressly forbids men and women of the ruling class to enter into anything but temporary sexual relations for the purpose of breeding.

Conspicuously absent anywhere in Plato is the notion that women might be equal partners in a love-match; or that they could be adequate, still less life-long, companions in higher endeavour. It is taken as axiomatic that homoerotic love is alone capable of nurturing – Plato does not say of *satisfying* – the noblest aspirations; and he will eventually prohibit carnal relations of this type. That this was not the whole truth of ancient Greece, that tenderly devoted and faithful male-female couples certainly existed, we have glimpses in the literary texts that have survived: Hector and Andromache (but they were Trojans), Ulysses and Penelope (but 'Que d'erreurs promises!'), Amphitryon and Alcmena (but the Greek gods are infinitely licentious and predatory: the entire mythical pantheon, to the modern eye, incorporates a free-ranging – in part, compensatory – male erotic fantasy, rather as present-day advertising images do).

The deeper logic of this socio-cultural order is, surely, that it reflects a latent, universally held 'anthropology', with its implied world-view. It proceeds, that is, from a pervasive sense of the *ultimate insignificance* of sex and gender differentiation for the 'definition' of human beings as such; hence for the realisation of their higher spiritual potential – and hence also for their loves. Eros is not (save in its threefold variety and its transcendent movement) itself *ordained*: it is 'as we find it', and therefore conforms merely to cultural convention, itself determined by biological and socio-economic realities.

All interlocutors of Plato's dialogue agree that sexual pairing actually occurs *ad libitum*, indifferently of gender: not only in the practice of lovers (male and, implicitly, female), but also in the ordering act of Zeus himself who made them – by way of the conspicuously makeshift afterthought we have noted. Women – and, with them, male–female sexual relations as such – fall on the 'wrong' side of the omnipresent fracture-line of a *dualism* which begins at this precise point. This dividing-line of value and appraisal separates male and female, higher and lower forms of eros, spirit and flesh, human and animal, the other world and this; in each case, disqualifying the 'lesser' term by comparison. By virtue of this 'genealogy', women thus all but fail, in the Greek philosopher's estimate, to cross the threshold of fully humane status at all. The most revealing and contestable sub-text of the *Symposium*, corrected only in part by the special decipherment or discernment of Eros referred to Diotima, might well lie in the thought that the heavenly Aphrodite has 'no female strain in her' (180e).[8]

To see just how distinctive this view is, and how far-reaching, we must turn to the contrast supplied by our second source text, which fulfils with paradigmatic splendour the expectation which the *Symposium* conspicuously disappoints.

Notes

1   Plato, *The Symposium*, trans. W. Hamilton (London: Penguin, 1951), p. 88, 207b. References are given in the form of the classic paragraph divisions of Plato's text.
2   S. Freud, *Beyond the Pleasure Principle*, in *The Standard Edition of the Complete Psychological Works of Sigmund Freud*, ed. J. Strachey & A. Freud (London: Hogarth Press and the Institute of Psycho-Analysis, 1953–66), Vol. 18 (1957), p. 57.
3   See *Éthique de la différence sexuelle*, discussed in Chapter 13, below.
4   Plato almost certainly has in mind the Principle of Being, which, in the *Phaedrus* and elsewhere, he hints at as containing the Forms. In the *Timaeus*, he writes: 'It is hard to find the maker and father of the universe, and having found him, it is impossible to speak of him at all' (*Tim.* 28c 3–5). Later neo-platonists refer to this ultimate ontological principle of which Plato refuses to speak as 'the One'; and this too, again despite the logic of analogy implied in the word 'father', is beyond all personality, as well as beyond all knowing and saying.
5   *The Republic of Plato*, trans. F. MacDonald (Cornford, NY: Oxford University Press, 1941), p. 208.
6   I. Singer, *The Nature of Love*, Vol. 1: *Plato to Luther* (Chicago & London: University of Chicago Press, 1984), pp. 82–3.
7   S. Freud, 'The Most Prevalent Form of Degradation in Erotic Life', in *The Standard Edition*, Vol. 11 (1910), p. 183.
8   She is said by Pausanias to spring 'entirely from the male': an allusion to the traditional myth that Aphrodite was born of the sea, into which had been thrown the severed members of her father Uranus when he was mutilated by his patricidal son Cronos.

Chapter 2

Nuptial Splendour: The Song of Songs

Like the *Symposium*, the Song of Songs treats erotic love; yet the total figure of sense offered is antipodally different. The lyric voice that speaks in this text is not a discursive abstraction from experience, nor any kind of speculative or logical construct. It is the utterance of first-person experiential knowledge of a type which, raising the sense of being to a hymnic exaltation, overflows in song. And the song sung is celebratory utterance, re-presenting the discovery of that which, marvellously, *is*. Lyricism, said Valéry memorably, is the development of an exclamation.

It does not matter, then, as it certainly would in Plato, that this text is a composite one, formed of originally autonomous oral poems and poetic fragments arranged many centuries later into a loosely-breathing but suggestive textual unity;[1] or that this edited compilation leaves zones of uncertainty (in relation to speaking personae, dramatic situation and action, allusion and reference). On the contrary: the difficulty of schematising the lyric voice intellectually, provides a haunting and resonant opacity. In conjunction with the insistently polysemic play of the original Hebrew text and its extraordinary metaphoricity, this mediates an intrinsic coherence of affirmation communicating from within the experienced depth and mystery of love itself; and it invites successive discernments of deeper layers of meaning.

There is no need, therefore, to preface the present reading with much scholarly attention to previous readings (which are legion: the reception history of this text retraces the story of Western thought), or to translational, exegetical and hermeneutical difficulties (which are formidable). In essence, two major impulses of interpretation have vied with each other: one, receiving the text according to the resonance established by its integration within the canon of the Scriptures (Jewish and Christian), has developed the symbolic, and later, allegorical, figure of a larger, founding love (that of Yaweh for the Jewish people; and subsequently, that of Christ for the new Israel, the Church). The other, secularising, tradition has wished to reclaim a literal, human and specifically erotic sense, comparable to that of the love lyrics found in Egyptian or Indian poetry, for this purpose detaching the text from its supposedly anomalous incorporation into the religious traditions of Judaism and of Christianity.

The only comment required here is to suggest that it may do more justice to the *Song*'s human significance as love poetry to seek understand why it has in fact been transmitted to us within the biblical canon than to decree that this ought not be so; and, conversely, that it may not best serve the 'religious' depth of the text today to allegorise it as the Christian Middle Ages did (largely in function of the syncretism this period effected with the Hellenic tradition of Eros). The residual dualism of the Western mind is writ large in such a polarity of interpretation; and the *Song*, as we shall see, rebukes the alternative put to it.

It seems likely that the singular *Song* we have belongs in genetic origin to the poetry recited and sung at village wedding feasts, very much like the songs of nuptial folklore used in Syria to this day. If so, it is probable that, as in Syria now, the Hebrew bride and groom were declared king and queen for a full week of festivities. This may explain how apparently royal personages originally came to be mingled with simple peasants in the text. It may also suggest a metaphoric 'hook' by which these erotic love-songs became attached to the Temple built by the theocratic King Solomon, despite their being clearly different in inspiration from the biblical Psalms (which were indeed used in temple liturgies); which in turn allows scholars to suppose that they became, over centuries, interpreted within the hypertext of re-read scriptures and rabbinical exegeses within the Temple and edited in function of a Messianic expectation of which an idealised Solomon was the focus.[2] In the canon of Jewish scriptures, the text appears with a subscript of attribution to Solomon, and in older versions of the English Bible it is still called the 'Song of Solomon'.

A more far-reaching suggestion regarding the genetic development of the text within this environment is that these songs became integrated into the liturgical tradition of the Passover. Into the commemoration of the central experience of the deliverance of Israel out of Egypt might thus be integrated the experience of encounter with the Canaanite fertility cults discovered on Israel's return to the Promised land. Together with a 'subversive' reference to the – notoriously licentious[3] –' real' Solomon himself, this encounter may be thought to have provided the counter-model of *inauthentic* love which the text proposes in counterpoint to its own song.[4]

In the end, however, we are obliged to regard all contextual and genetic hypothesising as part of the resonant opacity of the text rather than as providing an unequivocal 'key'. There is nothing for it but to become *readers* of the text we have.

***

The admirable title 'Song of Songs' exactly captures its innermost inspiration. Here is a Song speaking on behalf of all love-songs (as attested by the process of compilation itself) – the very paradigm of love sung. And this sense enfolds further senses: love-songs themselves are, generically speaking, paradigms of all lyric song, just as love is the paradigm of all celebratory experiences of being alive and human; the love of the male–female couple is the place in which all love is realised quintessentially and emerges to self-apprehension in the singing and celebration of it. In this way, the title is resonant with an almost infinite exemplarity. The potential intertext in literature, folklore, proverbs, the songs of contemporary pop culture, and the Bible itself, must be as extensive as that of any text ever written. Yet we hear everything afresh, as never before; which is to say that this is, additionally, a song of surpassing excellence – a 'transcending' song.

The received text takes the form of a dialogue, in which the female and male lovers speak alternately, with contributions by way of answer or commentary from a 'chorus', which is usually denoted female[5] and is addressed as 'daughters of Jerusalem'. Significantly, the female voice leads: traditionally described as that of the Sulamite or Shulamite (this name, mentioned twice, links her both to Solomon and to the Jewish greeting *shalom* –'peace').

No less significantly, it leads in the register of frankly erotic enchantment. The entire set of poems is predicated on a phase-change in feminine being and awareness: an awakening of the senses, a quickening initiation in and from sexuality, with all its sensual, romantic and erotic enhancement of life:

> Oh for your kiss! For your love
> More enticing than wine,
> For your scent and sweet name –
> For all this they love you.
> Take me to your room,
> Like a king to his rooms –
> We'll rejoice there with wine.
> No wonder they love you! (Falk, 13)[6]

Masculine charm, intoxicating, physically desirable, confirmed as such by the speaker's friends, is acknowledged; but playfully so, and with a metaphoricity of feeling and invocation which is indirect in its directness. This opening characterises the young woman who stands, perhaps, between fiancée and bride – part of a group of girls, yet already set apart in amorous choice and (soon or already) sexual initiation. The nuptial act (or its imagining) is clothed in royal splendour; which is no hindrance, on the contrary, to its understated meaning of physical consummation.

As the *Song* progresses, it will re-echo with other harmonics of awakening feminine eros: the longing of unaccompanied nights or of post-nuptial absence, and the plea for presence and intimacy. Ardent languor, oneiric in quality, though no doubt representing a waking reverie ('Je dors mais mon cœur veille' ['I sleep but my heart stirs/restless and dreams']), reveals both a powerful sexuality and an instinctively assured and ancestral pairing-instinct:

> I'll rise and search the city,
> Through the streets and squares
>
> Until the city watchmen
> Find me wandering there
>
> And I ask them – have you seen him?
> The one I love is not here.
>
> When they have gone, I find him
> And I won't let him go. (Falk, 25)
>
> Until he's in my mother's home,
> The room where I was born. (III: 1–4)

Later, the same dream(like) scenario is re-run: the Sulamite speaks of receiving a nocturnal visit from her fiancé; her entranced and transgressive excitement is first disavowed as she refuses to admit him; then it turns to acute anguish as he acquiesces in her dismissal, and fades away just as she manages to work open the bolts of the door. Here, the motif of her solitary quest in the nocturnal streets ends in social reprobation and punishment (V: 2–7).

Her 'fault' – perhaps enacted only in desirous imagining, but real enough to self-understanding – is that of de-regulation and *impudeur*; the veil removed is that covering the power of sexual eros in the speaker's own feminine nature. The whole scenario strikes us as shrewd, even contemporary (the feminine translator of the quoted modern version translates the tearing of the 'veil' as a tearing away of the 'robe', and comments that this violence of the guards connotes a [fear of?] rape). More strategically, we glimpse here the expansive resonance of the poem's insistent refrain: 'Who is it who...?' (III: 6; VI: 10; VIII: 5). Sexuality is a powerful spring that, once engaged, beckons gloriously, but also disturbingly and perilously, to an unknown Other within the self, thus triggering the entire question of human subject identity. Immediately, the drama of eros is to reconcile this powerful impulse of momentous personal and social significance with the avowable expressions of language and conduct as authorised within a given socio-cultural regulation (represented here by the nightwatchmen, who certainly mistake the Sulamite for a streetwalker).

One subterfuge of desire is to imagine the lover as brother:

Oh, if you were my brother
Nursed at my mother's breast,

I'd kiss you in the streets
And never suffer scorn

And give you wine and nectar
From my pomegranates.

O for his arms around me,
Beneath me and above. (Falk, 45)

Que sa main gauche soit sous ma tête, et que sa droite m'embrasse! (VIII: 1–3)

Both the touching *travestissement*, transparently confessed, and the simply stated goal of sexual intimacy-in-caring, are powerfully gender-differentiated; again we admire the fusion of 'Freudian' awareness and delicacy, often passing, as here, through the nature symbolism: all the poem's natural images (vineyard, fig tree, cleft mountain places), but also its human ones (eating, drinking, fruit-gathering, pasturing, etc.) project, as here, a fully conscious, venturesome-yet-innocent erotic sense.

Some caution, of course, is required: a danger of anachronism lurks in discovering the loves of the ancient world through the agendas of contemporary sexual politics and the prism of post-Freudian liberation of the libido from Victorian repression. The poem, precisely, has no self-conscious earnestness about 'writing female sexual pleasure'; nor is 'pleasure' an exact word for the nuptial delight envisaged. In an orally transmitted, collective and edited work, the concept of 'author' is, in any case, problematic and the question of authorship beyond empirical resolution. This said, the unveiled boldness of the speaker, like the leading role conferred on the feminine voice, is remarkable. If the *Song* is held to be no more than ritualised transmission of wedding folklore, it is, indeed, distinctly *curious*: we may well sense here the background of erotic self-discovery supposed by Israel's encounter with the fertility cults in which female protagonists had the leading role; but still, we are left to wonder how, within the regulating patriarchal tradition this voice emerged and survived.

The masculine voice is no less recognisable in gender difference. Quintessentially, it is the voice of wondering admiration for physical beauty in the feminine partner, and of erotico-romantic invitation. The excellences of the beloved are detailed in repeated litanies, poetically sincere and often moving, but not exempt from virile naivety and rhetorical *maladresse*:

Ma bien aimée, je te compare à ma cavale qu'on attèle aux chars de Pharaon.
Tes joues ont bonne grâce avec les atours, et ton cou avec les colliers.
Nous te ferons des atours d'or, avec des boutons d'argent. (I: 9–11)

My love I compare you to my mare harnessed to Pharaoh's chariots
Your cheeks are comely with their finery, and your neck with its necklaces.
We'll make you a golden harness, with buttons of silver.

In modern equivalence, 'his' first thought might be that she has all the speedy grace of a gleaming Yamaha 2000; his second, that one can and must gild the lily! Hebraic scholars point out that the image has a masculine and warlike connotation: the Isaraelites liberated from Egypt knew that only stallions were harnessed to Pharaoh's chariots. A well-known battle tactic against them was to release mares on heat among the stallions, plunging the superior 'cavalry' into wild confusion ('Like a mare among stallions/You lure, I am held ...' [Falk, 15]). We imagine the recipient of these compliments smiling slyly, as well as shyly, in accepting the unpractised words – wondering, clumsily earnest and a touch self-assertive – of the young shepherd who speaks.

But the litany, as it finds its voice, is also splendid. Precisely, it is resplendent with the beauties and the mystery of nature and the with glories of human conception in which the beloved is seen to be haloed, and which she recapitulates in her person, before and beyond any bedecking finery:

Striking as Tirza
    you are my love.
Bright as Jerusalem,
    frightening as visions!
Lower your eyes
    for they make me tremble.

Your hair –
    as black as goats
    winding down the slopes
Your teeth –
    a flock of sheep
    rising from the stream
    in twos, each with its twin
Your lips –
    like woven threads
    of crimson silk
A gleam of pomegranate—
    your forehead
    through your veil. (Falk, 39)

The awesome halo, concretely realised in the shapes, colours and light-values of pastoral Palestine, does not inhibit, but rather inhabits, a masculine erotic delight in feminine bodily form, seen within a real and concrete *pays qui te ressemble*. Masculine sensuality thus finds its answering amorous voice: rustic still, yet royally appreciative in praise, and hence already *poetic*.

The duo of feminine and masculine voices, differentiated, equal in weight and symmetrical in expression, points to the novelty not found in Plato. Even in its sublimated and dialectically 'higher' forms, Eros is a self-related quest for the objects of desire, and through them, its own 'good'; in relation to its human objects, it is specifically casual, promiscuous and nomadic. The 'love' sung here, by contrast, *responds* to its awakening and elected Other; and it seeks the *person as such*, not to pass through and on, but to create a sphere of bonded co-presence, in which erotic being-in-delight is contained and enhanced, complexified and returned. Inversely to the *Symposium*, the emphasis falls on the speakers' preference for, pursuit of, and rejoicing in, the amorous consent of a particular and chosen personal partner. The exuberant and playful glow of the poem's opening is predicated on singular choice, already operative at the level of sexual attraction, and already distinguishing ('among thousands'), but re-echoed at all levels of personality.

Symptomatic of this are the motifs which the Sulamite enunciates in response to the initiatives of the beloved, which are, just as often, her own initiatives: delight in gifting ('there ... I will give you my loving'); exaltation in mutual possession marked by faithful constancy ('I am my beloved's, and my beloved is mine'); the sense of excursion in novelty and of entry into the essential adventure *à deux* of every day

('Viens, mon bien-aimé, sortons aux champs ... Levons-nous le matin ... et voyons si la vigne est avancée', VII: 12 ['Come, my beloved, let us go out to the fields ... and see whether the vines have come on'); peace in bonded belonging ('j'ai été à ses yeux comme celle qui trouve la paix', VIII: 10 ['I was in his gaze as one who finds her peace']). The marvel, if recapitulative and universal, is resolutely particular. Without didacticism or theory, but nonetheless unmistakably, the Song articulates a *personalist* vision of love.

The sense of mutual election-in-delight will re-echo throughout the poems of the text in the litanies of poetic appreciation which the two lovers bestow upon each other – the so-called *wasfs* (i.e. poems following a set form of amorous praise common in the ancient Middle East, in which the excellences of the beloved are spelled out singularly in litanies that move from head to toe, or inversely). These reciprocal and ever-renascent outpourings of wonder are no less singularly Other-specific because they explore the 'I–Thou relationship' (Buber's personalist binome)[7] as a marvel of inter-gender complementarity and involve the cosmos in it metaphorically. On the contrary, to choose and be chosen across the great anthropological force-field of male–female difference is to exist, without paradox, in a circuit of desire bestowed and received by another person, yet precisely recapitulating the 'good' order of created things.

This is best expressed in the perfect lyricism of the 'bride's' most celebrated words, evoking a return to the recreating sources of being held in common with the world of nature, and bonding the new couple to each other within the natural mystery of cosmic renewal in springtime:

Come with me,
my love
come away

For the long wet months are past,
the rains have fed the earth
and left it bright with blossoms

Birds wing in the low sky,
dove and songbird singing
in the open air above

Earth nourishing tree and vine,
green fig and tender grape,
green and tender fragrance

Come with me,
my love,
come away. (Falk, 21)

The mobilising invitation epitomises the amorous feeling of the *Song*: its ever-fresh lilt of cosmically complicit romance and its age-old dynamic of Excursion and Return.

In purely socio-cultural terms, the bondedness envisaged implies conjugality. More importantly – to adopt a distinction elucidated by Paul Ricœur – it is *nuptial*.[8] The difference is worth grasping. Commentators who point out that nothing in the *Song* explicitly imposes the conclusion that the lovers are, or are about to be, married, are, literally speaking, correct: even the expression traditionally translated as 'my sister, my bride' may well be a term of endearment imitated from Egyptian love poetry referring to 'my beloved'. This does not mean that we are reading a subversive apology for free love, save possibly in respect of the interval between betrothal ceremony (which, in ancient Israel, was a decisive commitment and might be private), and wedding (which was a major public celebration of an often previously consummated commitment). Any such reading is likely to be a post-Romantic modern fantasy, ignoring a whole series of textual and contextual clues: the approval of the mother; the content of the relationship itself; the 'sapiential' message of the text; the likely context of origin in the wedding folklore of Israel; the distinctive and ethnically distinguishing emphasis of the ancient Hebrews on marriage (non-Jews might be referred to derisively as 'the fatherless'!);[9] and the acceptance of the text into the Jewish scriptural canon – to mention a few.

Simply: the *Song* is not interested in 'matrimony' – our Roman-derived word indicating the social regulation under the law of human reproduction (the disposal of bodies, names, goods and inheritance rights, etc.). It did not have to be – that dimension of things was provided for in ancient Israel by religious tradition and goes entirely without saying. The much-remarked absence in this text of any reference to the 'father' is symptomatic only of this *abstention*. It is significant, however, in a more subtle sense: it invites us to look beneath the public and patriarchal frame to something more fundamental. What intensely interests the *Song*'s textual voices – and its singers, writers and editors – is the subjective, but recognisably universal, experience of inter-gendered erotic love as such, and its human ('anthropological') meaning. It is this mysteriously emerging and pervasive *qualitative dimension* which the text's poetic language insistently designates as 'nuptial', that is: 'bonded', 'allied' or 'betrothed' not just individually, to each other, but to human life as such, affirmed as excellent, and of one weave with the 'good' being of things bestowed in creation. Ricœur speaks of this nuptial sense being 'in reserve' in the erotic tenor of the poem, and emerging dynamically thanks to the play of various elements of its textual functioning: narrative and dramatic imprecision, metaphoricity, the structures of movement. This insight, I suggest, – rather than the omni-present reference to sexuality as such – gives the true, meta-Freudian measure of the semantic dimension explored by the leitmotif-refrain: 'Who is this who…?'[10]

***

Ricœur's hermeneutical perspective also invites us to read anew what is sometimes called the 'sapiential' dimension of the poem: the dimension of reflective existential wisdom passed down to successive generations in the ancestral line (placed, we have seen, within the maternal 'lining' of a patriarchal society).

One key place to observe this dimension is the central image-cluster relating to the vine, the vineyard and wine. Wine is delicious and intoxicating, like the effect of love on the sexually awakened and amorously engaged powers of the lovers' entire being. This is the point of imaginative irradiation from which the text speaks so exuberantly: kisses are compared to wine; wine accompanies and favours the jubilant intimacy of the lovers; love's trysts are located as much in the 'winehall' as in the chamber or other external sites ('under the quince tree', 'in the room where my mother bore me'). Among the latter, the vineyard itself is a choice location, thrice evoked; because it envelops the love-play in complicit privacy and shade, but also as a fundamental analogue of the intoxicating desirability and potent fruitfulness, maturing with natural growth, of the sexual personae of the lovers:

> Viens, mon bien-aimé, sortons aux champs, passons la nuit aux villages.
> Levons-nous le matin pour aller aux vignes; et voyons si la vigne est avancée, et
> si la grappe est formée, et si les grenadiers sont fleuris; et c'est là que je te
> donnerai mes amours. (VII: 11–12)

> Come, my love, let's go out to the fields, let's spend the night in the villages./
> We'll rise in the morning and see whether the vines have come on, if the grapes
> are forming; and that's where I'll give you my loving.

The female persona (particularly) is herself a vineyard; and in sexual intimacy, 'my vineyard', with its tender leaves and young flowers, its hanging fruit and secret shade, becomes 'his vineyard'.

Within this symphonic metaphoricity, the selfsame source of enchantment is seen also to generate contrapuntally suggestions of danger – predation, violence and loss. These suggestions re-echo in the metaphoric tissue of the text, subterraneously linked to the themes of male power and the exploitation or control of female sexuality. So, in the opening dialogue with the 'daughters of Jerusalem', the Sulamite explains that her 'dark' complexion is due not only to working in the vineyards, but to her brothers who made her do so:

> And I have faced the angry glare
> Of others, even my mother's sons
> Who sent me out to watch their vines
> While I neglected all my own. (Falk, 13)

Declared beyond *pudeur*, female sexuality incurs reprobation. Freely bestowed, it becomes guilty unless or until it is sanctioned socially (as in the dream episode with the night watchmen). The same motif re-echoes in the 'boarding up' of the pre-pubertal 'little sister' and *her* vineyard against masculine predation. It is unclear whether the plural voice we hear at this point is that of the same 'brothers' speaking again to reprove the Sulamite's own 'opened door', or (more subtly) the voice of the two lovers themselves concerned for the next youthful female of the family line, and deciding, on the basis of her developing sexual persona, whether to enhance her beauty so as to attract suitors or to hide her away so as to save her from harm. Either way, 'foxes' prowl the vineyards and snatch the fruit. The metaphoric compass of the richly promising but ever-vulnerable place of human fruitfulness recalls, simultaneously and without paradox, 'the wine that entices/The lips of new lovers' *and* Solomon's harem *and* 'the fruit of the vine' used in the marriage celebrations of Israel.

In following this metaphoric network, we become aware of a minor tonality of wariness entering the radiant, private sphere of nuptial celebration. There is, indeed, a shadow side to the life-enhancing return to the sources of being held in common with all nature. The form it takes is a resonant counterpoint: on the one hand, the bonded-and-bounded intimacy between lover and beloved; on the other, the lure of unbounded erotic desire referred to the contrasting figure of the historical King Solomon.

The feminine beloved is unique among 'sixty wives, and eighty concubines and queens without number'; which is to say that when *desire* becomes 'fixated' in *love* there is a formidable, creative novelty – she becomes the new dawn, cosmic as stars, terrible as the vision of marching armies (VI: 8–10). Yet even here, there is a latent and secretly countervailing masculine dream-thought. It consists in the comparison– – and, implicitly, the choice – between his Beloved and the innumerable objects of sexual desire, such as are available to the powerful. If the shepherd's heart-chosen One is celebrated in the poem as preferable to all Solomon's concubines, and if the bondedness of the betrothed lovers is chosen above unlimited sexual adventure, these things are so by virtue of a more fundamental value-choice deliberately transcending the same awesome and ambivalent inner emergence that also troubled the waking-dreaming female speaker. In daylight translation, the poem's nocturnal dream-thought would appear to be that 'his' *powerful temptation of sexual nomadism* answers 'her' *desire to be desired by the powerful.*

This latter (feminine) ego-identification resonates in the evocation of Solomon's Egyptian bride and her escorted cortege, advancing imposingly in the desert haze, surrounded by regal finery and virile power, amid clouds of incense. This textual fragment, the oldest, is thought to have been composed originally in evocation of the historical Solomon's actual wedding to a daughter of one of the Pharaohs. The context of insertion, with its interweaving echoes and suggestive symmetries, however, creates an analogy-in-desire between the Sulamite and the literally 'royal' bride. In turn, this analogy gives a new depth of resonance and reflection to the organising leitmotif which questions the emergence of the unknown 'other of desire'. 'Who is this approaching, up from the desert ...? [...] Go out and see, o Jerusalem's daughters' (cf. III: 6–11).

If we hear the two voices, masculine and feminine, in their echoing and allusive reciprocity, a pattern of common affirmation seems to emerge, marvellously clarifying the entire relationship of 'love' and 'desire' in the biblical text. For 'him' as for 'her', the Song of love bonded and nuptial emerges precisely in answer to, and in exorcism of, the temptations of a sacralised sexual eros ever-latent in the archaic dream-thinking of humanity: temptations luridly presented to the Israelites, both in their collective *religious* expression (by the fertility rites of Canaan) and in an individual *socio-ethical* expression (by the sexual errancies of Israel's theocratic King).

The sapiential refrain, urged by the Sulamite on the 'daughters of Jerusalem', seems designed to articulate just this pattern of understanding:

Filles de Jérusalem, je vous adjure par les gazelles et les biches des champs, ne réveillez pas, ne réveillez pas celle que j'aime, avant qu'elle le veuille (II: 7; cf. III: 5 and VII: 4)

O women of the city,
Swear by the wild field doe

Not to wake or rouse us
Til we fulfil our love. (Falk, 25)

The latter (modern, Jewish-American) translation no doubt gets the gender of the speaker right; and, no doubt, it translates the first of the two senses generated by one of the most famous of the poem's double entendres. Erotic desire is to be *sated undisturbed*. But what, we may still ask, in this re-echoing and re-alerting text, is the '*fulfilment*' of 'love'? More, assuredly, than anything indicated by the sign 'Do not disturb' placed outside a modern motel room ...[11] The sense of not awakening the redoubtable power of sexual eros before *the time of secure, personal and mutual consent* seems in context to gain clear priority; and, the earlier translation, though less 'accurate', is indubitably more *faithful*.

The delicious erotic intimacy of the lovers is indeed predicated on a closure against predation and errancy, more or less visible according to the translator:

Ma sœur, mon épouse, tu es un jardin fermé, une source fermée, et une fontaine scellée. Tes plantes sont un jardin de grenadiers, avec des fruits délicieux, les troënes avec le nard;
le nard avec le saffran, la canne odorante et le cinnamome, avec toutes sortes d'arbres d'encens; le myrrhe et l'aloès, avec tous les plus excellents aromates.
O fontaine des jardins! O puits d'eau vive, et ruisseaux du Liban! (IV: 12–15)

Enclosed and hidden, you are a garden,
A still pool, a fountain.

Stretching your limbs, you open –
A field of pomegranate blooms,

Treasured fruit among the blossoms,
Henna, sweet cane, bark and saffron,

Fragrant woods and succulents,
The finest spices and perfumes.

Living water, you are a fountain,
A well, a river flowing from the mountains. (Falk, 33)

The 'jardin fermé' à deux, both recalled and longed-for, is well, if over-insistently, conveyed in the first ('traditional') translation as a private space of consensual and assured intimacy in which erotic sensuality is free to blossom in delight (it does so with perhaps excessive *pudeur* on the part of the translator). In the second, it is a place of esoterically fascinated sexuality, linked to a cosmically open nature feeling. Superimposing the first on the second perhaps gives us the biblical Song of the 'perfumed garden'.

The counterpoint between daylight understanding and nocturnal dream-thought focuses in this way the emergent secret wisdom of the *Song*: the shadow-love of *sacralised* or *power-bought eroticism* is exorcised – and Eros raised to nuptiality and to full humanity – only in its bonded and faithful–'conversion'. The 'brotherly' care of the true lover in this sense creates the real conditions for a 'nuptial' fulfilment of erotic desire. Reciprocally, the Sulamite, in her night of erotic langour, defends her elected One in terms that transfer to the beloved (and future husband) the many-splendoured dream of 'royalty'. Is this not also the point of her swearing by the – beautiful and vulnerable –'wild field doe', rather than by the city lights or by the savage gods of orgiastic ritual campfires?

The immanent royalty of Eros (Plato's half-god) is, in short, *re*-invested in the single, particular and embodied love to which it consents. In that particularising re-investment is refound the treasure that is not a transgressive and godlike regal dream, but a concrete and truly 'royal' experience of the splendour of being: analogical, indeed (as the prevalence of simile within the poem's overflowing metaphoricity already suggests), yet nevertheless a *real participation* in the mystery of created being as knowable to humankind, male and female (this is the exact sense of the Hebrew word 'Adam').

The 'search' or 'quest' of the Sulamite, with its answering echoes in her beloved, is best interpreted in terms of this same ultimate wisdom of the *Song*. It is the most resonant and enigmatic feature of the 'poem' *as a textual whole* that the two subjects of enunciation speak *both* as though they had not yet come together in sexual union *and* as though they already had. Certainly, a compilation of wedding songs may readily be supposed to include its own retrospect or re-capitulation: to evoke, that is, without excessive concern for rational chronology, the time of erotic privation and the time of erotic desire 'fulfilled' in physical intimacy. Yet the very characteristic structure and rhythm of our text are not simply those of linear dramatic progression. There is a present of anticipation contemporaneous with a celebration of desire already answered in delight; and the most satisfactory explanation is not anecdotal. It is, rather, that desire physically consummated remains desire; so that 'possession' (derisorily so *misnamed*, as Proust will point out)[12] does not extinguish it, except very temporarily, but rather sharpens and renews it. In this sense, the hymns of praise exchanged in the present tense between the two voices are neither those of fiancés merely, nor exclusively those of a married couple, but both at once, the *before* blending into an *after* distinguished from it only by the increase of intimacy and the deepening of presence-absence.

Similarly, the narrative perfect tense ('J'ai cherché durant des nuits sur ma couche celui qu'aime mon âme', III: 1 ['I have looked in the nights on my bed for my soul-love']) is not to be taken as a pre-nuptial languor only, but as a permanent feature of love, which is centrally and always an experience of *absence-in-presence,* hence an allusive and renewed referral of desire to an act or mode of co-being *other* and *more* than that already known. And this structural pattern itself can be seen as reworking or 'converting' the pattern of amorous passion, which spontaneously creates, through fixated desirous imagination, a *presence-in-absence*.

The alternation and co-existence of 'presence' and 'absence' in the text, composed by its hauntingly superimposed planes of temporality, are most satisfactorily seen, not as an element of psychological realism, therefore, but as a form of poetic suggestion attentive to the 'duration' of loving desire. What appears to our modern understanding as a casualness of narrative-dramatic framework on the part of the editor, may, on the contrary, be seen here as an expressive *trouvaille* offering insight into something the analytical mind readily passes over. Absence and presence, seeking and finding, longing and re-discovery, excursion and return, are the most basic 'durational' categories of the experience of loving – and of living. At least, they become so as soon as 'love' is envisaged, as we have here been led to see it: as a bonded and self-limiting reciprocity of desire, faithfully invested in an elected Other, and maturing in time. The play of presence and absence does not contradict, but rather exemplifies and signifies, the nuptial reciprocity of the 'I-and-Thou'.

Presence–absence, we may say, is the dynamic, subjective inner time (French says 'la durée') of the festal dwelling-in-reciprocity envisaged under the name of such a love: 'Il m'a mené dans la salle du festin, et l'étendard qu'il lève sur moi porte AMOUR' (II: 4) ['He brought me to the banqueting hall, and the standard he raised over me bears the name of LOVE'].

This 'time' of being also has its place. The banner raised like a symbolic tent is the named standard of all the many other dwelling places and spaces in the poem. Interiors or exteriors, these places of erotic desire and tenderly loving passion are all personal places, and, implicitly or potentially, conjugal as well; they also are set under the banner of love, to which they owe their freedom and their variety. All are enunciated, it will be observed, by the feminine voice: a further element of gender differentiation which we may register reductively (the 'nesting instinct'), or else more presciently, if we say that *she* knows better than *he* does what truly *liberates desire* and *transforms* it into love. The lover's willingness not to awaken desire '*before* it pleases' appears then implicit in his fading away from her nocturnal dream-thought: the sign of a caring and tender consent to *another* mode of co-presence.

In what we may call the coda of the poem, 'she' answers in just this way the jointly posed question of what to do with – and for – the 'little sister': 'Je suis comme un mur, et mes seins sont comme des tours; j'ai été à ses yeux comme celle qui trouve la paix' (VIII: 10) ['I am like a wall, and my breasts are towers; I have been in his gaze as one who finds her peace']. If we have followed the syntax of the nuptial dialogue of male and female voices in the poem, her *peace* lies in surmounting the danger, not just of predatory male eros, but of her own gender-specific temptation, essentially reciprocal to it: that of excursive passion in thrall to the erotic appetite of and for power. Is there, for 'love', any peaceful dwelling-place of being-in-joy unless the potent infinitism of Desire accepts embodiment in the limited and particular community of the I-and-Thou, socially inserted and witnessed?

The role of the chorus is that of witness to the emergence of love and its social insertion; and, if the 'daughters of Zion' are indeed to be associated *either* with the Temple *or* with the harem of Solomon (or, particularly, if textual imagination moves *between* these poles), the enigma of the genesis of the poem itself and of its integration into the canon of the Jewish scriptures seems a good deal less opaque and anomalous than many secularist readings have claimed. The religious sense of deliverance from the power of Egypt of the people beloved of Yahweh – his 'bride' and his 'vineyard' – would naturally include also deliverance from the unbridled and sacralised eroticism of the Canaanite fertility cults discovered in the land of the Promise. Sacred and profane might very well recognise a single law or pattern of wisdom:[13] namely, that desire must seek sublimation, so to speak, 'vertically', in the efflorescence of love, rather than 'laterally', in the idolatrous *débordements* of eroticism.

That 'consent' – that is, recognition of, and waiting upon, the Other of one's own desire – is the key to love, has been thrice proclaimed. There can be desire without love, and love outside, or at least beyond, desire; but the Song of Songs proclaims the message of messages. Love – bonded, nuptial and splendid – can be for humankind, and is called to be, the *fulfilment of* desire.

Is it because love thus understood is a treasure of great price, not to be bought with political power or with the potency of erotic sacralisations, that the *Song* ends with a parable-like vignette dismissing the mighty Solomon ('Ma vigne, qui est à moi, je la garde, ô Salomon', VIII: 12 ['My vine is mine and I shall keep it, o Solomon'])? And perhaps because the treasure defended is infinitely fragile before the power and worldly prestige of the counterfeit 'other love', there is, too, an urgent injunction for the safety of the beloved: 'Mon bien-aimé, enfuis-toi aussi vite qu'une gazelle, ou qu'un faon de biche, sur la montagne des aromates' (VIII: 14) [My love, flee like the gazelle, or the doe's fawn, to the bitter-scented mountain]. Is there, one wonders, something perennially contemporary in the suddenly chilly breeze of that minor ending? Its note of tender concern stamps it, at all events, with the name it gives itself: 'AMOUR'.

***

The 'emergence' in meaning of the *Song*, the response to its nuptial celebration and its enigma-freighted questioning, have not ceased over the centuries; and twentieth-century French recognitions are part of a vaster, ongoing posterity. Most commonly, they are mediated by the intervening religious and cultural tradition and are conspicuously self-situating. So Claudel, for instance, labours exegetically and poetically in the vineyard of 'figures' transmitted by the medieval allegorising which he inherits, illumined by insights belonging to the drama of romantic passion and Christian faith which is his own.[14] Gide, in the name of a (homo)sexual liberation, retains an imprint of voice, imagery and theme ('J'ai chanté pour vous, Sulamite')[15] in turning to the 'fruits of the earth'. Valéry, in consequence of his encounter with the *Song* as mediated in the imagery of the sixteenth-century mystic John of the Cross, hears the resonance of the voice acutely and scatters the *Song*'s voices and its images of eros throughout his poetry,[16] while interiorising, in secret rivalry, the enigma of erotic love and its emergence to self-understanding.[17] Julia Kristeva is dazzled and challenged by the *Song*: by its metaphoricity, its pertinence to the contemporary drama of Freudian eros, its improbable and marvellous feminism.[18] Luce Irigaray hears it more obliquely, in confirmation of her own ethic of sexual difference;[19] while the French-Jewish Hélène Cixous appropriates its nuptial song in transgressive bi-sexuality.[20] Paul Ricœur, protesting at one more 'subversive' modern reading (this time, by a theologian!), contributes a formidable and illuminating hermeneutics of emergent meaning to which the present study is indebted.

None, perhaps, echoes the *Song*'s sapiential understanding of itself better than Giraudoux, when he gives his lively, lovely and faithfully bonded Alcmène the following speech:

JUPITER: Pourquoi ne veux-tu pas d'amant?
ALCMÈNE: Parce que l'amant est toujours plus près de l'amour que de l'aimée. Parce que je ne supporte ma joie que sans limites, mon plaisir que sans réticence, mon abandon que sans bornes. Parce que je ne veux pas d'esclave et que je ne veux pas de maître ... Parce que j'aime les fenêtres ouvertes et les draps frais. (*Amphitryon 38*, Act I, sc. 9)

JUPITER: Why will you not have a lover?
ALCMÈNE: Because the lover is always closer to love than to the beloved. Because I can take my joy only unconfined, my pleasure uninhibited, my abandonment entire. Because I will have no slave and no master ... Because I like open windows and clean sheets.

Yet another, deeper, paradox begins here to emerge in turn: that of Western culture itself. The message so well heard by Giraudoux (at least in a polite, bourgeois projection) is not referred to any Judaeo-Christian source whatsoever. Quite the reverse: to speak it all, the mythical disguise of a *Hellenic* framing is required, together with a heroine who defends the human condition against the predation *of the gods*. The criss-cross of this paradox has a certain thickness which will provide a leitmotif in our own recognitions of cultural origins.

***

As a first step, we may enquire further about the logic of the *Song*'s incorporation into, and its transmission by, the canon of the Judaeo-Christian scriptures. If we follow Ricœur, the 'anthropological' question asked about human subject-identity is pushed towards ultimacy by the text's very 'failure' to be answerable in the dramatic and narrative patterns of expectation to which the *poem* stubbornly refuses to conform, and by its exuberant 'between-the-lines' realisation of metaphorical meanings. 'La métaphore vive', for Ricœur, is not only lively, but of quickening ontological penetration and pertinence.[21] It intuits what is true 'vertically' (ontically) from what is true 'horizontally' (humanly and existentially). This is a text looking for a transcending answer to its own emergent-and-transcending question.

We also know something of the environment of reception within Solomon's Temple and the cultural context of development it finds in Israel's return from captivity. What is decisive here is, of course, Israel's self-understanding as the people of the Covenant: both the 'vineyard'[22] and the 'bride'[23] of a high and demanding God ('jealous' is, in biblical speech, a conscious and quite unabashed anthropomorphism explicating this analogy). The most 'erotic' human love is seen here, precisely, as a real (if imperfect) *likeness* of the divine love, a lively metaphor of it (just as sexual errancy is *like* the religion of the golden calf, the 'idolatry' of Baal). It then also follows that human love can be used to speak of the antecedent, larger Love which seeks and calls it, as to its own fulfilment.

This final metaphoric 'emergence' is clearly present in the following verses in which, we may think, the amorous dialogue takes fullest cognisance reflectively of its own depths:

> Who is this approaching
>   Up from the wilderness
>   Arm on her lover's arm?
>
>
>   Under the quince tree
>   you woke
>   to my touch
>   there
>   where she conceived
>   where she who carried
>   and bore you
>   conceived

Stamp me in your heart,
Upon your limbs,
Sear my emblem deep
Into your skin.

For love is as strong as death,
Harsh as the grave.
Its tongues are flames, a fierce
And holy blaze.

Endless seas and floods,
Torrents and rivers
Never put out love's
Infinite fires.

Those who think that wealth
Can buy them love
Only play the fool
And meet with scorn. (Falk, 46–7 cf. VIII: 1–7)

This passage responds to the re-echoing motif of a mysterious subject-identity to be deciphered. Its last verse gathers up its sapiential message about the treasure of inestimable worth, to be infinitely respected, indefinitely preserved against its own perils, deviations and idolatries – 'Can't buy me love!' (John Lennon). But now there is something else. The dialogue of feminine and masculine voices is pursued *at the level of a 'vertical' (theological) reflection.* In the first-quoted stanza, we find the chorus rehearsing the enigma that now encompasses human subject-identity as such; in the second 'she' speaks to 'him', as initiatrix in carnal knowledge and inheritor of maternal wisdom; in the third, 'she' speaks again – but now, unmistakeably, with '*His*' voice, in an urgent plea that is at once that of human love and that of Israel's election. The seal to be set upon arm and heart (rather than on the '[fore]skin' merely) is the bond of fidelity, freely assumed in consent ('*mets-toi* un sceau'). The reason for the injunction to assume it is that in the flesh, always-already-there, resides a God-given flame of spirit-led sexuality ('flamme de l'éternel', VIII: 6) recognised as formidable, *both* in respect of its capacity for loving (said to be as strong as death) *and* in its 'infernal' virtuality of possessive passion and power-bought or power-led sexual dependency. The founding reality of human love and desire is seen here as the imprinted mark of a divine Covenant written in the organic and psychosexual human 'flesh',[24] such that no natural force can erase it.

All of which is a far cry from Plato. One world of experience encompasses loves human and divine, answering each other in metaphoric analogy and re-echoing allusion; the flesh is no obstacle to the spirit, but its home and locus of efflorescence; the spirit no hindrance to the flesh, but its very calling. And, without loss of mystery – *au contraire!* – the *Song* knows, very differently from Plato, what, in erotic love, *is* 'divine' – and what is *not*.

This 'alternative' account of love and desire offered by the Song of Songs is indeed embedded in *another* account of 'transcendence'. To this account, and to its evolving reception in Western cultural tradition, we must now turn.

Notes

1   It is not agreed among editors and exegetes whether the singular 'Song' represents an anthology of heterogeneous but related lyric fragments, loosely edited, or whether a single author, working with received materials, has fashioned a substantial unity, somewhat loosened by later additions and modification in the course of transmission. See the discussion of this point by Michael V. Fox, *The Song of Songs and the Ancient Egyptian Love Songs* (Madison, WI: University of Wisconsin Press, 1985).

2   See R. J. Tournay O.P., *Word of God, Song of Love: A Commentary on the Song of Songs*, trans. J. E. Crowley (New York: Paulist Press, 1988). Tournay is the former Director of the École biblique et archéologique française de Jérusalem.

3   1 Kings 11: 3 remembers him as having, in round figures, seven hundred wives and three hundred concubines.

4   See 'The Song of Songs' in G Buttrick (ed.), *The Interpreters Bible*, Vol. 5 (New York: Abingdon Press, 12 vols, 1952–57).

5   One of the significant features of the original Hebrew is that its pronominal suffixes can (usually) allow exegetes to determine grammatically the gender and number of the speakers.

6   No single translation is adequate. In the hope of reflecting the text's lyric voice, as well as its translational difficulties and its allusively re-echoing depths, we quote here, sometimes comparatively, two translations, one traditional: *La Sainte Bible*, Version d'Ostervald (Paris: rue de Clichy, 1903), the other modern and poetic: M. Falk, *Love Lyrics from the Bible: A Translation and Literary Study of the Song of Songs* (Sheffield: The Almond Press, 1982). The first is referenced in my text with traditional biblical verses; the second as 'Falk' followed by page number.

7   M. Buber, *I and Thou*, trans. W. Kaufmann (New York: Charles Scribner's Sons, 1970), see especially pp. 53–85.

8   See 'La métaphore nuptiale' in A. Lacoque & P. Ricœur, *Penser la Bible* (Paris: Seuil, 1998), pp. 411–56.

9   See G Knight & F. Golka, *The Song of Songs and Jonah: Revelation of God* (Edinburgh & Grand Rapids: Erdemans, 1988), p. 27.

10 Ricœur, *Penser la Bible*, p. 416.

11 This Interpretation is derived from R. Gordis, *The Song of Songs and Lamentations: A Study, Modern Translation and Commentary* (New York: Jewish Theological Seminary KATAV, 1954, 3rd edn 1974), who likens this refrain – questionably – to Ovid's '*O lente, lente, currite noctis equi*' (p. 55).

12 *A la Recherche du temps perdu*, ed. J.-Y. Tadié, Bibliothèque de la Pléiade (Paris: Gallimard, 1987), Vol. I, p. 230.

13 The biblical 'Book of Wisdom' contains a number of suggestive pointers as to how this interaction may have occurred: Wisdom is given a feminine personification; she is questioned by King Solomon; the review of Wisdom in the history of the chosen people includes the encounter with the idolatry of the Canaanites, and so on.

14 See *infra* Chapter 8.

15 A. Gide, *Les Nourritures terrestres* (Paris: Gallimard, 1935), p. 91.

16 See, in *La Jeune Parque*, Valéry's reworking of, for example, the motif 'Who is this…?'
    ('Dieux! dans ma lourde plaie une secrète sœur/Brûle …'), or of the unlocked fountains
    of springtime in the famous 'Primavera' fragment.

17 See *infra* Chapter 7.

18 See *infra* Chapter 15.

19 See *infra* Chapter 13.

20 See H. Cixous, *Vivre l'Orange* (Paris: Des Femmes, 1979).

21 P. Ricœur, *La Métaphore vive* (Paris: Seuil, 1975).

22 See Ps. 80: 14; Isaiah 5: 1–7; Jer. 2: 21, 6: 9, 12: 10; Hos. 10: 1, 14: 7.

23 See Isaiah 49: 18, 61: 10, 62: 3–5; Jer. 2: 32; Rev. 21: 2.

24 The biblical use of this word is by no means equivalent to Plato's 'body'. As we see from
    the *Song*, it designates the entire natural reality of the human composite: the spirit is –
    marvellously – incarnate, and the material body is spirit-written through and through.

Chapter 3

Shadow Upon Splendour: Genesis, Transgression and the West

If there is one text more fundamental to Western culture as a whole than the two previously considered it is the account of Creation and the Fall given in the first three chapters of the biblical Book of Genesis. In this chapter, we revisit the founding 'theological myth' and its echoes in certain twentieth-century French recognitions of origin. It is hoped to offer some account of the shadow of estrangement from the Judaeo-Christian matrix of our culture, which, as we will increasingly perceive, lies across the entire logical space of contemporary Western decipherments of Eros.

The first step will be to recognise the solidarity of this text with the wisdom-poem we have just read. The *Song of Songs* 'reads' the principal features of the founding myth of origins strikingly well; more percipiently, we may think, than the reductivist suspicion of post-Freudian 'deconstruction' on the one hand; and far better, on the other, than some traditional accounts which once passed in Western Christianity for 'orthodoxy'. This reading will offer us some basic ground from which to recognise and evaluate the tradition of contestatory counter-readings of the themes of Genesis which are so central to Western (and particularly French) cultural tradition. By way of *apéritif*, a brief hermeneutical prologue is required.

***

To understand that a myth is 'foundational' is of course to realise that it is likely to form an *enjeu* (stake) in the way everybody within a given culture construes his/her own preferred version of the collective identity. This means in turn that the decipherer is always mirrored in his/her decipherment: there is a hermeneutic circle. Twentieth-century deconstructionism responds to this considerable fact by saying that 'the text' has no mind of its own: what we construct out of it is an unstable and infinite play of self-generated meanings reflecting only our own meaning-making. If we mistrust the deconstructionist palace of mirrors, as there is good reason to do, the only recourse lies in hermeneutics itself.

My own reading is indebted to the most luminous of twentieth-century hermeneutic philosophers, Paul Ricœur, in particular to his remarkable study of Genesis 'Penser la creation'.[1] Ricœur's reading of the well-known text (but wait!...) rests on a splendid distinction between two narratological 'times': the *'primordial time' of myth* and the *time of historical narrative*; the first being distinguishable from the second, although calling to it and interpenetrating it in a *complex relation*, at once that of *inauguration* and that of *foundation*. Developed with rigorous patience by the master of *Temps et récit*, this distinction gently casts adrift, one after another, the most assured certainties of the post-Enlightenment quarrel over Genesis. No, says Ricœur, this text nowhere talks about creation *ex nihilo* (the very question of the radical origin of things did not arise before the inter-fertilisation of Greek and Hebraic thought in the Hellenistic era). No, there isn't one single act of global creation; rather, a series of creative beginnings, dynamically interlinked, some relating to cosmogenesis, others to anthropogenesis. No, we can't say either that this is a pre-scientific fable recounting the origin of things, since that is to confuse the 'primordial time' of myth with the 'time' of historical *récit* ('How liberating it is,' notes Ricœur mischievously, 'to confess that there is no call to date the creation of Adam relatively to Pitheanthropicus or Neanderthal man' [p. 59]!). No, we can't even say that there is in this text one model of the creating act, since there are several, all traditional. Westermann's typology is cited: creation by generation, by combat, by fabrication, by speech: the hermeneuticist points out that the only model missing here is creation by generation – the reserved space, perhaps, of a 'not-yet-said'?

And No, there is no reason, in respect of the Fall, to distinguish in the *historical* condition of humankind a *before* and an *after*. No: it isn't the Fall, therefore, that creates death – nowhere does the text say man was created immortal; rather, the Fall changes the sign under which death is experienced and viewed, its existential 'meaning'.

We might summarise this often surprising series of negatives by saying that, freed from the 'retrospective illusion' of an historical narration projected by readers of our culture onto the 'primordial time' of myth, the Book of Genesis does not recount divine creation as a constituted and closed action, nor as a form of divinely written 'finished work' mysteriously mortgaged to all the imperfections suffered by an unfortunate and accursed humanity.

Consternation! For this is very centrally what the thinkers of the French Enlightenment, the poets of the Romantic-Symbolist-Surrealist tradition and all the Masters of Suspicion who followed in twentieth-century critical theory actually thought, or still think, that it does say... And not without just cause, since this is somewhat, and on occasion a great deal, what they were hearing from the authorised interpreters of the text. Genesis, or the *much mystified* foundation ...

From the hermeneuticist's viewpoint, what is capital in this Judaeo-Christian myth is the original solution of the writers as confronted by the knot of the mystery of being itself: the knot in which is enfolded all thought of creation, and all creative thought. Of this original resolution, Ricœur writes: 'The religious presupposition here is that the origin itself speaks in letting itself be said. In this point, the origin of things and the origin of utterance coincide. This coincidence can only be received as a gift: the gift of being and the gift of the utterance of being. From this gift, all returns to the origin of things are possible, permitted, required, even though they risk losing themselves in the unseizable' (p. 85). Hence, in all serenity, the declaration in Genesis of a momentous thing, quite unwitnessed, entirely non-imaginable: 'In the beginning, God created the heavens and the earth' (Gen. 1: 1). A declaration which is *either* – hermeneutics always gives us choices! –'apodyptic' (i.e. self-authorising, like Descartes, *Cogito*) *or* 'kerygmatic' (i.e. gifted hearing, given proclamation).

The hermeneuticist's tabula rasa is helpful to us by way of refreshing our twenty-first-century act of attention to the foundational text. What account of transcendence, desire and love is there, then, to attend to?

***

Whatever status we decide to give them, the first words of the first book of the Judaeo-Christian scriptures affirm the Creator's transcendence over all existing things – all time and space, all of nature, the entirety of historical process. For the biblical writers, this 'given' is not something to be defined or demonstrated: rather, it is something always-already-there – encountered, acknowledged, responded to. In this perspective, human desiring and loving stand – and 'fall' – as they come to exist in the first place: in relation to a prior and ultimate Other. Within the 'good' creation, the human potential for transcendence is specified in function of this primary aptitude for relationality; yet all play is given to all virtualities of all freedoms (among these, of course, the human freedom to decipher – and dispose of – Eros).

'So God created man in his own image, in the image of God he created him; male and female He created him' (Gen. 1: 27). The divine image in humankind is its charter and first model of 'transcendence'. This imprint means that man, alone in nature, intrinsically transcends nature – including 'human nature'. We are endowed, that is, with a capacity for creatively self-determining freedom irreducible, in the ultimate, to all pre-determinations and constraints (of material necessity, economic law, sexual cause, social morality, political power, self-interest, past events, etc.); minimally and at least, we can always, as the *Song* suggests, 'flee to the mountains'. The divine imprint also conditions the human aptitude for relationality: both 'vertically' (as explicated by the entire drama of relational dealings recorded in the Bible); and 'horizontally' (including the individual love-bonding represented in the *Song*). It is the ground-in-possibility of all giving and forgiving, all promising and self-committal (cf. the *Song*'s 'seal' set on heart and arm). On this account, all 'other-encounters' will be configured in a *triangular form*, since all bear as their enabling first condition and deepest Other-indication the image of the transcendent God. As the *Song* allusively 'knows', in every relationship 'God is always the third party' (Kirkegaard).[2]

'Male and female He created him.' As acts of Creation go, this is a very much more purposeful policy of sexual differentiation than that attributed to Zeus. The divine image or likeness is *not* exclusively masculine; it rests upon the male-female dyad (the Hebrew word 'Adam' means, as we saw, humankind – *anthropos*). Sex-and-gender difference in humans is given as the finishing touch and the crowning glory of the 'work' in nature of the Creator. It recapitulates the purposive promise of the word which creates order-out-of-chaos, as it has already distinguished the geophysical elements from each other, living creatures from the world of things, and man from animals.

In this ancient myth of creation and fall, sexual differentiation is seen as a prime means by which the work of creation is continued in man creatively (i.e. not simply as a perpetuation of the aboriginal status quo). The call to relationship with the creating and transcendent Other has, as its charter of passage, the recognition of the sexually gendered, creaturely Other, from whom is learned the fact of incompleteness (in experienced *desire*) and the relational value of alterity (as experienced in *love*). French theologian Erich Fuchs comments:

> The 'goodness' of male–female unions refers to the goodness of creation, for sexuality is the sign of the difference by which God reveals his own Otherness. Thus in Gen. 2: 23 man's accession to communicative speech (as distinct from the mere naming of things [as in Gen. 2: 21]) is described as the result of his encounter with the woman. Man can speak to God only when he is revealed to himself by the alterity of the other (sex). This is to declare the positive function of desire, whenever it is recognition of the other.[3]

The hope of realising the potential for divinity written into the flesh integrally supposes sexual differentiation – not as an accident or afterthought, but as something primordially inscribed in the weave and texture of things written by the Creator's ongoingly writing hand. This view of the *transcendence immanent in humankind* adequately accounts, we might think, for the striking fact that, while the *Symposium* is not significantly 'about' male–female loves at all, the *Song of Songs*, right down to its gender-differentiated voices, with their answering symmetry and their structural complementarity-in-dialogue, is about nothing else. The antiphonal duo of the couple, exalting in the wonder and joy of their reciprocity-in-difference, and haloed in the glories of the natural world, is the faithful and moving expression of just this conception of Genesis. That 'profane love' is totally sacred in this sense (and *not* in the later sense of referring to a *reserved sphere* of religious acts and references set apart from the common world of human experience) may imply, according to Genesis, that it is 'sacred' in a manner that has all but ceased to be recognisable in our culture.

'And God saw everything that he had made, and behold, it was very good' (Gen. 1: 31). The *Song* develops this same idea: it is, indeed, the *point of exclamation* developed by the answering voice of humankind; an exclamation which embraces in principle – how would it fail, on this account of human 'transcendence', to do so? – the superlative splendour of the most embodied and erotic sexuality. Across the primary wonder of creation lies no shadow of shame or blame: 'And the man and his wife were naked and were not ashamed' (Gen. 2: 24). This edenic reality too finds its echo in the poem; the Sulamite is 'at peace' when she recognises that same grounding in 'goodness'.

Yet in the *Song*, we saw a shadow reality to be first confronted and overcome, a darkness in the paradise of created being. There, the temptation of human Eros is seen as the counterfeit love which mimics the treasure without price. If its symbolic embodiment is the kingly power of Solomon, it also inhabits the dream-thought of both lovers. Its form is the will to possession which, mitigated by whatever courtesy of social forms, believes it can ravish the crown, or buy it transactionally, with the 'royalty' that is wealth-and-power. It is the 'love' which – *as measured by its potential for that transcendence to which it is called*— suffers from not being *love*. It is the 'passion' of erotic desire experienced as autonomously god*like* and parodically mimicking deity: self-related, compulsive, objectifying, infinitist, predatory, concupiscent – and, somewhere in its own *telos*, having murder in mind.

Paradigmatically, Genesis offers a mythical account of this shadow. It shows the counterfeit love as a perverse deviancy of moral freedom within the created order: a disobedience of Eros in respect of its own charter, hence a betrayal or defacement of its own true godlikeness. The Serpent suggests it (Gen. 3: 1–5). He is a leading voice older than rational consciousness, an archaic presence 'always already there' in the space of the bountiful Garden of human living and loving. If we follow the metaphoric logic of the *Song*, he is the voice of the nocturnal dream-thought *always already there* in the human psyche. He presents the Creator as the metaphysical Solomon: that is, the Powerful One (in psychoanalytical terms, the castrating Oedipal Father or Superego; in the language of Girardian cultural anthropology, the mimetic Rival), whose jealous edicts exclude the human couple from access to the innermost life of paradise: that is, from the ultimately hidden Thing reserved within the life of the transcendent Creator, the ontological mystery itself. The Serpent speaks of this ultimate and defining limit as if it were a challenge to human desire *of the same order as the interdicts of man-made socio-cultural regulation*; that is, as if it were a limit *in culture* and not a limit *defining created nature*; hence, an intolerable restriction arbitrarily placed on human liberty. Transcendence, suggests the Serpent alternatively, lies in transgression. The quasi-divine ecstasy he promises beckons to a practice of Eros which, at whatever level of realisation (sexual, amorous, political, religious, etc.) has the *arrière-pensée* of an unmediated, self-procured experience of the divine: 'You shall be as gods, knowing good and evil' (Gen. 3: 5).

More quickly than her partner, Eve responds. Here, too, 'she' is the leading human voice – by virtue of a prompt complicity with vital forces and life-mysteries. Is this not, in the *Song of Songs* also, what makes 'her', with her immediate same-gender confidentiality and her articulate speech, the leading voice of love and desire? The Serpent is crafty enough to have *chosen* his Interlocutor: rather the intuitively swift and spiritually venturesome 'mare among stallions' than the leaden-footed author of that compliment![4] Perverse enough, too, to exploit the great anthropological Difference between them. Surely, he says, hissing suavely, she is too subtle to be taken in by all that Patriarchal Nonsense, and so unfair, about 'Transgression'? Are not all prohibitions, starting with this single quite incomprehensible Decree of His, invented to frustrate by intimidation one's very natural curiosity about life-mysteries? Indeed, alas, to put Her down; and precisely because She is a person of such Superior Sense and Sensibility? The Seducer's art, as we know from the *Song*, is a way of awakening desire prior to and beyond consent.

Eating the fruit of the Tree of the Knowledge of good and evil signifies, immediately, knowing the shadow-side of human eros, in both its sexual and its spiritual reaches: fear, shame, inhibition in respect of sexual difference; wariness of the knotted threats it poses of rivalry, resentment, jealousy, cruelty, exploitation, regression and violence – everything, in short, that caused the Sulamite her nocturnal misadventures and her daytime fears. 'Otherness' has dramatically changed its sign:

> from positive, it becomes negative; henceforth, everything must be done to reduce it. Thus to the falsified image of God (as jealous) corresponds a falsified image of the other sex, seen as threatening ... Loincloths of leaves have to hide what signals sexual alterity. Henceforth the sex of the other becomes the forbidden fruit, in relation to which the same play of greed and fear will be indefinitely worked out. Sex is thus subtly sacralised, taking the place of the founding limit, whereas it was meant to refer us to this limit.[5]

The same inversion of signs operates in the immediate self-disculpation and re-apportioning of blame: the man indicts 'the woman you [Yahweh] gave me' (Gen. 3: 12). The woman, who blames the serpent, is threatened with not being able to assume her femininity without enslavement to man: 'Thy desire shall be to thy husband and he shall rule over thee' (Gen. 3: 16). Sexuality is here evoked as a place, not of reciprocal and bonded dwelling-in-joy, but of co-habiting uneasily or conflictually under the curse of an eros directed towards self-gratifying and – explicitly male – power. This is an anthropological perspective of immense insight (anticipating feminism and Foucault), no doubt born out of much bitter human experience; but it is linked to the Creator only in the sense that it is what humankind, individually and collectively, is free to make, and predictably does make, out of the 'very good' thing purposed in creation.

Disconcertingly, however, at least to literalist modern eyes, the writer of the third chapter of Genesis (who is not the same person as the writer of chapter 1),[6] appears to attribute this threat and this shadow immediately to the 'cursing' decree of the Creator. At least, he shows us the latter speaking, to all seeming just like Solomon, sentencing humanity to hard labour and suffering for transgression of a royal interdict (Gen. 3: 14–24). In the wake of the Serpent's speech, appearances are deceptive. The contradictions, exegetical and logical, set up by a *literal* interpretation of the divine voice and viewpoint in this passage are insuperable. It is as if the Creator had suddenly become one of the 'gods', precisely in the sense the Serpent has suggested (and as the writer, by the very use of that plural form, attributed to the Serpent, has just told us he is *not*). Voice and viewpoint have to be regarded therefore as poetic anthropomorphisms of the type for which there is entire licence in myth, and which rarely troubles Old Testament writers generally. To each age its discernment: post-Freudian readers may well decode them as incorporating a fair dose of patriarchal severity and expressing the superego of the writer himself – an immediate symptom of the *inversion of signs* predictable from the Genesis narrative itself. 'Though guilty and punished, humanity is not, however, accursed.'[7]

If we are willing to read 'theological myth' as *myth* in which the *theology* still has to be done and re-done (rather than as primitive scientific cosmology, historical anthropology, moral treatise, *cinéma-vérité* or any form of naïve realism), the same writer has already given the real 'cause' of what follows: to taste transgressively is to die (Gen. 2: 17). The good fruit itself, once partaken of in concupiscence, is poisonous to man and gives the very genuine knowledge-by-acquaintance of evil, over and against the 'goodness' primordially purposed and 'previously' known. It follows that the shadow lying over love and desire is not, on this account, the consequence of any superadded act of condemnatory divine punishment. It is, here and always, the reified and 'fatal' consequence of human errancy. It is a self-inflicted wound to the created potential for transcendence; in which, theologically speaking, consists the 'Fall'.[8]

Genesis does not signify, just as the Song of Songs very transparently does not signify, that mankind is divinely condemned to a sexuality of sin and grief; or that human desire as such is evil; or that the children of the paradigmatic couple will never again know the 'goodness' of desire and the transcending excellence of love. In the religious and cultural traditions in which the Song of Songs stands, and from which we inherit, human eros *is*, however, seen decisively *in its ambivalence* – as shadow profiled against splendour. And the enigma of human subject-identity, freighted with its incoercible vocation of transcendence, will be inextricably linked to the same fractured and ambiguous emergence. We have not finished, therefore, with the Sulamite's question, which finds in the Genesis narrative its most radical paradigm of understanding: 'Who is this who…?'

***

Now the reading just offered of the most obviously founding myth of Western culture, though it may command wide recognition from readers who have followed the exegetical and hermeneutical revolution of the twentieth century, is by no means culturally evident common ground. In chapters to come, we shall discover ample evidence that the vision of this founding text, and of the Judaeo-Christian matrix as a whole, has come to be, as a source and resource, occluded almost beyond recognition – all but 'lost' to cultural memory and self-understanding. This estrangement is the very considerable phenomenon to which we must now attend.

As symptomatic pointer to the *explicandum*, we may consider the parodic and orphic variation on Genesis written in the latter days of the First World War by Paul Valéry in his poem 'Ébauche d'un Serpent'.[9] The poem is mischievously dedicated to a convert of the Catholic Revival of that period, Henri Ghéon. It represents a subversive re-writing of the founding myth into which Valéry, brilliantly, weaves his own heterodox decipherment of the inherited motifs of Creation, Fall and the human Adventure in history – all interpreted *from the viewpoint of the seducing Serpent*. As narrator and principal actor of the drama, the Serpent revisits the Garden of all things *in principio*. In a monologue which modulates from ringing cosmic denunciation, through jubilant and clowning sensuality to narcissistic self-applause, he relives his epic 'triumph' of seducing the mother of humankind from her primary allegiance to 'l'Etre vieil et pur' ['the old and pure Being']. Eve is the delectable figure of the first human psyche or 'soul'; the Serpent's seduction song infuses into her the awakening savour of critical self-awareness and autonomous Eros: 'La sinueuse amour/Que j'ai du père dérobé' ['the sinuous love/That I from the father stole']. Eve is re-fashioned spiritually in the image of the Serpent's reflexive self-love; she then becomes prey to a thirst for movement, transformation and growth. Her future visions of Ascent shake the great Tree of Knowledge itself, with a dark and prodigious dynamism, athirst for its own transcendence, overshadowing the heavens luminously, yet also bearing fruits of death, despair and disorder. So – as the finale of the poem asserts, in a defiance at once mystical and burlesque – the very thirst which has made mankind a giant-in-nature lifts up towards Being the strange power of negation or nothingness that is human consciousness:

> – Cette soif qui te fit géant
> Jusqu'à l'Etre exalte l'étrange
> Toute-puissance du néant! (Ébauche, st. 31)

> This thirst which made you a giant/Up to Being exalts the strange/Omnipotence of nothingness!

What has happened here to Genesis? We observe, first, that the biblical text itself has been multiply mediated through a number of identifiable cultural models and re-construed in their image. The poem's inverted counter-vision of creation as a Fall of God is the most striking example. The Creator of all things visible and invisible is anathematised by the Serpent for having failed to retain his perfect self-coincidence as absolute Being:

> Cieux, son erreur!
> Temps, sa ruine
> Et l'abîme animal, béant!
> Quelle chute dans l'origine
> Etincelle au lieu de néant! (st. 7)

> Heavens, his error!/Time, his ruin/And the animal abyss, gaping!/What a fall in the beginning/A spark instead of nothingness!

He is denounced for having created the human Other out of weakness, in despair at his own loss of perfection, and in order to procure the paltry consolations of servile human praise:

> Si profond fut votre malaise
> Que votre souffle sur la glaise
> Fut un soupir de désespoir! (st. 8)

> So deep was your malaise/That your breath upon the clay/Was a sigh of despair!

This – gnostic – reading of creation derives immediately from Baudelaire, who writes: 'What is the fall? If it is unity become duality, it is God who has fallen. In other

words, is not the creation the fall of God?'[10] Beyond Baudelaire, we hear echoes of
an orphic dissidence from Catholic orthodoxy which has been gathering momentum
in the whole Romantic-Symbolist tradition. Valéry's Serpent outdoes the Romantic
Lucifer in resplendent accusation of contingency and spiritual exile; just as his
designing eroticism of Intellect mockingly echoes Hugo's tender wonder at 'Le Sacre
de la Femme'. Like Mallarmé, his all-powerful Second Word *corrects* the divine
Word spoken in Creation, and proclaims the superiority of the conscious artist.
Specifically, he remembers Poe's exalted cosmogony of *Eureka*: if the Creation is
the sublime poem of the supreme Artist, then the Serpent, his Critic and Rival, will
do *better*.

Deciphered after the imprint of its mediating sources, Genesis is then contested
in its supposed affirmation. This *myth of origins* is what the Enlightenment thinkers
suspected all myths were: naïve fictions making irreceivable monotheistic nonsense
out of metaphysical conundrums on the provenance, finality and the nature of the
soul. In the – pre-reflexive – Garden of neo-scholastic Catholic orthodoxy, the Serpent
stands as subversive *farceur*: delighting in paradox and preferring his own dark
lucidity; yet taking care to cloak himself in Bossuet's cadences ('Celui qui règne
dans les cieux' ['He who reigns in the heavens']), and to wear the language of jesuitical
casuistry ('Pour cueillir ce que tu voudras/Ta belle main te fut donnée' ['To gather
what you will/Your beautiful hand was given you']). Globally, his dissidence displaces
from the human garden the traditional religious science of ontotheology (referrable
to 'L'Etre vieil et pur'), and actively replaces it with a 'neuve science' of autonomous
divinity, representing the affirmation ('Je suis! je serai!' ['I am, I will be']) of modern
times; a science of the self-cognisant human mind and spirit, subduing the world,
bearing the burden and the grandeur of its own idealisations ('songes') according to
its own – Hegelian – dynamic of upreaching transcendence.

We may suspect, if we are familiar with the more secret resonances of Valéry,
that the poem's foreboding about the human adventure as reconfigured by the Serpent
is more than a last virtuoso trick of this sinister, if clowning, *farceur*. The same
thought is suggested by the debonnaire apology offered at the end of the poem to the
outplayed and undone Creator of Genesis; and by the hints offered by the whole
poem that the Serpent's hatred is rooted in frustrated or disappointed love of the
Absolute. Still, the poem asserts unmistakably that there is no way back to the *in
principio* which is taken to be the religious affirmation of the received culture myth.
Nor, more insidiously, is there any way back to an exegetically accurate and
theologically re-informed reading of the actual text of Genesis. Precisely not: since
a new culture-story (essentially that of anthropocentric humanism since the
Renaissance) has become the prism through which the founding myth is decoded;
so that the founding myth itself acquires the new status of a *recapitulative symbol* of
the now rejected construct of human meaning; it now stands as *repoussoir*, or 'anti-
term', in an oppositional dialectic of auto-centred Eros. A new and rival foundation
myth is indeed inscribed in the emptied-out shell of the Judaeo-Christian story of
creation and fall. It is integral to the subject's own counter-project of transcendence;
and it is of one psychic substance with his grimly determined *fuite en avant*. 'I am

on the road which formerly led to paradise/But now I must find the strength to look upon the Nevermore.'[11] Like Orpheus, in short, Valéry's modern Faust must not, dare not, 'look back'.

At which point, the real biblical Beginning is refracted, scattered and buried beyond recall. The Serpent's sketch leaves an exact and haunting image of the larger *repudiating de-connection* of the Western mind, in the twentieth century of the Common Era, from its own sources of self-understanding.

***

The ground is thus prepared for the vengeful revisionist narrativising of love-and-desire in history which runs subterraneously through French nineteenth-century culture, exploding at the time of the First World War with Surrealism. Benjamin Péret offers an exemplar of this thinking in a late text, 'Le Noyau de la comète',[12] which envisages the celestial trail of Eros in history, leading up to the glowing heart of the Surrealist comet itself: 'sublime love'.

For Péret, the ancient world was already on the verge of carrying sexual relationality to a sublime fruition. 'But already, Christianity was there.' This grimly premonitory piano-roll ushers in the Villain of the piece:

> It was the prerogative of this religion to set against sexuality an entirely disincarnate love, transferred to the divinity alone [...]. To the free exercise of sexuality, having no other goal initially than its own satisfaction, the Church imposed an ineluctable task. It channelled the sex-drive without attempting any lifting up in the order of feeling, and confined itself to directing towards the divinity those spiritual forces which were tending obscurely towards the metamorphosis of love. (*Anthologie*, p. 33)

The main indictment is that of subjecting humanity for centuries to a deforming repression of sexuality, thus inhibiting the flowering within human love of an erotic sublimation – an efflorescence of love – that was otherwise in train. The mechanisms of this historic crime are multiply present, Péret asserts, in the traditional Catholic moral regulation of sexuality, itself rooted, so he believes, in the logic of revealed truth. He cites in particular: the subjection of woman to man within monogamous unions; prescriptive priestly intrusion, limiting the very form of the sexual act; policing by the intrusive confessor; the culpabilising of sexuality, diminished and overshadowed by an anguished and anguishing cult of sin (this, he claims, is already present in germ in the Mosaic law and is decreed out of the essence of Christianity's own cult of the wrathful Jehovah). The entire regulatory corset he sees as being imposed under the promise of 'illusory heavenly felicities' and – at least in the high Middle Ages – under the terrifying threat of Hell. 'Christianity became a religion of repression like no other' (*Anthologie*, p. 34).

Within the 'merciless Christian world', sexual communion has suffered a mutilation which reacts catastrophically on its sublimatory potential. Feminine eros in particular is thrust back into one of two derivative roles, splitting its thrust dualistically: maternal tenderness is all that is left to the flesh, disincarnate mysticism for the spirit. Under the influence of the Augustinian doctrine of original sin, woman becomes the mythic incarnation, not of beauty, but of sin and temptation. Moreover, this malignant development has a latent agenda of sinister intent:

> By transforming woman into a diabolical temptress and sexuality into a supreme sin, Christianity wanted above all to protect its dogma and the Church to strengthen its hold. Classical antiquity offered many myths directly issuing from desire and from woman in which it recognised the source of an unstoppable impetus, the transformations of which were likely to defeat Christianity ... The Church suspected that only woman could vanquish its God. This is why it attempted, later, to give human impulses an outlet in the myth of Mary. (*Anthologie*, p. 35)

Whereas the latter centuries of the Roman Empire brought merely the triumph of the flesh over a degraded spirit, Christianity repressed and corrupted the flesh the better to master the spirit in its very degradation. It compressed into a mould of mortality and mutilation 'all the forces of humanity aspiring to life' (*Anthologie*, p. 36), thus determining, in conjunction with the barbarian invasions, a cultural and social regression which culminated in the 'dark ages'. The heretical revolts of the period and, spectacularly, the Cathar epic, are interpreted by Péret (here following René Nelli)[13] as 'resurgences of the repressed'. According to this reading, Catharism taught that the love of and for woman was the means of rising towards spiritual love, and it enshrined an ideal femininity taken over from Gnostic tradition. Only the slow evolution of economic and social conditions could however, by stages, bring a complete transformation of sensibility and the longed-for rehabilitation of womankind and of natural human Eros.

This decipherment of gendered Eros and its alienation in history is a paradigmatic statement of a 'death-of-God' vision of the European past. Any watcher of popular TV presentations of love and desire,[14] any reader of *Playboy* or *Cosmopolitan* – or of a vast part of academic critical theory! – will be aware of its extensive field of persuasion in the century just closed. Is this not the ultimate Signified – if we except only relativising Irony itself – at the centre of the labyrinth of signs presented in a postmodern text such as Umberto Eco's *The Name of the Rose* (itself a symbolic mirror held up to the culture field of the contemporary West)?

Reviewed in twenty-first century retrospect, Péret's vehement pamphlet should, however, inspire the sort of reservations that go with its inspiration and genre. Is there not a dramatic foreshortening of temporal perspective in this exegesis of origins? (Is it the case, for instance, that late antiquity was ripe for the sublime transfiguration of liberated sexuality into love, or that the same love revolution was abortively prefigured in Catharism?) A darkening ideological simplification seems to be at work, too, in the account offered of the moral tutelage of sexuality exercised by the early Church: this is particularly clear in the charge of a fearful conspiracy to oppress womankind as the recognised Enemy of faith; and, in principle, in Péret's summary reduction of the logic of Christian Agape to a system of wrathful moralism and taboo. Is the author of this conspiracy theory not writhing in the shadow of the – literalistically interpreted and resentfully interiorised –'curse' of Genesis?

There are also unargued theoretical postulates of some substance. Is psychogenesis, in particular by the mechanism of disguised and sublimated sexuality, a sufficient account of the origin of religion and morality (Freud thought so; Bergson, we recall, speaks of the 'two sources')? Is all religion idealisation and projection? Does 'liberation' of the sexual communion inevitably produce a spiritual communion in love? Or is Péret here the victim of his Hegelian mindset: flesh as thesis, spirit as antithesis, finding their *Aufhebung* in the dialectic resolution of 'l'amour sublime'?

Above all, we are struck by a haunting circularity in the essayist's – anti-theistic – starting point. What Péret insistently calls 'l'amour divin' is in fact a *human* love for an imaginary divine Object; that is, a form of theistic Idealism; it is not a love bestowed by and returned to a real divine Subject. It *must* consequently be construed as a form of Eros detached from its *arrière-monde* and referred back to this world; which implies that it *can only* be a hateful rival to 'real' human love; which in turn rigorously *dictates* a certain reading of culture-history.

What seems incontestable is that Péret's incandescent liberation narrative, like the Valéryan Serpent's 'transgressive' spirituality of self-cognisant Intellect, refers us to a deep-seated and irradiating crisis of culture which finds its nerve point in the problematic nature and status of human Eros – problematic, above all, in its relation to the culturally received and formative faith-matrix.

***

It would be a brave critic who undertook, in a few pages, to make serene and transparent sense of this tangled knot of repudiating alienation. And yet: on the threshold of the third millennium, certain authentic insights are emerging which invite us to take a modest further step in recognition. I offer here some notes towards the full-dress study we require and lack.

Clearly, there is a background of socio-political and ideological struggle. France emerged from the Middle Ages via the Ancien Régime and its overthrow in the Revolution of 1789. As François Furet has shown,[15] this constituted a traumatic break in national memory: less because of the accompanying violence of the Terror, than because it split asunder the nation's collective identity-sense by the radicality of its anti-theistic and secularising societal project (very different, in this respect, from that of the American Revolution, which *continued elsewhere*, on virgin territory, both the 'glorious revolution' of English parliamentary liberties *and* the Protestant Reformation).

In matters of sexuality, as in matters political, the profound phase-change wrought by the Protestant Reformation (which addressed many of Péret's charges centuries before they were made) all but passed France by, leaving an *ancien régime* of Catholic socio-cultural regulation to face its libertine and rationalist demolishers in the eighteenth century. Catholics themselves were thrown back for 150 years into identification with a hierarchical, tutelary and dogmatically conservative ecclesiastical establishment, which, from the Restoration, sought its security in clerical alliance with right-wing regimes and in traditional, prescriptive sexual moralities. Conversely, Republican secularists plotted the progress of the Enlightenment project by the marginalisation of their 'foundational' Adversary. For them, in project and desire if not in realised fact, history had *begun again* in 1789; and 'religion' or 'monotheism' (the preferred terms for traditional Catholic Christianity) was equated with medieval Christendom as such; that is, they were relegated to the 'wrong' side of Valéry's time-line for the coming of 'modernity', 'emancipation' and 'progress'.

French post-Enlightenment thought has rarely, for this reason, been disinterested or serene, let alone sympathetically curious, in respect of its own formative faith-and-culture matrix. It has, more typically, been mobilised in militant suspicion or vibrant revolt against it – the case of Péret, and, more secretly, of Valéry, but also of the entire tradition of the writers and thinkers identified by Alexandrian as 'love's liberators'.[16] The interface between religion and sexuality, which concerns us here directly, is merely the most sensitive and enduring locus of this dynamic antipathy of belief-and-value.

Moreover, the ideological 'adversary' is here identified as an institutional power-structure, harnessing a theistic ideology to political influence and social control: such has remained the basic 'take' of radical French secularists in all matters of 'religion'. Under these conditions, reactions of contestation might readily espouse a dialectic of reversed or inverse signs – the very possibility to which Genesis itself alerts us. 'God' is then cast in the role of jealous Rival, inventor and guarantor of the interdict. The 'accursed' are identified with a constrained and victimised humanity, arbitrarily excluded from its own 'divine' potential. And 'transgression' itself – stepping defiantly over the 'received lines' drawn in moral space – then becomes a value-laden stance: an awakening challenge, a sacred duty of authenticity, a way towards the Promise (at the very least, the spice of intellectual life!). Love's 'liberators', accordingly, will often take up the position of enthusiastic 'first degree' hearers of the Serpent's song; particularly where they follow Freud in asserting there is No Other Song, or Nietzsche in proclaiming New-for-Old. Valéry is not the first, and will not be the last, to espouse explicitly the Serpent's 'trangressive' speaking position; we shall discover more radical reactions still, pushed well beyond Valéry's subtle sense of significant paradox and metaphysical farce.

Is there in this entire drama of reversed signs, a fundamental *quiproquo*: a misplacing of lines of distinction, a misidentification of persons, a misunderstanding of what is at stake and how to think of it – a kind of waking dream of collective 'teenage' confusion? Very possibly so; yet none, however, that is readily apparent on the basis of the Enlightenment's rationalist definition and discernment of 'myth'. Nor, perhaps, before the advent of psychoanalysis; and indeed, not cogently even then, perhaps, before modern critical reflexivity has been pushed to the point of sifting and testing psychoanalytic deconstructionism itself; which is what we find at the latter end of the twentieth century in the steely and rigorous hermeneutics of Paul Ricœur.[17]

Post-Enlightenment models of historical understanding, too, have allowed only partial recognition, or made for verifiable misrecognition, of cultural origins. So, for instance, writers on love and desire will often think of Christianity as arising against the background of social harmony and easy natural religion envisaged in Rousseau's myth of the noble savage; or, with nineteenth-century French poets of the Romantic-Symbolist tradition, set against a time of Orphic understanding between a serene humanity and its laughter-loving, mythological gods: an understanding which the advent of Christianity is seen to have grievously subverted and destroyed. Or with Auguste Comte, they will think of an age of religious metaphysics succeeding the 'ages of myth', to be itself superseded by the new and scientific Positive Era; or again, with Nietzsche, of a Judaeo-Christian transmutation of all ancient values, effecting an insidious and enfeebling inversion of a fundamentally healthy and virile paganism.

Insights of historical scholarship and cultural anthropology not available at the end of the nineteenth century now invite a markedly different account. We do know (as Péret did not) that the ancient world was intensely and endlessly 'religious' in deeply primitive ways. In Dionysian Greece, in the Canaan of the Old Testament, in the Nile Delta and in Celtic Britain, there were countless phallic cults, and fertility cults and mystery cults, all associating the energies of sexuality with the cosmic powers: 'the first properly human sense given to sexuality appears in the phallic cults in which it was associated with the cosmic powers leading the vertiginous dance of the cycles of life-and-death.'[18] Sexuality, symbolised or enacted in ritual or in festival, or perhaps through relations with sacred prostitutes, linked adepts to these resurrected and resurrecting forces that were held to be divine. The idea was to identify with the divinities in orgiastic frenzy and/or to control, appease and exorcise their baleful power by transactional ruse.

Sexual eros, that is, was, in all ambiguity, *sacralised* as the principle within man which, in a world 'full of the gods', offered immediate access to the divine life. It was a source of exaltation in the instant, precipitating an ecstatic return to an undifferentiated fusion, yet also a resurgence of the 'bad' forces which threatened to submerge the social community (as Euripides shows with incomparable power in the *Bacchantes*). Propitiatory animal sacrifice held such baleful resurgences at bay, discreetly recalling the human blood sacrifice on which, if we follow René Girard, has been ultimately based all social regulation of mimetic rivalry and violence; hence, all 'culture'.[19] Lifting in carefully delimited, ritualised ways the social interdicts or taboos that regulated sexuality, these cults opened for ancient man, albeit at great cost to himself, an ambiguous window of 'transcendence'.

These were, arguably, the true 'Dark Ages'; and it is now possible to recognise better than hitherto how the coming of Christianity, despite and beyond the breakdown of the *pax romana*, decisively ended them. With the transcendent Creator of Genesis, nature is emptied of its cosmic divinities, benign or pulsional, and loses its sacrality. The heavens might indeed 'declare the glory of God' (Ps. 19), but only as immensity, beauty and cosmic order point beyond themselves to the author of these things; they are henceforth *debarred* from themselves being divine. More radically, the incarnate and dying God of the New Testament replaces all transactional propitiation in its very principle with a new pact of relationship, centred in his person and in the sacrifice, freely offered, of the Love divine (known, in a special use of this rare Greek word, as *Agape*).

The immense release experienced in this novelty as received by faith re-echoes in St Paul's exultant hymn of assurance amid tribulation:

> For I am persuaded, that neither death, nor life, nor angels, nor principalities, nor powers, nor things present, nor things to come, Nor height nor depth nor any other creature, shall be able to separate us from the love of God which is in Christ Jesus our Lord. (Rom. 8: 38–9)

The same sense of the looming Sacred dismantled, of darkly soaring Eros brought down to earth, of reality touched and experienced as ultimate goodness – the sense of cosmic peace made – underlies the same writer's celebrated hymn to Love in the First Letter to the Corinthians. The city of Corinth, we may note, notoriously gave its name in the ancient world to the verb *korinthiazein*, signifying all the practices, both spiritual and carnal, of eros unbound and sacralised. It was to believers in this city that St Paul wrote of 'love' in its radically declared and newly bonding acceptance: 'If I speak with the tongues of men and of angels and have not charity...'"(1 Cor. 13: 1–13).

If modern cultural historiography modifies the narratives of indictment offered by Péret and other 'liberators', militant post-Enlightenment estimates of the Christian contribution to humane civilisation, particularly in respect of 'love', have also been much revised. It is recognised that, in a world emptied of the dark gods of the blood, sexual eros – now desacralised – underwent what we might today call 're-education' in the service of the new love for God and for neighbour: at first in small persecuted communities of faith, deeply at odds with their time, but then, from the conversion of Constantine, and by a fateful phase-change, as official religion of an entire temporal and socio-political order co-extensive with the Roman Empire and, later, with medieval Christendom.

This latter order represented a 'rule of God' (but *not* the 'Kingdom of heaven': something highly ambiguous, therefore, in Christian terms). In a real sense, 'Christendom' indeed inverted and traduced the Christian idea of love: from one of consent responding to divine invitation ('Do not awaken love before it pleases') to that of a temporal supremacy imposing obedience as supreme good – a regime in which the 'divine transformation' of human eros might be *made* to happen. Under this dispensation, human loving – and desiring – was, structurally, at risk of being administered as a pre-directed human quest for the ultimate Good-that-was-God. The extent to which this danger became in fact realised, was, of course, multiply conditioned: not least by the 'Freudian' fact that the 'pre-teenage' centuries of the 'Common Era' represented something analogous to a childlike 'period of latency'.

Viewed in Freudian terms, this period constituted perhaps the most remarkable case seen in human history of a civilising 'sublimation' – something of profound import for the whole subsequent evolution of culture and society in the West, and no doubt, in the longer term, for humanity at large. Its positive legacy (as recognised by such diverse inheritors as Levinas or Ricœur, Kristeva or Girard, George Steiner or Irving Singer), was and is of incalculable importance. Eros re-educated in the school of Christian ethics and spirituality permitted and prepared over time huge advances in cultural humanisation. 'There is neither Jew nor Greek, there is neither bond nor free, there is neither male nor female: for ye are all one in Christ Jesus' (Gal. 3: 28). We may speak here of the emergence, in the name of the divine Other, of an unprecedented recognition of the 'human other', with its constellation of far-flung consequences, many of them now labelled *secular*, in personal and in social life, to this day. Robert Wagoner speaks accurately of the Christian culture-matrix as creating 'the core of our moral consciousness'.[20]

We judge *anachronistically* if we suppose that the loving and directing discipline of 'Mother Church', or the transcendence of its 'heavenly Father', were typically or in principle experienced as repressive in the Medieval period. The problem of 'parental authority' did of course arise acutely in the 'teenage centuries': starting with the 'pre-Renaissance' of the thirteenth century and growing from the Renaissance of the late fifteenth century towards the declared 'death of God' of the end of the nineteenth century. Yet if the third millennium is no longer unanimously content to endorse Péret's global indictment, this is because a more complete memory of origins lightens the caricatural charge;[21] or because a certain growth crisis has now run its course; or perhaps, more radically, because the shorthand description of the Middle Ages as 'Christian' is itself recognised to be a falsifying misnomer.[22]

Nevertheless, it is the difficulties, ambiguities and failures of this process of emergence and sublimation that most invite attention. Many of the culturally inflected practices of the Western Church (though not necessarily of Eastern Orthodoxy) are by now well-catalogued and quite well understood (if not always well corrected).[23] Against the eroticism, sacred and profane, of the ancient world in general, the early Church sought moral discipline and holiness of life; the more so, in the earliest Christian era, since its dramatic re-appraisal of human sexuality reflected the premature expectation that the whole order of human time would be rapidly consummated in the Second Coming. Following this logic, it then inclined to the *puritan reaction* which had by then (again, all unsuspected by Péret) became characteristic of late Antiquity in general.[24]

Against the exaggerated asceticism of many forms of Neo-Platonic or Gnostic dualism, it vigorously defended the institution of marriage; but it did so by underlining, in the tradition of the Jewish patriarchs, its procreative finality; and thus paid the considerable price of evacuating the much more comprehensive vision of sexuality and gender difference expressed in Genesis and explicitly confirmed by Jesus. (In interpreting marriage, the founder of Christianity of course assumes, but nowhere underlines or foregrounds – or, indeed, even mentions – its reproductive finality.)[25] Against the Gnostics, those extreme dualists who believed in the irremediable corruption of the flesh, it borrowed arguments about 'natural law' from the Stoics and again commended marriage; but, this time, in terms virtually excluding sexual desire and bodily love, thus falling entirely short of the biblical promise of erotic desire fulfilled in love.

At work also was the ever-present temptation of a curious exchange of roles or reversal of identities, the possibility of which we have already glimpsed in reading our first two source texts. At first sight, the *Symposium* (in its second half) appears to be the more 'religious' and 'mystical' of the two; the *Song* the more concrete, sensuous and human. The difference between Eros and Agape, though tangible, is qualitative and profound, and not easily 'manageable' intellectually; whereas the two loves resembled each other enough, and complemented each other enough, to generate constant interchange and semi-permanent confusion. This was notably the case when Christianity began to encourage the ascesis of virginity in its religious communities, and, particularly, from the fourth century onwards, in an increasingly celibate priesthood.[26] Progressively, the ecclesial and sociological reality of the Christian religion became quasi-dualistic: on the one hand, a 'high-road' spirituality for the unmarried religious, for whom sexual abstinence was *de rigueur* (in theory, if not always in practice); on the other, a 'low-road' vocation attributed to the common lay people (to whom marriage was recommended as channelling sexuality towards the acceptable goal of procreation). In this frame of reference, marriage comes to resemble a (platonic) 'base love', dialectically set against an (equally platonic) 'high' or 'noble' love.

In the limit case of Christian mystics such as Dionysius the Areopagite, or later Eckhart and Ruysbroek, it became entirely natural to evoke spiritual experience in categories and structures borrowed from Plato, often via such Neo-Platonic mystics as Plotinus. The borrowings of language, thought and sensibility were blended with biblical motifs and thought-forms, including nuptial imagery, in an ambiguously synthetic language of inner experience. This blending of traditions is characteristic of what Nygren and others call 'the *caritas*-synthesis' (from the Latin word for 'love'); that is, the far-reaching attempt by the Medieval Church to think out the singular, 'revealed' logic of Christian love in the culturally received conceptual language and values of Greek thought. Certainly, the high-road of contemplative spirituality found less to change in the Hellenic *Symposium*, as refracted and re-expressed by Plotinus, than in the Hebrew *Song of Songs*. The Hebrew love-song, indeed, was read in an entirely transforming allegorical interpretation which accommodated it to the new, hybrid structures of transcendence.[27] It was seen as an allegory of the nuptial relationality between the soul (the female voice) and God (the male voice); or between God and the Church; or else as a prefiguration of the longing and delight of the Virgin Mary.

In a kind of illuminated retrospect revisiting the Hebrew poem, the Church of the 'latency period' discovered in the New Testament intertext just this 'vertical' dimension of analogy, this 'spiritual figure'. Such interpretations have their ever-respectable basis in the Judaeo-Christian postulate that human love is founded by the loving God, and that, by natural resemblance perfected through grace, it may partake of the same character and realise its God-given potential to know its own source and origin. The culturally determined specificity of such readings, as applied to the *Song of Songs*, was, however, to *allegorise the text with platonically 'ascendant' corridor vision*, so that the divine essence shone through the human accident – and abolished it. Allegorising, the Church's hellenically inflected hermeneutic machine all but severed the vital metaphoric connection with 'profane' love, and with sexuality as such. The model of 'the higher love' prevailed exclusively; so much so that it became anathema, for instance, to suggest that the *Song* was in any way about human, carnal relationships.[28] Ricœur speaks here of an appropriating *re-use* of the text.[29]

Enshrined as orthodoxy, and reinforced by the prestigious exemplifications it received from St Bernard of Clairvaux (twelfth century) to St John of the Cross (sixteenth century) the allegorical interpretation remained the exclusive and unquestioned one in Catholic France until well into the twentieth century. It is a suggestive pointer to this considerable *datum* that, as late as 1944, when the author of 'Ébauche d'un Serpent', Valéry, came to prepare a public lecture (never in fact given) on the *Song of Songs*, he noted the following words, designed to unveil with precautionary prudence the text's primary dimension as erotic poetry: 'May I be allowed to speak quite frankly of mystical things? ... The Song can be felt in more than one way, and one of these is extremely delicate to express.'[30] We glimpse here again – and not for the last time – the very French sense of an ecclesiastical veiling or occultation of sexual eros; this is one of the most powerful springs of modern French alienation from the Christian past in its entirety; perhaps, indeed, one of the occult reasons why 'French theory' after 1968 undergoes what Ricœur calls its 'Oedipal' moment.[31] What had to be unveiled was, in a real sense, the great Repressed-and-Forgotten of the institutional Church.

The hidden dynamic of the 'idealist shadow' within Christian spirituality often seems, to modern (post-Freudian) eyes, to be a self-culpabilising repression; and the basis of 'guilt' is the generalising association of sexuality with 'sin'. This association is to be traced back to the great moral theologians of the fourth and fifth centuries: Gregory of Nyssa, but also John Chrysostom, Ambrose, Jerome and (above all) Augustine. We are familiar with the insistent and often pertinent critiques of recent years made in this direction, particularly by contemporary feminism. Yet, in respect of their doctrine of love and desire, the most significant thing about the Greek and Latin Fathers is perhaps *not* that they were Fathers-in-patriarchy (that was effect, rather than cause). It is that they were, mostly, *not* fathers (in fact or desire) and that they *were* (in culturally conditioned thought and sensibility) Greek and Latin.

It belonged to Augustine to give its most abrupt formulation to patristic mistrust of sexuality, marked by original sin and identified almost exclusively with its shadow reality of lustful and acquisitive desire (*concupiscientia, cupiditas*). With Augustine, sexuality is seen as an essentially disruptive/transgressive force, the epitome of passion itself. Its defiance, in intimate respects, of reason and will are proofs of the ineradicable mark of sin:

> Human nature is without doubt ashamed of this desire, beyond all control of the will. For in the submission of the genital organs to the sole impulses of desire, outside the control of the will, there appears manifestly the punishment inflicted upon man for his first

disobedience. It is most significant that it should be manifested in that part of the body in which nature engenders, that nature corrupted by the terrible sin.[32]

'The terrible sin', we might think, could well refer more restrictively to Augustine's own youthful debauchery, with its multiple 'submissions' to the insubordinate organ. Yet this self-intimate 'original sin' is projected onto the third chapter of Genesis and becomes the basis of his reading of the myth; and via this reading, it is theologised and injected, fatefully, with irradiating consequences, into the bloodstream of Christendom.

Psychoanalytically, this case (at least) seems today transparent enough. Augustine's self-reproach, recognising its own superego condemnation in the 'cursing' voice of Genesis, identified with the defied Author of the Interdict, constructs a dramatic over-valuation of the intrinsic evil of sexual eros, and effects by this means a universalising transfer of guilt. When to this transfer was added the notion (derived from a pre-critical understanding of myth) of a historical *before* and *after* of the *original crime* of the first couple;[33] and when to this reading of 'the Fall' was added the juridical notion of inheritance (borrowed from Roman Law, and suggesting that guilt could be transmitted impersonally, like property), the classic – and classically objectionable – formulation of the doctrine of 'Original Sin' was born.

Even Augustine does not say – no more than do any of the patristic theologians – that sexuality is sin. But he stresses warily, as they all do, its links with sin, of which sexual desire, irrational instinct and pleasure are the signs. Sex would have existed, he considers, had there been no original sin, but without *libido*, i.e. pleasurable gratification in and of sexual desire (the term is Augustinian before being Freudian). It would have been the sign of an alterity or difference conducing to male–female relationality, but free of lust and purely a matter of willed choice and predilection.[34]

Remanded on suspicion of concupiscence, *libido* did also mobilise other shadows within its own: principally that of ancient misogyny. Here, too, the formative thought of the pre-Reformation Church bears the imprint of a dualist-idealist fracture; and this too may be read, as I have attempted to suggest, as the reverse side of a momentous cultural sublimation of human eros, within a childlike 'period of latency'.

***

Our all-too-rapid review of this vast dossier offers, it is hoped, some preliminary sense of what there was reasonably to object to in the formative faith-and-culture matrix; and of why, objecting 'transgressively' to the worst, secular thought from the Renaissance was likely, progressively, to lose all cognisant memory of the incomparable Judaeo-Christian best.

As viewed from the first 'post-teenage' century of the Common Era, the medieval Christian Church did a necessarily imperfect job (both flawed and unfinished). It left ambivalent memories in respect of all three of our themes: sexual desire might be held in suspicion (on occasion, literally demonised); transcendence might be asserted at the expense of the world of human experience; and love could be hybridised, in both 'low' and (particularly) 'high' variants, rather than fully exalted and transformed. Conversely, it knew (as we tend not to) that the Kingdom of heaven is not for consumption here and now; and that children do (despite Freud) respect and love their parents more fundamentally than they desire them.

The ambiguous legacy was remembered and represented within the – equally ambiguous – logic of 'transgression': a veritable Bermuda triangle of dream-encounter, Oedipal rivalry, dynamic mis-recognition and unreliable cultural memory. Retaining only the *shadow* of Genesis, Western humanity in its post-Renaissance growth years will seek – and increasingly struggle – to re-invent some half-remembered 'splendour'.

This strategic interaction of ambiguities was momentous in its consequences; and most sharply so in France. It ensured that the evolving cultural construct of 'love' would bear the hallmark of a mixed or hybrid parentage, in which Hellenic Eros and Judaeo-Christian Agape would explore every type of synthesis, create every 'model' open to their possibilities of recombination, and eventually become almost unrecognisable as separate motifs within the common culture. It meant that human erotic desire would develop in constant tension with ecclesiastical regulation and would eventually reject such regulation vomitively. At which point, Agape itself would be declared redundant – an illusory and suspect 'idealisation'; and self-reflecting Eros alone dominate the field of a prosaically secularised, scientifically enabled, consumerist culture.

All of which signified in turn that the promise of a transcendence through love, conceived as grounded, called and fulfilled desire, would, as reference, resource and model, for an indeterminate time recede – together with the splendour of the *Song of Songs*.

Notes

1 In A. Lacoque & P. Ricœur, *Penser la Bible* (Paris: Seuil, 1998), pp. 57–102.
2 S. Kirkegaard, *Works of Love*, trans. H. Hong & E. Hong (London: Collins, 1962), p. 124.
3 E. Fuchs, *Le Désir et la tendresse* (Geneva: Labor et Fides, 4th edn, 1982), p. 45.
4 Cf. the epigraph quotation of my chapter 13: 'Rien de plus spirituel ... que la sexualité féminine' (Irigaray).
5 Fuchs, p. 44.
6 Two distinct traditions are combined in the early chapters of Genesis. The liturgical hymn of creation (Genesis 1: 1–24) belongs to the 'Priestly' tradition and dates from the 6th century BC, whereas the account of humankind's opportunity and failure (Gen. 2: 4b – 3: 24) belongs to the 'Yahwist' tradition (10th century BC).
7 Ricœur, *Penser la Bible*, p. 66.
8 Cf. St Paul: 'All have sinned and fall short of the glory of God' (Rom 3: 23).
9 P. Valéry, *Œuvres*, 3 vols, ed. J. Hytier, Bibliothèque de la Pléaide (Paris: Gallimard), Vol. 1 (1957–60), pp. 138–46 .

10 C. Baudelaire, 'Mon cœur mis à nu', *Œuvres complètes*, ed. Y.-G. Le Dantec, Bibliothèque de la Pléiade (Paris: Gallimard, 1961), p. 1283.

11 P. Valéry, *Cahiers* (Paris: CNRS, 1957–61), Vol. XII, p. 783.

12 This essay is reprinted as the Introduction to Péret's *Anthologie de l'amour sublime* (Paris: Albin Michel, 1956). Further references to *Anthologie* will be given in the text.

13 See the references to R. Nelli, *L'Amour et les mythes du cœur*, quoted in *Anthologie*, pp. 42, 45, 46.

14 See e.g. S. Andreae, *Anatomy of Desire: The Science, and Psychology of Sex, Love and Marriage* (London: Little, Brown, 1998).

15 F. Furet, 'L'Ancien Régime et la Révolution', in: P. Nora (ed.), *Les Lieux de mémoire* Vol. 3: *Les France* (Paris: Gallimard, 1992), pp. 107–39.

16 S. Alexandrian, *Les Libérateurs de l'amour* (Paris: Seuil, 1977).

17 See in particular P. Ricœur, *De l'Interprétation: Essai sur Freud* (Paris: Seuil, 1965) and *Le Conflit des interprétations: Essais d'herméneutique* (Paris: Seuil, 1969).

18 A. Jeannière, *Anthropologie sexuelle*, Recherches économiques et sociales (Paris: Aubier, 1964), p. 54.

19 See R. Girard, *La Violence et le sacré* (Paris: Grasset, 1972), pp. 180–200 and *Des Choses cachées depuis la fondation du monde* (Paris: Grasset, 1978).

20 R. Wagoner, *The Meanings of Love: An Introduction to Philosophy of Love* (Westport, CT & London: Praeger, 1997), p. 45.

21 See e.g. J.-C. Guillebaud, *La Tyrannie du plaisir* (Paris: Seuil, 1998), especially Deuxième Partie: 'La Mémoire perdue'.

22 See R. Girard 'The Mimetic Theory of Religion: An Outline', in: P. Gifford (ed.), *2000 Years and Beyond: Faith, Identity and the 'Common Era'* (London: Routledge, 2002), pp. 187–8.

23 I am indebted here to Fuchs, *Le Désir et la tendresse*, Chap. 4, 'Le Christianisme et la sexualité'.

24 See P. Brown, *The Making of Late Antiquity* (Cambridge, MA: Harvard University Press, 1978).

25 The most important text of the New Testament on love and marriage is Matt. 19: 3–9 (cf. Mark 10: 2–9). Rejecting a fixed morality of the permitted and the forbidden, Jesus recalls and endorses the founding purposes of sexuality (the humanising and divinising encounter in alterity) as given in Genesis. He adds by way of commentary the notion of sexuality as a transcendence of infantile status and a passing-over into adulthood; and he solemnly warns against the ancient Jewish practice of 'repudiation' of the wife by a bill of divorce written by the husband: 'What therefore God has joined together, let no man put asunder.'

26 There were various codes of practice in Eastern and Western Christendom. In the West, celibacy of the clergy was increasingly praised as an ideal, but not legally enforced until the time of Hildebrand, Pope Gregory VII (1073–85).

27 The first allegorical treatment of the *Song* in the Church was that advanced in the commentary of Hypolytus of Rome early in the third century CE. Origen's classic commentary in five books, which gives both the Church and the soul as bride, opened the floodgates. The *Song* soon became an authoritative thesaurus of words, images and structures of mystical spirituality. See J. A. Montgomery, 'The Song of Songs in early and mediaeval Christian use', in: W. Scott (ed.), *The Song of Songs – A Symposium* (Philadelphia: The Commercial Museum, 1924).

28 This interpretation, advanced by Theodore of Mopsuestia, was declared heretical by the second Council of Constantinople in 353 CE.

29 Ricœur, *Penser la Bible*, p. 426ff.

30 '"Le Cantique des cantiques de Salomon". Notes pour une conférence demandée par les Cent Une', Département des Manuscrits, BNF, Paris.

31 See P. Gifford (ed.), *2000 Years*, p. 170.

32 Augustine, *De Civitatis Dei*, XIV, 20, 44, in: *Œuvres de Saint Augustin* Vol. 35 (Paris: Éditions de la Bibliothèque augustinienne, 1947), pp. 436–9.

33 Cf. Ricœur: 'It is entirely erroneous, and prejudicial to a theological understanding of this whole sequence, to consider transgression as an event separating two successive states: a state of Innocence, reckoned as primordial, and a fallen state supposed to belong henceforth to history' (*Penser la Bible*, p. 70).

34 Augustine, *De Genesi ad Litteram* III, 21, 33, in: *Œuvres de Saint Augustin* Vol. 48, pp. 264–5.

Love as Cultural Construct

Eros and Agape

In this section, we turn from recognitions of the culture-matrix to particular developmental realisations and effects within it: first, by reviewing the major myths and models of French tradition up to the eighteenth century; second, in examining more closely the nineteenth century crisis of Eros.

The preliminary mapping required here relates to concepts and definitions. If the shadow projected upon the splendour has to do with a hybridisation of sources at work historically, it will be worth pausing briefly in order to acknowledge some twentieth-century attempts to disentangle the threads of the richly ambiguous force-field of emergence. This will also help us recognise why the cultural constructs to be encountered are various and competing, yet also related; and why the word 'love' itself has a seemingly infinite plasticity of sense and application, while – arguably – retaining an ultimate coherence.

Few serious thinkers have doubted that the conceptual field is bounded by the two terms Eros and Agape, recapitulating the confluence of cultural sources we have (selectively) revisited. The relation between these two aspects of love was first addressed in a brilliant, limpid and scholarly book written before the Second World War by an otherwise little-known bishop of the Swedish Lutheran Church.[1] Modestly, but very radically, Anders Nygren suggested that Christianity had, in its twenty centuries of existence, given insufficient energy to defining the original coherence of what was, after all, its most central concept, since it had assumed that the Christian meaning of the word 'love' was sufficiently accessible to all from tradition, example and general current usage.

Nygren set himself to resolve the spectrum of extant loves into its pure colours. Whatever qualifications have been entered since by way of remixing them or of reconfiguring the field itself, the distinction he made between the two 'motifs' – i.e. the two moving intentions and organising logics – of Eros and Agape remains a classic reference point in any competent discussion of love and desire in the Western tradition. Nygren identifies the basic binome, allowing decipherment of the ever-inventive combinations and recombinations, subsequently formed or potentially formable.

Between the two motifs, Nygren sees a figure of inverse symmetry. Eros is an anthropocentric and ascendent love, focused in the individual psyche, moved by a negativity of desire; its transcendence is aspired to, grasped at, and conquered from below – the possession of, or fusion with, an impersonal Absolute. Agape, inversely, is an Other-centred love, whose content is personal self-bestowal or gifting by the lover. It does not begin as a sublimated form of sexual desire in search of an ever-transcendent ideal Object. In the language of transcendence, it comes 'from above', stooping in order to lift up the beloved into a communion of acceptance. Eros, even where referring to God as *telos* (as it usually does in the ever-ambiguous expression 'the love of God'), is always a human love. Agape, even where qualifying human subjects, always has the character (and, for Nygren, the agency) of the Love divine.

Its original (i.e. unoriginated and originating) character, as predicated of God, implies that Agape does not aspire to possess a good which it lacks; nor is it determined or motivated by the merit of the object it loves, or by any self-interest of possessing it. Rather, it moves autonomously, gratuitously, without extrinsic motive or foundation. By virtue of its own other-centred tendency, it creates and recreates in its object a value previously lacking or lost. In the logic of Agape, God is said to 'love' the world, not *because* the world, on inspection, presents an independent goodness of its own, meeting with divine approval; rather, the world is seen to be good *because God loves it*. It owes to the overflowing of divine generosity in creation its very existence, its entire character of goodness and its coming-to-be in love. The crucial difference from a logic of Eros is clear if we recall the derisive incredulity of Valéry or Baudelaire in considering that 'creation' might be any predicate of 'God', let alone an act of creation in, by and for 'love'. The same proposition, as conjugated within the dualist-idealist mindspace of Eros, here gives an antipodally different sense (or rather *non*-sense) from that obtaining within the field of Agape.

So much so that Nygren sees Agape as simply unrecognisable as such within a logic of Eros. Its 'excessive' character is always folly. 'Love your enemies', not because that is naturally just or wise, but because it is blessed, like the loving God. The labourers of the eleventh hour will be paid in full, just like the others who have laboured all day, not because that is 'fair', like some piece of distributive human justice, but because only giving all is in character with the Love divine. 'Your sins are forgiven', not as a reward for enhanced performance following Appraisal, but radically, as love-gift, recreating human value and restoring human potential where it was lost. Human love, in short, is motivated, conditional, transactional. Divine love is unconditional, purely given, as well as totally giving.[2]

Of course, Agape is declared in principle as a function of the Judaeo-Christian encounter between 'human' and 'divine' *styles of loving*; it is, in this important sense, a function of 'revelation'. Yet once culturally declared, this distinction allows us *consequently* to discern the double weave and the bi-polarity already at work *also* within *all human loves as such*. It describes, it configures, indeed it largely creates, the basic culture-matrix as such. It sets up bi-polar or binomial structure of self-recognition; something open, assuredly to re-interpretation, in a dozen culturally inflected styles; just as it is possible to discern unlimited figures of combination and recombination between the terms.

Nygren's formula *Eros><Agape* was and remains, then, in crucial respects, the $E = mc^2$ of the Western historico-cultural universe of love, desire and transcendence. Its sharp-edged radicality in this thinker belongs among the twentieth-century insights that may be said to have restored a measure of conceptual clarity within a culture inheriting from its own hybrid antecedence all syncretisms, all exchanges, and consequently also all confusions of terms and values. The general pertinence, in genetic and historico-cultural terms, of the model has been broadly recognised by 'erotologists' of all persuasions – until, that is, the 'libidinal economists' of the

'postmodern' twentieth century. The question raised then, as we shall come to see, is whether it is possible to evacuate the enabling binomial structure itself without putting conceptuality and cultural practice as a whole at risk of no longer being able to distinguish, discern or define (save in impoverished reduction) the meaning of the verb 'to love'.

Unsurprisingly, however, as successive theorists have shown, Nygren's conceptual and hermeneutic 'reduction' has distinct drawbacks and limitations. His account of historico-cultural realities is incomplete, over-systematic, inadequately functional in accounting for 'indeterminacy', that is for the aptitude of the pure colours to recombine within a re-echoing and complex unity which is not that of the conceptual spectrum merely, but that of actual human behaviour in historico-cultural time. Succeeding historians of ideas, erotologists, love-theorists and theologians of different persuasions have sought diversely to re-introduce into Nygren's account the required suppleness, rather as Einstein's disciples have sought to reconcile relativity and indeterminacy in physics.

So the Swiss Protestant culture theorist Denis de Rougemont, closely following Nygren, extends the scope of 'Eros' to include not only its luminously aspiring higher manifestations, but also the darker, pulsional and death-oriented (Freudian) virtualities which he finds in Plato's hinterland, the indo-European mystery religions, particularly Gnosticism; from which revision he derives a suggestive, if often schematic, account of a basic counterpoint within the culture of the West between a stabilising and healthy Christian realisation of love's 'transcendence', and its subterranean, subversive and finally catastrophic Romantic rival.[3]

Martin D'Arcy, the distinguished English Jesuit, reacts more radically in the name of Catholic humanism: to assert, within created nature, a principle of analogy, and of complementarity, between the Eros and Agape; such that the most fully natural human loves can show the other-centred, gift-like qualities of Agape as well as all the virtualities of Eros. In all polarities, through all the diverse reciprocities engendered within the force-field, D'Arcy sees still, in the end, 'one Love' where Nygren basically deals in two.[4]

The American moral philosopher Irving Singer, speaking from the viewpoint of a humanism that does not credit the Freudian reduction of Christian Agape, nor yet quite believe Nietzsche's vengeful account of its genealogy, wishes to retain the priceless singularity of a conception of love as enacted bestowal, creating value. Nygren – he complains reasonably – leaves human longing facing divine Love in a complementarity of antithesis (rather as nature faces Grace in Lutheran theology). He points, again reasonably, to the other elements (*philia*, *nomos*) that have entered into the historically affirmed make-up of 'Christian love'. Yet, like Freud and Nietzsche, Singer himself represents Agape as an 'idealisation' henceforth irreceivable in its own terms – that is, as a transcendence in the order of being; and he seeks a 'transvaluation' reclaiming its exclusively human meaning, in the mode of iconically-led artistic performance in self-fashioning – a design rehearsed throughout his monumental review of the love-philosophies of the West.[5] This response heralds a number of modern French patterns we shall encounter.

The most recent major study in this field, by Jean-Luc Marion, shows in practice how the logics of Eros and Agape are at every point present in human love-relationships, like an alternating current, conferring on the acts and feelings of love, in all its phases, a positive and a negative 'charge'. Their interplay constitutes a permanent psychic and moral ambiguity within amorous relationality, as well as a way of classifying its realised forms.[6] The binome, it appears, is written deep into atomic and cosmic textualities – and with it no doubt, the perennial uncertainty of our own central question: 'Who is this who...?'.

> The two poles of human love are fairly commonly opposed by giving them the Greek names Eros and Agape. Eros is desire-love, capturing and self-related, whereas Agape represents the altruistic forms which may reach the 'oblative' level of 'charity'... [but] their deeper unity should not be lost sight of.[7]

With this prudent and open-ended recognition, we may turn from the conceptual matrix of Western thought to the actual realisations of love and desire in French tradition.

Notes

1   A. Nygren, *Eros et Agape: La Notion chrétienne de l'Amour et ses transformations*, trans. P. Jundt (Paris: Aubier, 1943; 4th edn 1962). The two-volume Swedish original appeared in 1930 (Vol. 1) and 1936 (Vol. 2).

2   St Paul and St John are shown by Nygren to have synthesised in reflection, from faith-experience, the notion of Agape, so as to describe each term, human and divine, of the new love-bond or communion. The Pauline hymn to the 'greatest of these' (i.e. the participatory or 'theologal' virtues) spells out the other-centred and oblative qualities which signal Agape, as communicated to, and therefore active within, the 'new creation': 'Love bears all things, believes all things, hopes all things, endures all things. Love never ends' (1 Cor. 13: 4–8). Reciprocally, first Paul and then John think out the metaphysical credentials of Agape as enacted and revealed in the person of Jesus. The Father is Love (Rom. 5: 8; 1 John 4: 8, 9–10, 16). He loved the Son before the creation of the world (John 17: 24). In living and dying in the world, the Son gives back to the Father the Love received before the world was (John 17: 20–6). This circuit of exchange in love, enacted in the Incarnation, enables the Spirit to be given to the world, thus renewing the human creature and all of creation (John 14: 15–17, 25–6; 16: 13–15). Whoever loves (i.e. acts in the nature of Agape) is in God and knows God (1 John 4: 7).

3   D. de Rougemont, *Love in the Western World*, trans. M. Belgion (New York: Pantheon Books, 1956).

4   M. D'Arcy, *The Heart and Mind of Love: Lion and Unicorn – A Study in Eros and Agape* (London: Faber and Faber, 1945; revised edn 1954).

5   I. Singer, *The Nature of Love*, 3 vols. Vol. 1: *Plato to Luther* (New York: Random House, 1966); Vol. 2: *Courtly and Romantic* (Chicago: University of Chicago Press, 1984); Vol. 3: *The Modern World* (Chicago: University of Chicago Press, 1987).

6   J.-L. Marion, *Le Phénomène érotique: Six méditations* (Paris: Grasset, 2003).

7   P. Burney, *L'Amour*, Que sais-je? (Paris: PUF, 1984), p. 28.

Chapter 4

Love in French Literary Tradition: The Troubadours to Rousseau

The second millennium CE in Europe displays a close-set series of new impulses of intellect and sensibility. This phenomenon of cultural growth is, we have suggested, not unlike the growth-surge of adolescence in individuals, brought about by an influx of psychosexual energies and producing the emergence of an adult identity.

Even in the numerical designation of the centuries concerned, this developmental pattern is strongly reminiscent of the teenage years in adolescent individuals. We observe: a surge of acute 'pre-teen' idealisation in the twelfth and thirteenth centuries; a more radical 'Renaissance', bringing a richer blend of carnality and ideality in the late fifteenth and sixteenth centuries; a coming to self-awareness and a precarious balance in the seventeenth century; in the eighteenth, revolt against an inherited *ancien régime*, generating experimentation in ideas and sexuality; in the nineteenth, an ambiguous emergence to intellectual, moral and spiritual autonomy, expressing itself in an acute division of flesh and spirit and a romantically supercharged sense of transcendence. This tension finds release in a traumatic religious deconversion, repudiating not only the culture-matrix of the institutional Church ('secularisation'), but now also of a theistic Superego ('the death of God').

The major myths and models of love and desire explored by the French literary tradition may be seen as giving determinate form to this process of emergence. Indeed, they signally promote the process itself by lending it an ever-enriched self-representation in writing and cultural memory.

***

The French twelfth century has often been credited with having 'invented love'. This view is today relativised by the knowledge of what the 'pre-Renaissance' of this period owed to the aftermath of the crusades and to Hispano-Arabic influence.[1] More exactly stated: this developmental culture-moment coined and put into circulation an intensely enriched and novel conception of inter-gender relations – that of the romantic courtship by a gentle lover of an idealised lady, an attachment ritualised, devoted and tenderly sensuous – thus providing the foundation for the only model of love (apart from eroticism) widely recognised and culturally valued in our own times –'romantic love'.

This prototype is 'courtly love', developed by the aristocratic troubadour poets of Provence in the last years of the eleventh century, under the name of the *fin' amors*. From 1150, the model was picked up with significant modifications by the Northern poets and authors of the Breton romances, who blended it with a broader ethic of chivalry and with elements of Arthurian and Celtic folklore.[2]

Later writers will be hugely conscious of it: Madame de Scudéry, in mapping the country of the amorous heart; Laclos, who explores its inversion, 'libertinage'; Rousseau, who most fully develops its logic of deferral; Stendhal, who paradoxically laments that the positive and progressive nineteenth century has lost it; Proust, when he depicts his adolescent troubadour of the Champs Elysées. Perhaps human memory always retains the traces of a 'first love'. And this first notable adolescent stirring indeed presents, as we shall see, many features of pre-teen 'kiss-chase' feeling: acute idealisation, trembling devotion from afar, the sense of unworthiness, the need for trials, and so on.

In its own place and time, *fin' amors* was an enacted critique of the 'matrimonial' conjugality of feudal Europe. In the aristocratic warrior class of this period, marriage had little or nothing to do with personal feelings. It was determined by parental choice for reasons of dynastic advantage, political and financial. A wife was expected to produce heirs and provide for the material welfare of her husband, who was her moral tutor more than her lover or companion. He often neglected her in favour of more rewarding pursuits such as war, hunting or wenching, while imposing on her a requirement of fidelity dictated by concern for the blood-line. The theme of the 'mal mariée' understandably re-echoes in troubadour poetry; and it gave the troubadours – the often errant poets of the minor nobility – the structural vocation of making good the human deficiencies of this system and of entering a counter-proposal which rectified the contempts of brutal pragmatism and casual misogyny.

The ethic of the *fin' amors* radically disqualified marriage in respect of love; it disjoined and opposed the two.[3] Conjugal love was base; adulterous love was noble since realising the moral qualities of *cortezia*: generosity of spirit, loyalty, humility, bravery. A mere husband had access to his wife by permanent right of ownership, blessed by the Church; he had no need to win the consent of the heart or to solicit sexual favours. A married woman could accede to 'noble' love only by accepting service from a lover. Yet in the *consent* of the beloved resided both the torment and the exaltation of true love. Here was the spiritually vital nerve of the *fin' amors*; and it made the new construct into a love of approach and imploration, across a differential of social rank, in defiance of the matrimonial bond.

Considered as a dwelling place of the human spirit, *fin' amors* evokes a *topos* of separation, absence and waiting upon a recompense or recognition, a fulfilment that is tormentingly incomplete or deferred. Typically, this reward is envisioned half-oneirically, rather than claimed or even overtly named (as in the obsessional motif of being admitted to the alcove to observe the undressing of the Lady). The troubadours thus form a cortege of the incurably love-sick, often half in love with the torment itself:

Mon mal a bel aspect
car mon mal vaut mieux qu'un autre bien
et puisque mon mal est si bon pour moi
combien meilleur sera le bien après l'effort.[4]

My sickness is a fine thing/for my ill is worth more than some other good/and since my sickness is so good for me/how much better will the cure be for my striving after it.

Ideality, devotion, the inaccessible horizon, dreaming, love-sickness, a certain discrepancy between sexual and affective needs, endless inconsistencies or contradictions within desire itself: all these features characterise structurally the loves of adolescence. So, equally do the values of the troubadours, particularly their praise of *Jovens*: not just physical youth, but the youthfulness of the pure and generous spirit and a delight in love and springtime.

In what sense is this model of desiring and loving connected to the theme of transcendence? Indirectly, the troubadours were indeed reacting against the summary and loveless feudal marriage sacralised by the medieval Church. In demanding of love that it show an authentic spiritual component of praise and wonder, a mutual consent in joy, an enlivening human significance, they were demanding a form of transcendence native to it. Innocently, they 'remembered' some harmonic notes of the *Song of Songs;* and they sought, albeit 'transgressively', a natural state of grace in which to sing them.

It is particularly suggestive, moreover, that at the very moment when the Abbot of Cluny was transposing the highly erotic human love of the Song of Songs into an esoteric spiritual 'figure' to which scripture gave the key, and which signified the entire relational logic of the 'vertical' love, the troubadours, for their part, were re-inventing a transcendence of the natural heart which mimicked the union of the soul with God, required a language of adoration, and invoked a Presence (to say nothing of the divine aid and protection which, on occasion, they tranquilly sought in favour of their adulterous loves). Sacred mysticism and natural love mysticism, the love of God and the immanent god of Love, Cistercian contemplation in Agape, and romantic fervour with its tutelary divinity Eros thus mirror each other in haunting and ambiguous solidarity.

Was this isomorphism a gesture of appropriation or one of tribute? Did it represent progress or deviancy? Had human love begun to rival and replace religious love, within a single economy of idealisation; and which, in that case, was the 'true love'? Or was there, more radically, a principle of analogy embracing both forms as valid and mutually complementary expressions of a love-potential in the process of cultural emergence, a dynamically unfolding triangular figure of horizontal *and* vertical loves?[5]

It is no accident, at least, that this construct takes shape in near-symbiosis with Catholic liturgy and with Cistercian love mysticism; it is an effect of what culture theorists call the Medieval 'caritas synthesis' – i.e. the attempt of the Medieval Church to express Judaeo-Christian Agape in the thought forms of Hellenic Eros; it displays this culture matrix at work in a formative moment.

***

The dimension of transcendence is explored in three significant prolongations of the basic model of courtly love. The first is the fateful idolatry of *amour-passion*. This figure is developed with fullest intensity in the legend of Tristan and Iseult, particularly as treated in the spirit of the *fin' amors* by the poet Thomas. Here, the courtly ideal of a superior adulterous love is supercharged with a tragic fatalism borrowed from Celtic tradition. The story is well known: Tristan is charged with bringing to Cornwall from Ireland the bride of his uncle, King Mark; they drink in error the love potion meant for the married pair. Their treasonous passion has no peace; its threatened and tormented longing survives many vicissitudes (including Tristan's unconsummated marriage to another woman, also named Iseult), and they are united only in death. Love is portrayed as a fateful passion, commanding the will of the star-crossed lovers and leading them after multiple torments of jealousy and intrigue to their deaths.

The dramatic reading of the Tristan legend offered by Denis de Rougement is that we are here confronted with the paradigmatic myth of unlimited Desire. What is significant, he suggests, is the way in which self-exalting passion, superior to all conventional morality, lives and thrives upon obstacles. These are seen to be ingeniously invented by the protagonists, the better to separate them, as though the social and moral code of the feudal order were not obstacle enough. 'What is the true subject of the legend? The separation of the lovers? Yes, in the name of passion, and for love of the very love which torments them, to exalt and transfigure it – to the detriment of their happiness, even of their lives.'[6] Tristan and Iseult, de Rougemont asserts, are most fundamentally in love, not with each other, but with the divine delirium of feeling, the sense of *infinite transcendence* discovered in a *passion frustrated or denied*; and they follow the dark call of this transgressive transcendence towards the true and absolute consecration to which it secretly aspires, namely the effusion of being-in-death.

De Rougemont's thesis that *amour-passion* constitutes a form of 'transgressive' counter-religion endemic in the christianised Western psyche is, though over-systematised and not always reliable in scholarship, nevertheless a profound and suggestive one. Its general thrust can claim considerable support from twentieth-century psychology, anthropology and literature: namely, the assertion that *amour-passion* mobilises in the psyche a dark thirst for transcendence, which then functions like a primitive (i.e. archaic, natural) religion – intoxicated, violent, self-sacralising, idolatrous, nostalgic for the lost unity of the One, and 'half in love with easeful death'. The origin of this dark compulsion is to be discerned in the original vice of *amour-passion*: '[Tristan and Iseult] love each other, but each loves the other only for self's sake, not for the sake of the other. Their love takes its source in a distorted reciprocity, masking a double narcissism' (p. 55). Tristan and Iseult are, that is, archetypally, *in love with love*; 'In fact, like all the great lovers, they feel snatched up "beyond good and evil", into a sort of transcendence of our common conditions of life, into an unsayable absolute experienced as more real than the real world' (ibid.). The 'lover' envisaged here is distinctly related to the reckless, self-consuming and fatal idealism of the modern suicide-bomber.

The fruitfulness of this perspective is, in part, that it takes account of the imaginative and experimental 'modelling' that literature always undertakes. There is an observable fascination binding writer and readers in the pact of what has become the European, and particularly French, literary tradition. 'Happy love has no history in Western literature,' says de Rougemont acutely (ibid.).[7] On the other hand, we are all fascinated by, and indulgent towards, the ever-remodelled imaginary *adventure* that is 'transgressive' *amour passion*: 'Knowing through pain-and-grief, that is the secret of the Tristan myth, passion-love both shared and combated, anxious for a happiness which it thrusts away, and which is magnified in its catastrophe – unhappy reciprocal love' (ibid.). The formula certainly describes a major part of the 'suffering', 'tragic' or 'infernal' face of amorous relationalities in French literature, from *Phèdre* to *Madame Bovary* and beyond, as well as the remarkably constant fascination in French tradition for specifically adulterous forms.

A second paradigm, complementary in its affirmation, is that of Héloïse and Abelard: a 'true story', for which the Church itself is the setting. The brilliant young philosopher and cleric Abelard is retained by the Canon of Notre Dame to tutor his talented and beautiful niece. The pair fall in love; scandal follows, but also popular endorsement for this real-life exemplification of the Tristan and Iseult myth. Héloïse's pregnancy, however, leads to a secret marriage, then to her taking the veil; meanwhile, Abelard's supposed abrogation of this marriage is 'avenged' by her uncle in assault and castration practised against the 'offender' by hired thugs. The lovers' passion survives the ecclesiastical career which then secludes each from the other, only to bring them together again by chance ten years later. As their letters show, travail, separation, impotence and the monastic vows taken have served only to heighten an enduring attachment of passionate devotion which outlives any possibility of sexual communion between the lovers.

Are this star-crossed pair noble victims or impenitent transgressors? Both, of course; and the story will sit exactly on the cusp of a bi-polar and evolving French discernment of *amour-passion*. Their transgression is social, but, more significantly, religious. The absolute devotion to a transcendent Other is called forth in a Christian ethos (are 'horizontal' romantic attachments either conceivable or compelling *apart from* this 'vertical' framing?); but here, absolute devotion is re-invested horizontally in a substitute, finite object. Héloïse knows her passion is idolatrous: 'At every stage of my life up to now, I have feared to offend you rather than God, and tried to please you more than him' (*Letters* 134). Irving Singer suggests, indeed, that Héloïse's love 'patterns itself on the dogmas of the man she reveres'.[8]

Yet her absoluteness of bestowal creates in return an absolute claim, asserted possessively. Bestowal and claim are then fortified by all obstacles to passion, which are experienced as 'trials' – new occasions to surpass oneself. However 'driven', the amorous subject experiences a real and immediate, if purely negative, apprehension of his/her own spiritual *freedom* to overstep the limits (of reason, self-interest, social or moral code, or simply of prosaic self-identity). This *excursion*, however perverse or painful, is what is thrilling – and compelling – about passion. Transgression must be accounted an immediate experience of 'transcendence'.

'Romantic love' here retraces meta-sexually, in a larger space and for greater stakes, the pattern of sexual eros itself. Like sexual desire, it lives in want and invention (as Plato declared); the worst that could happen to it is to 'succeed' – for then it is no longer *passion*. What ultimately differentiates it and certifies it as 'romantic' is its own carrying intensity, its own 'transcending', all-justifying imperative. This is already true of sexual eros; but, being goal-limited, sexual eros can re-appraise, re-adjust and move on. The romantico-spiritual realisation of Eros, by contrast, is liable to obey a dynamic of unlimited self-sacrifice, potentially unto death: 'I was powerless to oppose you in anything,' says Héloïse. 'I found strength at your command to destroy myself' (*Letters* 113).

However, a precisely inverse figure may also be seen to develop from the model of the *fin' amors*: the myth of a *celestial love*. That is: love seen as an adventure of the immortal soul, encountering – and rejoining *beyond death* – its twinned Other, by whose mediating inspiration as intercessor and guide the lover ascends to the knowledge of ultimate truth and beauty. This myth, arising in the Neo-Platonic, but still deeply Catholic, climate of the early Renaissance, represents a cult of the Lady in which amorous and religious feeling are ambiguously fused. Dante and Petrarch opened up this mythical space of the male imaginary. The Lady, though encountered originally as a genuinely embodied partner, comes, in the separation imposed by her death, to represent a tutelary projection invested with care of the 'better' part of the poet; she answers for his aspiration towards the ideal and to Heaven itself. Beatrice (the 'dispenser of bliss') is for Dante the lost and looked-for angel watching over the poet in the presence of the Virgin and of God. The same is true of Petrarch's Laura (in Italian: the aura, the laurel and the inspiring breath): 'She is the source of that uplifting grace/That guides you by the proper path to heaven/So that I go already proud in hope.'[9]

Both poets assert the transcendent glory of a love stronger than death and the assurance of spiritual salvation through a veritable *mediation* of the Beloved. This is, as D. D. R. Owen has remarked, the ultimate consecration of courtly love: 'ma Dame' has become the 'ornament of heaven beside whom even the Virgin pales a little'.[10] Or alternatively, as Martin D'Arcy has it: 'The highest motion of the human mind, Eros, as some understand it, at its best, has to give way to Agape. The way to heaven is reserved to the divine Beatrice. It is she, the symbol of grace and heavenly wisdom, who leads man beyond the rainbow, over the water, out of the swing of the sea.'[11]

***

The equivocal synthesis of loves sacred and profane found precise ideological decipherment in a work which was hugely influential throughout Renaissance Europe, particularly in the France of Marguerite de Navarre and the Pléiade poets, and which exercised a pervasive influence for very much longer on the transcendent loves of the Romantic generation and well into the twentieth century. Marsilio Ficino's *Commentary on Plato's 'Symposium'* gives a summarily Christianised reading of

Plato's text, incorporating Neo-Platonic elaborations derived from Plotinus and Dionysus the Aeropagite. What emerges from this syncretism of Hellenistic metaphysics and Christian doctrine is an exalted and expansive charter for human love in the image of the Renaissance itself: an ontology sacralising the natural appetites that lead the world: to respond to beauty is to experience the captivating glow of divinity ('lo splendore del divino'); an account of the elective affinity of twin souls; of their magnetic attraction, with its energising virtues of elevation; and of the vocation of Platonic ascent articulating the four cognate forms of 'divine frenzy' – poetic, religious, prophetic and amorous. The thrust of the work is well summarised by Marcel Raymond:

> What we in fact see developing in Ficino is, in Platonic terms, a history of the soul: a soul which, created by love, has sinned through pride but regathers itself in order to pursue the way of the Beautiful, hoping that, at the limit of its strength, the God whom it no longer knows except through images, will restore to it the lost light, leading it from 'frenzy' to 'frenzy' as far as the frenzy of Love, which will allow those who have sought God in everything to refind everything in God.[12]

Ficino's idealist 'come-back of the fallen soul' marks the end-point of the long conceptual dilution of Agape by Eros which Nygren detects as operating throughout the Middle Ages.[13] Despite intentionally Christian forms and references, it signifies a decisive shift from an ontologically 'realist', to an anthropocentric and immanentist account of divinity and transcendence. The spirit of the Renaissance is epitomised in the byword of Ficino's theology: 'Know thyself, race divine under a perishable garment'.[14] To an age wearied with the dry rationality of scholasticism on the one hand, and on the other by an orthodox love-mysticism which evacuated all attachment to the human creature, together with all worldly images that would sully the purity of the 'mirror of the soul', Ficino's metaphysic of Love did, however, represent a dynamic starburst signalling a new dawn of human possibility.

In many ways, sixteenth-century love poetry is the child of the liberating confidence of the new ideology. It is, at once or by turns, upreaching and earthy, idealistic and cynical, rhetorically subtle and yet appetitive in roguish sexual conquest. Baif, Scève, Louise Labé and the major voice of Ronsard impress us as striking a marvellous balance between a fresh and frank sexuality and reflexive awareness of the 'metaphysical' aspects of desire. These poets are both universalising in mythological reference, yet also personal in poetic voice. They know and say the solidarity between the two 'divine frenzies' of poetic creativity and love, linked in the conquering persuasion of Eros. In Louise Labé, in Erasmus and in Marguerite de Navarre, this new sense of possibility extends even to redressing something of the anti-feminism implicit in male-dominated models of love (as Ronsard's certainly is). The same sense of starburst and invitation is of course born also out of the Protestant Reformation, though here with deeper background shadows of polemic, political struggle and war. The *Heptameron* chronicles with rare lucidity and non-judgemental concern the inconsistencies of marriage without love; and no less those of a religious piety yoked to the disorders of sexual eros within the unstable psyche of a turbulent age.

Many of these co-ordinates are still recognisably present in the seventeenth century. On the incompatibility of love and marriage, at least as reflected in major literature, little changes: 'M. de Clèves was perhaps the only man in the world capable of conserving love within marriage ... perhaps also his passion had endured only because it had encountered none in me',[15] confides the heroine of *La Princesse de Clèves*. In the earlier part of the century, in d'Urfé's *L'Astrée*, marriage figures, more optimistically, as the ideal horizon of love, though it is unclear whether the much-tried hero will ever actually benefit from it, and there is much indication that the heroine is about to turn *précieuse* and declare the whole elaborate courtship a platonic charade.

The latter work of course echoes the courtly tradition in presenting the relationship of a demanding and capricious mistress with a docile and unshakeably faithful aspirant. It also bathes in a climate of lightly Christianised Platonism: all beauty is the reflection of divinity; love is an aspiration to the divine; to love is to die to self and relive in the beloved.[16] Yet other currents also surface: the *libertinage* of Hylas who defends the rights of the senses and of multiple loves; the neo-stoicism of du Vair for whom love is a passion to be mastered as inimical to rationality. The whole work became a manual of behaviour for polite lovers in an age which, in salon and in court, intensively socialised – and endlessly discussed— all matters amorous. If the seventeenth century added to the existing range of courtly, passionate and celestial loves, it was, first of all, the *model of 'galanterie'* (a notion covering high-society flirting, amorous intrigue, and sexual liaisons).[17]

Socialising love implied giving it psychological mapping and moral codification. Mlle de Scudéry's allegorical 'Carte du tendre' was typical of this movement, at least in its most refined development, towards *préciosité*. Illustrative of the process of psychological and moral mapping, and most fully 'classical' in its content, was the *heroic and virtuous love* of Corneille. This model reflected neo-stoical mastery of passion and drew inspiration from the political model of the strong centralised state. Inversely, Racine maps the downward gravitation of erotic *amour-passion*. His tragedies explore its propensity to psychological violence and moral evil: its cruelty to those whom it 'loves' under the sign of deceit, surveillance, blackmail, torture and death; also, its degrading effect on the lover whom it blinds and leads to self-destruction.

La Princesse de Clèves, too, offers a disillusioned mapping of *amour-passion*. Love is here a war of conquest and possession fought between champions in male and female beauty. The heroine is the prey, her virtue a besieged city. Each dialogue is a duel; and the prospect of defeat, in the form of dishonour, or of subjection to the torments of impotent jealousy, proves finally intolerable. Mme de La Fayette's heroine displays a heroism of renunciation in breaking off a relationship of 'fatal attraction', subversive of moral autonomy and self-esteem; but she is in turn broken by it, and we retain from this most subtle and poignant of seventeenth-century fictional studies its keynote of pathos, classically understated. Desire-in-passion fails to achieve any transcendence of its own destructive virtualities, or to realise its own promise of happiness. The female protagonist is thrown back into ultimate mistrust of a 'love' that is not yet loving enough to be faithful to its object rather than to itself.

How far, in the face of the demonic virtualities of the inner god of *amour-passion,* does rational control or self-mastery reach? Can reason and passion, love and marriage, be reconciled? Can there be love without a corrupting self-love? Is there a 'pur amour'? Around these questions moralists, philosophers and theologians turned.[18]

***

The eighteenth century explores the virtualities of Eros in the form of a new cultural love-paradigm – that of *libertinage.* Originally pejorative in sense, the term *libertin* was coined around 1620 to denote free-thinking, free-living young noblemen of deistic or even atheistic persuasion, such as Théophile de Viau, who mocked preachers, failed to observe the rules of abstinence and frequented bawdy taverns. Molière's *Dom Juan* has more than an echo of their actual words and behaviour. After the death of Louis XIV in 1714, the Regency brought an unbuttoning. Contained sexual energies overflowed in debauchery, which was widespread throughout the aristocracy; it also brought a thoroughgoing assault of thought, epicurean and materialistic in orientation, against the moral teaching and authority of the Church. Spirituality, the immortality of the soul, the divine origin and sanction of morality are denied; man is conceived as animal or as machine. Whether these developments in thought preceded and prepared, or whether they followed from, sexual licence is difficult to say; they were its reflective counterpart.

Crébillon fils was the first to define the *libertin* systematically: he is a man – Laclos will innovate in respect of the essentially masculine definition— who uses his sexual power or prowess to work out his erotic will, in all its developments, on successive partners, if necessary without their consent and usually to their harm. Inconstancy is a matter of principle: the satisfactions sought have nothing to do with the heart, and everything to do with sensual pleasure and the satisfactions of vanity in conquest. Eros is a game of seduction and abandonment, in which delight in the game well played is completed by public scandal, received as a homage to the libertine's powers.

'To conquer is our destiny'[19] says Laclos' hero Valmont in what is deservedly the most famous of the novels of *libertinage.* Other valid analogies include sporting performance or theatrical triumph. Thus Valmont will seduce the Comtesse de M. whose bedroom is sandwiched between that of her husband and that of her current lover, and will manage to retain the goodwill of all three. In relation to courtly love, the wheel has come full circle. Laclos is at pains to remind us, ironically, of this inversion.[20]

Morally, this behaviour implies a ruthless and cynical egoism which Laclos is concerned to explore. Yet his couple of seducers, male and female, are also genuinely superior in certain ways: resolution, energy, gifts of analysis and lucidity. The game of eros is played with unclouded subtlety and exquisite enjoyment precisely because of their remarkable emotional detachment. In its intellectuality, *libertinage* is the equivalent of erotic chess, and characteristically French (not to be confused with good-natured British 'rumpy-pumpy in the hay' in the style of *Tom Jones*). Feeling, which connotes dependency in relation to the erotic Other, figures in the libertine code as ultimate weakness. Laclos' genius, in a book which is in the end a subtle critique of the humanly deformed eros it explores, consists in having his hero 'fall in love' with the virtuous Mme de Tourvel whom he has already succeeded in seducing. Under the taunts of his accomplice, he dispatches the humiliating note that will kill the beloved and precipitate his own destruction.

Les Liaisons dangereuses is a keywork in respect of our themes: it explores the most recognisably modern form of eros, its connection with liberated intellectuality, its fundamental association with power and the sex war (waged against the victims of *libertinage*, but also between libertine accomplices, male and female). It also opens towards a perversity of aggression, cruelty and humiliation in 'love' which the eighteenth century also memorably explores in the writings of the Marquis de Sade.

Before Freud, this disturbingly sane prophet of unlimited libidinal pleasure espouses the whole inventive range of sexual expression normally confined and sifted by personal morality or by socio-cultural regulation. His fantasy scenarios – many enacted in reality, though mostly belonging to a fantasised psychodrama written in prison – offer a kind of reverse transcendence, effected by a willed regression to the most primitive roots of libidinal energy. 'One of the great conversions of the Western imagination', concludes Foucault: 'Unreason, become a delirium of the heart, a madness of desire, an insensate dialogue of love and death, in the boundless presumption of appetite.'[21]

A little more, perhaps. For de Sade's sanity (and his 'perversion') lies in the insistent, indeed obsessional, intellectual counterpoint proclaiming – against Voltaire and most rationalist philosophers of the Enlightenment – that morality divorced from its metaphysical and religious origins must wither like a flower cut from its root. Either there is God, and 'sadism' is then profanation or blasphemy; or else there is only the moral indifferentism of nature, in which case all expressions of libido are permitted and equivalent; it is as *moral* to rape, sodomise, defile, ingeniously torture and kill as it is to 'make love'. De Sade's career as erotic practitioner, theorist and writer asserts the latter hypothesis:

Je prétends expirer au sein de l'athéisme
Et que l'infâme Dieu dont on veut m'alarmer
Ne soit conçu par moi que pour le blasphémer.
Oui, vaine illusion, mon âme te déteste,
Et pour mieux te convaincre ici je le proteste
Je voudrais qu'un moment tu pusses exister
Pour jouir du plaisir de te mieux insulter.[22]

I wish to expire within atheism/And that the infamous God with whom they seek to frighten me/Should be conceived by me only the better to blaspheme him./Yes, vain illusion, my soul hates you,/And the better to indict you I here protest/I would that you might for one instant exist/To enjoy the pleasure of better insulting you.

De Sade's obsession with a God whose inexistence he has proclaimed evident relates to the motif of libidinal violence and power. His vehement apostrophe to the non-existent God suggests that transgression of sexual norms is fundamentally a form of profanation exercised against the creature, enhancing erotic pleasure precisely to the extent that it represents a form of defiance of, and vengeance against, some monstrous superego representation of the Deity. This haunting 'Third Party' invites Blanchot's view of his atheism as a nexus of pulsional, semi-lucid hatreds directed against the power bond of a Transcendence that negates man.[23]

The eighteenth century's antipode both to calculating eroticism and to blasphemously transgressive sadism is Rousseau's model of *passionate but virtuous natural love*. Heartfelt, idealistic, innocent, the reciprocal passion of Julie and Saint Preux presented in *La Nouvelle Héloïse* (1761) in many ways represents a return to the tradition of courtly love, with its Neo-Platonic prolongations. Behind it lies the persuasion that true love, the indestructible bond uniting the lovers in their innermost being, is incompatible with the social obligation of marriage. The novelty here is that an adulterous consummation is equally ruled out – a 'sin' against the essence of love *as experienced by the lovers themselves*. 'Take away the idea of perfection and you take away the enthusiasm; take away esteem and love is no longer anything' (3^e Partie, Lettre XVIII).

The courtly motif of the love-obstacle is here interiorised. Before her arranged marriage takes her away from Saint Preux, Julie indeed surrenders carnally to him, less through sensuality than from a tender concern to reward his devotion. Yet the experienced violence of physical desire sullies the pure flame of spiritual communion and incurs moral guilt in hastening the death of Mme d'Étanges, so that the relationship develops, beyond Julie's arranged marriage, under the sign of incompleteness and of distant devotion to an imaginary model of the Beloved: 'Let us forget the rest and be the lover of my soul' (3e Partie, Lettre XVIII).

The new Héloïse thus accomplishes the sacrifice of 'love' to Love, renouncing the transports of a passion which, since it is inconsistent with her other social relations and duties, creates only disturbance and disarray. More fundamentally, perhaps, earthly loving as such is branded indelibly with the anxiety of privation and the need to possess; so that the fusion to which passion tends is seen as incompatible with the aspiration to a communion of the spirit, seen to be more central to love. (Rousseau wrote to Sophie de Houdetot that he loved her too much ever to possess her.) The only way out lies in the heroine's death, authenticating the triumph of her life. 'No, I am not leaving you, I will wait for you. The virtue which separated us on earth will unite us in eternity' (6e Partie, Lettre XII). At once pathetic and exalting, the love-death of *La Nouvelle Héloïse* answers the stoicism of Mme de La Fayette's heroine with an essential affirmation of pre-Romantic spirituality: natural religion can, in evolved souls, purify both passionate love and honourable marriage, integrating both in an Ideal that the universe will endorse.

A century that contained both de Sade and Rousseau is astonishing enough. It belonged to Marivaux to show how the spectrum of natural loves, explored in its breadth, still held together. A play such as *La Double inconstance* echoes Laclos in its themes: love as game, the masks and disguises of seduction, the influence of power relationships (all here benignly deployed), and inconstancy itself. Yet the register is light, bantering, comic – and, in the end, optimistic, the order of the heart being, here at least, reconcilable with the social order and quite unthreatened by the metaphysical order of things. The theme of inconstancy has the status of piquant dramatic paradox: Marivaux gives us a subtle study of falling out of love and into it again under the influence of a new environment. At the same time, there is such a thing as an 'order of love' whose truth is known to the natural heart divested of social prejudice. In which respect, Marivaux's orthodoxy joins hands with Rousseau's natural religion.

***

'O God of peace, God of goodness, it is Thee I adore! Thine I am, I feel it, Thy work; and I hope to find Thee in the last judgment as Thou speakest to my heart in life.'[24] It is possible to think Neo-Platonically about the immortality of 'true love': providing the metaphysical order of things is still felt, confusedly, to have *consistency* given to it by its undergirding Judaeo-Christian Creator and Judge. The cultural construction of love in the West has taken shape in the sheltering cultural space of this formative faith-matrix, often mirroring the hybrid ambiguities of the matrix itself, while developing in increasingly 'transgressive' tension with Church tutelage.

This genetic filiation and belonging are about to be repudiated. The culture-narrative of love and desire thus reaches a point of crisis, affecting its most secret intimacy – the crisis of 'transcendence'.

Notes

1   See M. Lazar, *Amour courtois et Fin' amors dans la littérature du XIIe siecle* (Paris: Klincksieck, 1964), pp. 12–13.
2   See Lazar, *Amour courtois*, pp. 171–2, and B. Frappier, 'Vues sur les conceptions courtoises dans les littératures d'Oc et d'Oil au XIIe siècle', *Cahiers de Civilisation médiévale*, IIe année, no. 2 (April–June 1959), pp. 135–56.
3   Marie de Champagne, patroness of the Northern poet Chrétien de Troyes, held that true love between a man and wife was impossible, since he who is not jealous cannot love. Codifying fin' amors at the end of the twelfth century in the 31 rules of love of his *Ars amandi*, André de Chapelin declares intransigently that 'marriage for reasons of love is not a valid excuse' (rule 1) and 'it is improper to love ladies whose *pudeur* aspires to marriage' (rule 11).

4   Bernard de Ventadour, *Chansons d'amour*, ed. C. Appel (Halle: Niemayer, 1915), p. 186, ll.25–32.

5   See I. Singer, *The Nature of Love*, Vol. 2: *Courtly and Romantic*, Part 1: 'Humanism in the Middle Ages'. Singer's preference – urged against C. S. Lewis, Nygren, and particularly de Rougemont – is for the hypothesis of a humanistic autonomy.

6   D. de Rougemont, *L'Amour et l'Occident* (Paris: Plon, 1938); definitive edn Coll. 10/18 (Paris: Minuit, 1972), p. 39. Further references will be given in the text.

7   This is not to say that happiness in love has no voice (Éluard, Aragon, Giraudoux and others would refute this interpretation); but it has no narrative dimension worth remembering, no *recorded story*.

8   I. Singer, *The Nature of Love*, Vol. 2: *Courtly and Romantic*, p. 96.

9   F. Neri (ed.), *Francesco Petrarca, Rime, Trionfi e Poesie latine* (Milan & Naples, 1951), quoted by D. D. R. Owen, *Noble Lovers* (London: Phaedon, 1975), p. 155.

10 Owen, *Noble Lovers*, p. 160.

11 M. D'Arcy, *The Heart and Mind of Love: Lion and Unicorn – A Study of Eros and Agape* (London: Faber & Faber, 1945; revised edn 1954), p. 163.

12 M. Raymond, *Marsile Ficin: Commentaire sur le 'Banquet' de Platon* (Paris: Les Belles Lettres, 1978), p. 112.

13 See A. Ngyren, *Eros et Agape*, vols 2 and 3. Nygren sees the focus of this development in the syncretic Catholic notion of *caritas*.

14 M. Ficino, in *Letters of Marsilio Ficino* (London: Shepheard Welwyn, 1975), Epist. I,1, p. 642 a.

15 Mme de La Fayette, *La Princesse de Clèves* (Paris: Le Livre de poche, 1972), p. 256.

16 This notion is borrowed from Ficino; it is a good example of the transposition of Christian theological structures in the service of 'profane' loves.

17 See N. Hepp, 'La Galanterie' in: P. Nora (ed.), *Les Lieux de mémoire*, Vol 3: *Les France*, pp. 745–87.

18 See e.g. Descartes, *Les Passions de l'âme*, art. LXXXI: '[L'amour de bienveillance] incite à vouloir du bien à ce qu'on aime', whereas 'l'amour de concupiscence' limits itself to desiring its object for its own satisfaction (*Œuvres choisis de Descartes* [Paris: Garnier, 1916]).

19 C. de Laclos, *Les Liaisons dangereueses* (Paris: Garnier, 1961), Première Partie, Lettre 4.

20 So Valmont's former lover, accomplice and rival, Mme de Merteuil, compares herself to the 'belle Dame sans merci' (Premiere Partie, Lettre 20).

21 M. Foucault, *Histoire de la folie à l'âge classique* (Paris: Plon, 1961), p. 347.

22 Marquis de Sade, 'La Vérité' (1787), in *Œuvres complètes*, Vol. 14 (Paris: Cercle du livre précieux, 1966–70), pp. 82–3.

23 M. Blanchot, Sade et Restif de la Bretonne (Paris: Éditions Complexe, 1986), pp. 44–59.

24 J.-J. Rousseau, *La Nouvelle Héloïse* (Paris: Garnier, 1988), Sixième Partie, Lettre VIII.

Chapter 5

The Crisis of Eros and the 'Death of God'

The moment of breakdown intervenes at the end of the nineteenth century, establishing the landscape of twentieth-century Eros. It is a determining moment that will repay particular attention.

The underlying drama of Romantic Love, as we shall see, is to be idealistically supercharged with the sense of its own potential for transcendence. This overbid, generated within an increasingly anthropocentric, rationalised, technically masterful and materialistic culture, produces tensions which are both external and internal. As the century progresses, bourgeois materialism in all its forms denies and chokes the over-extended and increasingly unsupported idealism of Romantic Eros, which is recognised with deepening *ennui* to be non-viable. Its inner spring of spiritual aspiration buckles and twists under the weight of its own dreams – attaining, no doubt, a singular depth of self-reflection in the process – yet falling apart into disjointed and disarticulated urges, mystical and carnal.

This is indeed a dualist drama. The post-Renaissance adventure of growth-in-individuation, though humanistically enriching in its exploration of what human loves are and can be, has been pursued at the price of a progressive deepening of the ancient, inherited Platonic fracture-line. The overt Accused will, however, be – not the contradictions of Romantic Eros itself, nor its philosophic overbid of transcendental idealism, nor even the Platonic mind-frame which has beckoned to both of these – but rather the Judaeo-Christian faith-matrix from which the Promise was legitimately inherited and within which it is non-dualistically founded.

The end-loser will be the ever-ambiguous and perpetually unfulfilled sense that in love, is somehow encountered a promise of human transcendence; it will be the modern human subject of loving.

***

Developing under the influence of *La Nouvelle Héloïse* and *Werther*, French Romanticism re-invested in the passion of love an aspiration to transcendence increasingly de-invested from traditional religion. Though frequently couched in quasi-Catholic forms, and borrowing still from this cultural environment some ultimate providentialist 'guarantee', the Christian substance of these constructs was almost entirely evacuated in favour of a wide variety of spiritualisms and idealisms, the metaphysics of which were largely 'made in Germany'.

The century as a whole is reflected quintessentially in the paradigm of Goethe's Faust and his twin souls (recalling Plato and his charioteer): one sensually clinging to the earth, the other striving heavenwards and invoking a providentialist confidence in the rightly aspiring transcendence of the human spirit. This figure of sense is evoked in the Prologue of *Faust, Part I* and consecrated in the operatic Finale of *Part II*. It places nineteenth-century loves under the sign of the *'twin-souls' paradigm* and that of an – equally Platonic – *myth of the Eternal Feminine*. We may speak here of Romantic love as a fully-fledged parallel religion: no longer requiring the sanction of the Judaeo-Christian proposal that 'God is love', but exploring instead the logic and meaning of the inverse – anthropocentric – proposition, 'love is God'.

That the interpersonal communion and the power of feeling generated by human loves are literally 'salvational' was an intuition developed by German Romanticism. The hero of Novalis' novel of initiation *Heinrich von Ofterdingen*, for instance, discovers the fullness of his powers as poet-magus through the juxtaposed experiences of love and death. (To view the first in the perspective of the second is the secret of the omnipresent nineteenth-century motif of the *Liebestod*: love becomes the symbol of being in its ideal potency insofar as it strives to nullify death through the destruction of all separability between individuals and between the individual and the cosmos; for the same reason, the goal of love is frequently represented as a fusion of identities or 'merging'.) The hero's first kiss is a revelation of the spiritual force that moves the stars in their courses; with this extension, love survives the grave – no longer in vague poetic aspiration, but now in an actualised rite of spiritualistic communion with the lost beloved, penetrating the veil between this world and the next. Its first fruits are the hero's initiation into his Orphic vocation. Composing the magical dream-sphere of the novel and of the world, Heinrich-the-initiate henceforth discerns and declares the hidden Sense of Things. (The Orpheus myth will have a long innings throughout the Romantic-Symbolist tradition in signifying just this function of magus-like potency attributed to the poetic imagination.) Human love is indeed seen as a foretaste of divine love, the presentment of total union, dissolving the individual in the vaster reality of the Absolute.

Love is henceforth advisedly 'infinitist': first, in the transcendentalist sense; but, from now on, the sense of an eschatological absolute is just as likely to be projected horizontally, along the line of historical becoming. Here we discover the imprint of German metaphysics: Schelling, Fichte, Schopenhauer, for the former sense – but also, and very influentially in respect of the latter sense, Hegel. These idealist metaphysicians explain and justify dialectically to the Romantic soul the salvational rightness of its 'infinite longings', its 'intimations of immortality', its 'yearning for transcendence', particularly as experienced through what Ficino had already called the 'divine frenzy' of love.

Spirit, says Fichte, mentor of Novalis, is animated by 'the desire for something entirely unknown which is revealed only by a need, a malaise, a void in search of what would fill it, all unknowing whence it may come'.[1] For Schelling, to love is to participate, in all joyful innocence, in 'the world's holy, elemental and primal energy which engenders and actively brings forth all things out of itself'.[2] It links human interiority to the current of cosmic life and energy that traverses the apparently materialistic and mechanistic appearances of nature. For the Protestant ex-theologian Hegel, Romantic love is a secular religion that justifies itself purely through the irrationality of subjective passion.

Hegel's speculative narrativisation of the entire historical process dynamised by *Geist* (both 'mind' and 'spirit') is, in the last resort, an attempt to replicate, in idealist and immanentist categories, an *equivalence* of the saving incarnation of Christian Agape. Just as the Christian God descends into the world in an outpouring of love, so, in the closing pages of the *Phenomenology of Mind*, the Hegelian Absolute is seen to infuse its spiritual being into all particulars and then progressively return to itself through the evolutionary growth within history of self-knowledge (*Bewusstsein*). The lack of equivalence – the loss – involved in this transaction are not immediately apparent. Provisionally, transcendentalist Eros, can still count on its unexamined *correspondence* with the being of things – a confidence borrowed from a syncretic culture-matrix that is, in increasingly secularised memory, indistinctly Platonic and Judaeo-Christian. This fiduciary credit enables it to assume the status of essential Initiation: it is held to be an immediate experience of the Absolute. This latter concept, as Singer points out, fulfils in respect of the self-referring Romantic heart the same function as 'God' in the theistic world-view of the mediaeval Christian thought: it is the basis for all knowing, and the cipher of the totality of being. It 'procures the benefits of Western religion without the Bible'.[3]

Not all loves of the Romantic generation, of course, are explicitly conceptualised in metaphysical terms; yet all play themselves out, at least in their first movement, *as if* they were metaphysically significant, lacking only a German penchant for philosophical abstraction to declare themselves so. Nerval, who was closest to the German source, so describes the generation of 1830: 'Love, alas! Of vague forms, of pink and blue hues, of metaphysical phantoms! Seen close-to, real woman disgusted our ingenuous innocence; she had to appear a queen or a goddess, and, please, no approaching her!'[4]

In Lamartine, 'love' is indeed an ethereal 'Invocation':

O toi qui m'apparus dans ce désert du monde,
Habitante du ciel, passagère en ces lieux!
O toi qui fis briller dans cette nuit profonde
    Un rayon d'amour à mes yeux;

A mes yeux étonnés montre-toi tout entière;
Dis-moi quel est ton nom, ton pays, ton destin:
    Ton berceau fut-il sur la terre?
    Ou n'es-tu qu'un souffle divin?[5]

O you who appeared in this desert of the world/Inhabitant of heaven, passing through this place/O you who caused to shine in the deep night/A love-ray to my sight;
To my startled eyes appear entire;/Tell me your name, your country, your destiny:/Was your cradle of the earth?/Or are you merely a breath divine?

For Chateaubriand's doomed and incestuously driven hero René, love is even less substantial: a Nostalgia born of pantheist mysticity and a quasi-gnostic sense of exile, heralding a release in death and a flight towards 'those unknown regions that my heart demands'.[6]

In all these writers, a mystico-sentimental religiosity mirrors, under the cover of Catholic forms, the natural thought of Platonic Eros: that the Good is elsewhere, and that She, the image of the Eternal Feminine invoked by the gloom-stricken and adoring lover, is – or would have been – the supernatural mediation leading to it. If human loves are mysteriously flawed – subject to the scandal of time and death, and scarred by the misfortune of unfulfilment – they nevertheless represent a luminous clue to the enigma of being and the nature of things. Accordingly, the image of the beloved as inspiration, mediation or regeneration undergoes a hundred variations from Nerval's Aurelia to Auguste Comte's Clothilde.

***

The mid-century novel, bending to the evolving ethos of the century, strikes a more realistic note, showing a line of mediocre and divided heroes, torn between tender adoration of a married inspiratrix and the more or less inhibited desires of the flesh: Sainte-Beuve's *Volupté* (1834), Balzac's *Le Lys dans la vallée* (1835), Fromentin's *Dominique* (1862), Flaubert's *L'Éducation sentimentale* (1869), like the narrator-hero of *Sylvie* and *Aurélia* (both 1853), diversely exemplify this line. Faithful to its eternal rendezvous with adulterous passion, the French novel of the mid-century explores the inhibitions of its heroes and their divided loyalties as a function of an idealising fixation of desire upon an inaccessible woman. Thus Félix Vandenesse, complacently explaining to the chaste Mme de Mortsauf his attentions to the unchaste Arabella Dudley:

> She is a daughter of the earth, a daughter of fallen races, and you are a daughter of the heavens, the adored angel ... you have all my heart ... she only has my flesh [...]. Yours are my soul, my thoughts, my pure love, yours my youth and old age; hers the desires and pleasures of passing passion; yours my memory in all its extent, hers the deepest forgetting.[7]

Yet, as Mme de Mortsauf's posthumous letter makes clear in revealing the repressed sensuality of her passion, this dualism of flesh and spirit is a convenient and hypocritical male convention. Woman here appears as doubly victimised: corseted and confined in the strict convention of *bourgeois marriage*, as defined by the Code Napoléon and sacralised by the Church, a condition which subjects her to exclusive possession and genteel slavery; but also alienated by her lover's projection onto her of a masculine myth of the Eternal Feminine. Strategically, this myth reacts against, but also belongs to and confirms, the dominant ethos of industrialisation, technological advance and Progress. Romantic idealism in and about love and the narrowly prosaic pragmatism governing bourgeois marriage in fact answer each other Janus-like, as opposed but secretly related facets of the acute dualism of the century.

French traditions of Enlightenment scepticism and psychologist reflexivity increasingly lead the myth back, however, to its genesis in the lover's psyche; just as they cruelly recall the para-religious dream to its prosaic conditions of social insertion. The ideologico-political persuasions left in its wake by the Revolution and the Napoleonic adventure, then, typically determine whether the 'religion of love' becomes the foretaste of a this-worldly Utopia of universal loving-kindness to be realised in history (as in Fourier, Saint-Simon or Enfantin), or else (as in Chateaubriand) the clue to an otherworldly 'Elsewhere', repudiating the century of Progress.

Despite the apparently contrasting affirmations thus delivered, the intuition of amorous transcendence, promoted – however confusedly or impotently – as key to human existence as such is a fundamental constant. Love immanentalised and exalted is obscurely felt still to be a symbol of Being – the Absolute. As such, it serves as the magical paradigm of all creative idealisations, capable of reconfiguring in its own image the writer's vision of the social order or of unveiling immediately the metaphysical order of things.

This underlying movement towards a hyper-valuation of amorous feeling and of its human-cosmic significance is, however, essentially fragile and vulnerable to disillusion. On the one hand, a hostile empirical reality submits it to multiple trials of incarnation; on the other, it is an ideal house built upon shifting metaphysical quicksands. Increasingly, as post-Enlightenment scepticism bites, 'there is no goodness prior to love and nothing for it to see or to contemplate before it creates its own perfections'.[8] Estimates of love, accordingly, oscillate wildly between extreme optimism of an eschatological tenor and an acutely disillusioned, world-renouncing pessimism.

Disarticulated Eros has its trail of omnipresent signs. Stendhal, cynical and atheistic son of the Enlightenment, yet has his nostalgia for the 'transcending' adventure of *amour-passion* (distinguished in *De l'Amour* from the more superficial forms arising out of physical appetite, sympathy and social vanity). His celebrated theory of 'crystallisation' looks towards it by investing the game of love, through creative imagination, with psychic depth and compulsion: 'What I call crystallisation is the operation of the mind which draws from what is presented the discovery that the loved object has new perfections.'[9] His reflection on the *Fin'Amors* is, accordingly, a lament for a lost capacity of devotion, admiration and self-surrender seen to have been sterilised by the calculating, moralistic prudence of his own time: 'We have harvested from our hypocrisy and our asceticism not a homage rendered to virtue – nature is never contradicted with impunity – but simply that there is less happiness on earth and infinitely fewer generous aspirations.'[10] The calculating and role-playing heroes of his novels are caught by the generous 'madness' of love and find in it the only happiness.

Yet they do so paradoxically, against the dominant mind-set of their creator, in defiance of their bourgeois century – and of any sustainable philosophic consistency. The key analogy Stendhal offers for the process of crystallisation goes to the heart of the matter: the glittering deposit of salt crystals which covers the twigs of the salt-mine makes them objectively beautiful. They are not merely beautiful in the subjective eye of the beholder; whereas Stendhal's mocking commentary as novelist on his heroes' inconsistencies, errors, inner knots and deviations from reality point, on the contrary, to his hyper-awareness that love is indeed a delusional fantasy, an exhilarating game played in obedience to biological irrationalities. Stendhal *believes* only in the 'coup de foudre', in the objective chance of mutuality and the knife-edge of amorous insecurity, artistically stage-managed. It is a precarious paradox for the – perhaps –'Happy Few'.

In Zola, the soaring spirituality of Romantic Eros is brought sharply down to the brutish reality of its sexual origin. *Nana* is, implacably, a novel of earth-bound desire: 'the poem of male desires'.[11] It explores, that is, the psychic complications and the irradiating social consequences of a basic animal instinct. The reality is that of 'a pack of dogs after a bitch who isn't even on heat';[12] the psychic complication, a fascinated male complicity in a high-society prostitute's stage-managed myth of *Volupté*. That the highest-placed of all Nana's lovers should be Comte Muffat is doubly significant. Sociologically, this Minister from the Catholic *haute-bourgeoisie* exemplifies the destructive dynamic of animal libido, seen as a power of nature capable of corrupting the governing class, destroying a régime and enfeebling an entire society. The second puberty experienced by this repressed son of Catholic misogyny and asceticism, as Zola sees it, also illustrates the *reconvertibility* of a mystical eros illegitimately invested in the Catholic religion. Religious faith and sexual desire are presented as 'the twofold lever which lifts the world';[13] and Zola is concerned to show the first dynamic as reducible to the second. The god in the animal flesh is the only god.

The whole cultural construct of love as we have followed it in French tradition has tended precisely to *re-imagine* the 'other' love (Agape) according to the native logic of Eros. Zola perfects this process as surely as Hegel: the distinctiveness of Christian Agape is here absorbed, philosophically speaking, as an epiphenomenon of Plato's 'common Aphrodite', leaving a residual shadow only – the misogynistic blame his own novel projects onto Nana herself, avatar of 'fallen Eve'.

Flaubert is more subtle but no less radical in subversion. If *Madame Bovary* is the finest of all French novels of adulterous passion, this is precisely because the contradictions of Eros are scrutinised in multi-layered subtlety, with an analytic precision matching the depth of insight conferred by Flaubert's imaginative self-identification with his heroine ('Madame Bovary, c'est moi'). Emma is exhibited, certainly, as the victim of male superficiality and egoism, as personified by her lovers; of the stifling prosaism of bourgeois marriage as represented by Charles, and of a thoroughly mediocre social regulation epitomised by Homais. Yet her internal inconsistencies are greater still. Her transgressive dream of love is pre-programmed, by her Romantic reading; and it is supercharged with a mysticity imbibed without theological understanding from her convent upbringing. In the crisis of her first abandonment, and again later in her death throes, her yearning for a 'transcending' ecstasy reverts equivocally to a language of Catholic devotion. The confusion involved is superbly drawn. Flaubert, in these episodes, goes to the nerve-centre of a *quiproquo* central to his heroine, to the Romantic ideal and, indeed, to the entire cultural construct we have been following. Whether addressed to her lovers, to the celestial Deity or to the representation of the Crucified, Emma's dream always supposes an ideal Other, a romanticised phantom born of her most ardent memories and longings.[14] Always, it looks to a consummation beyond any that reality could supply. She desires, in fact, infinitely, with the infinity of Desire itself – yet also 'horizontally', with immediate, appetitive gluttony –'drying up all felicity in advance by wishing it too great'.[15] This last subordinate clause captures the ever-frustrated, and finally self-destructive, essence of Romantic *amour-passion* as viewed by Flaubert.

Baudelaire, too, is haunted and condemned by a devouring ideality. 'Hymne à la Beauté', devoted to his adoration of the heavenly Aphrodite, already betrays intimations of a horror of incarnation:

L'amoureux pantelant incliné sur sa belle
A l'air d'un moribond caressant son tombeau.[16]

The panting lover bent over his lovely/Looks like a dying man caressing his tomb.

Symetrically, in 'Aube spirituelle':

Quand chez les débauchés l'aube blanche et vermeille
Entre en société de l'Idéal rongeur,
Par l'opération d'un mystère vengeur
Dans la brute assoupie un ange se réveille.[17]

When in the house of debauchery the white and scarlet dawn/Enters into company with the gnawing Ideal,/By a vengeful mystery/In the somnolent brute an angel wakens.

Whereupon the unquenchable thirst for the Ideal derides 'the prostrate man who dreams still and suffers'. The 'two souls paradigm' here grasps its own formula as logical paradox and spiritual contradiction.

Moreover, both paradox and contradiction are projected onto the feminine Other. 'Woman,' writes Pierre Emmanuel acutely, 'is merely the mortal envelope of Being, which has engulfed within itself the image of heaven ... she points to this essential because she attests the loss of it.'[18] Extreme fascination, voluptuous and spiritual, thus wars with an extreme misogyny that *both* resents the self-centred idol defying male desire *and* mistrusts the unspiritual female animal who entraps spiritual man in the toils of the flesh. Woman is both 'a mediatrix towards being' and at the same time a 'castrating amputatrix of being'; she is a 'stage-decor absolute, Doorway to the forbidden Grand Return'.[19]

Both these roles are linked to a radical experience of human time:

> Radical because Baudelaire seeks in vain in her the prior root of being, its unity, its eternity. Yet, always, even and especially in voluptuous ecstasy, is heralded, declared or accomplished a fateful tearing away ... the abrupt loss of the absolute within the lightening flash that reveals it.[20]

Here, the innermost spring of Desire is seen, as it will often appear in the twentieth century, as a pursuit of gnosis: saving illumination, direct and immediate apprehension of Being. By the same token, the haunting lure of such Knowledge appears as an eternal mirage, infinitely generative of frustration and *ennui*. In Baudelaire, the breakdown of Romantic spirituality as a quest for the absolute is patent.

The underlying spiritual quest finds its paroxysm in Wagner, the artist who gave, as Valéry was later to remark, the consummate image of everything the nineteenth century desired and sought to accomplish. Wagner resurrects the Tristan myth in all its potency. Indeed, according to Denis de Rougemont, he lifts the in-built taboo which has meant that the deepest sense of the myth – the secret death-wish inhabiting *amour-passion* – has hitherto been allowed to surface only allusively. 'Delivered from the world, I possess you at last,/O you who fill up my soul,/Supreme voluptuous ecstasy of love.' The love duet of Act II of *Tristan and Isolde* is the song of two souls imprisoned in their fleshly envelopes, yearning, as towards an orgasmic consummation in the order of spirit, to transcend their individualised and limited identities. De Rougemont comments:

> It is the desire of the flesh that separates them still. They are together, and yet, they are two. There is this 'and' of Tristan *and* Isolde which signifies their created duality. At this point, the music alone can express the substance and the certainty of this double nostalgia to be one.[21]

What we see on stage, no doubt, is a stout lady and a Teutonic warrior in a strange torment of desire. But, says de Rougemont, it is enough for the spectator to close his eyes and listen to the music for the whole drama to become clear. 'The overwhelming morbidity of the music reveals a world in which carnal desire is now merely a last burning languor in a soul which is being cured of living.'[22] What we hear is a mystical invocation to death: a death-in-apotheosis conceived as the fulfilment of the promise of passion, as the transcendence of pure spirit and as a liberating fusion of Self in the Absolute.

Wagner marks an apex. Yet the nineteenth century as a whole, if we listen to the underlying concert of its literary voices, bears witness overwhelmingly to a gathering and generalised crisis of the idealist-dualist culture of Eros. Anthropological dualism, pushed to its limits, has become paradox. The desire of the natural flesh wars with the transcendent desire of spirit; sexual eros is increasingly impatient of a socio-cultural regulation imposed by the dominant bourgeois ideology (a regulation felt to rest ultimately on a Catholic sacralisation of marriage and nothing else); while spiritual eros declares a secret spring of mystical absolutism which not only rejects all moral regulation, but yearns in world-denying purity for an Unsayable Beyond. The Ideal condemns the real, while the real dissolves the Ideal. The anthropological composite of beast-angel has fallen into a condition of unliveable contradiction. The sign and symptom is the great Romantic-Symbolist motif of *ennui*, with its twin faces: the difficulty of material incarnation and the absurdity of spirit.

***

There had to be a resolution, and there is one; although, as we may judge a century later, inevitably more symptomatic of the crisis than truly judicious or healing. It is known to historians of culture, following Nietzsche's passionate cry of atheism and metaphysical autonomy, as the 'death of God'. This 'event' is rightly seen as marking symbolically a sea-change in culture separating the twentieth century from the previous nineteen of our era, since it tends to eliminate the great Explicator-Respondent of Western culture to which all human phenomena – including those of love, desire and transcendence – had been, proximately or ultimately, referrable.

As an event occurring within the dualist-idealist mindsphere, it displays in an extreme form the same character of ambiguity we have come to associate with all phenomena expressing the cultural emergence and development of Eros. The 'ambiguity' has the character of a confusion about identity; and it is worth examining closely, both in Nietzsche himself, and in Mallarmé, Rimbaud and Valéry, all of whom refract the same ambiguity in the French cultural mindspace.

Apparently, there is not the slightest doubt about the God-who-is-dead, or the meaning of his being so. Writing in *Ecce Homo*, Nietzsche himself describes his mission as an 'unreserved onslaught against the Crucified',[23] and as an attempt to liquidate the fictions of God, morality, immortality, grace and redemption which, for Nietzsche, set up a mind-created other-worldliness, inhibiting to the creative will and possibility of mankind. Or again, he writes: 'I call Christianity, and it alone, the great calamity, the great perversion of mind, the great vindictive instinct which finds no means venomous enough, underhand enough, stealthy enough, mean enough, I call it the one mortal stain upon humanity.'[24] That he should so express his revolt is perhaps comprehensible in psychological terms: as Jaspers points out, Nietzsche was a pastor's son, reared amid quietistic nineteenth-century pietism, who was disappointed by the failure of those he observed at first-hand to embody a spiritual heroism he never ceased, despite all his denunciations, to expect of Christianity.[25] 'Have I been understood? – Dionysos [invoked] against the Crucified.'[26]

Yet, hermeneutically speaking, the case is a good deal less clear. Invariably, Nietszche treats Christianity as a popular Platonism (just as he treats Platonism as a Christianity for intellectuals).[27] In the great inversion of values which he accuses Christianity of having thrust upon the ancient world, the specifically Christian role consists in having metaphysically confirmed and universalised a slave morality, the invention of which he traces back to the resentment of the Jews in the time of their Assyrian captivity. Strikingly, his reading of this phenomenon moves from the Jews to Paul, whom he regards, like Freud, and many contemporaries of early liberal protestant exegesis (but against all modern biblical scholarship), as real founder and true inventor of the Christian belief-system; it skirts notably around Jesus of Nazareth, whom Nietzsche treats as a quietistic Buddha figure concerned merely with a rule of life conducive to inward beatitude, and who died, on this account, not to save men from the sin which prevents them from knowing God, but in an attempt to show them how to live 'morally' (i.e. unresistingly, in suffering, loving those who persecute them). In all of this, Christianity is seen, as it were, through an inverted telescope: in dramatically reduced perspective, with near-zero recognition of its constituting logic of Agape and of the original project of its first Founder. It becomes, on this account, a mere peg for the subsequent invention of a hellenistic faith; a construct which seeks, with the low cunning of the vanquished, to recuperate failure and transform the defeat of an inferior morality into a posthumous metaphysical victory.

It is of course possible to share, as many modern intellectuals have done, the excitement generated by the passionate and iconoclastic – i.e. intellectually *erotic*[28] – Nietzschean leitmotif: a new transcendence of human creative energy springing out of Nihilism itself. Without that carrying persuasion, however, it must be doubtful whether Nietzsche's basic identification of Judaeo-Christianity could appear judicious or cogent to a well-informed contemporary mind literate in the twentieth-century scholarship of cultural sources and origins.[29] On the other hand, Nietzsche does strike home with power and pertinence at precisely the 'God' of a cultural hybridisation we have observed throughout the present chapter: a hybridisation invited in the first place by Christian theologians, but then exponentially magnified in its effects by accumulated secular attempts, both naive and philosophic, to conjugate 'the divine' in the logic and categories of Hellenic Eros: that is, in function of aspiring human loves pursuing the other-worldly *telos* of human desire. It is clear enough, in the poem by Lamartine quoted above – but also in Baudelaire and in Zola – that such cultural hybridisation results, by the end of the nineteenth century, in a near-complete 'white-out' of the ability of the most highly cultured and intelligent minds to distinguish any longer between the fundamental motifs of Eros and Agape, or to know Christianity from its idealist accretions and spiritualistic shadows.[30]

It might even be argued that Nietzsche is in fact less securely a prey to this confusion than many of his contemporaries. One finds in his *Volonté de puissance,* for instance, the surprising (and revealing) concession: 'Christianity is still possible at any moment. It is not bound to any of the shameless doctrines which have usurped its name; it has no need of a personal God, nor of sin, nor of immortality, nor of redemption, nor of faith; it has no need of any metaphysic.'[31] His ultimate, unpredictable, identification of Dionysos and the Crucified is well-known: it marks perhaps, on the threshold of madness, a last throw at asserting a self-generated counter-thesis to the logic of his own (mis)identification of his true adversary.

The meaning of the proposition 'God is dead' is of course crucially inflected by the recognition that Nietzsche strikes validly at what he understands well; and that what he understands well is in fact a life-denying, other-worldly, ascetic and moralistic transcription, a pale offprint, enacted in idealist-dualist categories, of the faith of

Agape. In general terms, it is clear, as many writers have pointed out, that Zarathoustra's momentous pronouncement is an uneasily ambivalent figure of speech: it cannot be *literally* meaningful or true that 'God is dead' or that 'we have killed him', since any recognisable or competent concept of God as 'transcendent' *ontologically* must set him beyond such accidents. There is, of course, an important sense in which both propositions *can* be received integrally; but this sense is entirely un-Nietzschean. It refers us, precisely, to the incarnate and crucified God of the New Testament, and is thinkable *only* in the logic of Agape; it represents, in fact, a specifically *Christian* sense.

What may be true in Nietzsche's prophecy is something of lesser, though still momentous, significance: that the *theistic* idea of *a* God, conceived in the terms of *transcendental idealism*, is no longer 'live' in human consciousness; or that a certain form of *hybridised religious metaphysics* is culturally repudiated and dead; or that cultural memory *no longer retains any accurate sense* of the meaning of Christian 'Agape'.

The Nietzschean declaration, in sum, says a considerable something about Eros and its hybrids, but very little about Agape. It signifies validly the disappearance of the horizon of thought and action provided by a superficially Christianised Platonism: 'the notion of a "Beyond", of a "true world", invented with the sole aim of devaluing the only world which exists, of no longer retaining for our terrestrial reality any goal, any task!'[32] Yet this meaning also confirms as judicious the following conclusion, which I would propose to follow for the purpose of the present readings: 'Far from neutralising the question of God, Nietzsche's critique restores to it its innocence, safeguarding for a more essential meditation an ultimate still-to-be-thought.'[33]

These judicious retrospective distinctions and evaluations do not however belong to the mental horizon of *fin-de-siècle* France. They are excluded, both by reason of the still rudimentary state of critical exegesis of cultural sources and by the entire nexus of counter-persuasions most characteristic of the Symbolist moment. What ultimately weighs in the mental horizon of a Mallarmé, a Rimbaud, a Valéry is indeed the sense of an awesome metaphysical decease forever neutralising the question of God, relegating the believing past of mankind to pre-history and re-posing dramatically, in purely human terms, the question of an *autonomous human transcendence*.

Mallarmé's historical reading of Western cultural origins shows 'Beauty bitten to the heart since Christianity by chimera'[34] – that is, by the tragic consciousness of death and afterlife. Like the Serpent of Genesis, the triumph of the so-called 'ages of faith' is seen to have destroyed the quasi-edenic innocence of pagan antiquity; whereas the Renaissance, in restoring a living continuity with the mythology of antiquity, and by inaugurating a critical spirit, is perceived to have heralded the end of Christianity and, with it, of 'the mind of misfortune'. Christianity, for Mallarmé, as for Rimbaud, and later in Valéry's private reflections 'On things divine'[35] is identified with a Baudelairean consciousness of exile and fallenness. This is seen to have generated, by way of symbolic compensation, its dreams of eternity and of an objectively existent, personal (i.e. 'anthropomorphic') God. It is significant that, in translating Cox's treatise on ancient mythology, the translator of *Les Dieux antiques* discreetly corrects the believing and theocentric perspective of the English author so as to reflect his own anthropocentric theory of the divine.[36]

Behind this striking case of *traduttore traditore*, lies a tradition of early comparative religion and mythology, the guiding intuition of which had been the notion of an 'underlying single religion' reflecting the perennial religious genius of the human psyche. In effect, this was a theory of the natural parthenogenesis in the human psyche of supposedly 'revealed' monotheisms and of the equivalence of all 'mythologies of the gods'. It authorised the view, widely held by French Symbolists, that all constituted dogmatic religions had hypostasised and appropriated to themselves a central power of infinite dynamism and insight proper to the matricial psyche; and that the human psyche itself, considered in its ill-elucidated depths, constituted the only true mystery.

More simply and directly, the Romantic and Parnassian predecessors of Mallarmé, Rimbaud and Valéry had overwhelmingly read the Christian gospels as a self-related human tragedy. Jesus, hero of the Christian Fable, appeared to their vision like a Romantic or Parnassian poet, set against a décor of Absence, abandonment and cosmic void, bearing not so much the sins of the world as the melancholy of a metaphysically orphaned generation of poets. Reciprocally, the artist's perception of organised Catholicism in the late nineteenth century is the one well epitomised by Flaubert: 'Pius IX – the martyr of the Vatican – will have been fatal to Catholicism. The devotions he has instituted: – hideous! Sacred heart, Saint Joseph, Mary's womb, Salette, etc; it's like the cult of Isis and Bellone in the latter days of paganism.'[37] As the century advanced, the besieged citadel, with its hideous devotions, its apologetically exploited miracles and late doctrinal developments, looked fatally degenerescent, a condemned dinosaur venerable only for the consummate aesthetic magic of its revised liturgies.

In all these ways, the drama of 'the death of God' as refracted in France may be expressed as a reflexive regathering into the psychic source itself of all the idealistic aspirations and all the sublimated thirst for transcendence characteristic of nineteenth-century Eros in general. Of Christianity as the faith of Agape this development in culture had little perception and nothing to say, save by way of immediate generic dismissal. The Love divine figures simply as one of the mind-generated 'glorious lies' which Mallarmé wished to refer to human invention and to proclaim such 'before the Nothingness which is the truth'.[38] We have already noted a parallel phenomenon in the case of Valéry.[39] Pierre Emmanuel, pointing out that the word love does not figure in Baudelaire's religion even as an attribute (let alone as the *Ipse*) of God, explains this phenomenon as a sort of tautology: 'Under the name of God, the mind plays out its own myth and endlessly reinvents it. Orphism is the favourite dream of poets and philosophers, and often enough the very foundation and pattern of their thought-forming.'[40]

Everything happens, in short, as though the insecure idealism of the age were unable to conceive of a love that was *not* a reflection in the mirror of mind, secondary to, and dependent upon, the mirror itself; as though it could not accede, consequently, to the notion of Agape, except as remade in the likeness of a cracked and deficient construct of human Eros. Here, perhaps, we have the explicative formula which tells us why the crisis of natural Eros is experienced and recorded overwhelmingly in French cultural tradition as a crisis of the religion of revealed Agape.

***

The conceptually ambivalent nature of the 'death of God' does not, of course, diminish in any way the trauma of loss. Nietzsche himself spoke of the event as tremendous beyond the comprehension of contemporary atheists. (René Girard, in our own time, has roundly denounced the mediocre *contresens* made of this by the 'vulgar atheism' of French secularists – the belief that God has died 'naturally', without violence – *of senescence*.)[41] Rimbaud, by no means mediocre, passed through his *Saison en Enfer*, including the temptation of a capitulation restoring him to the safety of the Catholic womb and denial of his Orphic genius. Mallarmé underwent a prolonged spiritual crisis before proclaiming he had 'laid low, victoriously, God'[42] and founded a new poetics upon the twin pillars of the science of language and of the immanent divinity of human Desire.

As for Valéry, the event and its trauma find memorable expression in a still unpublished prose poem of 1888, dedicated to Mallarmé and entitled 'L'Enterrement de Dieu'. The narrator, beset, as in a dream, by a sense of constriction and foreboding, comes as bemused spectator across a strange funeral, whose subject is, so he is informed by a heedless crowd of merry-makers, 'God'. At the sound of earth falling upon the coffin, the masked drama of contemporary culture becomes, with surging insight, a vast drama in cosmic nature. The whole Universe suffers apocalyptic dislocation:

> Then it was that the Sun, after a last radiancy, paled and disappeared. Something warned me that it would not return and that we should not see it more.
> The moon herself had melted from the skies. The sombre firmament held no more stars. It was a cold, dark hole. And at that moment I felt falling onto my hands from above a few icy drops, like liquid diamonds and I knew that all those stars had just come loose and that I was witnessing the tears of Heaven flow...
> ...A great cry rent the air.
> ...A great wind stirred up the leaves which covered the Earth... And it seemed to me that this wind was blowing within me, that it extinguished my Being.[43]

This remarkable text, written by a seventeen-year old schoolboy, is, in one sense, an extreme case of the Pathetic Fallacy: it involves the cosmos in the consternation of the human subject. In this respect, it perpetuates the essential ambiguity surrounding the 'death of God'. Yet its adequate Symbolist music and powerful apocalyptic imagery sit directly upon the springs of the unconscious; and perhaps, in fallacy, they speak greater poetic truth than merely factual discourse could.

The adventure of modernity, of metaphysically autonomous self-awareness, is heralded under the redoubtable sign of Absence. More than mere anguish at the 'ways of liberty', the tears of the mind, the great cry of abandonment, the nocturnal wind extinguishing the flame of Being express horror at the ontological void and a sense of irreparable loss which strikes at the innermost being of Desire. The 'death of God' is experienced not merely as a withdrawal of order and purpose from the cosmos; it signifies also for the human subject a momentous fall from Being to existence. It is a mortal wound in respect of the innermost need for life and light and love, constitutive of the human *ipse* as such. There is grievous trauma in being amputated from the 'other world' posited and desired by human Eros; such that the cosmos itself is put out of joint – and it is Night.

Of such intuitions, proper to the primitive *anima religiosa* whose signature is given in the primitive (and allusively Platonic) metaphor of the eclipse of the Sun, will be made the deep-seated knot of the modern imaginary. We glimpse here for the first time the landscape of twentieth-century desiring and loving.

Notes

1   Quoted by I. Singer in *The Nature of Love*, Vol. 3: *The Modern World* (Chicago: University of Chicago Press, 1987), pp. 187-8.
2   Quoted by Singer in ibid., p. 387.
3   I. Singer, *The Nature of Love*, Vol. 2: *Courtly and Romantic*, p. 383.
4   G. de Nerval, *Sylvie* (Paris: Larousse, 1973), p. 46.
5   Lamartine, 'Invocation' (1817).
6   A. de Chateaubriand, *René* (Paris: Bordas, 1976), p. 82.
7   H. de Balzac, *Le Lys dans la vallée* (Paris: Garnier, 1966), p. 248.
8   Singer, Vol. 2, p. 292.
9   Stendhal, *De l'Amour*, in *Œuvres complètes* (Paris: Champion, 1972), Vol. 3, Livre 1er, chap. 2, p. 20.
10 Ibid., Livre II, Vol 4, *passim.*
11 H. Mitterrand in his editor's preface to É. Zola, *Nana* Folio (Paris: Gallimard, 1977), p. 14.
12 Ibid.
13 See *Nana*, pp. 444–5.
14 See G. Flaubert, *Madame Bovary* (Paris: Garnier Flammarion, 1979), pp. 342–3.
15 Ibid., p. 312.
16 C. Baudelaire, *Les Fleurs du Mal*, XXI, Bibliothèque de la Pléiade, ed. Y. Le Dantec (Paris: Gallimard, 1961), p. 44.
17 *Les Fleurs du mal*, XLVI, in ibid., p. 44.
18 P. Emmanuel, *Baudelaire, la Femme et Dieu* Points (Paris: Seuil, 1982), p. 6.
19 Ibid., pp. 9, 11.
20 Ibid., p. 7.
21 D. de Rougemont, *L'Amour et l'Occident* 10/18 (Paris: Minuit, 1972), p. 250.
22 Ibid., p. 252.
23 Letter to Georg Brandes, 20 November 1888, quoted by J. Natanson, *La Mort de Dieu: Essai sur l'athéisme moderne* (Paris: Presses Universitaires de France, 1975), p. 178.
24 F. Nietzsche, *L'Antétchrist* (Paris: J.-J. Pauvert, 1967), para. 62.

25 K. Jaspers, *Nietzsche et le christianisme* (Paris: Minuit, 1949), pp. 11–14.

26 F. Nietzsche, *Ecce homo* Idées (Paris: Gallimard, 1974), p. 155.

27 See F. Nietzsche, Preface, *Par delà le bien et le mal* trans. G. Bianquis (Paris: Union générale des Éditeurs, 1962).

28 Nietzsche writes of the Dionysian soul as 'wanting to accede to will and desire'. Zarathoustra says: 'Something unsatisfied and unsatisfiable is in me, which wills to be heard. A desire for love is in me, which speaks the language of love' (*Ecce homo*, pp. 117, 119).

29 See e.g. C. H. Dodd, *The Founder of Christianity* (London: Collins-Fontana, 1971) and *The Interpretation of the Fourth Gospel* (Cambridge: Cambridge University Press, 1960).

30 Cf. Natanson: 'I think too that the theme of the death of God has to do with the relationship of modern culture with the historic symbiosis of Christianity and Platonism. More exactly, it is the "mortal collusion" ... between classical philosophy and faith which is responsible for the absence of God characteristic of the modern world, and of nihilism' (*La Mort de Dieu: Essai sur l'athéisme moderne* [Paris: PUF, 1975], p. 191).

31 F. Nietzsche, *La Volonté de Puissance* (Paris: Gallimard, 1995), Vol. 2, p. 329, para. 407.

32 F. Nietzsche, *Ecce Homo*, p. 154.

33 J. Granier, 'La Critique nietzschéenne du Dieu de la métaphysique', in *Procès de l'objectivité de Dieu* (Paris: Éditions du Cerf, 1969), p. 79.

34 S. Mallarmé, *Correspondance 1862–1871*, ed. H. Mondor (Paris: Gallimard, 1959), p. 246.

35 Valéry projected in 1921, but never wrote, a Socratic dialogue 'Peri tôn tou theou', the voluminous notes for which form a very substantial rubric in the 28,000 pages of his *Cahiers*. See P. Gifford, *Valéry: Le Dialogue des choses divines* (Paris: Corti, 1989), pp. 345-69.

36 See B. Marchal, *La Religion de Mallarmé* (Paris: Corti, 1988), pp. 118–22.

37 G. Flaubert, *Œuvres complètes: Correspondance, série 1877–1880* (Paris: Connard, 1930), p. 343.

38 S. Mallarmé, *Correspondance*, Vol. I, pp. 207–8.

39 See chap. 3, p. 51.

40 P. Emmanuel, *Baudelaire*, p. 149.

41 R. Girard, 'Le meurtre fondateur' P. Dumouchel (éd.), in *Violence et Vérité Autour de René Girard* (Paris: Grasset, 1985), p. 603.

42 S. Mallarmé, *Correspondance*, Vol. I, p. 241.

43 Unpublished ms., Dossier 'Proses. Anciennes', ff.115–16, BNF, Paris.

Deconstructing Romantic Transcendence

Eros Under Suspicion

The 'death of God' as we have decoded it signifies the repudiating loss of the 'ontic logos' (Charles Taylor's term),[1] which gave the pre-twentieth-century psyche its confidently assumed hold upon the world. Eros ceases to be able to count on its pre-known or intuited *correspondence* with the being of things. The nineteenth century had believed 'transcendentally' in Eros – and suffered in consequence transcending traumas of disenchantment. Twentieth-century rebeginnings start at the other end – –'from below', often in a spirit of vengeful demystification. Deprived of an objective correlate in the non-self, and finding no sanction in any purposive ordering of things, the promise of metaphysical transcendence previously intuited through love, and posited as a basis for love, slips away. The arrow of infinite longing then turns back upon itself in reactive – and often hyperbolic – self-suspicion.

Has love any ethical dimension? Not obviously, if all morality is socially coded inhibition. Has it any sense or consistency? Perhaps only as a pathology of feeling, and then only in rhetorical terms, if language as such is merely conventional and arbitrary, a system of 'broken' signs without intrinsic referential pertinence. Is the concept of love even thinkable? With extreme difficulty, given the fatal slippage, now so acutely perceived, in the gearing of mind onto things; and then only with elaborate precautions of scientific method. Will it, at least, be theorisable? Only on the hypothesis that we secrete, by parthenogenesis, through the operation of a mythically powerful but naive nominalism (belief-upon-names), our own gods, referable entirely to the single source of subjective, sexually stimulated imagination. Is not love, the first among these secreted goods or half-gods, 'really' a complicated biological interest – reducible, in materially realistic fact, to sex?

More exactly, 'love' (with suitably distancing and sense-deferring inverted commas) is now envisaged purely as 'idealisation' i.e. an imaginative valuation of a creative and mytho-poetic type, secretly obeying vital ego-interests. This will become the norm-setting twentieth-century view. For its best-known twentieth-century prophet, Freud, 'Idealisation is a process that concerns the [sexual] object; by it, that object, without any alteration in its nature, is aggrandised and exalted in the subject's mind.'[2] It obeys, says Freud, a logic of narcissism, which is the primal condition underlying all states of love: we pursue libidinal pleasure and self-concern through the circuitous device of the Other who happens to meet the requirements of the ego-ideal we ourselves construct, while supplying by replacement our need to be loved maternally. As such, it constitutes a misappraisal, an illogical delusion determining a form of behaviour which is essentially viewed by this post-Romantic rationalist as a debilitating waste of energy of the compulsive-neurotic kind.

Freud considers that the coalescence of object-libido and ego-libido in the service of the 'drives' of a pan-sexual energy ('libido') coincides with 'the all-inclusive and all-preserving eros of Plato's *Symposium*'.[3] In hermeneutical terms, the equivalence asserted is entirely problematic: as we have suggested, Freudian psycho-decipherment turns upside-down Plato's dialectic of ascent towards an antecedently real truth and beauty. Yet how *unproblematically* the equivalence is asserted by Freud the meta-psychologist! The psychoanalyst's reflexive, criticist and positivist suspicion of Romanticism, harbinger of all twentieth-century 'deconstructions', is simply held to offer an adequate explanatory formula, mopping up all 'transcendentalism'. The psychoanalytical 'sub-text' is taken to represent what Plato 'really meant' and would, with scientific enlightenment, have said; a regressive aetiology is a sufficient hermeneutic truth ...

Our series of twentieth-century essays opens with the generation of Proust, Valéry and Claudel. While not yet reliably cognisant of Freud's writings – and by no means organised by 'Freudian theory' – early-century French writers are often moved, in differing degrees, by insights analogous to his. Proust shows greatest direct affinity: to a Freudian pan-sexualism (which he escapes perhaps only in his half-platonising account of art and human value); to the polymorphous perversity of Freudian desire (including its directly sexual expressions – homosexuality, incest, profanation, paedophilia); to a sense of the ultimate narcissism and fragility of human loves (even if Proust does enquire about 'love', and not just about 'Sex').[4]

Even where acutely mistrustful of Freudian reductivism (as Valéry and Claudel certainly are), all wrestle with 'idealisation'; all strip down the erotico-romantic construct of Eros before rebuilding it in personal decipherment. All have their own version of what later theory, following Freud, will call a 'libidinal economy', a single-sourced budget of desirous energy animating all enterprises of the individual and collective mind, hence also of culture, and admitting a harmonic inter-resonance between desire-forms: 'Our slightest desire, although unique as a chord, admits within it the fundamental notes of which our lives are constructed,'[5] writes Proust, echoing Freud – albeit more subtly, and in a way all three of our writers might have recognised.

The contours of a twentieth-century French mindscape begin to emerge here; we are entering the 'time of desire'.[6] The precursor signs are all present. As the 'reality quotient' accorded to Eros dips down towards the point of its phenomenal emergence, identified as sexual, and as the mind is seen to be sexually energised, so the sexual body is accorded a prominence and a cognitive status occluded by Romantic spiritualism and idealism. There is a desire to reconnect higher mental function to a resurgent underlayer of libidinal feeling, particularly in artistic activity. Eros becomes the attribute of the writing subject, as well as of the subject written; it may, indeed, provide the artist with a substitute object of love. The writing itself often has self-consciously erotic textures; to the point of creating a hermeneutic 'circularity' of its own. By century's end, we shall be asking: what, then, belongs to the reflective experience of love, and what to the rendering of it imaginatively in the language-woven text?

In the post-Romantic context, the focus falls on the idolatries of Eros: on the power of desire energising the human psyche and fabricating a deviant transcendence, a false sacrality, and in the end a counterfeit love. The notion of the *eidolon* implies a false representation, determining an illusory self-investment: an *image* which is also an *idol*. Yet the deconstruction of idolatries still leaves, ambiguously, something else-and-more; something non-Freudian, known primarily in its metasexual transcendence, as a mysteriously allusive sign or trace to be deciphered.

Notes

1 See C. Taylor, *Sources of the Self: The Making of Modern Identity* (Cambridge: Cambridge University Press, 1989).

2 S. Freud, *Three Essays on Sexuality*, in *The Standard Edition of the Complete Works of Sigmund Freud* (London: Hogarth Press and the Institute of Psycho-Analysis, 1953–66), Vol. 7 (1959), p. 150.

3 Ibid. 19: 218.

4 See M. Bowie, *Proust Among the Stars* (London: Harper Collins, 1998), Chap. 6: 'Sex'.

5 M. Proust, *A la Recherche du temps perdu*, 4 vols, ed. J.-Y. Tadié, Bibliothèque de la Pléiade (Paris: Gallimard, 1987–89), Vol. IV, p. 206.

6 D. Vasse, *Le Temps du désir* (Paris: Seuil, 1969).

Chapter 6

Marcel Proust: The Idolatries of Eros

*L'amour le plus exclusif pour une personne est toujours
l'amour d'autre chose. (II, 189)*

Proustian love may be a thing of the mind – *cosa mentale* – but this is not to say it represents a minor matter in the economy of *A la Recherche du temps perdu*.[1] Within the lexical field of Proust's novel, statistical analysis of frequencies puts the words 'love' and 'desire' in first and second places respectively (ahead of 'memory' and 'time').[2] Perhaps more than any other writer, Proust indeed strikes us as a novelist of total libidinal awareness, whose writing consists in perpetually retracing, reflecting upon, and deciphering human Eros apprehended in the diversity of its forms and questioned in its deeper unity, as a problem of both self-understanding and existential self-realisation.[3]

Readers and critics have of course long recognised the unrivalled subtlety, penetration and range of Proust's analysis. Not only is love viewed, for the first time, entirely within the fourth dimension of Time, it is referred as never before to the unconscious depths of the mind; examined as interplay of eroticism and imagination; tracked in its full range of 'deviant' or 'regressive' expressions, as also in a founding dimension of androgyny. 'The over-narrow boundary lines we draw around love derive simply from our great ignorance of life' (II, 763), says Proust, heralding presciently the vast continent uncovered by modern psychoanalysis. On the other hand, there is a residual problem about the 'validity' of the total figure of Proustian love. Moral and philosophic judgements have often seen it as an over-sombre, basically aberrant account of this most central human potential, redeemed only by the author's probing and heroic honesty; an account of the 'passionate' more than of the properly 'loving' (tender, concerned or altruistic) virtualities of love; and, for some, admissible under the name of 'love' only in the looser, generic sense applying to any and every sexually-based attachment involving a powerful object-cathexis.

Reasons have been sought variously: in Proust's chronic hypersensitivity of temperament; in the artistic detachment intervening between himself and the objects of his affections; in the novelist's 'bi-valent' sexual orientation; in the superficiality of his time and milieu; and in the internal dialectics of time lost and regained, which gives love the peculiar status of depreciated 'false path' on the itinerary towards the spiritual homeland. Thus Jean Rousset writes of the functional place of Proust's study of love in the structure of the novel: 'we can understand perfectly well why it is limited and systematic and has to be so.'[4]

What is seen through the psychologist's microscope and what is seen through the ethico-philosophic telescope may, in short, differ antipodally: a Proustian paradox with a wider, and characteristically modern, resonance. A point of unitary understanding is to be found, however, in the development of Rousset's point just stated. In the novel's dialectic of quest, the experience of *amour-passion*, as recounted and commented on by the narrator, represents in fact a 'lower love' viewed from the standpoint of the 'higher love' discovered in and through art. 'Proustian love' is a progressively unfolding existential experiment, motivating and promoting through self-decipherment its own self-transcendence.

***

The dialectic of higher and lower loves is brilliantly adumbrated in *Un Amour de Swann*. Here, the course of Swann's love for Odette is set in structurally significant counterpoint with successive appearances of the 'little phrase' from Vinteuil's sonata, for which Swann experiences 'a sort of love unknown' (I, 206). Entwined with his affair, first as witness and accomplice, then as spiritual confidante and consoler, the 'petite phrase' acquires, in the divine retrospect of its last appearance, the status of a veritable alternative to the all-too-human Other pursued in passion. It thus emerges as the true contender for his affections; it becomes, in fact, the second of the novel's two 'elle's, and a superior rival to Odette. This dialectic relationship is maintained in each of the succeeding major loves, failure and suffering generating an ever-deeper awareness of the message and the call of the higher love. So in this provisional account of narrator's spiritual progress:

> This was not the first time that I felt that those who love and those who take pleasure are not the same. [...] I had already learned, even before going to see la Berma, that, whatever the object of any future loves, this would be set at the end of a painful pursuit, in the course of which I should have first of all to sacrifice my pleasure to this supreme good, instead of seeking my pleasure in it. (II, 7)

This inverse reciprocity between 'love' and 'pleasure' is completed in *Le Temps retrouvé*, where the discovery of the novel's most regressive pleasure-love – the masochistic flagellation scene, set in a homosexual brothel at the heart of the nocturnal labyrinth that is wartime Paris – prepares the most significant renunciation, which is also the most 'celestial' moment of annunciation, liberation and rebirth.

The relation of ascesis between 'lower' and 'higher' loves is, of course, significantly Platonic in conception; and it is visibly related – albeit in the mode of insight gained through suffering – to the dialectics of ascent in the *Symposium*. Proust, that is, is not simply a libidinal writer and theorist; he is a modern re-decipherer standing within the Eros tradition as such. This insight is crucial to our recognition, not only of the place of love in the novel, but, more centrally still, of what Proust actually means by 'love' and of how we may view his account of it. *La Recherche* offers a recapitulative account of *amour-passion* as constructed throughout Western cultural tradition. This model is re-enacted by the 'Marcel' whose autobiography is presented, and by his fictional avatars in the story; it is reflexively theorised by the narrator whose commentary unfolds the sense of the latter's adventure of desire and quest. It should be no surprise that many of the myths and models we have encountered in explaining this construct are present in one or another guise in Proust's text: the fervent and trembling 'amor de lohn' with which the adolescent troubadour of the Champs Elysées waits for Gilberte and for Odette; the guilty and fated passion of Phèdre, invoked by the narrator as prophetic for his own loves; the Wagner of Tristan, alchemist and transmuter of passion. Implicitly present are the group of nineteenth-century writers who stand behind the fictive Bergotte – the Stendhal of 'crystallisation', the Flaubert of 'bovarysme', the Nerval of nominalist loves and ideal feminine essences, the Baudelaire of perverse and platonic ones. Swann is both *libertin* and high-society *galant*; the hero practises a psychological version of exactions of the Marquis de Sade's underground chambers; Charlus, Morel and others take them more literally. The *Symposium* is the live and operative source text for the exegesis of homosexuality, and the controlling myths of both sexuality and spirituality; and its dualist-idealist framework provides, albeit with notably criticist, post-'death of God' hesitations, the philosophic parameters for the dialectics of time lost and regained.

The cultural intertext of Proust's omnivorously literate novel leaves no doubt, therefore, *which* concept of love, interiorised by the hero of the novel, is brought, recapitulatively, into question and explored as *cosa mentale*. The same conception will provide the controlling referent of Proust's own critique of idolatry and of his own quest for a human transcendence. In this perspective, it is possible to recognise the full merit of Proust's virtues, while seeing his 'limitations' as belonging in part to the concept of love which his critique envisages, and in part as motivating his dialectical movement beyond this culturally received model.

***

'The most exclusive love' is of course a definition of just this model of *amour-passion*, with its concentrational focus on the one-and-only Object and its obsessional, sacralising intensity. It is, comments Proust subversively, always a love of 'something else': something *other*, that is, than the unique object intended by its adoration. It is, therefore, not self-cognisant or well-advised in the absolute commitment it makes; it is errant, self-alienating, idolatrous and a source of profound suffering. Such is the – characteristically understated – conclusion of Swann in the first full-dress exploration of love that defines the paradigm which other love-affairs of the novel will explore with enriched harmonics, in ever more fully demonstrative range and confirmatory depth: 'To think that I've wasted years of my life, that I've wished to die, that I've had my greatest love for a woman I didn't like and who wasn't my type!' (I, 375).

The genesis of the *cosa mentale* that is Swann's love for Odette provides the classic Proustian account of the unperceived 'something else'. The novelist's illustrative choice of a mature man of the world, hardened *galant-libertin* of countless amorous conquests, is certainly deliberate: Proust requires, and means here, to avoid the suspicion of Romantic immaturity that his psychopoetics of amorous illusion might very well arouse if attached immediately to his imaginatively precocious and suggestible adolescent hero. Swann, given as Marcel's alter ego and prototype, deflects any such reproach. He is awakened to a grand passion against the odds, by a chemistry of creative imagination which promotes to this status a desultory liaison already begun mechanically, in response to the availability of the lady and out of sheer familiarity with the music of sentimental intimacy. This throws into relief the alchemy of aesthetic suggestion and psychic transfiguration which the novelist has to show us. The 'little phrase' by Vinteuil renews the lover's spiritual energy and idealism, opening up a space of belief and need for self-dedication which had long since disappeared from his existence. In this enlarged inner space, a second artist, Boticelli, helps Swann to inscribe the name of Odette. He does so by offering in his portrait 'Zephora, daughter of Jethro', the prestigious and cherished *idea* of a feminine beauty, which Swann – half-unconsciously, half-knowingly, with a kind of artistic instinct to re-arrange and enhance the raw material of life – fuses and confuses in imagination with the real-life object of his affections. 'Her type was becoming intelligible and clear. [...] The word "Florentine work" [...] allowed him to introduce Odette into a world of dreams to which she previously had no access, within which it became imbued with nobility' (I, 220–1). Thus Swann forges a vivid, poetically enhanced and morally justifying myth of the beloved; and she becomes the fatally desirable respondent of a re-energised dream of passion. This mind-generated magic, with its hidden poetry of association, this call to transcend the self in response to the supreme good of these perceived values of beauty, mystery and magic which henceforth halo the object, constitute, we may say, the kernel of Proust's account, at least in its negative aspect, of the 'something else'.

All loves (and indeed and all fixated desires in the novel) provide a vast symphony of variations on this theme of mytho-poetic projection and dream pursuit. The youthful narrator as we discover him in childhood at Combray, then in early adolescence on the Champs Elysées and in late adolescence at Balbec, is the perfect and original 'saline solution'. He possesses all the factors of romanticism inherent in youth and in what Proust calls 'creating faith': imaginative vitality, philosophic innocence and nominalist belief (names hold the key to things); the stirrings of (pre-)adolescent sensuality, stimulated by natural beauty or the ideal objects encountered through reading. He embodies, too, that essential multiplier of desire: the space of dream left by age and inexperience between himself and the objects of desire. His exalted imagination is spontaneously transcending, naturally infinitist:

> Yet if this desire that a woman should appear added to the charms I experienced in nature an element of exaltation, the charms of nature, conversely, opened up the over-specific element there might have been in the woman's charm [...] and, my imagination taking new strength from my sensuality, my sensuality spreading out into the whole realm of my imagination, my desire no longer had any limits. (I, 154)

The expansive power of sensually charged dream-desire pre-exists in us, says Proust; it needs only the hint of a pretext from the external world – the merest twig inserted by reality into our psychic space – for a compelling mytho-poetic crystallisation to occur. Gilberte, glimpsed for an instant, is haloed by the glory of the hawthorn hedge which frames her first appearance, but also by the prestige of Bergotte whom she knows, and by the fascination of forbidden sexual delights suggested by the father's association with the 'lady in pink'. Albertine, likewise, is a mere silhouette momentarily outlined against the sea; but in her mental persona and name as recreated by Marcel lies a whole world of speed, of grace and insolent assurance, of summer playfulness and sensual indulgence, together with a disconcertion at the shifting frontiers of land and sea which derives from Elstir's paintings; the entire nexus shot through with the tumultuous, sparkling, peacock-tail beauty of the waves. In each case, a psychic complex of poetic associations coheres into a mythic essence which is a reflection of the beholding mind projected onto the bearer of the name.

'We seek to rediscover in things, thereby rendered precious, the reflection our psyche has projected onto them' (I, 86). The narrator in fact makes this remark in commenting on the power to enchant and fascinate of the mental images of the natural landscapes which we form through the imaginary, dreamlike experience of reading. Yet the enchantment of essentialised mental images in the economy of desire is for Proust a truth of the desiring psyche as such, and is entirely transferable: it applies to the names of places we long to visit, to the social milieux whose embrace we covet, and above all to the partners of our amorous desire.

Mytho-poetic projection not only transfigures the object perceived; it reacts upon and modifies desire itself, thus transforming the whole subject–object relationship. Crucial to this process is the word 'mystery'. Many things in the world remain opaque or quite unknown to us, without arousing the intensely fascinated and compulsively specialised curiosity connoted by this Proustian term. Mystery for Proust always implies a desired contact of penetration, initiation and fusion with something of immense significance that is felt to be hidden or concealed in the mytho-poetic object. It measures a 'differential of transcendence': that is, the distance by which the object is felt to be more and other than the desiring subject, the extent to which it stands higher in the order of being, closer to the ontological mystery as such (hence the – Platonically – numinous language we shall come to see as inseparably associated with this sentiment in its ultimate developments). So the landscapes conjured up in Bergotte's books are felt by Marcel to be 'a true part of Nature itself'. Had he been able to visit them, he says, 'I should have thought I was making a priceless step forward in the conquest of truth' (I, 85).

So it is, in a more dramatic and fateful sense, with the mytho-poetically transfigured beloved. As the narrator of *Le Temps retrouvé*, speaking of his 'feeling of idolatry for the future Gilbertes, the future Duchesses of Guermantes, the future Albertines', will come to recognise: 'I should however have considered that preceding each of these was my own sense of the mystery in which they were bathed' (IV, 566). Not only is the lover's attraction recognised retrospectively as more than physical or sexual; the mytho-poetic 'added value' of the object highlighted by desire is seen as unambiguously initiatory:

> Imagination, awakened by the uncertainty of being able to attain its object, creates one goal which conceals from us another, and, substituting for sensual pleasure the idea of penetrating into a life, prevents us from recognising this pleasure, from experiencing its true taste, of restricting it to its specific importance. What is required is that, between oneself and the fish which, were we to see it for the first time served up on the dining-table, would not seem to be worth the infinite wiles and stratagems needed for us to catch it, should be interposed, in those fishing afternoons, while we still had no idea what we meant to do with it, a surface swirl occasioned by the emergence of polished flesh, a half-glimpsed form, amid the fluidity of a transparent and shifting blue sky. (II, 154)

To the rational intelligence, settled stolidly at the table of life, the beloved has the prosaic virtue of a nourishing meal or a gastronomic pleasure; but to the being of desire awakened in passion, she is the essential excitement of the quarry half-perceived in another element, a tantalising allusion to some ill-defined and unlimited secret, breaking surface from the depths or reflected out of the sky and pursued amid the flux and vagaries of existential adventure. The role of uncertainty, here and always, is to tease and re-activate the obscurely allusive sense of initiatory transcendence-in-mystery; Proust tells us here why desire intensifies in proportion as it is frustrated.

The lover's excitement of initiation fails in fact to deliver any insight into the order of the world; the sense of numinous allusion is, in this sense, a broken sign – and the beloved an *eidolon*, a phantom beautified and essentialised by the alchemy of suspenseful imagination. On the other hand, this illusion says a great deal, more than any other experience, about the order of the desiring psyche. It declares the need and aptitude for transcendence as the very being of human desire. It tells us, reflexively, about the 'something else' of passion: the essential and indubitable *promise* pursued –'the most mysterious element offered us by the beauty we desire and which we console ourselves for not possessing when we ask for pleasure' (II, 155). To designate, comprehend, and renounce the 'illusion' exemplified in all the multiple forms it assumes throughout 'the inhuman world of pleasure' (I, 162) will thus be to denude in its human authenticity the indubitable 'allusion' to be deciphered. From the outset, the Proustian lover is suspended in anguish upon the 'differential of transcendence', seeking to penetrate and possess the mystery hidden in the beloved precisely in proportion as it escapes him:

> Of all the modes of production of love, of all the agents for disseminating the sacred ill, there is indeed one more effective than all others, that great breath of agitation which sometimes passes over us. At that point the die is cast in favour of the being whose company we had merely enjoyed up until then; that person it is we shall love. It is not even necessary for us to have liked them more or even as much as others. What is required is that our taste for them should become exclusive. And this condition is realised when

[…], seeking the pleasures given us by their charm, we find abruptly substituted within us an anxious need to possess focused on this very person […], the insensate and painful need to possess them. (I, 227)

The 'god' inherent in Eros – the exalted, compulsive, tyrannical, absolutist, the frustrated and perverse mystic willing to adore to the point of martyrdom and murder – rises up at this point from the underworld of the psyche, taking over the hedonist in Swann, commandeering the aesthete and artist of feeling, radicalising the romantic who dreamed of initiation. The rest of Swann's love for Odette, and the entire episode of Marcel's sequestration of Albertine in Paris, like the novel's series of homosexual love-affairs, unfold and explore this determining moment. Proust's vision of love – 'the sacred ill'– is likewise fixed in the same moment; save only that the philtre of *amour-passion* itself ultimately obeys one higher law conditioning all human phenomena, that of the successive and multiple self immersed in time; so that it, too, will yield at length, painfully, to forgetfulness, as the 'self of love' dies.

***

Proust's psychopoetics of love thus revolves around two essential accidents – the fabrication and transfiguring projection onto the beloved of a mind-generated myth, and the transforming fixation within the lover of 'le mal sacré'. Both alert us to the Proustian definition of passion-love as a radically subjective phenomenon and as delusional and tragic error; and both herald the general sense of his study of *amour-passion* – that of a thoroughgoing critique, born of post-Romantic disenchantment.

On the radical subjectivity of love, the narrator of *La Recherche* comments obsessionally, etching for us the most fundamental sense realised by each successive love-affair enacted or recounted. The substance is contained in this decisive paragraph, which reviews (in terms paralleling Swann's love for Odette) the birth of Marcel's long fixation upon Albertine:

> Worthlessness of love, also, when, pre-existing and unfixed, it settles on the image of a woman simply because that woman will be almost impossible to get to ... An entire process of anguish develops and suffices to fix our love upon her, who is an object almost unknown to us. Love then becomes immense, and we do not consider how little place the real woman has in it ... What did I know of Albertine? One or two profiles against the sea. That Albertine was barely more than a silhouette, and everything superimposed on it of my own confection, since in love what comes from ourselves is so much greater than what derives from the person loved. (II, 213)

Through thousands of pages, this same analysis of idealism and delusional specularity is varied, deepened, systematised. The message is constant, only the tone changes: now persuasively diadactic, now clinical, now elegaic; now vehement in radical philosophical pessimism and denegation ('Man is the being who cannot emerge from himself, who knows the other only in himself and who, declaring the contrary, lies' [IV, 34]). True, Proust does not quite disavow love in principle, as reality or as value.[5] Yet in his role as moralist, he is overwhelmingly dedicated to deconstructing psychogenetically the most tenacious and widespread of Western versions of it, the romantic delusion that the beloved is the unique and predestined âme sœur, to encounter whom constitutes in itself a decipherment of the text of the universe and an initiation prefiguring celestial bliss. Such is the naïve metaphysic of the wishful heart, latter-day inheritor of the dualist-idealist culture of Eros:

> But at the time when I knew Gilberte, I believed that Love existed really outside ourselves; that, allowing us at most to set aside obstacles, it offered its joys within an order in which one was free to change nothing; it seemed to me that if I had, on my own initiative, replaced the sweetness of avowal by the pretence of indifference, I would not simply have lost the joys I most dreamed of, but that I would have fabricated arbitrarily an artificial and worthless love, unconnected to the true love, the mysterious and pre-existent paths of which I would have given up following. (I, 393)

Between the narrator and his adolescent self, as between Proust and the Romantics, intervenes the devastating awareness of psychopoetic contingency. If 'love' is the creation and anguished pursuit of a mind-generated phantom, it can only be a formula for tragic soul-error and suffering. The lover is condemned, then, to explore indefinitely, until time and the psychic death of forgetting finally release him, the multi-levelled discrepancy between inner and outer worlds, image and Other, desire and fulfilment. There are for Swann two Odettes, for Marcel two Gilbertes, two Orianes, two Albertines: one growing in him, formed by his thoughts, the other outside, defiant or compliant, but always finally strange, remote, unfathomable. Reciprocity, happiness in love, can only be a fragile and temporary paradox: 'In non-reciprocal love – let's just say in love as such – the only taste of happiness lies in this simulacrum of it, offered to me in one of those unique moments when the kindness of a woman, or her caprice, apply to our desires, in perfect coincidence, the same words, the same actions, as if we were truly loved' (III, 229). Swann, too, knows fleeting moments of a quietening satisfaction 'so sweet that it could pass for happiness' (I, 232). Yet the essential and permanent experience of the Proustian lover is that of a vertiginous and ever renewed insecurity: of reaching out to grasp and possess a 'being of flight' (III, 600) who forever eludes his embrace; of the extenuating effort to conquer and reduce the alterity of the Other – an effort doomed in its very principle, since to succeed would be to kill the desire which alone feeds the flame of passion, while to fail is to suffer torment without limit: 'that immense anguish of not possessing her everywhere and always' (I, 340).

'Passion', etymologically understood, connotes passivity, impotent suffering; and this is indeed the experience of Proust's lovers, for all the treasures of strategic intelligence and energy expended on neutralising the tormenting mystery of the elusive fish. 'Passion', in Western culture, also has a sacred or religious sense, and

Proust's critics, often enough, have been tempted to think that 'the cross becomes the accurate symbol of it',[6] or to describe the tormenting ascesis suffered by libidinal pleasure in becoming 'love' as a 'Via Dolorosa'.[7] This view itself, however, betrays a post-Romantic *confusion* of some moment. The Proustian lover actually provides a spectral parody of the Christian cross (at least if we prefer the plain sense of the gospels to the introverted and doom-laden poetic projections of Vigny). In the logic of Agape, suffering implies self-possessed, resolute and dedicated *action*, rather than feverish and despairing activism; its cross is a *work* which obeys no other compulsion than the non-needy, gift-like imperative of Agape itself, which in humility consents to suffer for the beloved *because it loves*. What Proust shows, by contrast, is the self-sacralising absolutism of Romantic Eros: not that God is love, but that 'Love' is, devastatingly and infernally, god.

***

It is importantly true, as we see here, that Proust is concerned less with 'love' than with its inseparable shadow-reality of romantico-erotic 'passion'. His *Recherche* deals predominantly with the negativities, deficiencies and deviations by reason of which *amour-passion* is no longer, or not yet, love, or with the infernal virtualities which threaten to destroy it as love.

The experience of Proust's lovers is exactly the contrary of what love aspires and seeks to be (as reference to the *Song of Songs* will remind us): there is no mutual recognition in delight and praise by answering subjects, but instead only the lover's unilateral attempt to capture, sequester and possess the evasive object; this brings suffering in place of joy; suspicion and jealousy submerge tenderness; 'douceurs' change into 'douleurs'; a sense of vertiginous insecurity proliferates at the expense of peace; consent yields to a relationship of power and dependency; there is aggravated isolation and exclusion instead of reciprocity and communion-in-presence; the end-product is not enhancement of life, but a degrading and tragic alienation, from the lover's own deeper self, from nature and from the order of things. Not only does Proust give us a full and exact symmetry of inversion, negative for positive, but the negative is developed and accentuated progressively through *Sodome et Gomorrhe*, *La Prisonnière*, *La Fugitive* and *Le Temps retrouvé*. That it does so signals Proust's original and heroic enterprise: to explore *all* the consequences of 'le mal sacré' and chart the psychic underworld of *all* its desire.

The origins of erotic negativity outstrip knowledge; they are, in Proust as in Valéry, 'too remotely lost in the heavens'.[8] Malraux, considering with Schopenhaurian pessimism that 'the consciousness of life is and can only be anguish',[9] captures the Proustian sense of the incomprehensibly primordial nature of the negativities of love when he writes: 'The knowledge of someone is the negative feeling; what is positive, the reality, is the anguish of being always foreign to that which [sic] one loves.'[10] True, Proust gives us a more proximate origin, within range of affective memory, and even of voluntary recall, in the *drame du coucher*, which is presented – and recalled in the novel – as the prototype of all the subsequent dramas of passion-love. In this key episode, primordial existential anguish is expressed as the delicate child's need for the love of its mother. This is sharpened by the refusal of the ritual goodnight kiss, and characteristically specified as 'the anguish of sensing that the person we love is in some place of pleasure where we are not, where we cannot join her' (I, 30). Yet we notice what anguish decisively misses and seeks: 'the communion of peace from which my lips draw her real presence and the power of going to sleep' (I, 13). The religious language indicates the extent and nature of the need; and for the first and last time in the itinerary of *La Recherche*, gift-love ('her loving face proffered like a eucharistic host' [ibid.]) is experienced as an available and adequate fulfilment. Mother-love is, in this sense, a 'figure' of paradise lost; resembling in this respect the matricial childhood world of Combray itself, symbolically dominated by the Church. (The hidden Oedipal overtones of this episode provide an alternative, shadow paradigm of interpretation.) Extending the maternal gift-love, Combray offers, as long as childhood innocence lasts, rootedness, harmony, integration, order, reassuring acceptance – circumstantially answering a sense of Being still unshadowed, for the most part, by the vertiginous sense of contingency and time.

This other face of experience, that of ontic uprootedness, is supplied by the nocturnal world of the novel's prelude, where the sleeping-waking consciousness of the narrator experiences in dizzying anguish the kaleidoscope of moments contingently composing the sense of 'self-in-time'. Valéry will offer us in *La Jeune Parque* a strikingly parallel account of selfhood: a poetic phenomenology of identity-perception shot through with ontic negativity. To awaken-in-desire from the 'time of innocence' is to be cut off from all rootedness in Being. Both writers are, in effect, offering us auto-centred and momentously 'orphic' re-writings of Genesis. In both, the twentieth century is declared in the passage from womblike implacentation in cosmic process to a tormented and isolating extrusion.

Nor is there anything in Proust to disavow Valéry's bold and surprising assertion: 'We have to recognise and confess that the deepest basis of all our ideas has to do with some metaphysic [...] every need of the mind is metaphysical.'[11] This perspective best apprehends, perhaps, the more specific exclusion which haunts Proustian love. The 'mystery' which mytho-poetic imagination projects in love is the perpetually regenerated shadow of its own ontological sense of Being lost. It is always, in this crucial sense, *allusive*: it stirs – very platonically, in haunting 'reminiscence' – the metaphysical needs of the deep psyche. It is thus supercharged with the need to recreate the sacrality and the transcendence which it 'remembers'; it is exigent in proportion to its absolute, that is *ontological* need; and it is desperate, regressive and violent to the extent that it is turned away in failure, by the perpetual 'flight' of the beloved, from the lost paradise of its desiring. Proust does not state these implicit things in relation to the false path of *amour-passion* (as he certainly does in relation to the 'true way' of art); but he displays them again and again in the resonant immensity of the psychic shadow cast by the words: 'No, tonight I won't be free' (III, 193).

Is this not also the deeper logic by virtue of which Proustian passion is most deeply felt when thwarted, threatened, forbidden? Its negativity consists precisely in thriving on all forms of exclusion: *unavailability* (as in the chance absence that transforms Odette into the mythical Eurydice of a grand passion); *social inaccessibility* or remoteness (from which Oriane de Guermantes benefits, as does Odette once Swann is 'excommunicated' from the Verdurin salon); *affective non-reciprocity* (the fundamental obstacle in all loves, of which the signs are the pretexts and lies which seek to justify the beloved's 'absence'); *intellectual opacity* (which is the translation given by the lover to the 'mystery' of the beloved – ever misguidedly, since objective 'knowledge about' somebody is in fact a parody of the interpersonal communion truly sought); and *sexual deviance* (Odette, Albertine and Morel are all essentially *êtres de fuite* in the very basic sense that a dis-valence of sexual orientation turns them away from the lover's embrace, not towards it). If we have correctly followed Proust's deeper discernment of Eros, the logic of this very striking pattern lies in the 'differential of transcendence': the more-and-otherness of the beloved, her power to excite and engage the (metaphysical) need for Being is what profoundly determines her desirability, so that desire grows as this differential increases. Proust shows us the full psychic complexity – and the basic simplicity – of the most fundamental law of *amour-passion*: the less I have, the more I need, want and desire.

It follows also that the more the amorous subject seeks, the more the bearer of the mystery sought becomes, in her tantalising elusiveness, a defiance of desire and a threat. The 'alterity' of the Other at this point changes its sign; it reverts to a negative value: no longer a 'good' to be loved, but an immense ill to be feared and resisted in struggle. From this inversion derives the Proustian lover's ambivalence of feeling, his rivalry with and tyranny over her, together with two-thirds of his jealousy concerning her (and *a fortiori*, in the case of Charlus, concerning *him*).

The following passage from *La Prisonnière* takes us to the heart of the matter. It evokes the relative remediation of suffering procured by Marcel's sequestration in Paris of Albertine, the immediate context being his crucial discovery that Albertine had been brought up by the lesbian friend of Mlle Vinteuil:

> If earlier I had been excited in perceiving mystery in the eyes of Albertine, now I was happy only in those moments when, from those eyes, even from those cheeks, reflecting as the eyes, sometimes so sweet but quickly turning gruff, I managed to expel all mystery. The image I sought, in which I could rest, and up against which I should have wished to die, was no longer the Albertine with an unknown life, it was an Albertine as well-known to me as might be possible (which is why this love could not last except in unhappiness, since by definition it would not contain the need for mystery), it was an Albertine not reflecting a distant world, desiring nothing else – there were moments when this indeed seemed true – than to be with me, just like me, an Albertine who was the image of what was specifically mine, and not of the unknown. (III, 583)

The 'differential of transcendence' is reversible: once exalting (since perceived as the sign of a world of exotic delight and adventure), it here becomes charged with anguish and converted into an infernal sign (by the revelation which has set the differential at infinity). Insecurity must be reduced to the greatest possible extent by the physical proximity of sequestration and skin contact (procuring the illusion that the beloved is of the same substance as the lover's desire for her, and that she is consequently transparent and assimilable). Yet the underlying desperation of the sequestering lover, his hidden charge of violence, his latent sacrality – his essential *idolatry* – are suggested in his clutching to himself a tangible metonymy of Albertine, those cheeks 'up against which I should have wished to die'. At the same time, the narrator is aware that, could such an embrace succeed durably, the transcendent butterfly would lose the very charge of transcendence, both celestial and demonic, which makes her desirable. Only unhappy passion still has a 'distant world' to cherish, and is still passion.

The tyranny of sequestration, with the labyrinthine web it spreads of dissimulation, lies, ruses and inquisitorial cross-questioning, is a direct measure of the infernal and infinitist 'something else' into which desire deviates. Moreover, as René Girard points out, Proustian desire, like all human desire, is 'triangular' in the sense that it links together with the desiring subject and the desired object a real or imaginary third party, who is both mediator (he suggests and re-suggests to us, by a sort of mimicry, how and what to desire) and rival (in that he bids to possess the object for himself). On this basis, Proust's lovers are deeply pitiable. The mediator/rival is both real and declared (Forcheville, Andrée), but also, more importantly, imaginary and quite indeterminate, since virtually any male or any female encountered by the beloved is a potential rival, past, present or future. Proust's lovers, accordingly, often appear as paranoiacs caught in a generalised conspiracy of libidinal threat.

Worse still: mediator and rival actually coincide in the person of the beloved herself (or himself); for, as we have seen, the Proustian lover desires the body of the beloved as a talisman to the same mysterious inner space which the latter also covets and so denies to him – 'for no human being wishes to deliver their soul' (III, 656). There is rivalry for the 'same' treasure, accurately represented or not; a rivalry which is intensified by an effect of mimetism, since as the lover attempts to capture it, so the beloved withdraws to preserve it (i.e., to re-assert possession of it). The status of the beloved as mimetic rival of the lover is confirmed in the remarkable phenomenon of Marcel's elaborate comedy of feigned indifference towards his long-term partner in cohabitation. He will never confess the extent of his feeling for Albertine, or say he loves her, fearing (rightly) to lose his desirability for her, and hoping (vainly) to whip up her desire for him mimetically (i.e., to act as mediator, manipulating in his own favour the 'differential of transcendence'). 'Love' here signifies mutual torture. 'All communion has disappeared from a feeling which is defined by that very communion. [...]. The word survives the thing it points to, but it means the opposite. Deviated transcendence is expressed by a deviancy of language.'[12]

Projecting the energies of psychosexual eros absolutely upon a human Other, the lover indeed courts and cultivates hidden virtualities of both masochism and sadism. These are by no means confined to the homosexual couples of the novel; they characterise 'le mal sacré' as such. Marcel himself, for instance, appears as an artist in both moral torture and self-flagellation when, manipulating the logic of mimetic rivalry, he writes to his fugitive mistress Albertine that he has decided to replace her with her own suspected lesbian lover Andrée (IV, 51–2). Yet it is true that such virtualities are most fully illustrated between homosexual lovers. The profanation of her dead father's portrait by Mlle Vinteuil, like Morel's attempt to whip up the passion of Charlus by promising to seduce and abandon young girls, and the actual flagellation Charlus pays to receive in a male brothel, all involve creating, in an overtly theatrical or ritual manner, a perversely exalting 'differential of transcendence'. What distinguishes these role-play scenarios is that the effect of transcendence is derived, transgressively, from an 'infernal' mytho-poetry of power and submission, divinity and abasement; the principle of mimetic rivalry here *inverts* the 'celestial' mytho-poetry from which other loves start. The effect of this specificity is to explore the deepest and darkest negativities of *amour-passion*, while demonstrating, through a series of homologies-in-desire, the essential solidarity of all manifestations of human eros. Marcel himself is *like* Charlus in his restless and devious efforts to enslave the beloved; yet only in Charlus does the alienating sickness of a deviant transcendence culminate over time in total degradation and madness.

The narrator sees that, 'beneath the slight differentiation occasioned by sexual similitude [i.e. homosexuality]', the case of Charlus conforms to 'the general laws of love' (IV, 399). It illustrates the relationship of power and dependency, capture and flight, rivalry and struggle, impotence and suffering, weakness and moral decline, which characterises all forms of erotico-romantic passion. Functionally, the novel's homosexual affairs thus carry to its conclusion Proust's demonstration of love as tragic illusion on the road to a true realisation of desire. They act as one of the 'magnifying glasses' by which the narrator aspires to help future readers of his narrative to 'read within themselves' (IV, 610), recognising the idolatrous errancy of *amour-passion* as such and detecting, with a compassion born of liberal understanding, the root of this aberrant form: namely, the flawed nature of human psychosexuality as such. We may in turn agree with those critics who have stressed that homosexuality is not an appendage to Proust's vision of love, but a fundamental and crucial revealer of it.[13]

In the theoretical essay of *Sodome and Gomorrhe*, Proust speaks for and from a position, not of homosexuality, but of sexual bi-valence or androgyny. He invokes both the diverse and ambiguous sexualities of pre-human nature and a re-unitive human eros, complete with sexual indifferentism, as in Plato's myth. Mytho-poetic and Darwinian perspectives combine in his postulation of an initial hermaphroditism in all of nature, such that anatomical (and, implicitly, psychological) vestiges of each sexual kind or gender remain in the other (III, 31): a complexity well-recognised by psychologists and sexologists today. The androgynous viewpoint is certainly consonant with the spectrum of sexual types and loves displayed in the novel. The centre of the spectrum is occupied by an ambiguous 'intersexuality', which is destabilised by the siren call of Gomorrah and parodied by that of Sodom; but the fictional spectrum also shows eddying currents of cross-fascination and permutation. The novel's closing stages produce, notoriously, cascading revelations of concealed homosexual tendencies. As the 'infernal' shadow is explored, so it appears increasingly that the centre cannot hold and that the two sexes will indeed die 'each apart and alone', as predicted in Vigny's apocalyptic vision (III, 17).

The androgynous viewpoint and vision, with its radical insecurity about sexual identity and orientation (cf. III, 190–8 etc.), its inability to valorise and build on the complementarity of sexual difference, or, consequently, to envisage the creative maturation of love in time, constitutes the philosophic substratum of Proustian *amour-passion*. Reciprocally, as Rivers has argued, sexual ambiguity finds a platonic resolution, uniting the psychic masculine and feminine at a higher level, not in inter-personal love, but in artistic creativity itself.[14]

Almost as significant as Proust's explicit philosophic belonging to the homeland of dualist-idealist Eros is the bleak and oblique vision of the other great Western source. From Genesis, the novelist retains only culturally mediated fragments charged with negative, superego connotations. The keynote retained is the divine malediction which the biblical text seems to pronounce on transgressive human desire. This is writ large in the volume's title alluding to the cities of the plain, and again in the Romantic motif of the fiery angel of interdiction who guards against any return to Eden, specifically, as a warning against any return of the homosexual diaspora. The sense of condemnatory (self-)judgement, even of malediction, is powerful. Proust the infinitely subtle deconstructor of mytho-poetry thus reads Genesis literally and culture-conventionally, as a *moral fable*, taking from it lessons of mistrust, misogyny and accursedness highlighted by his own unconscious (cf. I, 4–5; III, 32–4; III, 587). This paradox is no doubt rooted in its place and time. It is also symptomatic of Western cultural memory at large. It is not otherwise easy to explain how this incomparable analyst of the shadow lying across human desire might fail to recognise in Genesis the prefigure of his own finest insights, or to decipher beyond the ghostly shadow retained by collective memory within our culture any signs to a foundational hopefulness about love.

The haunted and tragic idealism of the Proustian account of love is in the end (like Proust's reading of Genesis) profoundly rooted in the same cultural construct whose idolatry he so brilliantly deconstructs. His pessimism about the shadow love is, genetically speaking, a form of post-Romantic disenchantment. *La Recherche* works out this suspicion of 'creating faith' in a cycle of reflectively analysed experience which parallels Comte's theory of the three intellectual ages of humanity: the lively childhood faith of mytho-poetic belief; rationalist maturity, bringing a long apprenticeship in the poetics of scepticism; and an old-age of positivist disenchantment. As the sacred fades, so the world is filled with a false or corrupt sacrality which, deciphered, declares the idolatry into which we are led by the incoercible need for transcendence experienced within human desire itself. *Amour-passion* provides the richest and most searching of Proust's enacted illustrations. 'Under the guise of woman, we address ourselves to the forces by which she is accessorily accompanied, as to obscure divinities' (III, 511).

***

Proustian disenchantment leaves intact – and the writing of Proustian love demands – one 'higher' love. From dispersion, alienation and nothingness a single, authentic, 're-verticalised' form of transcendence – this, too, retrieved from Romantic-Symbolist tradition – is asserted. As expounded in the long coda of *Le Temps retrouvé*, Proust's salvational mystique of art might appear to constitute a slightly disjointed proposal on aesthetics, linked to an exalted ethic of literary vocation of a type since repudiated by the more radical suspicion of contemporary postmodernism. Perhaps, however, we should read it rather as a tribute to the perennial persuasiveness of Platonic Eros and of its dialectic of ascent – albeit now fraught with formidable twentieth-century ambiguities of affirmation.

As we would expect, the counterpoint between the two Aphrodites of Proust's novel is focused most crucially by the music of Vinteuil. As introduced in *Un Amour de Swann,* the 'little phrase' of the Sonata occasions in the alienated and exiled lover a self-recognition derived less from its complicit association with the story of a passion than from the music's power to re-express essentially, and so to communicate transparently, the deepest joy and suffering of love. Transcending these lived experiences and containing them, it also relativises, exorcises and heals. It speaks, as it were, from a higher plane and another time, which are experienced by Swann as the true homeland of the psychic subject, the essential being of desire. In return, he becomes capable, in transcending his own passion-bound ego, of recognising disinterestedly for the first time something of the heavenly Aphrodite who addresses him (she is described successively as 'captive genie', 'supernatural being', 'tutelary and confidential goddess of their love'). Her invisible and gracious presence in sound unfolds to the newly contemplative lover her status as a 'mysterious entity' capable of unveiling one of the 'true ideas, of another world, of another order' (I, 34–45). Thanks to the highest form of aesthetic experience, Swann is thus seen to move through a kind of inward regathering which leads him in ascendant steps towards a form of ontological intuition. His furthest step in spiritual awakening and decipherment is to speak, platonically, of such musical phrases as the 'divine captives who will follow our fate': death, which as a biological event is certain, yet holds, with the caution of these tutelary hostages, something less bitter, less inglorious, and perhaps (as ultimate nothingness) less probable. As ever in Proust, mystical and religious language intervenes to signal an affinity which finds its principle in an immediately experienced perception of transcendence.

The Septet unfolds a different world from the Sonata: 'yet it was a same prayer, called forth by different risings of inner suns' (III, 759). This profound and mysterious kinship signals to the artist's inward ear the depth of essence, an inner duration or 'spiritual homeland', which each great artist 'remembers' singularly, effecting communication of some 'unsayable' reality antecedent to all common speech and discourse. True art, that is, finding here its purely essential and spiritual medium, gives us to apprehend that mystery which was vainly pursued in the ever-opaque object of passion. The *Septuor* declares 'the promise that there existed something else, realisable through art no doubt, than the nothingness I had found in pleasure and in love itself' (III, 767).

Its prayer, we may say, is for all the metaphysical 'good' that Eros lacks. And it is in token of Vinteuil's – and Proust's – ultimate faith in (at least) the worth of that 'good', and of the significance of the prayer for it, that the *Septuor* develops the motif of metaphysical joy:

> Finally, the motif of joy remained triumphant; it was no longer an almost anxious appeal thrown out from behind an empty sky, it was an unspeakable joy which seemed to proceed from paradise [...]. I knew that this new inflexion of joy, this summons to a supra-terrestrial joy, was something I would never forget. Yet would it ever be realisable for me? (III, 764–5)

Here is the 'lively' intuition on which Proust's higher love rests, and of which the narrator's 'literary vocation', the future work of the novel, and the existence itself of *La Recherche*, are the material effects. The dialectic of the 'time regained' argues that the idolatries of Eros are but the shadows of a transcendence lost; but that, by the gracious mediation of art, they are salvationally regained; and with it, the 'communion' – or at least the 'communication' – lost to love (IV, 474).

This assertion is, of course, intensely problematic. Is Proust, in the end, a fully-fledged Platonist, affirming an ontological depth of psychic experience and a subsistent, foundational order of reality? Are we, on the contrary, to decipher the sense of the transcendent experienced in music in purely psychologist terms, jettisoning as hyperbolic 'metaphor' the persistently allusive appeal to an intuited world of essence? Is artistic creativity no longer being proclaimed as 'glorious lie'; and is 'Nothingness' not quite, after all, 'the truth'? What is the status of Proust's 'essences' – and the thickness of Proustian metaphoricity? The novelist himself struggles to theorise the knot of ambiguities emanating from this vital imaginative centre of his work;[15] and his critics have variously followed suit. The answers are not, in either case, entirely philosophically or hermeneutically cogent.[16]

Perhaps we ask too much in insisting that they should be. It was never easy to decipher, in its ever-ambiguous emergence, the most fundamentally constitutive principle of human subject identity; and the crisis of the dualist-idealist framework of thought in which such answers were, in previous ages, sought and framed, introduces a formidable new dimension of difficulty. Henceforth, what is felt to be indubitably transcendent in Eros must construct its own hermeneutic framework; it must say how and why it ventures to cross the chasm between subject and object, mind and world. Our residual idealism is left, vulnerably, to resolve the problem of its own inveterate dualism and to placate the super-ego god of its own self-suspicion.

What is not doubtful is that, in this very difficulty, Proust prefigures the twentieth century's rendezvous with Eros, with its mysterious density, emanating from the very roots of human psychosexuality; with its spiritual and philosophic ambiguity; with its incoercible spring of transcendence. Out of the encounter has come a work which is at once a modern critical theory of human desire, a searching account of the shadow over human loves, and one of the greatest of novels.

Notes

1   M. Proust, *A la Recherche du Temps perdu*, 4 vols, ed. J.-Y. Tadié, Bibliothèque de la Pléiade (Paris: Gallimard, 1987–89). References in the text are to this edition, given as volume and page number.
2   See P. Newman, *Dictionnaire des idées* (Paris & The Hague: Mouton, 1968).
3   The best extended account of the unified vision running through the erotics, aesthetics and ethics of Proust is G. Florival, *Le Désir chez Proust* (Louvain & Paris: Nauvelaerts, 1971).
4   J. Rousset, *Forme et signification* (Paris: Corti, 1962), pp. 166–7.
5   See B. Pluchart-Simon, *Proust: L'Amour comme verité humaine et romanesque* (Paris: Larousse Université, 1975), pp. 146–54.
6   Ibid., p. 28.
7   M. Bowie, *Proust Among the Stars* (London: HarperCollins, 1998), p. 259.
8   P. Valéry, 'La Pythie', *Charmes* (1922).
9   A. Malraux, *La Condition humaine*, Livre de poche (Paris: Gallimard, 1971), p. 273.
10 Ibid., p. 183.
11 P. Valéry, *Cahiers* (C2, 489; *C*, XI, 808); see Chapter 7, note 2, *infra*.
12 R. Girard, *Mensonge romantique et vérité romanesque* (Paris: Grasset, 1961), p. 113.
13 See R. Fernandez: 'Inverted love accentuates naturally the imaginative or imaginary character of the amorous subject, while ... maximising the disconcerting or divisive effects of passion. If love is a sickness, it is in the sicknesses of the amorous form (inversion or sadism) that it will assert its nature most visibly' (*A la Gloire de Proust* [Paris: *Nouvelle Revue critique*, 1943], pp. 75–6). G. Deleuze sees 'inverted' passion as 'the very truth of love': *Proust et les signes* (Paris: PUF, 1970), p. 72.
14 J. E. Rivers, *Proust and the Art of Love: The Aesthetics of Sexuality in the Life and Times of Marcel Proust* (New York: Columbia University Press, 1980).
15 See for instance 'Given that the world of differences does not exist on the surface of the earth among all those countries which our perception renders uniform, all the less does it exist in 'the world'. Does it indeed exist anywhere? The Septet by Vinteuil had seemed to tell me so. But where?' (III, 781); or 'But it is not possible that a sculpture, a piece of music, which imparts an emotion that we feel to be higher, purer, truer, does not correspond to a certain spiritual reality, or life would be without any meaning' (III, 876).
16 G. Deleuze sees an unveiling of Being 'which cannot be reduced to a psychological state, nor to a psychological subjectivity, nor even to a form of higher subjectivity'. The essence, for this writer, implicates, envelops and enrols itself in the subject, rather than the reverse (*Proust et les signes*, pp. 54–5). For the opposite view, see S. Doubrovsky: 'Art does not liberate sublimate or heal anything; it is entirely a *neurotic passion*': 'La place de la madeleine. Écriture et fantasme chez Proust', *Mercure de France* (1974), p. 148.

Chapter 7

Paul Valéry: Eros Unveiled and the Re-imagining of Love

Il faut parvenir à visiter son être, jusqu'à toucher le dieu avec le dieu.
Comprendre l'amour.

'Myths are the soul of our actions and of our loves. We can act only in moving towards a phantom. We can love only something we create.'[1] Thus Paul Valéry, offering what looks like a recapitulative definition of Proustian *amour-passion*, with its diagnosis of 'idealisation', its disenchanted judgement of soul-error, its *temps perdu*.

Yet if Valéry retraces this Proustian figure of sense, he also develops it. He indeed unveils the sexual basis of Eros and minutely deconstructs its mind-spun idolatries; but he also comes to discern, as Proust barely does, its human potential; and, discerning it, he enters a proposal for the re-working of the inherited construct. This leads him, as we shall see, to re-invest existentially in the poem of amorous relationality that intuition of inner time redeemed which Proust refers solely to art.

His credentials for this role differ from the novelist's. Combining poetry and analysis, Valéry encompasses the paradox of a brutally objectivising, exceptionally 'masculine', intellect associated with an extraordinary depth of mystico-lyrical, 'feminine' sensibility. 'Strange it is that this icy fury of extermination should in me be linked to an infinitely tender tenderness' (C2, 111; *C* XII, 352).[2] We shall hear both these voices; and Valéry's generalised psychopoetics, like his poetry, is a quest for the highest degree of integration of these psychic forces within himself. Yet inner complexity does not, in his case, signify ambiguity or equivocation in respect of sexual identity. While Valéry may, as a poet, transpose that identity into a string of feminine personae, his sense of male-female complementarity is strongly established and underlies everything he writes on love and desire. Conspicuously, he retains from Plato's myth of the Androgyne nothing whatever about hermaphroditism, but only about the re-unitive tendency between male and female: 'Male and female form a complete system like Wegener's continents![3] Plato had the right idea [...] present attraction 'explained' by an original unity' (C2, 495; *C* XIII, 315).

The fragmented cosmos of Valéry's writings, together with the laboratory status of his most central thought, mean that what the poet-analyst himself has to say on love and desire is still an almost entirely unknown continent. It will help to achieve strategic understanding if we start here by offering what Proust's novel gives us ready-made: a biography of the poet-analyst's engagement with Eros.

***

'I sent myself crazy, made myself desperately unhappy for years – imagining that woman to whom I never even spoke' (C2, 534; *C* XXIII, 589), writes Valéry, reviewing (in echo to Proust's Swann) the 'great mental sickness of love' of his twenty-first year. His passionate fixation upon the barely glimpsed silhouette of the *dame catalane*, Mme de R., is experienced by Valéry as a shameful obsession; the more horrifying since it resonates subterraneously with the sense of ontological void experienced three years previously at the 'Enterrement de Dieu'.[4]

Masked in his earliest poems by a platonising spirituality, libidinal energies here erupt disturbingly, producing a reaction proportional to their invasive violence. An inner abyss opens up, displaying within the self a writhing inner monster of erotic sensibility, at once carnal and 'infinitist'. Not the least afflicting pain of this 'absurd' revelation is the phantomatic and fallacious character of the imaginary idol of which one is oneself the creator. The 'idol' (Greek: *eidolon*) is a Valéryan keyword. It signifies the shadowy complement fabricated by occult mental process, alienating the desiring subject from himself. The hallucinatory silhouette of the *dame catalane* points to the gaping discrepancy between what is in the mind ('*intra*') and what is outside it ('*extra*'), and to the human propensity for secreting naturally and perpetually all forms of false transcendence. Valéry's first notion of desire is fixed at this point; and it catalyses reactively the entire chain of consequences which form the foundation of his intellectual life: the conversion to a Cartesian and positivistic rigour; the Copernican revolution of critical consciousness; the 'guillotining' of literature and all youthful idols in favour of a new cult of pure Intellect; the disciplined mental time of the *Cahiers* and a twenty-year analytical 'Silence'.

What begins under the new régime of thought is a systematic attempt to effect a phenomenological and functional reduction of all 'transcending' values ('les transcendantes') naively formed and cultivated by the nineteenth century, but dynamically latent also in himself and in the human psyche as such. Master of the laboratory of pure thought, Valéry sees himself as 'the metaphysical Michelson'[5] repeating in the domain of mind-made things the Michelson-Morley experiment disproving the existence of 'ether' in the physical world (that is, the idea of a universal fluid medium, posited by nineteenth-century physics in accounting for electro-magnetic effects at a distance). Monsieur Teste sets himself the task of evacuating from the pysche every last trace of idealist transcendentalism and spiritualist 'depth'.

Brutally, almost vengefully, *amour-passion* is then amputated from its Platonic other world; it is despiritualised, demystified. What remains is an animal instinct with culturally determined psychic complications: a physiological mechanism (taken as 'real') enveloped in a mind-generated mystique (held to be 'imaginary' and culture-conventional). The latter part – the cult of the one-and-only Object, the predestined union of souls, the intimations of immortality – are swept aside as a 'one vast joke for popular consumption' (C2, 396; *C* II, 499), 'a ridiculous literary fabrication' (*C* II, 559). 'Saying to somebody *I love you* is just reciting a lesson. Nobody would ever have genuinely thought of that. The notion of entering into complicity with the policies of the Universe … by imitation' (C2, 396; *C* VII, 143).

Envisaging love reduced to its most 'real' expression, that is, the sex act itself, Valéry writes:

> What has civilisation made out of this? – Has made it difficult, *needing to be hidden*; delayed it; more or less *sacralised* it; set it apart from all other functions; introduced consensus into the matter; more or less decorated it with multifarious *spiritual* ornaments; made it a cult, a genuine illness, ... a fault, a taboo; dressed up the physiological thing as a psychological one...
> And love has followed pretty much the same destiny as the notions of divinity and of the state... It has waxed strong and become a monster under veils. (C2, 486; *C* XI, 15)

This is as sharp a diagnosis as we shall find of love as cultural value in pre-Freudian France or Victorian/Edwardian Britain. It goes a long way to explaining why Valéry will appear as the analyst, poet, lover, and finally mystic, of *eros unveiled*.

The inventor of the System certainly intended that his positivistic 'self-science' should not only lay bare the authentic psychosexual reality cloaked within the received cultural construct, but also that it should contain, control and direct this same principle within himself. The latter proposal was to prove the more problematic of the two. We shall see Valéry progressively taking the measure of a confounding mystery, which, far from yielding to psychogenetic reduction, proves always one step ahead of his efforts to comprehend and master it.

The first indication of this comes in the earliest manuscripts of *La Jeune Parque*. The poetic voice, re-solicited after long neglect, emerges within him orphically laden with the oldest and deepest psychic tensions, unresolved – indeed, exacerbated – by the twenty-year adventure of pure thought. The self-decipherment proceeding in these manuscripts uncovers something deeply disturbing: far from containing Eros, the twenty-year adventure in pure thought has itself been a secretly sublimated waking dream of desire, a covertly mystical quest for the Absolute: 'Je retrouve l'empreinte sur le sable de mon désir Comme le pied d'inconnu non aboli' (*JP* ms. III, f.11v) ['I rediscover the imprint on the sand of my desire/Like the surviving footprint of someone unknown'].[6] 'I am an other', as Rimbaud had said – or rather, here, *une autre*.

This is a second defining moment. The decipherment of this erotic 'figure voilée' [veiled figure] commanding the exercise of intellect itself initiates an effort of creative writing that is also and inseparably an exegesis of the poet's own spiritual biography. The outcome is one of the very greatest of twentieth-century poems, *La Jeune Parque* in which the veiled 'figure' is unfolded, but also transmuted in the writing of it, by the play of musical and architectural form.[7] The finished poem will give back a mythic-universal biography of the modern psyche of Desire, mirroring the entire modern adventure of reflexive Awakening.

The original shock of erotic self-recognition is picked up in the lines:

Dieux! Dans ma lourde plaie une secrète sœur
Brûle, qui se préfère à l'extrême attentive! (*JP* ll.48–9)[8]

Great gods! In my heavy wound a secret sister/Burns, tending in attention to the extreme!

The second line is a latinism: *se ad extremum praeferre attendens*. Attentive to the extreme limits of mental power, a hidden Other within now lusts for ultimate initiation and gnosis. In the most intimate places of the Parque's psychic hurt, out of the very gaping of her wound, there arises a burning Other of secretly erotico-mystical determination, which the Serpent's venom has released in her.

The wound is to be understood in terms of the inner division of the self introduced by consciousness; it is also, in the ultimate, a tearing-away from the childhood paradise of Being. The 'time' of Being – historical memory, dream-reminiscence or ontological intuition? – is represented in the poem's fifth episode. The 'Harmonieuse MOI', unified and peacefully at one with the world, represents the Self the protagonist remembers having been 'before' her seduction by the Serpent of reflexive desire, of autonomous consciousness and knowledge. The capital letters designate a real and substantial presence, divinely founded by the love of the cosmic god who enfolds and penetrates her in Light:

Dites!... J'étais l'égale et l'épouse du jour,
Seul support souriant que je formais d'amour
A la toute-puissante altitude adorée... (*JP* ll.107–9)

Say!... I was the equal and the spouse of day,/Only support in love that smilingly/I offered to the all-powerful altitude adored...

Her unreflecting co-presence to the world is celebrated in gestures of religious adoration ('in your shadows of gold I prayed gropingly' [*JP* l.112]); and in the sunlight of being she dances her innocent joy. Her dancing form is, however, veiled in a linen dress, which covers her budding adolescent form. Catching on the flowers of paradise, this 'veil' contours the *jeune fille en fleur* and hints at her emergent adolescent sexuality:

Si la robe s'arrache à la rebelle ronce,
L'arc de mon brusque corps s'accuse et me prononce
Nu sous le voile enfleé de vivantes couleurs
Que dispute ma race aux longs liens de fleurs (*JP* ll.134–7)

If the dress snatches away from the springing briar,/The arc of my suddenly contoured body declares me/Naked beneath the veil swelling with living colours/By which my race outdoes the trailing flowers

The way in which her own sexuality comes to be expressed in the conscious psyche is figured in the Serpent of reflexive awareness and the thirst for knowledge. His wounding and desirable bite is, in fact, like the returning arrow of her own sublimated libidinal energies (the later image of her as 'winged huntress' confirms this linkage precisely). Valéry is here designating the sexual spring of all mysticism, including his own mysticism of the Intellect. Once awakened to lucid thought, the Parque can dismiss the Serpent in his traditional mythic persona. He is merely a player in the eternal dream-thought of Psyche, a figment of her own desire. There is Freudian prescience here: both in the Parque's horror of sexuality – she will later speak of her –'divine disgust which gave wings to [her] rising' (*JP* 1.363) – and in her phallic representation of the dream-seducer as a bejewelled and fascinating arm, raised, snake-like, to strike:

> Laisse donc défaillir ce bras de pierreries
> Qui menace d'amour mon sort spirituel...
> [...]
>   ... Apaise alors, calme ces ondes,
> Rappelle ces remous, ces promesses immondes.
> Ma surprise s'abrège, et mes yeux sont ouverts. (*JP* ll.58–63)

So let the bejewelled arm subside/Which with love threatens my spiritual fate.../[...]/
... Quieten then, calm those convulsive waves,/Summon back those ripples of commotion, those filthy promises.../My surprise is cut short, and my eyes are opened.

At this point, the 'mysterious Self' of the poem has begun to decipher a logic of her own continuity-in-time, answering in part the tear-choked question of identity with which the poetic monologue opens ('Who weeps there ...?' [*JP* l.1]). The veil covering her own psychosexual personality has been torn to reveal the monstrous ferment of the 'animal woman' beneath. Eros is, to this extent, unveiled. Thus, the half-denuded figure of the prelude is replaced in the finale by the fully denuded figure who accepts the caress of the sunlight (now no longer connoted sacred, or a sign of Being),[9] and who runs to the sea in refound erotic delight at existing:

> O, sur toute la mer, sur mes pieds, qu'il est beau!
> Tu viens!... Je suis toujours celle que tu respires,
> Mon voile évaporé me fuit vers tes empires... (*JP* ll.492–4)

Oh, over the whole sea, over my feet, how fine he is!/You're coming!... I am still the love whom you breathe in,/My wind-blown veil flees from me towards your domains...

Yet still the mystery of *metasexual* Eros subsists. *Who is this* who is so grievously wounded at having lost the paradise of Being? What 'reminiscence' (*JP* 1.406) is this; and 'what grief' (*JP* 1.26)? What 'vain and vain expectation' (*JP* 1.384) of initiation? Why, if of the flesh, does the Eros of the mind reject contingent embodiment, seeking luminous disincarnation and the fusion of pure spirit with the Absolute? Why, dismissing the Serpent and claiming the autonomous possession of her own inner mystery, can she not penetrate beyond the 'fiery door' (*JP* 1.76, cf. 1.461) which would yield final initiation? None of these questions which belong to the 'mystery' of the Young Fate – and to the drama of twentieth-century Eros—will be answered in the poem. In place of any essentialist resolution, there is the *form* – an ever-open existential reconciliation enshrining the dynamic enigma itself.

Valéry will remain, always and essentially, a poet of Desire, forever retracing and unveiling the 'figure' of sense, carried by the mysterious and 'feminine' Other within the psyche. In his *Cahiers* he writes revealingly of his ceaseless attempt to represent in the poem itself the mysterious and no doubt unknowable psychic springs out of which creativity issues and the poem is born:

> How I understand – often – that an artist may spend his entire life seeking to trace the same figure, ever more closely approaching – ... what?
> And I would wish to arrive at it by an ever more subtle analysis of my desire.
> The work must be (and be only) the maturity of desire itself. All effort previous to it. Effort merely spent to disengage that desire.
> Instead of writing the poem straight away, write the desire of it, hold it back, live it out...
> (*C* VI, 664)

The unveiling of the erotic spring of the human psyche, the enigmatic key to all forms of its creative 'poetry', is crucial to Valéry's vision of love, particularly as mediated by a third essential accident. A *surprise de l'amour* followed hard on the heels of the writing of *Charmes*. In 1920–21, under the spell of an enchantment due in part to his own creative triumph as a poet, Valéry discovered in the person of Catherine Pozzi an Other whom he could regard as perfect complement. An intense love-affair followed, of soaring ambition as regards its aspirations of intimacy. It declared its contradictions, disintegrated amid deepest spiritual despair in 1922 and was liquidated after long trauma in 1928.

Valéry speaks of the 'two or three formidable events of my secret life' (C2, 460; *C* VIII, 762) – there were to be others in 1932 and 1940. They were formidable principally because each occasion, but most particularly the first, produced a radical dislocation of inner syntax. The circuit of the 'curious love' which Valéry attributes to his Narcissus – the intellect's reflexive love for its own mystery, and the circuit of amorously intellective self-attention – reformed itself in each case on the new axis of a living bi-polarity. Momentarily, his own Eros agreed to understand something taken from the very different logic of Agape: that human subject-identity is not a possession of the self, but is something given and received in a relationship of exchange.

Four passages from the *Cahiers* capture memorably the respects in which this experience was 'transcendent'. The first declares the onset of *le mal sacré* in Hellenic imagery, borrowed from the myth of Orpheus in the underworld:

> Crossing in appalling darkness through the grotto of Tears [...]. This is the gateway to what they call 'the great Questions' [...] Smoke rises. A smell of wood attacked by flame. A doorway opens. Enter the most terrible thing in the world: Happiness; being not of this world, hence terrible when entering it [...] come from some other system of relations to bring an unknown standard, an *paradigm event*, a new *unit of reality*. (C2, 427; *C* VIII, 310)

The second enters, remarkably, into the once-ironised 'politics of the Universe' (albeit still understood as proceeding from need-love):

> To be profoundly loved is the most   —   thing in the world. That was the impossible goal of God.
> 'Profoundly', it's not a question of pleasure, not even of pride.
> But of receiving that obscure soul-warmth. (C2, 409; *C* VII, 659)

Fleetingly, in the glow of what he calls 'love-glory', Valéry even glimpses the novelty, the persuasive possibility, of Christian Agape:

> What novelty, what strangeness to attach to the God goodness, justice, truth.
> The gods were magnificently simple...
> Then the strange thing. Tenderness and universe. Idea of sacrifice, no longer by man to God, but now from God to God. (*C* VII, 801)

The fourth, as if by the operation of some profoundly cogent inner homophony, expresses the song of the 'ineffable transformation' esoterically, in terms borrowed from the mystics of communion in Agape (the imagery of the 'dwellings of the soul' comes from Theresa of Avila):[10]

> My life was like a house known to me in its tiniest parts. And so well did I know it that I barely noticed it any more. Its regular forms, its advantages and drawbacks, seemed to belong to my body itself and to my very time. I couldn't conceive of any other dwellings. My soul was there and so habitually there that it wasn't actually anywhere. One day I touched by chance some spring or other and, there, a secret door opened. I entered into strange and infinite apartments. I was overwhelmed by my discoveries. I felt in moving within these unknown and mysterious chambers that they were the true dwelling-places of my soul. (*C* VIII, 778)

The awakening of sensibility and intellect occasioned by the event was, in turn, formidable. The liberation of unsuspected energies, although quickly damned up again by the violent reaction which followed in the name of self-defensive mastery of irrational forces, re-echoes in prolonged subterranean resonance throughout the entire mindsphere of the *Cahiers*. Henceforth the analyst is dedicated to the imperative of elucidating, in the language of his own neo-cartesian 'clear god', the darker, subterranean 'god' declared in love, the enigma of its transcendence, the mystery of its disappointed unitive tenderness: 'Get to explore one's being to the point of touching the god with the god. *Understand love*' (*C* IX, 304).

***

'Understanding' love means for the psychogenetician of the *Cahiers* stripping down the inner mechanisms and springs of passion. This involves prodigies of analysis, unravelling fibre by fibre 'the clump of obscure roots', in particular those of the strangely persuasive 'idol-poetry' (*C* XIX, 723) by which *amour-passion* betrays its 'intimate relations with mysticism' (*C* XXVI, 92). It means re-evaluating its potential as appraised by the mind. And, in the end, it involves 'understanding' in the very strongest sense (*cumprehendere*): reconstituting, within the self, the inherent Idea or Ideal of love. For convenience of exposition, we may separate these three aspects of Valéry's thought. But in reality, they are complementary moments or movements of a unified enterprise, held together in a form of ascendent dialectic – the re-imagining of love itself.

The 'basic' or 'real' part of *amour-passion*, for the analyst of the *Cahiers*, already contains a strange and arbitrary 'excess' of mobilised energy and spiritual quest, bafflingly beyond reproductive usefulness (C2, 404; *C* VII, 36). The psychic dimension of love, in his view, moulds itself to the physical act, propagating its irrationality and its excess:

> – The mechanics of Eros represent the finest example of 'transcendence' – that is, the passing into all registers and instruments of our being – demands and responses, levels and thresholds. One can't meditate enough on this transforming propagation, spreading through all our functions, scales, reactive durations... (C2, 543; *C* XXV, 477)

The 'mystical' quality of love is a phenomenon which Valéry analyses under the name of the 'aesthesic infinite', that is: the power of a psychic stimulus to re-excite itself and thus to resonate indefinitely within our sensibility. The resonant energy-excess is projected onto the chosen Object, which it converts into an inexhaustible sign (C2, 543; *C* XXVI, 92). This projection is necessarily an improvised poem, however, and a blind creation, since it precedes and exceeds knowledge of the Object which it beautifies mythically (C2, 544; *C* XXVI, 211).

If love were merely blind, its self-regenerating phantom-pursuit might be merely absurd; but, tragically, it also engages a dependency on the Other, magically invested with the key to our own being:

Love – Power of presence
The Key-being.
The one object capable of drawing from the Self the greatest sensation of being alive.
Man doesn't attain to this by himself. He needs an external occasion, an Other.
And he considers this Other as Self. He says 'My soul' – what animates me.
The Key which opens for me the myself. (C2, 481; *C* X, 336)

Outside the self the way to the Self
But, you damn fool, can't you see there is only you? (C2, 430; *C* VIII, 366)

The 'transcending' other-relation is, in this second entry, transparently self-referred and seen in its perilous ambivalence. No less for Valéry than for Proust, the 'idolopoésie' of passion carries, in practice, the risk of tragic soul-error. 'All loves end badly. It is impossible to think of an ongoing development without arriving necessarily at disgust, treachery, lies, dissolution in boredom, instability' (C2, 438; *C* VIII, 459). 'Love consists in thinking one has yielded willy-nilly to the Other what was only for oneself' (C2, 467; *C* IX, 127). This is the controlling vision expressed in the second of Valéry's 'Fragments du Narcisse' (*Charmes*). The mirroring pool, a coldly ironic witness to many lovers' trysts, here reflects the complete cycle of amorous enchantment and disenchantment accomplished by 'those madmen who believed people love each other' – the quasi-algebraic, anti-Romantic counter-formula of passion-love as it appears to the self-aware Intellect.

The mind's negative evaluation of love arises from an essential *mistrust* – of 'the poisoned sting of sex' (C2, 474; *C* IX, 640), of 'the fearsome trap of tenderness' (C2, 481; *C* X, 203) – and of the obscurely cosmic forces of life itself. There is in Valéry a residual undertow of Schopenhauerian pessimism, already expressed in the Young Fate's anguished refusal to transmit or perpetuate life:

Non! L'horreur m'illumine, exécrable harmonie!
Chaque baiser présage une neuve agonie...
[...]
Non, vous ne tiendrez pas de mes lèvres l'éclair!... (*JP*, ll.259–71)

No! Horror illuminates me, execrable harmony!/Each kiss foretells a new death-agony.../
[...]/No, from my lips you shall not receive the flash of life!

***

This first refusal of the appraising intellect is however balanced from 1921 onwards by a countervailing exploration of human love as a value: a haunting Idea that floats free of the shipwreck of Valéry's affair with Catherine Pozzi.[11] What Valéry habitually calls 'the divine element in love' is *also* explored in memorably positive terms. The analyst of the *Cahiers* speaks of 'that exultant life produced by the presence of another human self' (*C* XXVIII, 901); and of 'that virtue of generalised excitement which may be of the highest value in developing the energies of action and creation' (*C* XX, 909). In this respect, amorous transcendence is obscurely linked, like religious faith, to human potential as such: 'thus "faith", thus anything which causes us to accomplish great things and effects astonishing transformations in someone who didn't know he contained them' (C2, 471; *C* IX, 435). It represents, at the least, a hope – 'the only thing which can count for the soul that is not base' (C2, 449; *C* VIII, 501) – of believing one is not alone and that it is possible to 'truly exchange the soul's most precious substance for the most precious substance that is within another' (C2, 449; *C* VIII, 501). Against the persuasion of rationalist appraisal and of its essential Mistrust, love is seen to hold the last chance offered to the mind itself of 'feeling intelligently complicit with life' (*C* XIV, 262).

Love, in short, is – or might have been, or could be – a refounding counter-value, correcting the negativity of pure intellect and signifying 'the return or the re-attachment to one's condition as living being, to the energy given by an external source' (*C* XIV, 268). More simply, Valéry writes:

> Turning over inwardly this strange question: If one had to choose between love – and the possession of the intellect as clarity, fruitfulness, extent and depth – what should one choose?
> It is probable that somebody already 'spoiled' in respect of intellect, would choose love, and somebody already spoiled for love, would choose love as well. (C2, 412; *C* VII, 697)

Yet this dialectic of evaluation leaves in suspense the fundamental question: what *is* 'love'? More precisely: what is it that love seeks, above and beyond sexual possession; and what is its fulfilment?

> Possession itself cannot satisfy extreme love. It is, indeed, a sort of mad wish for adapting. The most intimate touching serves merely as a stimulus to its energies, and is not a finite resolution of them.
> But without this touching, it believes/ would believe/ that touching might satisfy/ quieten/ the infinite value which belongs legitimately only to the true god and not to the idol. The 'true god' being the absolutely originating point of all desires. (C2, 469; *C* IX, 289)

> Isn't there, in this tendency towards the act, a very complex act with two heads to it, two sensibilities, two forms and orders of existence – isn't there an excitement towards the wholly real [le réel complet] which all our senses are attempting to compose by means of X? And not our senses only, but everything in us that requires response – from the need for tenderness right up to metaphysical appetite. (C2, 489; *C* IX, 808)

I am, she says, that real Being, of which the being known to you, whom you love, which you edify within yourself, which tears and delights you – is but the dream. Wake up. Dispel my phantom. You will see what I am like. (C2, 487; *C* XI, 421)

The 'metaphysical' substratum of amorous desire is brilliantly illuminated by these remarks. What love seeks and loves is indeed 'le réel complet', 'l'Etre' as experienced reality. But, we notice, appetitively so, in the mode of deficiency and need. To profoundly ambiguous effect, moreover, since to awaken from the mind-made phantom may be to discover the plenitude of the 'real' Object, satisfying the whole measure of the appetitive need-god within; but it may also be to fall from this hope, and encounter the Other in his/her 'actual' imperfection and contingency. The greatest Hope may also be the most appalling Trap, the essential Disappointment.

The same haunting uncertainty moves through the most beautiful of Valéry's love poems, 'Les Pas' (*Charmes*). The Beloved approaches, absent still, announced only by the soft footfalls that emerge from the silence of the night as though born of the expectant desire that strains to catch them. *She* is the 'Ombre divine' [divine Shadow] bearing the promise of a totally real Presence, laden with the grace of gifts for body and soul. The spiritual place of waiting – 'le lit de ma vigilance' [the bed of my wakefulness] – is a patterned and directed tension, a fervour in the order of the sacred; *cor meum vigilat*, notes the poet (*C* VIII, 496), quoting from the *Song of Songs*. 'Mon cœur' [my heart] lives only for the imagined rite of encounter and communion at the limit-power of feeling, where delight in being verges, in its very extremity, on a negation of all known reality. What is divined and sought is a consummation pacifying the whole measure of the hunger and thirst of the unknown central 'I'.

The poem anticipates consummation; but it also defers the consummation it invokes:

Si, de tes lèvres avancées,
Tu prépares pour l'apaiser,
A l'habitant de mes pensées
La nourriture d'un baiser,

Ne hâte pas cet acte tendre,
Douceur d'être et de n'être pas,
Car j'ai vécu de vous attendre
Et mon cœur n'était que vos pas. (*Œ* I, pp. 120–1)

If, with ready lips,/You are preparing/For the dweller in my thoughts/The nourishing communion of a kiss,

Do not hasten the tender act,/Sweetness of being and of being not,/For I have waited on your coming/And my whole heart was but your steps.

If the Shadow quits the sphere of ideality and imminence, will she not disappoint the hunger and thirst that have consecrated her as divine? The Complement of all our longing cannot *exist*. The switch from the ardent 'tu' of the first quoted stanza to the more reverential 'vous' of the second, the syntax of conditional subordination, the restraining injunction, all set at a distance the object of the murmured prayer, so that this poem of Eros closes upon itself in a quivering balance of countervailing negativities, suspended entirely on the footsteps of awakening and promise that gave it birth. Such is the delectable and tenuous divinity of Eros.

***

The third movement or moment of Valéry's ascendant dialectic derives from precisely this extreme tension between the indubitable need for transcendence in its fullest metaphysical sense and the extreme mistrust of the intellect at the promise which *amour-passion* awakens but cannot fulfil. Valéry's deconstructive critique of passion viewed as 'idolopoésie' and his counter-affirmation of love as value find their articulating coherence in his mystique of the 'higher love'.

This construct is admitted to be a conscious creation of the poet-lover: 'we can love only what we create'. Valéry speaks of it as an exercise in self-awareness and imagination, recasting the Idea or Ideal of love in conformity with what the mind can know of its own Desire. Two texts of his old age, defining the project of the unfinished fourth Act of the Faust play 'Lust ou la Demoiselle de Cristal' lay out the grand design:

> I have done what I could to ensure that the monotonous theme of love re-appear and be heard in a higher octave [...] and that the theme of Intellect/ mind/ be disengaged from its 'useful' applications and be married with the first theme. (C2, 546; *C* XXVII, 417)

> That is indeed what I have desired and solely desired. Experience, alas, is not too encouraging. My faith is that this is possible, that it is possible to give a higher meaning to this damn silly life by essaying with all the combined forces of the heart, the flesh and the intelligence to realise a higher truth of sensibilities, a total resonance between human selves equating to a resolution of their difference, each becoming ever more the complement and necessary perfection of the other, and so less and less other ...
> This effort against nature (which demands there be between living selves an unscaleable barrier and which subjects them to an irreducible condition of egoism) is obviously of the same essence as the effort we call mystical in its crude state. (*MF* ms III, f.8)

Despite the simplicity of enunciation, the higher love is an extraordinary conception, at once a studied work of art remodelling the idea of love, a singular form of mysticism and a Valéryan psychodrama, which finds its creative expression in the experimental writing of his last play, *Mon Faust*.

In its artistic aspect, we can see it as related to 'ordinary' loves, and to Valéry's own unfinished or abortive sketches of real-life passion,[12] rather as his 'pure' poetry relates to that of his Romantic predecessors. It is a mind-distilled essence of higher necessity and beauty, which seeks to 'make something of this strange commotion (*C* VII, 627). 'But the mind can transport our transports into a domain of the extraordinary'', says the aesthetic technician in Valéry. 'For instance, make out of something linear a multi-dimensional construction – *sic* music. Wagner and his Tristan. Passion plus technical meditation' (C2, 405; *C* XVI, 506).

The basis and model for this multidimensional enhancement is, as ever, the act of sexual love-making, with its inherent virtue of 'transcendence', that is of an energetic propagation through functions, scales, levels and thresholds of the psycho-organic system, engaging an ever more all-encompassing, ever more intense and focussed collaboration of the lover's whole being. So the lovers of *Beatrice*, for instance, have sought to make sexual ecstasy, not an end in itself, but 'a sort of step or stage towards the perfecting of the deepest intimacy' (C2, 548; *C* XXVII, 715):

> Sexual delight was for them not the goal of all their tenderness, but a means of losing together as much as might be of their difference; for body with body may sometimes find understanding, responsiveness and a divine reciprocal divination; and there remains of this moment a sensitive presence of each in the other, and the memory of a silent comprehension which may serve as model for the relations between minds and therefore, in the end, between the Same and the Same. (C2, 546; *C* VIII, 594)[13]

This communion of essences, limited only by ontological difference, has as its finality the creation of 'moments of eternity': fragments of a privileged duration extracted from and lifted above ordinary time. Valéry always refers to this time in terms of the 'aesthetic infinite' (cf. C2, 971–2; *C* XVIII, 350 etc.), as experienced in poetry and music. Thus for the lovers of *Mon Faust*:

> We would be like gods, *intelligent Harmonics* in direct correspondence of our sensitive lives, whose accordedness would sound forth as thought, ideas.
> Summit of poetry which is after all communion.
> Making hours which would be fragments of eternity. (*C* XXI, 836)

The love envisaged is an existential projection of the promise of poetry itself: '"Love" – total singing state' (*C* XXIV, 660). More strikingly still: for Valéry as for Proust, 'the divine element in love is music, has no expression other than musical' (*C* XXIII, 910). Whereas for Proust music transcends, integrates and replaces love, in Valéry it is a sign of the human potential of love itself; it is a call to become – rather than a reproach for love's failure to be – 'transcendent' and 'essential'. Thus Valéry records a moment of supremely concentrated energy experienced in following a sublime performance of the role of Sieglinde in *Die Walküre*; and he notes without transition:

– That love might be a fine, peerless thing, an act-action of praise for having understood together – and a recompense, a mutual administration sharing the same bread of sexual delight taken by a single mouth at the zenith of mind… (C2, 473; *C* IX, 525)[14]

The sacramental language of this last proposal indicates that the Valéryan construct refers to a second major analogue or model, found in the Catholic mystics of love union such as Theresa of Avila and John of the Cross. The higher love is seen as a reworking or transposition of this model, producing a purely naturalistic *equivalence*. 'Mysticism without God', he notes in the *Cahiers*, 'cf. Synthesis of emotion by musical means' (*C* XI, 22); and again, 'I can make a mystic [*sic*] as exercise'.[15] More surprisingly still, he writes of the higher love as a deliberate attempt to replace the supernatural Object which the religions have proffered to the human need for transcendence: 'If God does not exist, this task remains to us of acting so that he should exist' (*C* VI, 753); 'what mysticism has taken as goal, that is, life in God, attempt it by substituting for God another living being' (C2 444; *C* VIII, 473).

The last declaration of intent of course rests on the post-'death of God' postulate that 'mysticism' is a form of *erotic idealisation* projecting, replaceably, its own divine Other. As Valéry expresses it, the notion of a 'divine substitution' marks the metaphysical gap or 'gaping' out of which the 'secret sister' of erotico-mystic sensibility in his work has always spoken. It is a highly significant gap, hermeneutically speaking, since it renders fragile the metaphorical equivalence sought. Without the *real presence* of the divine Other, what becomes of the mystic's legitimising invitation to unitive tenderness and of his grace of fulfilment? Can there be any order of love to fulfil or any genuine hope of the longed-for marriage of Being? As Valéry's Demoiselle de Cristal will say: 'After all, the soul is perhaps a void? It is perhaps what ceaselessly demands what is not?' (*Œ* II, 317). Deprived of any force of *allusion* to an antecedent and ultimate Reality, the 'Promise' of love must be precisely that power of *illusion* – and Desire in its infinity that principle of *soul error* – that Valéry most deeply feared and mistrusted all his life. In this sense, his para-religious love mysticism knows itself to be a paradox, a vulnerable Poem. His sense of rivalry with traditional Catholic spirituality is perhaps sharpened by this consciousness of fragility.

The theme of *voluptas ab opprobriis vindicata* (*C* VII, 748) has a particular resonance and a justifying density in this context. Valéry sees in orthodox belief a travesty to be resisted. Sexual delight (he dismisses the word 'pleasure') is vigorously defended against moral condemnation, spiritualistic scorn and confusion with procreative function. Insistently, Valéry presents it as a sign of true humanity and of true human transcendence:

The mystics who condemn the flesh, are they not in more distinguished but no less real error than that of the followers of the flesh? […] they mutilate the true nature of man. They refuse him first the intercourse of bodies and the profound intimacy of persons which this renders possible, and that coadaptation which may develop towards the mutual intelligence of organisms and of the reciprocity or alliance of weaknesses and strengths [...]. (C2, 538–9; *C* XXIV, 239)

Not only so, but 'sexual ecstasy itself is a symbol, a sacrament, a – figure'. For if only procreation is at stake in sexual love-making, 'all the psychic and super-affective part with its idolatry of the one being becomes inexplicable.' But, says Valéry, 'those who understand this thing place on it a higher value' (C2, 556–7; *C* XXIX, 805).

The 'figurative' promise of love is something Valéry is inclined to take seriously. In one curious and vibrant anagogic tale from the *Cahiers*, an appearing Angel reproaches two lovers with having sinfully stolen from the Lord by fornication 'the power of fire that was in you'. He is told firmly that this 'fragment detached from I-know-not-what instantaneous eternity and which resembles nothing on earth' is the only sign mortal man has of the God, who is also unlike anything to be found in the world. In other words, it is a more cogent theistic sign – there can be no question of *proof* – than any of the traditional 'five ways' of Aquinas! (C2, 537; *C* XXIV, 21–3).

What makes Valéry's fascination for the higher love into a form of mysticism, albeit counter-orthodox, is his sense of the mystery of being to which sexual love and the co-presence of lovers gives access. In the neuro-critical instants situated at the extremes of human physiological and psychic response, at the limit of the mind's potential of sensation, feeling and intellection, the veil between being and knowing seems about to part. The most intimate spring of Valéry's mystique of love, as also of his previous mystique of pure intellect, lies in 'a pursuit of the contour of things or the outline trace of being, a knocking at the doors of the knowable' (C2, 399; *C* IV, 722), motivated in depth by the ontological curiosity of which the Young Fate spoke, 'bound to this unknown sky' (*JP*, l.16). 'Ultra-sexual love' (C2, 524; *C* XVIII, 14) is probed in the same gnostic tension reaching out after the mysterious X beyond the Limit set, 'the Boundary', marking that which is forbidden, or at least hidden, by the very structure of the human psyche.

Yet more and more in Valéry's maturity, there is a subtle modulation of attitude, heralded by the gesture of abstention and deferral of 'Les Pas'. A receptive listening to the deep places of psychic desire seems to balance the acuity of masculine penetration and possession. The key player in the Poem of the higher love becomes the 'veiled figure' of that feminine part of the psyche, with its inherent nostalgia for a communion at source, for a lost integrity of being and for that 'réel complet' which supposes a genuine alterity and a living presence. Between these two interlocutors will be rehearsed Valéry's ultimate debate about the ontological status of love.

***

Is love, in the ultimate, a phantom or a reality? The question of how the mind *can* entertain and maintain this value, of whether it is *able* to love only as it creates, is at the heart of Valéry's Faust play, *Lust ou la Demoiselle de Cristal*. This partly published, partly private and experimental work occupied the last five years of his life right up to his death in 1945: a moving tribute to the steadfastness of his design of 'writing desire'. It is most rewardingly read as a psychodrama exploring the tensions of the long-interiorised Idea or Ideal of the higher love.

The four published Acts of the play offer a specifically 'modern' mental space, mortal to all the energising myths of Romantic subjectivity: confessional literature, autobiography, genius, the soul, love as redemptive force, and of course, providentialist Design. Revisited a hundred years later, Goethe's protagonist appears as a giant in consciousness, capable of putting God and the Devil in his pocket. Yet, by the same token, he is an alienated giant condemned to 'relive' within a fatally demystified mindsphere, lacking vital appetite and spiritual joy. He thus dismisses the suggestion of 'a new Gretchen affair' by which Mephisto, up to his old tricks, seeks to rewin his soul (it is Mephisto who slips into Faust's papers the suggestive notion of 'éros énergumène' – sexual love as a source of extreme energy).

Valéry's first idea, realised in the brilliant improvisation which gives us the first two published Acts, is that of a comic and poignant *surprise de l'amour*. Casually, Faust controls the subterranean current of attraction which unites him to the natural gaiety of his desirable young secretary. The dictation of his Memoirs tends to instrumentalise and distance Luste; yet her tender concern at his account of his past amorous conquests begins to fissure the sphere of the mind's self-sufficiency, opening up disturbing and desirable horizons of relationality. In the well-known scene of Act II, Faust yields to the melting beauty of sunset and a sweet-scented Garden, secretly charged with the energising presence of the human Other. His famous hymn to Living (recalling the supreme 'instant' of Goethe's protagonist) expresses a moment of perfect, quasi-mystical self-coincidence and plenitude, in which all the lack and longing of Desire seems to be cancelled out. Yet by an exquisite irony, the Faustian instant is presented as a masterpiece of the solitary Mind. At Faust's definition of 'reality' – 'I touch, I am touched' – Luste acquiesces with a gentle hand laid on his shoulder, soliciting exchange between them of the deepest feeling of living and offering a higher dimension of contact with reality. Faust hesitates between intimacy and distance, the 'tu' and the 'vous'; then retracts, fearful of the devastating 'totality' involved in the play of the flesh and the dependency of the heart. Yet he consents, finally, to share the peach plucked from the Tree, and to enter the ambiguous and troubled logic of Relationality. 'I felt myself a perfect work,' he will say in the Duo of the unfinished fourth Act, 'but you were close to me' (*MF* ms. III, f.59).

Valéry's second idea, emerging in the very process of writing desire, here breaks surface: to rewrite the *Gretchentragödie* in the image of the Valéryan 'higher love', showing it to be the only value capable of redeeming the alienation of the modern mind. Act III, from which Faust is entirely absent, prepares this conception. It offers a concerted play of reflections which compose the suggestion of the 'something else' in love: that part of libidinal energy irreducible to the 'gross convulsion' to which Mephisto would reduce it. The devil declares himself lost – but who in this play truly understands? – the obscure will and tendency of the supposedly transparent Crystal Girl:

I can't see what she wants from Faust. Between man and woman, there aren't three possibilities. She doesn't know herself. If she did, I'd know at once. But she doesn't know: so she is obscure to me [...]. She doesn't know what she wants and wants it with all her might. [...] Could this be some fire I don't know about? (C2, 354)

What Luste intuits in herself is an obscure need and potential for transcendence: 'there is in me something which is obscure and that nothing, nothing human can satisfy' (Œ II, 378). And divining, she demands that the hymn to Living be enacted *à deux*, each bringing to the other what is lacking in human desire, and that without limit, to the measure of the reminiscence of the paradise of Being. Thus the third Act anticipates, as it were negatively, *en creux*, the great Love of which the unfinished fourth Act was to have realised the dramatically embodied figure.

At which point, the published texts stops: not because Valéry lost interest in it, but, on the contrary, because it represented the supreme challenge to him both as an artist and as the decipherer of Eros. We know from the now partially published studies and scenarios how he wrestled with both of these interlinked problems. The fourth Act becomes the imaginary and experimental space in which the 'amorous attempt' pursues its elaboration: first, within a prescribed framework, but increasingly, escaping any framework.

Under the title 'Ulysse et la Sirène', Ned Bastet has brilliantly reconstructed the strange drama of the act of writing, whereby the text, in the process of constituting itself, suffers the reactive contagion of its own depths. The originally foreseen dramatic framework was the failure of the 'tentative amoureuse': Faust and Luste realise in part the Idea of a higher love: its aspiration to an infinitely reflecting mirror-play formed by each subjectivity in the other. Yet this attempt was to have yielded at length to the realisation that the Poem of Eros is not to be inscribed into reality; and the lovers' failure would then have led them to a 'Lebewohl' of desperate tenderness modelled on the parting of Wotan and Brunnehilde (rather than the mystic flight into death of Tristan and Isolde). Valéry would have shown the most powerful of all 'affections' incapable of undoing the ultimate resistance of the hero of Intellect, who, never ceasing to perceive the psychic nature of the mind's own Ideas and Ideals, can never consent, either, to the fatally flawed and limited nature of any relational bond.

However, this first scenario falters, then spectacularly *reverses* its project. The 'calculated dialogue' in which Faust 'objectifies' the Temptation of Tenderness is gradually invaded and taken over by the 'lyric Duo' in which the two voices re-echo in harmony the same themes of aspiration and exaltation, creating the emergence, as a pure precipitate, of a mystical impulse as imperious as it is, within the 'single horizon' of a world without God, impossible to satisfy. The last texts of the fourth Act 'seem to escape all problematics of the theatre and all insertion in any real psychological and dramatic development; they are no longer anything except a celebration "once and for all, transcending all" of a sort of pure beyond of the human, of an intentionality without content, perhaps a tangent of flight towards infinity, no longer finding any expression save in the universe of sound.'[16]

What are we to make of this strange reversal? Bastet suggests that the poet succumbs, in the act of writing, to the siren of libidinal fascination and finishes in magic, bewitched by the music of his own psychic depths. That figure of sense is remarkable enough. Yet one is reluctant to concur that this genuinely is the case of the most resolutely lucid of all twentieth-century writers, who has explicitly set himself the task of deciphering the 'veiled figure' of the Desire that dwells in Psyche. Bastet's reading seems incomplete, notably, if taken as an account of the theme of transcendence, ever associated with Eros. Pointedly so when we remember that Valéry himself links the ideal of the higher love with the spiritual dimension of Eros which, from 'L'Enterrement de Dieu' of 1887, belongs centrally to his entire work. If the the manuscripts of Act IV represent a fragmented space which 'Desire .... traverses but cannot inhabit',[17] is this not rather because the strange 'procreation of the Ideal' sought gropingly the ways of its own coherence, drawn, as in the dark night of *La Jeune Parque*, by the silent but irrepressible music of Being? 'Oh, Light' begs Luste in the Duo; 'Oh, Warmth' replies Faust (f.80). The siren that calls seems strangely like the golden song, lost as a known melody, yet ineffaceable within the psyche, of the 'Harmonieuse MOI'.

Scriptor of his own psychodrama, Valéry does nothing other than retrace the approaching steps of a shadow of Divinity, suspended upon the famous 'IF' on which pivots the little poem of *Charmes*. And if Luste's voice nevertheless prevails in the manuscripts, it does so to the extent that she expresses, with a force of strangeness ever less reducible to the translation operated by the logocentrism of Faust, the prayer for Life which is latent also in him:

> Nothing can have been like this: a force without a name, and which the word love veils more than it points to... This is what I implore. I pray to whatever I can. I pray to what I feel in my whole being should be prayed to... Oh, my principle of Me who art in Faust, do this. I would that he should love himself as I love myself, and that he should love me as I love him. (f.12)

All is in the quality of the loving: its confident simplicity, its transparency, its benevolence. One is unsurpised to find Luste declaring that her exigency 'runs so far, so high, that I cannot confess it to myself' (f.63). If she is heard, it is that the Faustian intellect consents at the last to recognise, valorise and welcome in its mysterious alterity the obscure expectation 'at the wellsprings of the poem':

> Daughter, child of what was proceeding in the shadow of my lucid thought...whereas I thought I was making thought, you the power of thinking. (f.92)

> Rise, little Luste... You are great, little Luste, very great. And for all my grasping you with my whole thought, understanding you with all my experience, foreseeing your movements, I whom nothing human escapes, I whom nothing human can surprise or touch any more yet...
> Yes, here now is a love which is like no other... (f.65)

This recognition of the unconscious and preconscious determinants of the rational Mind is unparalleled in Valéry. We may recognise here a 'turning point' (*C* XXIX, 783), a pivot around which the sense and intent of Act IV turns, looking now towards an affirmation of the totality of Desire.

Yet the veiled figure of human desiring is still ambiguous. Two melodies of desire, two imaginative persuasions, two figures of trancendence, mingle their voices in the Duo. The first is Tristanian. Plaintive, fevered, fusional, blessed-in-suffering, it is the song of *amour-passion* as it seeks at the limit of its range to achieve a climax of intensity having the power to eclipse the nothingness of the real world:

> Don't you understand that two beings of equal disgust, disdain, detachment from everything that repeats the same gestures... and who cancel out at a glance all the base commonality of life, should find in their embrace solely a clue inviting them towards an approach of infinitely greater intimacy, an image of a supreme exchange and that they should become some unknown focus point of living difference at the limit separating being from being. There is a despair... which is beyond price. Yet there too is a source, a strength, a summit... Oh, Faust, suffer what I suffer, and we shall be the most alive of beings in the world, amidst the talking mechanicals you hate...[18]

This is, fundamentally, the music of Absence, born of the need to compensate, by a desperate leap beyond the world, for the lack of sense, value and substance within it; the need to snatch, in the fleetingly possessed super-instant, at an immediate sense of divine Life or Transcendence. In the horizon of Absence, 'all other is but absence', as Valéry's Narcissus says; for nothing can truly found the relation of self to Other, and the love we experience is, necessarily and always, idolatry and soul error. It is clear that the attempt to represent in scenic terms what the writer of these manuscript drafts calls 'the divine substitution' (f.95) invokes the sense of ontological Absence in its original vigour, displaying in fullest, strategic relief the underlying paradox of all human love as such.

In counterpoint, we hear a music of Presence: the Other is here really given, truly present – both as the mysterious power of life pre-existing the sources of ideality and desire in oneself, and as living reciprocity and exchange, mediating the same mystery, in the person of the Beloved:

> And now I tell you that what is most precious in life... is found or refound in the presence and the correspondence or in the unheard of, silent exchange between what I do not know within myself or about myself and what I do not know in you or of you... Oh! that you might feel what I feel, that is a prayer to your profound life. I want to make you declare, without words, who you are. (C2, 1453)

This second soul music has a non-Wagnerian model, that of the mystic marriage according to St John of the Cross; that is, the immediate reciprocal knowledge procured by communion with the intimate Stranger present within the soul (or psyche), the Being creative of my being. We know that this model was very much in Valéry's mind, both in the writing of the fragment of *La Jeune Parque* devoted to the 'Harmonieuse MOI' and again in the writing of the unfinished *Lust IV*, from 1942, when he devoted an essay to the French translator of the *Cantiques spirituels*.[19] The reference to this model is attested in the motifs of the flower-strewn breast, of silence, of streaming light, of touching, and in the tones of gentle fervour, marvelling at the mystery that the imagined Other actually exists: 'You are the Other – that impossibility! What a wonder!' (f.25).

The writing of the veiled figure of desire thus ends in a defined alternative: less a matter of literature than of deciphering, in literature as in life, the foundations of love, desire and transcendence. *Either* it is Absence which is the truth; in which case nothing can make up for the missing lost Object of human desire or found the hope of that reciprocity in exchange which is the very condition of love – and the Poem of a 'higher love' is then destined to remain a splendid mystico-poetic firework-display emprisoned within the mirror of the Mind. *Or else* the intimate music of Presence is a better-than-illusory promise, a presentiment or intuition of the admirable Object secretly expected and waited upon by our whole psychic being. ('For nothing can attract us... that is not either pre-felt by our being or secretely awaited by our nature,' says Valéry's Socrates [Œ, I, 149]).

***

If we are willing to believe the evidence of the last things confided to his *Cahiers*, the sense of Valéry's own dice-throw seems clear enough. No fourth Act of 'Lust' exists; but there are a series of written traces of its writer's inner steps. A testamentary entry 'In which I sum up myself' speaks of an apocalypse of the heart: 'It prevails. Stronger than everything, than the mind, than the organism. That is the fact, the most obscure of facts. Stronger than the will to live and than the power to understand is, then, this damn-sacred H — [ce sacré C—]' (*C* XXIX, 909). The penultimate entry, barely decipherable, probably reads: 'Redo Theta' (*C* XXIX, 911), that is to say, the Platonic dialogue 'On things divine', which is the *other* unfinished masterproject of the *Cahiers*.[20] The very last trace reads: 'The word love has been associated with the name of God only since Xrist' (C2, 718; *C* XXIX, 911).

We cannot know whether this point of stasis constitutes an act of religious self-committal, nor to what effect. The most relentlessly sceptical of modern writers does not escape a final ambiguity, which is that of human Eros as such ('Who is this who...?'). Yet there is every sign that Valéry, at the extreme limit of his turning in conscious and lucid reflection around the spring of his own rising, did glimpse and, perhaps, embrace an intrinsic order of Love not created by the mind.

If literature is the entertaining of possibilities, it must be seen and said that this lifelong writer of Desire did, at the last, discern a 'Key which opens for me the myself'.

Notes

1   Paul Valéry, *Œuvres* Bibliothèque de la Pléiade, 2 vols, ed. J. Hytier (Paris: Gallimard, 1957, 1960), Vol. I, 967. Further references will be given in the text as *Œ* I or II followed by page number.

2   References to Valéry's *Cahiers* are given in this double form: the first reference is to the two-volume Pléiade edition, ed. J. Robinson (Vol. I, 1972; Vol. II, 1974), used whenever the quoted material forms part of this edition; the second reference refers to the integral facsimile edition (Paris: CNRS, 29 vols, 1957–61). Pléiade references are given as C2 followed by page number; CNRS references are given as *C* followed by volume and page number.

3   The German geo-physicist Alfred Wegener (1880–1930) propounded the theory of continental drift, according to which all continents originally formed part of a single land-mass.

4   See supra, chapter 5.

5   Cf. *C* IX, 297; X, 499; X, 715.

6   The three ms. dossiers of 'La Jeune Parque', together with a substantial and significant collection of other Valéry manuscripts, are held at the Bibliothèque nationale de France.

7   See the poet's declaration: 'Whoever manages to read me will read an autobiography in the form' (*Œ* I, 1631–2).

8   See 'La Jeune Parque' in *Œ* I, pp. 96–110.

9   This is clearly expressed in the lines, addressed to the luminous Beloved of episode V, which relocate the sacred not in the order of being, but in that of the desiring sensibility itself: 'Alors, malgré moi-même, il le faut, ô Soleil/Que j'adore mon cœur, où tu te viens connaître' ['So then, despite myself, o Sun/ I must adore my heart in which you come to know yourself'] (*JP*, ll.508–9).

10 Cf. 'Le château intérieur ou les demeures', in *Thérèse d'Avila, Œuvres complètes*, trans. M. Auclair (Paris: Desclée de Brouwer, 1964), p. 871 and *passim*.

11 Cf. C2, 487; *C* XI, 139: 'I will consecrate you as Eternal – Image – I shall name you with this name and you shall be before me for ever and ever, until the consummation of my centuries of thoughts, of grievings, of memories and of movements.'

12 Cf. C2, 502; *C* XV, 300: '*What has been lived is always a sketch*. The inner artist always goes back over it.'

13 Valéry's expression 'du Même au Même' has the same Neo-Platonic resonance as his term 'le Singulier universel' (*C* VIII, 344).

14 Valéry speaks of the death song of Isolde in *Tristan* as exemplifying the love which makes physical possession a 'stage towards the perfecting of the deepest intimacy' (C2, 548; *C* XXVII, 715).

15 See ms. dossier 'Dieu', Bibliothèque nationale de France (note of January, 1929).

16 N. Bastet, 'Ulysse et la Sirène. Le quatrième acte de *Lust*', in *Cahiers Paul Valéry* 2: *Mes théâtres* (Paris: Gallimard, NRF, 1977), p. 130.

17 Ibid., p. 136.

18 Quoted by Bastet, ibid., p. 58.

19 See *Cantiques spirituels* (*Œ* I, 445–57).

20 See my *Valéry: le Dialogue des choses divines* (Paris: Corti, 1989), pp. 400–07.

Chapter 8

Paul Claudel: Transgression and Promise

Je suis la promesse qui ne peut être tenue et ma grâce consiste en cela même.

It might be tempting to suppose that Claudel starts where Valéry leaves off: from the notion that human Eros finds the key to its own nature and movement in 'the love of God'. Certainly, his religious faith is for Claudel the delivering 'key':

Ouvre la porte! et la Sagesse de Dieu est
  devant toi comme une tour de gloire et comme
  une reine couronnée!
O ami, je ne suis point un homme ni une
  femme, je suis l'amour qui est au-dessus de
  toute parole.[1]

Open the door! and the Wisdom of God is before you like a tower of glory and like a crowned queen!/O my friend, I am not a man nor a woman, I am the love which is beyond all saying.

Yet it would be premature to conclude that Claudel is the poet not of Eros but of Agape; or to expect that the ambiguously interlinked themes of this book find ready-made within the ambience of the 'divine Wisdom' a formulary of unerring decipherment.

It is not about the Love divine, envisaged, precisely, as ineffable and ultimate (and invariably addressed by Claudel as 'Vous'), that the poet-dramatist actually writes. His real theme is Eros in its most passionately natural forms, now held to include 'love of God' (i.e., *human* desire *for*, and devotion *to*, God). If Agape is ultimate reality, known and unknown, human desiring, in its total range and depth, remains throughout his work the foregrounded topos. Like Valéry, Claudel 'writes desire', revisiting it, figuring and refiguring the movement of transcendence within it; but the distinctive axis is his lifelong struggle to integrate his own compulsional erotic drives and aspirations within the Catholic frame of belief and value to which he came through his conversion. It is his struggles in faith which generate his much reworked, never finally decisive, insight.

Specifically, from 1905, Claudel seeks to come to terms with a transgressive experience of *amour-passion*. The singularity of his work, we may suggest, lies in his attempt – in part orthodox, in part culture-conditioned, in part personal and idiosyncratic – to project in his writing a Christian redemption of Eros.

***

The essential Claudelian drama of desire is entirely prefigured in the evocation by the poet of the *Cinq Grandes Odes* of his conversion experience:

Vous m'avez appelé par mon nom [...]
O que je suis bien le fils de la femme!
    car voici que la raison, et la leçon des maîtres,
    et l'absurdité, tout cela ne tient pas un rien
Contre la violence de mon cœur et contre
    les mains tendues de ce petit enfant!
O larmes! ô cœur trop faible! ô mine de larmes qui saute! ('Magnificat', *OP*, 249)

You have called me by my name [...]/Oh, how much I am the son of woman! for now reason and the lesson of my teachers, and the absurdity, all that counting not a jot against the violence of my heart and the outstretched arms of this little child!/Oh tears! Oh breaking heart! Oh erupting mine of tears!

This text strangely echoes Valéry's 'Enterrement de Dieu'. In both cases, the quick of the poet's being is touched. A veiled and unknown self of desire answers, fraught with violence and tears, at odds with the *Zeitgeist*, uncomfortably 'other'; here, too, the feminine is stressed. Yet Claudel's experience is the inverse of Valéry's sense of dereliction and cosmic catastrophe. It is an explosively affirmative response to the sense of being addressed and loved, delivered in his innermost human identity by the indubitably present divine Other (the famous text of 'Ma Conversion' speaks of an overwhelming realisation of the innocence, the eternal childlikeness, of the Christmas-come God).

The exploding mine, with its associated imagery of flame and fire, is a highly significant metaphor. It will recur in a 'demonic' projection in the deaths by explosion of the lovers in *Partage de Midi*, and again in *Le Soulier de satin*. Whenever it is frustrated of the deliverance and joy offered by encounter with the Love divine, human desire is always, in its very principle, liable to be a destructive force. 'There is in humankind a fearsome need for happiness and it must have nourishment, or it will devour like fire! We have to get back to the notion of an imperative truth.'[2] Rooted in his own imperative moment, Claudel can have no truck with the twentieth-century enterprise of re-interpreting *a-religiously* the 'transcending' need of the human spirit for light and love, of turning aside toward some lesser end the constituting desire for God.

His refound Catholic acceptance initiated 'a campaign progressively evangelising all regions of [his] intelligence'.[3] The study of the liturgy and of the ontotheology of St Thomas formed a founding initiation, showing how the 'essentialist' spirituality of French Symbolism might be fulfilled within the very different perspective of ontological realism, as illumined by faith. The most crucial contribution of St Thomas is indeed to lift Claudel above the dualist-idealist divorce between mind and world, the shadow of which lies so heavily across the work of Proust and Valéry. The believing intelligence is not self-enclosed, not isolated within its own self-generated 'representations'; it can, by virtue of an analogy of being (*analogia entis*) quickened by Grace, have access to the signifying processes at work in Creation and to the patterns of salvation by which divine Providence operates in the world. (Thus, within the psyche itself, Memory, eldest of the Muses, is said to be 'placed in a manner ineffable/On the very pulse of Being' ['Les Muses', *OP*, 223].) All is not phenomenal *illusion*, but rather *allusion* to its objectively real origin and end; and the divine symphony is potentially decipherable by the poet in symbolic 'figures'. The *Cinq Grandes Odes* re-echo with triumphant jubilation at this deliverance out of meaninglessness, this 'co-naissance' into a universal, founding reality.

Yet the evangelisation of intellect is far from synonymous with the conversion of the whole personality, still less of its psycho-organic unconscious. Conversion never, for Claudel, eliminates desire as fact or as value ('And if desire were to cease with God,/Ah, I should envy Hell' [*OP*, 364]). And Claudelian desire is fraught with knots of psychosexual tension: deprivation of manifested affection in his strife-torn family; humiliated adoration for his sister Camille, whose erotic errancy fascinated and alarmed him; and a frustrated, fearful and self-condemning sexuality. The starched collar of the rising professional diplomat and *grand bourgeois* will be the sign of a perilous containment of psychic energies (the photos of the youthful Claudel, with their stubborn resolution and inner-burning fire, are singularly eloquent in this respect, and again parallel the illuminated intensity visible in the face of the young Valéry). The same energies are supercharged with the spiritual electricity of the time: negatively so, in resentful disappointment at the collapse of metaphysics and the triumph of a materialistic and mechanistic scientism; positively so, in mimetic contagion, at discovering the sacred fury of the prophets of 'the true life absent': Rimbaud's magic idealism and Wagner's 'summons of the hunting-horn' (strongly reminiscent by its *timbre* of the 'voice so rough, with love/horror/so veiled' of Valéry's poetic manuscripts (*JP* ms II, f.33).

Claudel's temperament is too earth-bound, too beset by coarse-grained, appetitive drives, for him to be anything other than a limping hybrid of spirit and mortal clay. If Erato, muse of mystico-lyric utterance and of passion, has her part in what he calls 'spirit', it is as a forked flame: too impatient, too flickering, too concupiscent and too grievance-haunted to be readily evangelised. All the more so since the reflexive finesse of Proust and Valéry, their subtle art of self-suspicion and self-discernment, are not immediate in Claudel.

The convert is thus very much open to the *surprise de l'amour* which came upon him in 1900. We know that this adulterous affair detained him, in flagrant contradiction with the moral ordering of love as defined by his new faith, for no less than four years of quasi-conjugal co-habitation. The affair ended, not by Claudel's volition, but by the departure in 1904 of his mistress, at that time expecting his child:

[...] J'ai connu cette femme. J'ai connu la mort de la femme.
J'ai possédé l'interdiction. J'ai connu cette source de soif!

J'ai voulu l'âme, la savoir, cette eau qui ne connaît point la mort! J'ai tenu entre mes bras l'astre humain!
O amie, je ne suis pas un dieu
Et mon âme, je ne puis te la partager et tu ne peux me prendre et me contenir et me posséder
Et voici que, comme quelqu'un qui se détourne, tu m'as trahi, tu n'es nulle part, ô rose!...
('L'Esprit et l'eau', *OP*, 245)

I knew that woman. I have known death brought by woman./I have possessed the thing forbidden. I have known that source of thirst!/I wanted your soul, to grasp it, that water which knows not death! I have held in my arms the human star!/Oh my darling, I am not a god/And my soul I cannot share with you and you cannot take and contain and possess me./And now, like someone turning away, you have betrayed me, and you are nowhere to be found, my rose!...

The sense of betrayal is very strong; and it is in many ways the key to what follows. It was lifted only in 1921, when Claudel came to understand that his lover's 'treachery' was motivated in part by the very reticence he himself expresses here and by her – perceptive and altruistic – determination to spare *him* the betrayal of his own deeper religious vocation.

His sense of resentful disarray was, however, tenacious and ramifying: Claudel felt that the 'human star' had been placed in his path, following the 'rejection' of his vocation at the Benedictine Abbey of Liguge, where he had presented himself as postulant immediately prior to the encounter of 1900. Immediately after the affair, and, at some level, for many years beyond that, he seems to have held against the Almighty a double grievance: that of rejecting his self-offering for the priestly and contemplative vocation; but also that of ordaining the fatality of his transgressive love-affair 'on the rebound', which he deemed to have finally destroyed it. This is the biographical origin of the adversarial interpellations in the *Cantique de Mesa*, which have understandably startled critics: 'Why are you playing the God with me?', 'And above Love/There is nothing, not even You!'[4]

At which point, he experienced a crisis of absence and darkness apparently undoing all his progress in faith since conversion:

Maintenant jaillissent
Les sources profondes, jaillit mon âme salée,
éclate en un grand cri la poche profonde de la pureté séminale!
Maintenant je me suis parfaitement clair, tout
Amèrement clair, et il n'y a plus rien en moi
Qu'une parfaite privation de Vous seul!... (*OP*, 246)

Now burst forth the deep wellsprings, now springs my salty soul, bursts in a great cry the deep-seated pocket of seminal purity!/Now I am entirely clear unto myself, quite/Bitterly clear, and there is within me/Just the perfect privation of You alone!...

One is reminded of Valéry's parallel 'awakening' of 1921: 'Alas my soul (ego) has plumbed the depths of its depth.' Valéry's reaction is to denounce in fury the deceptive tricks of the psyche which fashions in its own image the Complement of its own lack and longing ('The God is made of our impotency and our abandonment, taken in reverse').[5] By contrast, the bottom of Claudel's depth – the 'parfaite privation de Vous seul'– is a purification of the waters of desire, bringing a death of pride and a penitential rebeginning. The image of the 'poche profonde de la pureté séminale' brilliantly suggests psychosexual eros, but in its originally created, therefore good or 'pure', depth.

This re-beginning was to lead to the conviction that the trauma of unhappy passion had, after all, been a providential event, awakening him fully to the reality of divine Love of which the human 'star' was the sign and the mediating promise. Moreover, Claudel never ceased to be convinced that, far from being alone, his painful re-evaluation had benefited from the intercession of his confessor, whose death intervened two months after the departure of 'Ysé'.[6]

***

The figure of Eros redeemed in his work arises very directly from this experience. The effort to integrate transgressive *amour-passion* redemptively into his religious understanding is pursued in the first version of *Partage de Midi* (1905), conceived in the turmoil of the event by way of confession and exorcism. It is perfected and amplified in the more serene distance of *Le Soulier de satin* (1919–24). It is retraced in his commentary of 1943–45 on the *Cantique des Cantiques*; and receives a last reworking in the revised stage version of *Partage de Midi* of 1949. 'My whole life is involved, is the sense I have been led to understand' (*TH*, 1, 1344).

The basic figure is sketched in his work well before the crisis of 1900–04. In *La Ville* (1897), Lala says:

Je suis la promesse qui ne peut être tenue et ma grâce consiste en cela même
Je suis la douceur de ce qui est et le regret de ce qui n'est pas.
Je suis la vérité avec le visage de l'erreur, et qui m'aime n'a point souci de démêler l'une
de l'autre. (2e version, Acte III, *TH*, 1, 490)

I am the promise which cannot be kept and my grace consists in that very fact./I am the sweetness of what is and the regret of what is not./I am the truth with the face of error, and whoever loves me is not concerned to distinguish between them.

Her *raison d'être* in the order of creation is to awaken a desire which, though sweet and good in its proximate reality, points essentially beyond itself. The mystery of love exceeds every lover; and this very excess is a vector of transcendence, a 'grace' given in natural creation to all human beings. Yet because passion is blind, the risk lovers run is, idolatrously, to mistake for the transcendent Signified the human love-object, which is but the mediating sign. Claudel thus agrees with Valéry about the intimate relations between love and mysticism; but instead of reading mysticism as a reducible figure of the sex drive, he takes sexual passion, inversely, as an incomplete figure of love-union with God. Claudelian lovers are all potential mystics, the real question being whether they truly distinguish the shadow from the splendour – and how the Promise achieves its created calling.

Expressed in these terms, Claudel's basic figure certainly belongs within Christian orthodoxy. But it has many possible developments, many different cultural inflections and refractions. One of these, born of a syncretism with Neo-Platonic thought and already straining at the limits of orthodoxy, makes the Beloved a kind of appointed guide and mediatrix of divine grace: this is the Beatrice theme as invented by Dante. A further development, present in Novalis, Lamartine and Baudelaire (among others), makes the Beloved a pre-destined essence on the Plotinan model, sufficiently mediating between the human and the divine and representing the true goal of the unitive tension of human desire. On this account, to be with the human beloved eternally defines heaven, and Love is god: propositions entirely natural to Eros, and still commanding residual acceptance in Western culture, but falling outside Christian orthodoxy. (Gide's Pastor, in *La Symphonie pastorale*, strays in romantic bedazzlement across this same frontier.)

Inheriting from the '*caritas* synthesis' and affirming with St Augustine that 'There is only one Love', Claudel's many reworkings of the same figure of Eros redeemed trace a somewhat tortuous path, weaving in and out of the various possibilities outlined above. Fr André Blanchet recounts that he once recalled to Claudel Lacordaire's Augustinian maxim (often quoted by Claudel himself): 'There aren't two loves.' He received the interesting answer: 'I don't quite think that any more. Eros and Agape don't go together.'[7] The general sense of the dramatist's evolving vision of the case is perhaps contained in these words unpicking a culturally transmitted and temperamentally cherished temptation towards syncretism.

***

Certainly, *Partage de Midi* offers a profoundly hybrid figure. Romantic Eros is indeed understood in the perspective of the Promise which cannot be kept; but its attempted Christian redemption is realised in a hauntingly ambiguous and contestable form.

Mesa is the essential lover in Claudel's original and searching sense. He has loved God as earth-bound sons-of-Eve tend to do, demanding satisfaction of the totality of need and gift in himself:

> O la joie d'être pleinement aimé! ô le désir de s'ouvrir par le milieu comme un livre!
> [...]
> Moi qui aimais tellement ces choses visibles, ô j'aurais
> Voulu tout voir, avoir avec appropriation,

Non point avec les yeux seulement, ou les sens seulement, mais avec l'intelligence de
l'esprit,
Et tout connaître afin d'être tout connu. (*TH*, 1, 1001–2)

Oh the joy of being fully loved! Oh, the desire of opening up from the middle like a
book!/[…]/I who loved so much these visible things, Oh, I should have wished to see
everything, possess everything appropriatively,/Not with my eyes only, or my senses
only, but with spirit-led intelligence,/And to know everything so as to be entirely known.

His self-offering in religious vocation has, in this sense, been a self-related attempt
to reach out and grasp the mystic totality of the Promise. His concupiscent essentialism
makes him contemptuous of merely human loves ('but all loves are mere pretence/
Between man and woman the real questions are not even asked' [*TH*, 1, 996]) and
proudly separate from others ('I have a great seeding to defend' [*TH*, 1, 993]). At the
same time, his sense of incomprehensible 'rejection' leaves him devastatingly open
to an *amour* 'on the rebound'. Valéry's formula is integrally applicable: there will
be a projection of all deficiency and transcendence 'from the need for tenderness
right up to metaphysical appetite' (*C* XI, 808).

Ysé, too, is an essential lover, in a different sense. Her marriage to the weak,
vain and grasping de Ciz, has left her with a dissatisfaction which the passing of
youth transforms into an imperative demand: 'There is a certain totality of myself/
Which I have not yet given' (*TH*, 1, 1018). Just as Ysé represents for Mesa the
promise of an available transcendence, so he is for her, in his very unavailability, the
tantalising talisman to the missing totality. Hence the attraction felt by the lovers,
which Claudel underlines in the leitmotif of 'recognition': 'Mesa, I am Ysé, it is I
[…]. I am the one you would have loved' (*TH*, 1, 1003). Her version of their common
idolatry is the need to enfold and possess the human other with the same exigency of
total embrace with which Mesa had sought to compel the Love divine. The parallelism
is sharply etched when she says: 'Learn something from women! Ah, whoever gives
themselves will force acceptance of the gift' (*TH*, 1, 1008).

Yet if each recognises the other as unique key, each also represents a forbidden
love-object: she by virtue of her married status, he by reason of his prior and higher
calling, which preserves an inalienable claim upon him despite the crisis of failed
vocation. The sense of 'the impossible' determines the pact of Act I by which the
couple pledge themselves not to love. Mirroring Romantic tradition, however, this
very vow of separation also creates a transgressive fascination that precipitates the
lovers into the abyss. Under the searching midday sun of Act I, on the slow boat to
China, they speak of what is forbidden; in Act II, under the leaden skies of Hong
Kong, they will enact vertiginously that of which they speak.

The portrait of *amour-passion* in Act II is among the most memorable in French
literature: recapitulatively essentialised, lyrically vibrant – the Claudelian equivalent
of the second of Valéry's *Fragments du Narcisse*. Yet the presentation here is
controlled not by intellectual objectivity and mistrust of the supreme irrational value,

but by a theologically profound understanding, firmly drawn, of the mystery of an *idolatrous transcendence* within passion. The symbolic setting (curiously missed by most of Claudel's commentators) is a controlled allusion to Genesis. Stormy sky, shadow over the earth, wan daylight and graveyard recall the exile from paradise of the first couple and the transgression by which sin and death enter the world —'this accursed garden' (*TH*, 1, 1028). Mesa and Ysé slide towards consent in a kind of despairing semi-paralysis: he oppressed by exile and unfulfilment, she turned over to a fearsome liberty by the defection of her husband de Ciz, who remains more interested in his schemes for gain than in her confessed longing for a reckless and generous passion. Claudel shows us an explosive release in the lovers, as resistance ends and each is overwhelmed at the sense of completion found in the embrace of the other.

The delight of tenderness and intimacy follow. The ever-marvellous encounter with the sexual Other issues in a tumultuous Song of Songs:

> MESA: Tu es fraîche comme une rose sous la rosée! et tu es comme l'arbre cassie et comme la fleur sentante! et tu es comme un faisan, et comme l'aurore, et comme la mer verte au matin, pareillle à un grand acacia en fleurs et comme un paon dans le paradis. (*TH*, 1, 1025)

> MESA: You are fresh as a rose bedewed! And you are like the cassia-tree and the scenting flower! And you are like a pheasant, and like the dawn, and like the green sea in the morning, like an acacia in bloom and like a peacock in paradise.

Each is shown to remain a voluntary agent, conscious in transgression. Yet the call of reciprocal election in passionate sexual desire (the phenomenon known to film-makers as 'fatal attraction') is an all-powerful philtre: we remember, as does Claudel, the love potion taken by Tristan and Iseult on the slow boat from Ireland to Cornwall. Progressively, each answers the other in a crescendo of mimetic enfeverment. The forbidden fruit is tasted in a sphere of sacrality that is self-sufficient and relegates the world to inexistence:

> MESA: Je te préfère Ysé.
> YSÉ: O parole comme un coup à mon flanc! ô main de l'amour! ô déplacement de notre cœur!
> O ineffable iniquité! Ah viens donc et mange-moi comme une mangue! Tout, tout, et moi!
> Il est donc vrai, Mesa, que j'existe seule et voilà le monde répudié, et à quoi est-ce que notre amour sert aux autres? Et voilà le passé et l'avenir en un même temps
> Renoncés, et il n'y a plus de famille, et d'enfants et de mari et d'amis
> Et tout l'univers autour de nous
> Vidé de nous comme une chose incapable de comprendre et qui demande raison! (*TH*, 1, 1026)

MESA: I prefer you, Ysé.

YSÉ: Oh, the word that strikes a blow in my side! Oh hand of love! Oh the displacement of our heart!/Oh, unsayable iniquity! Ah, come then and devour me like a mango! Everything, everything, and myself!/Is it then true, Mesa, that I alone exist and that now the world is/Repudiated, and what use is our love to other people? And now the past and future are renounced both, and there no longer exists family, children, husband or friends/ And the whole universe around us is emptied of ourselves as something unable to understand, but importuning us with questions!

The essence of passion, for Claudel as for Valéry, is the call, not to sexual conjunction, but to spiritual fusion between reciprocal 'uniques'. Claudel displays it as a bid for godlikeness: spiritually stripping down and transgressing the limits of creaturely identity, in much the same way as the tearing off of clothes is demanded by impatience for physical union. Romantic Eros, on this account, is a reckless, violent and destructive soul-mysticism, infinitely transcending the search for sexual pleasure or even happiness:

YSÉ: Ah, ce n'est point le bonheur que je t'apporte, mais ta mort, et la mienne avec elle,
Mais qu'est-ce que cela me fait à moi que je te fasse mourir,
Et moi, et tout, et tant pis! pourvu qu'à ce prix qui est toi et moi,
Donnés, jetés, arrachés, consumés,
Je sente ton âme, un moment qui est toute l'éternité, toucher,
Prendre,
La mienne comme la chaux astreint le sable en brûlant et sifflant. (*TH*, 1, 1026–7)

YSÉ: Ah, it is not happiness I bring you, but death and mine along with it,/But what does it matter to me that I cause your death/And mine and the death of everything – who cares! Provided that at this cost which is the price of you and me,/Given, thrown out, snatched up and consumed,/I feel your soul, for a moment which is eternity, touch and take mine, as quicklime embraces the burning, bubbling sand.

To which mystical summons, also likened to a black flame of the soul, burning in a devastated city, the male voice answers with demiurgic consent. To experience passion is to know a power of exultant *revolt against the order of created nature*, undoing the work of differentiation which divided the waters from the dry land, male from female, I from Thou:

MESA: Voici entre mes bras l'âme qui a un autre sexe et je suis son mâle.
Et je te sens sous moi passionnément qui abjure, et en moi le profond dérangement
De la création, comme la Terre

Lorsque l'écume aux lèvres elle produisait la chose aride, et que dans un rétrécissement
effroyable
Elle faisait sortir sa substance et le repli des monts comme de la pâte!
Et voici une sécession dans mon cœur, et tu es
Ysé, et je me retourne monstrueusement
Vers toi et tu es Ysé!
Et tout m'est égal, et tu m'aimes, et je suis le plus fort! (*TH*, 1, 1027)

Now within my arms the soul which has another sex and I am its male./And I feel you
under me passionately abjuring, and in myself the profound dislocation/Of the created
world, as of the Earth/When with foam-flecked lips/It produced the dry land, and when
with a terrible contraction/It brought forth its substance and the folding of mountains
like paste!/And now the secession in my heart, and you are/Ysé!, and turn monstrously/
Towards you and you are Ysé/And nothing matters, and you love me, and I am the stronger
of us!

The holocaust of passion, coveting the communion of essences in defiance of the
ordering of the Creation, is chosen and sworn to by the lovers. At once, it re-orders
the small matter of their morality: Ysé henceforth wishes her husband dead, and
Mesa, in a masterly piece of hypocritical counsel to de Ciz, ensures that it will be so.
Claudel proposes in this scene a re-reading of Wagner in the light of Genesis – and
of his own transgressive passion.

If Act II is Fall, Act III is meant as Redemption. What figure of meaning did
Claudel intend? First, straightfowardly, he meant to show that the wages of sin is
irradiating death. The first movement of Act III accomplishes this. A *coup de théâtre*
reveals a new couple, Ysé and Amalric: the Promise has failed between the
transgressive lovers of Act II. Mesa has been unable to give the totality of himself;
Ysé has withdrawn in betrayal, abandoning both Mesa and her children by de Ciz,
and has sought the protection of the conqueror Amalric. The new couple, too, is
presently threatened with imminent death in the Boxer uprising, a death Ysé will
welcome as a release from obscure shame and nostalgia for the Promise lost. The
child born of her union with Mesa will also die. (Critics attuned to the violence of
transgressive desire in Claudel supply the thought that Ysé kills him in order to
liquidate the past; but the text of 1905 gives no clear warrant for this and later versions
remove any suggestion of it.) By another *coup de théâtre*, Mesa returns to contest
the possession of Ysé and the child; but his pleas and reproaches have no power to
resurrect the lost Promise, even though a legitimate union could now be formed,
given the death of Ysé's husband. He is, however, broken in violent struggle with
Amalric and again abandoned, this time to certain death, by the flight of his mistress
with his rival.

The *Cantique de Mesa* in the second movement of Act III has a pivotal function.
In ultimate communion with the splendour of the starry heavens, Mesa here sounds
the depths of despair, but also undergoes spiritual rebirth. His own suffering at betrayal
gives him insight into the nature of the Love always shown by the silent God, and he

abjures both his resentment at rejection and his transgressive passion. Through the suffering which unhappy passion brings, Mesa has learned how to give himself truly; his female Other has, in this sense, been the instrument of his eternal salvation.

And he of hers. For, Grace abounding, Ysé returns penitent to die with him, sacrificing her own life to the call of the true Promise reborn – a third *coup de théâtre*. In the final movement of the Act, the transgressive pact of Midday is replaced by a Midnight pact of a mystical marriage between the predestined lovers. The Promise will be fulfilled in eternal beatitude beyond the grave: this perspective animates a second love duo of operatic altitude and Wagnerian ambition – the duo of Eros redeemed.

'This is a sublimation,' explains the most orthodox of Claudel's commentators, Jacques Madaule, drawing out Claudel's meaning with strenuous – but confusing? – goodwill. 'For we have passed from the order of nature to that of Grace. The body no longer hides the soul but signifies it.' Despite 'serious failings', Mesa, in dereliction, has refound God; Ysé, for her part, has loved much. The triumph of the Catholic dramatist is to express the ineffable: 'the embrace of two souls, co-born without intermediary agency.' The finale shows us the true marriage, that of the Spouse and Bridegroom according to the *Song of Songs. Etiam peccata! Felix culpa!*[8]

Most subsequent commentators have been less receptive; not to mention the legion of those who habitually find Claudel 'unreadable', since they only ever discern an imperialistic Ego bizarrely rehearsing an incomprehensible or thoroughly objectionable theology. The closest the present reader can get to an exact assessment of this vexed case is to suggest that, because of his nearness to the event, and his anxiety to assert a happy outcome out of his own *infelix culpa,* the dramatist snatches at the desired figure of Eros redeemed – and misses it by a margin which is grievous, though it does not exclude flickering prophecy.

There is, first, an indubitable deficiency of incarnation. The pivotal pattern of penitence and consequent Grace is hardly made intelligible, let alone cogent, in psychological and dramatic terms. Only the Claudelian intertext will tell us, for instance, that the 'great, fearsomely melodious and shrill woman's cry' (*TH*, 1, 105) which accompanies Ysé's return expresses efficacious penitence in relation to her 'serious failings' (these include the essential sin of idolatry, and its moral consequences – double adultery, homicidal intent, treachery, abandonment of her children). Without such understanding, an audience will be hard put to imagine that Mesa's penitence has been for Ysé an efficacious channel of the Grace which has led her back.

The third and fourth of these 'failings' are repudiated later in Yse's 'confession' to Mesa. Yet the deficit here lies in his response:

MESA: C'est l'amour qui a tout fait. Eh, quoi? N'est-il donc pas pour nous la seule chose bonne et vraie et juste et signifiante?
Est-ce que les mots ont perdu leur sens? et n'appelons- nous plus
Le bien, ce qui facilite
Notre amour, et mal ce qui lui est opposé?

Dis, on l'appelle 'le triomphe de la nature et de la vie'. Et la mort même ne tranche pas
mieux les liens.
Que ne méritait pas entre nous une union si juste et si pure? Fort pure.
Certes, nous n'avons pas ménagé
Les autres; et, nous-mêmes, est-ce que nous nous sommes ménagés?
Me voici les membres rompus, comme un criminel sur la roue,
Et toi, l'âme outrée, sortie de ton corps comme une épée à demi dégainée! (*TH*, 1, 1057)

MESA: It is love which has done everything. Well, what of it? Isn't love for us the only
good and true and just and meaningful thing?/Have words lost their meaning? And do we
not call/Good what facilitates our love and evil what opposes it?/Say, don't they even
call it 'the triumph of nature and life'. And death itself does not better cut our links./What
did such a just and pure union not deserve between us? Very pure/Certainly, we did not
spare others; and did we spare ourselves? Here I am with broken limbs, like a criminal on
the rack,/And you, with soul distended, emerging form your body like a half-unsheathed
sword.

Some sophistries of the Romantic heart are pertinently displayed as such in this
bitter railing; but further layers of sophistry surround the surprising self-justification
which the dramatist appears to ventriloquise through his dramatic persona. We had
not noticed from the play that the passion of the lovers was 'so just and so pure'; or
that the damage inflicted on their own lives in any way made amends for the harm
wrought around them. If the emergent soul of Ysé is half-unsheathed from her body,
the sarcasm of the passage also reveals a half-hidden sword of phantasmal
compensation in the psyche of her creator, avenging humiliation and failure.

Mesa's own penitence and accession to Grace can be understood less prejudicially
than is sometimes claimed by Claudelophobe critics. It may not be true, for instance,
that Mesa decrees himself the cosmic funeral rites of the Romantic hero; merely
that, in exile, far from the sacramental help and comfort of his Church, the starry
heavens offer 'co-naissance' into the divine intelligibility, thus posing most
dramatically the problem of divine 'silence' as experienced by the man of faith. Nor
is it necessary to suppose that all the successive stages of Mesa's painful re-awakening
to Christian understanding and obedience equally represent exemplary attitudes,
expressing the finished pattern of meaning intended by the dramatist. Mesa is shown
to go through moments of revolt and grievance, in which his struggle with the angel
of divine Silence produces deeply jarring notes (in the very last version of the play,
Claudel uses Honneger's 'music of the stars' to mark out, and comment upon, the
successive phases involved). Most signally, it is unjust to Claudel to suggest that
Mesa's meditation fails to unearth the root of his sense of rejection by God, or to
achieve a genuine sense of penitence for pride, or to perceive how the suffering of
passion has been addressed precisely to his case: that of the 'sacré petit bourgeois'
whose greatest need was to learn how to love outside and beyond himself, and to
seek God for something more than 'an increase of my knowledge and my pleasure'
(*TH*, 1, 1050–1).

The enigmatic role of woman in his destiny is, in all these ways, firmly deciphered. The difficulty comes, however, in the adjustment of the two loves. Mesa declares that the misfortunes and sufferings of romantic *amour-passion* have enabled him to grasp the nature of the Passion of Christ, hence the meaning of the Love divine (Agape) and its redemptive efficacy:

Ah! je sais maintenant
Ce que c'est que l'amour! et je sais ce que vous avez enduré sur votre croix, dans ton Cœur,
Si vous avez aimé chacun de nous,
Terriblement comme j'ai aimé cette femme, et le râle et l'asphyxie et l'étau!
Mais je l'aimais, ô mon Dieu, et elle m'a fait cela!
Je l'aimais et je n'ai point peur de Vous,
Et au-dessus de l'amour, il n'y a rien, et pas Vous-même!
[...]
Mon crime est grand et mon amour est plus grand, et votre mort seule, ô mon Père,
La mort que vous m'accordez, la mort seule est à la mesure de tous deux. (*TH*, 1, 1051)

Ah! now I know/What love is! And I know what you endured on your cross, in your Heart,/If you loved each of us,/Terribly as I have loved this woman, and the death rattle and the asphyxia and the vice-grip of agony!/But I loved her, oh my God, and she, she did that to me!/I loved her and I do not fear You,/And above love, there is nothing, not even Yourself!/[...]/My crime is great and my love is greater, and your death alone, oh Father,/The death you grant to me, this death alone is of the measure of both of us.

This tormented harangue conflates a dolorist Christ and the suffering ego of the Romantic hero. Both innocent Victims are seen to illustrate the pain of rejection that the One Love always encounters in the world. (In the final version of the play, self-identification with the Crucified is even more abrupt: 'I loved her and she did that to me! You hear? That was done to both of us, comrade!') Claudel never, indeed, quite manages an 'I did that to you' or an 'Our love betrayed your love'. What is ambiguously called 'Love' is taken as *always-already cognate* with ultimate reality, and invokes its own source with assurance, even with a note of challenge. The filiation discovered between loves human and divine may well, of course, be significant in respect of the dramatist's own inner dealings with inherited guilt about sex, or the fear of hell, or superego images of God; but, however personally liberating to the dramatist, it provides a flawed theological basis for his artistic enterprise of displaying a Christian redemption of Eros. For, by virtue of the deficient likeness posited, 'redemption' itself is equated with *suffering* offered by way of *expiatory compensation or debt-repayment* —an all-too-human caricature of what New Testament writers mean by 'the Agape of the Cross'.

The finale, too, brings a problematic apotheosis. The controlling images are those of the great eagle lifting heavenwards the heavy and vanquished female clay, and of transfiguring fire, revealing 'the great male in the glory of God' (*TH*, 1, 1054, 1053). These images, recalling *Tête d'Or*, conjure up a scenario of longed-for vindication: no doubt Claudel's secret desire for a salvational role in bringing to God his unbelieving mistress... The scene as a whole lifts up operatically, like some symbolist 'monstrance', the Idea of the once-forbidden passion legitimised and fulfilled on the plane of eternity.

Marianne Mercier-Campiche comments tartly:

> Mesa ... fixes upon God the conditions of his rehabilitation. Is God an Avenger who requires propitiation? Mesa no longer has any assets to pay with save his [celestial] marriage programme. So let God consider this marriage as a penitence [...]. In fact, as 'penitence' for having coveted his neighbour's wife, Mesa attributes her to himself for eternity.[9]

Earnest Beaumont, for his part, ironises on the panoply of sacramental and sacerdotal functions which Claudel deploys in this scene: '[The lovers] embrace, in grandiose fashion, albeit quite untheologically, all the sacramental virtues which their 'mutual consent' suffices to confer on them.'[10]

Symptomatic of the ambiguities underlying the entire final scene is indeed Claudel's 'sacerdotal' re-use as between the Romantic lovers of words borrowed from the synoptic Christ: 'How long now, oh woman, before I drink you new in the Kingdom of God?' (*TH*, 1, 1060). Moreover, Ysé's response, 'Nothing except love forever, nothing save eternity with you' (*TH*, 1, 1054) sits uncomfortably with the words of Mesa's divine 'comrade' about marriage and the life everlasting ('They are neither married nor given in marriage').[11] On the best hypothesis, the dramatist is summoning the lovers to an ontic-nuptial soul-union 'in God'; but this notion, derived from the traditional Catholic reading of the *Song of Songs*, remains obscure in content and under-realised dramatically, as well as unexplored in its theological credentials.

In short, the lyrico-theological rocket of 1905, despite developing powerful vertical thrust on take-off, falters in the launch and, arguably, self-destructs. There is a deficit of dramatic incarnation, much vitiated pseudo-theology, over-visible patterns of moral sophistry and psychological compensation, an excess of fevered love-rhetoric in emulation of Wagner (not yet declared 'poisonous' by Claudel).[12] Yet the finale remains the abortive monument to a profoundly respectable aspiration. The Catholic dramatist had wished to suggest the transfigured splendour of human love, viewed in its created potential and its divine fulfilment:

> YSÉ: Mais maintenant je vois tout et je suis vue toute, et il n'y a qu'amour entre nous,
> Nets et nus, faisant l'un de l'autre vie, dans une interpénétration
> Inexprimable, dans la volupté de la différence conjugale, l'homme et la femme, comme deux grands animaux spirituels. (*TH*, 1, 1059)

But now I see everything and I am entirely seen, and only love subsists between us,/ Clean and naked, bringing life each to the other, and an interpenetration/Which is ineffable, in the delight of conjugal difference,/Man and woman, like two great spiritual animals.

What falls to earth is the duo of Love redeemed and glorious, answering the splendidly realised duo of Act II, of fallen and deviant love. Yet Erato's forked flame is still perhaps, even on this accountancy, half-prophetic. How well, it asks, and with what legitimacy, does nuptial Eros allow us to imagine by analogy the eschatological form of Agape? No doubt 'as in a glass darkly'...

**

The challenge, and the ambiguity, at least, are not forgettable; nor are they forgotten by Claudel. The decisive explanation of 1921 with the real-life 'Ysé' liberated him,[13] inviting him to apply for the first time to his own inner drama the reconciling inspiration explored in *L'Annonce faite à Marie*. The redemptive antidote in that play is the willing renunciation of concupiscence and an acceptance of the need to love altruistically, generously, at the cost of personal sacrifice. The significance of non-gratification, unfulfilment and absence as a factor in the divinisation of love was also confirmed by the dramatist's re-reading of Dante. In the *Ode Jubilaire*, he has Dante's Beatrice explain the necessity of her withdrawal in death from her lover: it takes a profound wound to ensure that the latter cannot give himself over to ephemeral things; he will, as poet, only give back the world to God when it does not appear to him complete or self-sufficient. If human lovers would shine with the radiance of the creating Love, they must learn to strip down appetitive and self-centred desire, and regain the integrity of their created nature. The terrible suffering and loss of a great passion unfulfilled can be an apprenticeship in and for the Love divine.

Le Soulier de satin shares with *Partage de Midi* the theme of an impossible passion. Deepest reciprocal attachment is here destined to unfulfilment – at least, in the normal sense of mutual presence, physical communion, the attempt to achieve human happiness together. Prouhèze, twice married, but never to the man she loves, will live out her life half a world away from Rodrigue, and the play will present only two encounters between them. In part the obstacle is the respect due, and here given, to the sacrament of marriage; more secretly, it lies in the logic of the Promise of love itself. The love-bond, reduced to its pure form of reciprocal desire and other-centred devotion, is presented as a kind of marriage of the heart: 'Are [lovers] not the work each of the other, in a word, is there not between them a true marriage the form of which is, not a *yes*, but a *no*, a refusal declared to the flesh in the name of the star?'[14] Constrained, heroic, and exceptional in its forms, this love is nevertheless for Claudel the limit case which allows a fundamental truth to emerge about the nature and potential of all human Eros.

An abyss of virtue, literally ocean-wide, replaces the erotic errancy of the earlier play. The action is concerned rather with how the lovers cope redemptively with the misfortune of impossibility and separation; in particular, it explores how Romantic passion, not succumbing to its darker, idolatrous virtualities and renouncing sexual expression, is transformed into love, and how it achieves *in absentia* the transcendent Promise carried within it. In relation to the earlier figure, there is also a significant reversal of roles: it is Prouhèze who leads the way, Beatrice-like, in showing that the lover must become mystic; and Rodrigue, the earth-bound Conquistador who follows, bruised and limping. There is also a shift in theological focus: this second figure of Eros redeemed will speak from what is undoubtedly the centre of Claudel's Catholic faith, the doctrine of creation (understood in ontotheological terms) and that of the communion of saints. The sense of providential patterns, discernable in individual destinies and in the larger canvas of history, sustains the whole composition.

In presenting the lovers, the dramatist makes it clear that the mystical impulse is not an artifical appendage, but the natural heart of love:

> DON CAMILLE: Celle qui aime, les poètes ne disent-ils pas qu'elle gémit de n'être pas toute chose pour l'être qu'elle a choisi? Il faut qu'il n'ait plus besoin que d'elle seule […].
> DONA PROUHEZE: Ah! ce n'est pas la mort, mais la vie que je voudrais apporter à celui que j'aime,
> La vie, fût-ce au prix de la mienne. (*TH*, 2, Version int., 676)

> DON CAMILLE: Do not the poets say of the woman who loves that she laments at not being everything to her chosen One? He should need only her […].
> DONA PROUHEZE: Ah! It is not death, but life that I should wish to give to the man I love. Life, even at the price of my own.

The self-giving instinct of the lover can be channelled towards life (as in Prouhèze), or towards possessive appropriation and death (as it will be in the significantly named Don Camille);[15] but overflowing generosity is at all events a defining attribute of the 'transcendence' experienced by those who love. Replying later to her chaperone Don Balthasar, Prouhèze confirms that her impulse is to give body and soul to Rodrigue: 'What have I of my own that does not belong to him? I would give him the entire world if I could' [683]. It is this self-same logic that will command her eventual decision to dismiss her beloved and to 'betray' him:

> DONA PROUHEZE: Il y a quelqu'un pour toujours de la part de Dieu qui lui interdit la présence de mon corps
> Parce qu'il l'aurait trop aimé. Ah! je veux lui donner beaucoup plus!
> Que tiendrait-il si je le lui donnais? comme si ce que je lis dans ses yeux qu'il me demande pouvait avoir une fin! (779)

DONA PROUHEZE: There is someone, forever put there by God, who forbids [Rodrigue] the presence of my body/Because he would have loved it too much. Ah! I want to give him much more!/What would he have if I were to give it to him? As though what I read in his eyes that he asks of me could have an end!

Nor is she mistaken about Rodrigue. The male Conquistador – the expression is almost a pleonasm in Claudel's view of the sexes in this play – is shown to experience in admiration for her beauty a sense of self-transcendence. Between his discovery of Prouhèze and the sense of cosmic beauty that had overwhelmed him at the sight of the queenly star during a night watch on his ship in the Caribbean, he draws this parallel:

DON RODRIGUE: Ah! c'était le même saisissement au cœur une seconde, la même joie immense et folle!
Aucun homme ne peut vivre sans admiration. Il y a en nous l'âme qui a horreur de nous-mêmes,
Il y a cette prison dont nous avons assez, il y a ces yeux qui ont le droit de voir à la fin! Il y a un cœur qui demande à être rassasié! (*TH*, 2, version int., 695–6)

DON RODRIGUE: Ah! I felt the same instantaneous seizure of the heart, the same immense, wild joy!/No man can live without admiration. There is in us a soul which is in horror of ourselves,/There is that prison of the self which palls, there are those eyes which have a right, after all, to their seeing!/There is a heart which demands its fullness.

The 'romance' of love reveals this imperative truth of the human spirit more fundamentally than it shows man to be a libidinal animal: the whole of this shrewdly humorous scene, in which the star-struck lover confides in his caustic Chinese attendant, turns on this point. To fall in love is to be co-born into the melody of the created universe, repeating (like the poet of the *Cinq Grandes Odes*) its splendour and its gift. Rodrigue's desire is not for the body of the beloved, but – with a radicalism outstripping anything in Proust or Valéry – for 'what is the cause of herself ... producing life under my kisses and not death' (698). Only 'that star which, in the depths of herself, unknown to herself, she is' (698) can content the lover's thirst in him; a thirst he already sees as 'impossible in this life'. Yet nothing else will do.

Rodrigue does not always speak at this altitude. The play will display him as mimetic rival to Camille, proposing to seduce and abandon Prouhèze if only he can get her into his power. Yet for Claudel, the most earth-bound and concupiscent love cannot help knowing in privileged instants that what it truly desires in the beloved is the creative source in Being from which her brilliancy springs; it is this Promise which she allusively signifies. The play's discourse on desire, and indeed the entire action, are to be understood in the perspective of the Promise which cannot be kept, and of the strange, unlikely grace that this promise may constitute precisely for the most earth-bound among humankind.

Against all modern instincts, Claudel will not let us think that sexual unfulfilment is necessarily a crippling and masochistic perversity. Prouhèze's Guardian Angel clarifies her own intuition in a key exchange which is strangely neglected by critics:

L'ANGE GARDIEN: Il était bon que tu lui apprennes le désir.
DONA PROUHEZE: Le désir d'une illusion? d'une ombre qui pour toujours lui échappe?
L'ANGE GARDIEN: Le désir est de ce qui est, l'illusion de ce qui n'est pas. Le désir au travers de l'illusion
Est de ce qui est au travers de ce qui n'est pas.
DONA PROUHEZE: Mais je ne suis pas une illusion, j'existe! Le bien que je puis seule lui donner existe.
L'ANGE GARDIEN: C'est pourquoi il faut lui donner le bien et aucunement le mal.
(819)

GUARDIAN ANGEL: It was good that you should teach him desire.
DONA PROUHEZE: The desire of an illusion? Of an ever-fugitive shadow?
GUARDIAN ANGEL: Desire is for what is, illusion for what is not. Desire through illusion is for what is through what is not.
DONA PROUHEZE: But I am no illusion, I exist! The good which I alone can give him exists!
GUARDIAN ANGEL: That is why you must give him the good and not at all the ill.

There is water for the thirst of the creature; thirst itself, in the good order of Creation, is a sign of it. She herself escapes illusion, sterility, and ultimate nothingness in so far as she points to it and mediates Rodrigue's acceptance of it. She must become a star in the created brilliancy which she carries within herself – what the Angel calls 'this child of God in the light, whom I salute'. Will it be the *same* Prouhèze, she asks – and still beautiful, still lovely to Rodrigue?

L'ANGE GARDIEN: Ce qui te rend si belle ne peut mourir. Ce qui fait qu'il t'aime ne peut mourir.
[...]
DONA PROUHEZE: C'était beau d'être pour lui une femme
L'ANGE GARDIEN: Et moi je ferai de toi une étoile
DONA PROUHEZE: Une étoile! C'est le nom dont il m'appelle toujours dans la nuit.
Et mon cœur tressaillit profondément de l'entendre
L'ANGE GARDIEN: N'as-tu donc pas toujours été comme une étoile pour lui?
DONA PROUHEZE: Séparée!
L'ANGE GARDIEN: Conductrice. (820)

GUARDIAN ANGEL: What makes you so beautiful cannot die. What makes him love you cannot die.
[...]
DONA PROUHEZE: It was fine to be a woman for him.
GUARDIAN ANGEL: And I will make you a star.
DONA PROUHEZE: A star! That's the name he always calls me by in the night. And my heart quivers to hear it.
GUARDIAN ANGEL: Have you not, then, always been a sort of star to him?
DONA PROUHEZE: Remote!
GUARDIAN ANGEL: Guiding!

This exchange, simple and profound in its poetry, establishes the 'good' Prouhéze can and must do for her beloved. It determines the conversion of desire into 'love', for to *love* is to desire the good of the beloved, rather than any self-related possession. At the same time it gives no theological hostages to fortune: Prouhéze and Rodrigue are not predestined *âmes sœur.* Their destinies are linked, not before all worlds, but in the particularised providence of Grace; and they will ultimately know each other as risen stars by participation in the recreating Light (the highly orthodox Angel even suggests that the resurrection of the flesh comes later!). Nothing is proposed but a transcendent fulfilment of created nature; and this itself does no violence to the creaturely humanity of the characters. Clearly, this discourse on the nature and meaning of human desire conditions the entire action of the play; and the play itself is readable or not according as we follow it.

***

It lies beyond the scope of this book to examine whether readability, in this impressive but sprawling work, signifies entire conviction in dramatic terms. Claudelophobes may find themselves consenting beyond expectation to the shrewdness and vigour of the psychology, or drawn by the visionary sweep of historical imagination; even, perhaps, projected beyond secure modern *évidences* by the persuasion of the period ethos, powerfully realised, or by the poetry of Claudel's lyric voice. The residual difficulty lies in the 'providential' patterns showing Eros in its travail of redemption within the larger love bond of mystic solidarity which Claudel's Catholic faith calls the 'communion of saints'.

This bondedness allows unsuspected interactions within a single 'economy' of Grace. It is as universal as the oceans which, visibly, link the separated lovers and as the overarching heavens by which, from continent to continent, they commune with each other. The Prologue establishes these two controlling metaphors. Rodrigue's brother, the Jesuit priest, drifts on the hulk of a ransacked galleon in mid ocean, under starry heavens. He is himself the victim of the violence and death generated by the struggle for domination of the Americas. His dying prayer sets the entire action of the play in the perspective of the fundamental pattern Claudel sees at work in all events: the redemptive transformation by which evil, with its trail of violence and disruption, is rewoven ceaselessly into new figures of a providential good.

It is in this perspective that we are invited to view Rodrigue's own career and, implicitly, the drama of the age. The Conquistador, the man of large scale appetitive desire, is himself (like every human soul) the object of a Desire which seeks to win him in love. Grace is seen as the secretly operative presence of the God who is 'absent' to all earth bound senses, discernable only to the heart of faith. Its instrument is the love-wound of absence: the more the lovers love in dedicated separation, the more they are conformed to 'their original wholeness and very essence', which is the likeness of God himself, written into the flesh. Claudel wishes to show 'sublimation', chosen and guided by Grace, producing sanctification.

The pattern is original (beyond Corneille and Rousseau, and quite unimagined by Freud); but it is also problematic in its dramatic embodiment. The star struck lover and mystic, as we have already noticed, is also the potential ravisher and destroyer. The King shrewdly exploits the frustration of the hero's love wound in the service of Catholic Spain, seeing in it a dynamic purged of the merely personal temptations of greed and debauchery. In the post colonial era, we are more reticent of the will to dominion, however disinterested and visionary – particularly where sexual frustration may be suspected as its mainspring. No doubt one should allow Claudel to claim in reply that his play is excited by the possibilities of a united world (the value of Catholic universality), rather than those of subjugation (theocratic totalitarianism). And no doubt it is possible to allow him more credit than is sometimes given for pertinent historical realism: the sixteenth century did indeed cover with the Christian cross its own quasi-erotic dream of 'the power and glory'.

In this world, however, the Conquistador hero evolves amid ambiguities. Rodrigue is seen as the brutal visionary of total conquest, destroying Almagro's civilising colony, and using calculated injury and injustice to extend to the entire continent a domination of fire and blood. If the crooked lines in which unregenerate humanity writes history are unattractive, the straighter lines of super-writing Providence, into which Rodrigue enters from Prouèze's death, are inadequately realised. No less an authority than the Guardian Angel tells us that the Conquistador's subsequent adventures in Japan make him an ambassador to those who dwell in darkness: 'he brings with him enough sin to understand their darkness. God has given him joy enough to understand their despair' (825). We readily admit the first proposition, but are left by Claudel to imagine the second.

The conversion of desire does achieve a certain degree of plausible consistency in the sequence of the fourth Day, centring on the misreported conquest of England by the Armada. Claudel uses this counter-historical hypothesis very imaginatively to ironise the attempt of the age of conquest to write the playscript of history. Rodrigue appears here as the liberal visionary who envisages a non-military solution for governing England, and who preaches a co-sharing of the Americas, healing in the New World the bloody conflicts of the Old. For which insolence, he pays with final disgrace and imprisonment. At this point, we can conceive of him as the object of the prayers focused upon him, even if his geo-political vision is never less than imperial: 'I cannot ensure peace except you give me the entire world' (933). His evolution is completed as, stripped of all power and all glory, he awaits death humbly as the servant of Theresa of Avila.

The dramatist's renewed plea, registered in the epigraph to the play, is 'Etiam peccata': even the tortuous ways of sinful human desire pre-trace the straight paths of salvation and serve obliquely the good purposes in history of God. Yet the translation of the deeds of earth into the patterns of heaven still remains, arguably, flawed and ambiguous. Claudel's own counter reformation faith hardly allows it to be otherwise. Is he too eager to espouse the divine viewpoint; too avid for Catholic supremacy; too indifferent to the means of its accomplishment, or too complacent about the economy of compensation between high mystical contemplation and worldly *realpolitik* – too prompt, perhaps, in assuming the seamless robe of the One Love?

***

That Claudel himself knew the limitations of his figure of love's redemption is attested by the very last reworking of the problematic final scene of *Partage de Midi*. In the revised 1949 version, all operatic pseudo theology drops away, the divine viewpoint is eschewed. A sober and symbolic stage language is entrusted with conveying, in directly personal terms, the decanted aspirations of the original finale. Ysé returns in compassion and kneels – 'no penitential idea being implied' – beside her stricken lover: 'I couldn't leave you like this.' The chair in the form of an Omega expresses a togetherness in the ultimate of the lovers who in life held the key to the spiritual destinies of each other. Ysé has taught Mesa to ask and to give all that was in him. He says still: 'I cannot give you heaven and earth.' 'You need only hold out your hand,' she replies. And she pleads (perhaps in echo to the penitent thief of Luke's gospel): 'Remember me, in the darkness, who was once your vine.' For the rest, the ultimate mystery of Love in its triangularity is respected. The play ends with the luminous uplifted hand that pleads for mercy and which points to glory. And there is a brusque curtain (*Nouvelle version, TH*, 1, 1228).

This poignant sobriety, so moving after the baroque exuberance of *Le Soulier de satin*, bespeaks a dramatist who has painfully come to terms with the ambiguities of his own figure of Eros redeemed. It is not difficult to fault Claudel's figure for its sins of commission (its psychological shadows, its theologico-cultural confusions, its overbidding) or of omission (the Promise is overwhelmingly transcendent: of earthly joys and time-bound relationships – including marriage – it has little to say). Yet Claudel's singular charge of lyrico-dramatic electricity is born of a vitalising contact established between the poles of Eros and Agape, constitutive of the entire force-field of Western culture. Can we even regret his prematurely reconciling synthesis between them? The struggle with inevitable deficiencies is, for this poet-dramatist of unique range and ambition, the source of perhaps the profoundest, as well as the most contestable, of our three explorations of the idolatries of Eros.

Claudel alone dares to imagine that the Romantic notion of love was, in its idolatry, too pinched and too small. Questioning Erato, he reads: 'An answer in your eyes! An answer and a question in your eyes' ('Les Muses', *OP*, 233).

Notes

1 P. Claudel, *Cinq Grandes Odes*: 'L'esprit et l'eau', in: *Œuvre poétique* ed. J. Petit, Bibliothèque de la Pléiade (Paris: Gallimard, 1967), p. 248. Further references will be given in the text as *OP* followed by page number.
2 *Cahiers Paul Claudel* II (Paris: Gallimard, 1960), pp. 171–3.
3 Letter to P. de Tonquédec, 13 June 1917, quoted by P. de Tonquedec, *L'Œuvre de Paul Claudel* (Paris: Beauchesne), p. 196.
4 P. Claudel, *Théâtre*, 2 vols, ed. J. Madaule & J. Petit, Bibliothèque de la Pléiade (Paris: Gallimard, 1965–67), Vol. 1 (1965), p. 1051. Further references will be given in the text as *TH* followed by volume and page number.
5 P. Valéry, *Cahiers* (*C* VIII, 139 and 466); see Chapter 7, note 2, *supra*.
6 See F. Varillon, *Claudel: 'Les Écrivains devant Dieu'* (Paris: Desclée de Brouwer, 1967). Varillon quotes (p. 62) his confessor's letter to Claudel of 3 December 1903, and (p. 60) Claudel's letter to G. Frizeau, 6 September 1905.
7 Quoted by A. Blanchet, *La Littérature et le spirituel* (Paris: Aubier, 1961), p. 321, note 5.
8 J. Madaule, *Le Drame de Paul Claudel* (Paris: Desclée de Brouwer, new edn, 1964), p. 217ff.
9 M. Mercier-Campiche, *Le Théâtre de Claudel, ou la puissance du grief et de la passion* (Paris: Pauvert, 1954), pp. 149–50.
10 E. Beaumont, *Le Sens de l'amour dans le théâtre de Claudel* (Paris: Les Lettres Modernes, 1958), p. 55.
11 Luke 20: 35.
12 See P. Claudel, 'Le Poison wagnérien' (1938), in: *Œuvres en prose*, ed. J. Petit & C. Galoperine, Bibliothèque de la Plèiade (Paris: Gallimard, 1965), pp. 367–72.
13 P. Claudel, *Mémoires improvisés recueillis par Jean Amrouche* (Paris: Gallimard, 1954), p. 269.
14 P. Claudel, 'Paul Claudel interroge le "Cantique des cantiques"', *Œuvres complètes* (Paris: Gallimard, 1963), Vol. XXII, p. 1963.
15 Claudel's sister Camille had reacted in savage revolt to her abandonment by her lover Rodin in favour of a previous mistress. Don Camille recalls the cruelty and ultimate madness her brother perceived in Camille's pagan drive to possess or re-possess her lover.

The Immanent Beyond

Libido Liberated and Love Sublime

The constellation of experimental art, thought and existential invention known as Surrealism is prophetic for the twentieth-century decipherment of Eros. The Surrealists drew a line under the culture and civilisation that had come to a terminal expression in the First World War. Explosively and publicly, they declared a rebeginning. Theirs was the first movement to incorporate the Freudian discovery of the unconscious and of the world of dream; and the first to link Freudian perspectives and insights with those of Marx and, more implicitly, of Nietzsche, in the triangular matrix of influence that formatively impressed a vast part of France's intellectual élite throughout the century just closed.

In a climate made momentous by the Great War and by the shock-waves it sent throughout the entire sphere of assumptions about 'Western civilisation', the starched collar of polite bourgeois constraint was torn off, and all veils removed. In and through the exercise of imagination, the young Surrealist grouping revelled in sexual energy and its irradiating virtue of 'sublimation'. In the feminised Paris of *Poisson Soluble*, in the 'automatic' poems of Breton's *Immaculée conception*, as in the paintings of Magritte or Dali, we encounter, hauntingly allusive or scandalously flaunted, a totally 'libidinal' mindsphere. The poet or painter was called to restore sexual eros, long repressed and culpabilised, to full innocence and to the playful inheritance of both body and deep psyche; art being, as Freud proclaimed, the domain of the pleasure principle. The hidden continent which psychoanalysis had opened up to view was thus joyfully annexed in the service of the Surrealist project of emancipation ('Huge joy, like the balls of Hercules').[1]

Yet the libidinal 'tail' of the Surrealist comet was truly significant only in relation to its incandescent spiritual 'heart'. The 'sublimity' of Surrealist love lies in the quest for a sublimation of sexual energies which, in bonding with the sexual Other, produces an intensity of apotheosis, surmounting all experienced dualities in a total and totally transforming expenditure of psychic possibility: 'the highest degree of elevation, the limit-point where the conjunction of all sublimations occurs, the geometric point in which are forged together, diamond-like and unalterable ... the flesh and the heart.'[2]

That this 'point limite' is nothing other than a super-volted distillation of Romantic *amour-passion* is confirmed by the defining features which Péret's grand narrative immediately adds: permanent fixation of desire on the one-and-only object; the transfiguring sense of the marvellous produced by 'crystallisation'; the catalysing role of the heart, transforming sexual attraction into something different in nature; the necessary complementarity of the lovers, mysterious and pre-ordained; the imperative relational need, more vital than oxygen, thus created; the goal of totally fulfilling happiness, and so on. Yet Romantic *amour-passion* is here radicalised both by its adaptation to an experimental framework (non-metaphysical and atheistic) and by its espousal of the principle of Eros in a post-Freudian, radically libertarian understanding. Where Proust, Valéry and Claudel mistrustfully disengage from the Romantic model, Surrealism will be concerned purely and simply to discern in it the whole will of the immanent god, and to raise Eros to the highest power of expression that is his due.

This project constitutes a bid for a human transcendence out of immanent depths. Sublimation of instinctual drives will be possible once the Christian shadow of 'sin' is lifted and the moral goodness attributed by Rousseau to the original and pre-civilised depth of nature in humankind is allowed free-play. The 'little desire' of the flesh will lift up the 'Grand Desire' of the spirit to the extent that sexual energy is recognised as its true fount and origin. Sublimity in love, that is, is seen to follow unproblematically from the sublimation of instinctual drives. The weight of Surrealist prophecy consists, therefore, in denouncing love's extrinsic alienations: social conditions, the inequality of the sexes, and, primordially, the repressive phantom of the metaphysical Other. 'In order to form the perfect androgyne, the symbolic system for generating happiness, humankind must bring its gaze back from heaven to earth and seek there the being which will allow it to reconstitute itself whole' (AAS, 49).

The articulating syntax of this dream is made in the nineteenth century, and, as we saw in Benjamin Péret, it is basically Hegelian. In Péret's grand liberation narrative, Abelard and Héloïse are the precursors. With courtly love, history reaches the equivalent of Columbus' cry of 'Land!' De Sade, however ambiguously, is the encyclopdaedist and prophet-martyr of libido unlimited (though was he not tempted, asks Péret, by sublime love in his late attachment to Marie Quesnet? [AAS, 56]).

Predictably, the nineteenth century represents – if not the promised Land – at least the homeland of the Promise (it supplies, as such, two thirds of Péret's anthologised texts). Its depth of religious inwardness is centred on the angelic unconscious, a flowering of the marvellous and a dream of the restored golden age. In spiritual and metaphysical terms, it accomplishes the displacement or transfer of the deepest affects of desire from an illusory collective divinity to the individual human Other: 'Formerly, it was in the depths of the divinity that man attempted to lose himself in order to acquire something of this. Henceforth it is from someone of the opposite sex that divinity is to be obtained, by conferring it on her. This twofold operation, by its irrational character, participates in the marvellous' (AAS, 61). Its love-ethic rises up against the prudential and hypocritical model of bourgeois marriage: 'The bourgeois could only offer a caricature of love, conjugal by day, libertine by night' (AAS, 62). In social and political terms, the current of utopian socialism (Saint-Simon, Fourier, Enfantin) reaches out to relieve the inferiority of woman; humanitarian solidarity is henceforth the necessary corollary of sublime love. In the words of Rimbaud ('in other respects a stranger to sublime love'): 'love is to be re-invented like all the rest' (AAS, 62–3).

In its retrospective retelling of 1956, this imperative call, with its sense of momentous possibility, encounters, however, a significant moment of disenchantment. Love remains the obsessive preoccupation of all manifestations of popular culture, but it consistently does so, notes Péret platonically, in the mode of aspiration and privation. Sexual differentiation, far from progressing, is in inverse evolution; there is 'an alarming aggravation of disorders of affectivity'; and the disappointments experienced in derisory experiences of love are reflected in recrimination between the sexes.

Strategically, Péret sees a disjunction, a discordance of rhythm, between the new sensibility and 'the liberation, now complete in our own day, of sexual relations' (*AAS*, 64). He repeats, for the avoidance of doubt, that 'sublime love implies the greatest sexual liberty', the *sine qua non* of meaningful encounter and recognition. Yet the necessary condition, being fulfilled, turns out not to have been a sufficient one:

> The rampart of sexual prejudices has been overrun, but it concealed a marsh, previously unsuspected, in which people are tending to become bogged down. Instead of the ascent to which sublime love invites us, sexual licence with no other horizon can only diminish human beings just as much as the severest taboo; but whereas taboo sometimes has the power to tense the springs of the human being, licence can only wear them out and may prepare the way for a new age of sexual constraint. (*AAS*, 64)

The Surrealist task has been to rehabilitate the flesh in its splendour, and to dissolve 'the grimacing phantom of sin in a daylight illumined by the beauty of woman'. Yet in the glowering mid-twentieth-century horizon, only 'a severe ascesis' ('une ascèse sévère') can procure 'the conditions of amorous grace' (*AAS*, 67).

Logically, this retrospective disenchantment opens up the possibility of a very different Grand Narrative from the one Péret has in fact given us. Yet no revisionism is in fact possible. Plato's demi-god – however *half*-godlike – is still sacred:

> Of all feelings, I see only love as sacred. If love is sacred, this is because the notion of the sacred derives so directly from love that, without it, no sacredness is conceivable (divine love being merely a confiscation of human love for, in effect, privative purposes). (*AAS*, 72)

The second great impulse of liberationist thinking, which intervened in France after the explosion of May 1968, happening on a much larger scale and with far wider societal effects, will yet happen in perceptible continuity with Surrealism: with its psychoanalytical springboard, its narrativisation of history, its aspirational dream-syntax, its displacements, its sacrality – and its haunting shadow of discrepancy between intention and achievement.

We may follow this curve in the work of Breton, Bataille and Duras.

Notes

1   Benayoun, *Érotique du Surréalisme* (Paris: Pauvert, 1957), p. 95.
2   B. Péret, *Anthologie de l'amour sublime* (Paris: Albin Michel, 1956), p. 9. Further references will be given in the text as *AAS* followed by page number.

Chapter 9

André Breton's Starry Castle

A flanc d'abîme, construit en pierre philosophale, s'ouvre le château étoilé. [1]

Founder and high priest of Surrealism, Breton drew from the poets of 'la vraie vie absente' and from the earliest French translations of Freud[2] an existentially assumed poetics of desire, signalling a new starburst of human possibility.

Freud had made a new economy of desirousness thinkable. 'Libido', ramifying in infinitely inventive disguises out of the dynamic unconscious, as in dream, is perceived by Breton to be the energy behind all psychic life and the force that makes history. Bound and unbound, desire is, definitively, the essence of man. The cult of it, eroticism – 'magic of life-energy expressed principally by the awakening of sexual potency'[3] – is held to deliver man from prohibitions and taboos. Reconnection to the libidinal unconscious is the Key, releasing human potential as such.

Clearly, Breton's erotology moves, in its magic idealism, well beyond Freud, whose clinical rationalism, moral pessimism and therapeutic concern for re-adapting libidinal excess or dysfunction to 'normality' represented in many respects the reverse of everything Breton sought. More than a new clinical therapy, Breton sees as akin to a new religion for modern times something emanating from the crypt of the psyche, just as primitive Christianity emerged from the catacombs of Rome. The *Dictionnaire abrégé du Surréalisme* (1938) defines eroticism, with jubilantly esoteric hints, as a subversive and sacralising cult: 'Sumptuous ceremony in an underground place' (II, 808).

Gathering (with Freud) the tangled threads of human desire into a single immanent source, posited to be henceforth decipherable, Breton re-projects these energies (like Rimbaud) into a life-transfiguring alchemy of poetic imagination. His projected figure is resolutely 'ascendant'. Eros is embraced above all in its 'sublime' (aspirational) potential, affirmatively linked to Freudian 'sublimation'. Here is the true formulary of all humanity's waking dreams of transcendence:

> It was to be expected that sexual desire, previously more or less thrust back into troubled or unhappy consciousness by taboos, should turn out, in the last resort, as it unbound desire, to be the vertiginous, the priceless 'this side', by prolonging which, without limitation, human dreams have constructed all 'beyonds'. (III, 8)

> Not only must the exploitation of man [...] by the supposed 'God' of absurd and provoking memory cease. The problem of the relations of men and women must, without the slightest residual hypocrisy and in a manner that brooks no delay, be revised from top to bottom.[4]

Breton is thus the explorer of an immanent human Beyond. Its most fully realised form is 'the mysterious, improbable, unique, confounding and unsayable love' of which he already speaks in *Nadja* (I, 736).

He is also the stern guardian of that dream. What has often appeared to later 'libido liberators' as an inexplicable conservatism in matters of sexuality is very directly accounted for in the logic of this implicit bid for a 'horizontal' transcendence. Wishing to give love its 'strict and threatening sense of total attachment to one human being, founded on the imperious recognition of our truth, of our own truth in a body and a soul' (II, 832), he is critically severe towards those who mistake 'eroticism' for the unfettered operation of the pleasure principle.[5] Sexuality, if it is to be liberated from the straitjacket of reproductive function within consecrated bourgeois marriage, can only be so delivered in the name of intensified spiritual desires, for the purpose of self-transcendence and to the benefit of Love. Its goal is not mere enjoyment, but Eros sublimated and 'admirable'.

Given this fundamental intention, Breton's dream of love, despite its anti-theistic posture and its experimental spirit, is always implicitly mystical. What he expects of love is an immediately 'divinising' experience: ecstasy, illumination, the reconciliation of contradictions in harmony, the revelation of essence. All these things are no doubt, to some extent, prefigured in the common experience of 'falling in love' romantically (we remember Valéry's definition: 'le seul échantillon de mystique que tous ou presque tous connaissent'). Yet in Breton, these common intuitions are espoused with total poetic intensity and complete existential seriousness. They are read as clues to an achievable, if mysterious, absolute ('le surréel', 'le point limite') to be attained within human existence; and they are principles of a revolution in morality and feeling which is parallel and complementary – albeit with acute tensions – to the Marxist project of structurally altering the conditions of social and political life.

Breton's language of love, while ever ready to disavow the metaphysics of its own mysticism, will be consistently mystical in tenor. It is the language of rapture, trance, cosmic intelligence, absolute presence, communion, adoration, invocation. The structures of desire, too – expectancy, availability to the signs of the Promise, quest in ardent passivity, ascent to the summit, plenitude, irradiating vision – will be consistently para-mystical (usually invoking an initiatory or alchemical frame of reference). Woman, the feminine Other who is sought as complement and real object of the dream of desire, will be mythologised as an ultimate referent, displacing and replacing the traditional mystic's 'God'. Thus the narrator of *Nadja* addresses the unnamed 'Tu' whose advent is seen to close the series of 'signs' presented in that book:

All I know is that this substitution comes to an end with you, because nothing can be substituted for you, and because for me it was from all eternity, with you, that this succession of enigmas had to end.
You are not an enigma for me.
I say you are what turns me away from enigmas. (I, 752)

She is the immanently transcendent Signified of all *his* obscure presentments, the Presence which disarms the torment of all ultimate unknowing about the human condition.

Breton thus reconfigures the structural 'triangle' of agents traditionally assumed in Western accounts of Eros, re-investing in the 'human Other' the transcendence previously reserved for the higher 'Third Term'. His variation on the Platonic triangle consists in a 'post-death-of-God' inversion, referring back to the psychic unconscious all the movements, intuitions and feelings which Plato and his Romantic descendents in idealism had read teleologically, as signs of an essentialist 'other world'. Love is here envisaged solely as a formation of the psyche itself, a sort of *poetic creation* all the more fascinating in that it finds mysterious and magical correspondences in the world outside the mind.

Love and poetry are, in this same resolutely psychogenetic perspective, exchangeable values. Both are rooted in the same affective disturbance induced by 'beauty'; both declare the same expectancy of desire; and each constantly encounters the central enigma of the relationship between the mind and external reality. Beauty is continuously encountered in both modes, mediated not merely through objects and persons, but in the events and processes of everyday experience, in so far as these produce the *frisson* of allusive promise, electrifying immanent libidinal depths, or else the shock of outright recognition. 'I have never been able to prevent myself from establishing a relation between this sensation,' says Breton of poetic emotion, 'and that of erotic pleasure and I find between these only differences of degree' (II, 678). In the same way, *Nadja* declares beauty itself to be 'convulsive', that is, implicitly homologous in nature and effect to a sexual climax (I, 753).

***

In the first chapter of *L'Amour fou*, beauty is compared to a high-speed locomotive abandoned in a forest: an object offering the image of potent dynamism, process, movement, yet fixed, paradoxically, in a recapitulative expression which is both surprising and revelatory, like some 'marvellous precipitate of desire' (II, 682). Its effect on us is to enlarge the universe and, partially, to remedy its opacity, declaring an unsuspected depth of things that answers the deeper needs of the human psyche (with Péret, and indeed like Plato, Breton thinks that the recognition of beauty engages more than merely aesthetic perception). Beauty in its surrealist acceptance is said to be 'erotic-veiled, exploding-fixed, magic-circumstantial' (687): Breton's famous trinity. The book presents *l'amour fou* as an encounter with beauty in just this manner; and we may grasp its defining quality of 'madness' by attending to these three compound adjectives.

Structurally, the work is articulated around three lyrical moments, all featuring excursions with the beloved: the magic errancy in nocturnal Paris upon first meeting; the summit experience of intensity and expanded consciousness as the honeymooners ascend by cable-car and on foot towards the summit of the volcanic peak of the Teide, on Tenerife; and the walk by the sea in Brittany, where this 'summit experience' falls victim to the baleful platitudes of the plain and of prosaic conjugality. There are two framing sequences: the first, evoking the mental theatre of the writer's confrontation with previous lovers, and the last, where Breton writes to his daughter to commend *l'amour fou*. These have the character of stock-takings in which a discrepancy is registered between the 'starry castle' of Surrealist love considered as poetic project, and the existential status of this construct reviewed in real time. Throughout, Breton is concerned not just to evoke lyrically, but to understand and to theorise; and his narrative of the love-encounter thus re-implicates itself in the decipherment of its own causes and meaning.

The origin of Bretonian love, as we have noted, lies in the poetic and creative virtualities of the deep psyche. Antecedent to any encounter with the beloved is for Breton the potentiality of, and the call to, a transfiguring relationship – an expectancy of Desire which reaches out in attention towards an answering echo from the world of the non-self; there is even, we are told in the opening pages, a pre-disposition towards a particular physical type, re-affirmed and re-presented to conscious experience thanks to 'an ever-enhanced subjectivisation of desire' (II, 678).

A revealing metaphor speaks here in alchemical terms of the deep-lying crucible in which is prepared an elective fusion of two beings, restoring to all things a colour otherwise lost and a sunlight eclipsed. Clearly, Breton believes, like Desnos, in the moving power of 'la Mystérieuse', the ideal Other inhabiting consciousness, and, like Valéry, in the 'Ombre divine' whose approach is intuited by an equally mysterious Dweller of desire within consciousness itself. The question is: how is pre-existent subjective expectancy answered; in what way is the gulf bridged between self and non-self?

Breton's response is given in his treatment of his encounter, outside a café in 1934, with the 'scandalously beautiful young woman' whose destiny was to 'enter into composition with mine' (II, 713). This event represents a prime illustration of circumstantial magic and is itself 'beautiful' in the revelatory and transfiguring sense outlined above. The encounter is evoked with memorable lyric resonance: the imprint of a face, the fugitive impression of a body; a first paralysing contact through speech, with its terror and gaucheness; then a first midnight assignation exploring the nocturnal world of the fruit-and-flower market of Les Halles, a world illuminated by a reciprocated attraction and poetically charged with floral enchantment, magical abundance, rejuvenating innocence, cosmic depth:

> Clear fountain in which all desire to draw along with me a new being is reflected and comes to drink, all my desire to retrace *à deux*, since this has proved still possible, the lost way leading out of childhood and which winds in and out, perfuming this woman still unknown, this woman still to come, between the meadows. (720)

As well as any writer since the *Cantique*, Breton here captures 'the lost grace of the first moment in which we love' (715).

Yet his rememoration is prompted also by a problematising curiosity about the subterranean logic of this grace. Within the moment itself, there is a message to decipher: that conveyed by the Tour Saint Jacques, pointed out to him by the 'beautiful wanderer' at his side, and already celebrated by Breton himself in the metaphor of the 'tournesol'. This image transforms the tower at once into both an urban sunflower turned towards light and life, and a chemical reactive agent recalling an historical association with 'the age-old dream of the transmutation of metals' (II, 717). The message of this complex poetry is symbolic. It urges a regenerating liberation from past affective failure: 'Let this curtain of shadows part and may I let myself be led without fear towards the light! Turn, sun, and you, great night, banish from my heart all that is not faith in my new star!' (720).

Moreover, the timeliness and pertinence of the message are amplified by the uncanny predictive power of another poem of exactly this title, 'Tournesol', written some eleven years earlier. In this text, Breton is astounded to discern retrospectively a precise and cogent presentment, albeit in coded terms, of the encounter of 1934. This lends a disturbing character of esoteric depth to the beauty of the event. It is this feature which, beyond the lyric content of the moment, poses the problem of self and non-self in a manner which evokes a powerful reaction of primitive religious awe:

> It is indeed impossible that [the mind] should not find here a feeling of extraordinary felicity and anguish, a mixture of *panic* joy and terror. It is as if, all of a sudden the dark night of human existence were pierced, as if, natural necessity consenting to become one with logical necessity, all things were delivered in total transparency, joined in a glass chain without a single missing link. (II, 711)

It is *as if* an initiatic or magic contact had occurred, evoking an occult harmony of psyche and world-process: 'the beginning of a supremely dazzling contact, between man and the world of things' (711). Its revelatory character, on which Breton insists despite evident nervousness as to the reaction of his Marxist friends, incites him to 'bring out the law of the production of these mysterious exchanges between the material and the mental' (711).

It also inspires, more immediately, a flight of didactic-prophetic fervour. One must not despair of love: 'for each of us, the promise of any hour to come contains the whole secret of life, potentially revealable one day in another being' (II, 714). Only the lingering atavisms of a religious education prevent modern man from reaching out for a Beyond in the here-and-now; the entire conception of love is to be revised; the ill-founded distinction of subject and object must disappear; the rationalist account of causality has been wrong-footed; the 'lyric behaviour' of Surrealism – its surrender to the flux of things, as in a waking dream of existential expectancy – stands vindicated by such divinatory encounters (721–2).

What are we to make of all this? In one sense, Breton's magic-circumstantial beauty indeed belongs to the universal experience of love. Every lover, presented with an Other coincident with inner expectancy acknowledges a marvellous correspondence between mind and world. Moreover, as Valéry points out, the persuasion of idealism in us – what emanates from our own mind being so much more intimately convincing than all the rest! – is such that it actually requires an act of faith to believe in the coincident but independent existence of the real object. The exclamation 'I still can't believe it!' belongs to every *surprise de l'amour*. Yet the meaning of this star-struck magic is more problematic. The writers of the *Song of Songs* might well have asked Breton whether it was really *magic* he meant, and whether truly a magic of *circumstance*. Love, in the *Song*, exemplifies a vaster *mystery* encountered in *wonder*: that of the superabundantly good order of creation which answers man's expectancy of spirit, as it does his human bodily needs, with the possibility of a real (i.e. non-phantasmatic) satisfaction. Novalis, to offer a second parallel case, is more idealistic, but equally consistent philosophically: the complicity of mind and world is founded on a World-Soul or Spirit expressing itself both within and without the self, such that the deep psyche is a cipher to the macrocosm of events and things; so that psychology *is* cosmology.

Breton's position is more paradoxical and tenuous. Novalis' mentor Fichte is explicitly set aside.[6] The magic idealism of the German Romantic poet is dismissed, at least as metaphysic, though not as religious sensibility (it is still 'as if...'). In Breton's world, belief in a pre-existent reciprocity of mind and things figures an unguarded and unliveable absolutism of the type that unhinges the sanity of Nadja. Instead, Breton appeals to the notion of 'objective chance'.[7] This covers a motivated but ultimately groundless act of faith in the immanent god of psychic Desire, obscurely but beneficently interacting with an ultimately random order of things. As Alquié suggests, the Surrealist commitment to this notion is in the nature of an invocation.[8] That it lacks any thinkable justification in the world outside the mind is, indeed, part of the 'madness' of existential attitude that makes up the starry splendour of *l'amour fou*.

Yet neither Surrealist expectancy nor the magic it seeks to conjure up out of circumstance are quite devoid of an explanatory, motivating logic: that of the mind-generated 'veiled erotics' which Breton is at pains to decipher experimentally ('I forbid myself anxiously to be taken in by desire' [II, 730]). The basic assumption is that amorous expectancy is a state comparable to dream, a state in which, says the author of *Les Vases communicants*:

> What desire demands from the quest for the desire-object disposes strangely of external data by tending egoistically to retain in them only what can serve its cause. Desire, which in essence is the same, lays hold randomly of what is useful to its satisfaction ... if it is truly vital, it refuses itself nothing. (180)

In the same way, the auto-decipherments of *L'Amour fou* are attempts to refer the magic play of prophecy and circumstantial coincidence to a common denominator of subliminal desire, by following its 'ruses and precautions for tacking in preconscious waters' (696). The aim is to 'discover the fine-pointed paintbrush of fire which brings out or perfects the meaning of life ... [so as] not to let the paths of desire become overgrown behind us' (697).

This suggests a twofold dialectic of subject-identity. On the one hand, the writer espouses a tension of expectancy open to the creative novelty of desire, as it interacts 'magically' with the world of events and things. On the other, he directs a reflexive and retrospective critical attention towards the 'crypt': the underground chamber of psychic Desire, upon which is edified the construct of acts and interpretations making up the narrator's conscious existence. Most signally, this is the crypt of the 'starry castle' of love, with its rejuvenating and expansive world of symbolic meanings and satisfactions. The subject of writing is thus a pure questioning form, doubly 'attentive' to what haunts him *a tergo* and to the poetic novelty this haunting can inject into a life lived as existential project.

The 'crypt' is most fully explored in the long *explication* Breton performs on his dreamlike automatic poem of 1923, 'Tournesol' (II, 717–35). He is seeking here to elucidate the *cryptic* (in all senses) 'prophecy' which, retrospectively, the earlier poem appears to offer of the Encounter of 1934. Some of the conformities between text and event are indeed striking: the central feminine figure of the poem – but Breton is present in it too – crosses the Halles, with timid steps (of hope?), under a sky of despair; the rustic-floral motif appears ('a farm prospered in the heart of Paris'); the chestnut-tree candles can be read as prefiguring the highlights in the chestnut-coloured hair of the real girl of 1934; the allusion to the breast of 'la belle inconnue' fits the real-life scenario; the title of the poem allusively evokes the Tour Saint Jacques and its associations on that occasion, and so on. The more room we allow to the displacements, symbolic disguises, ellipses and puns which Freud teaches us to recognise in dream imagery, the more the network of correspondences proliferates convincingly. So, for instance, Breton claims that the 'great, oh-so-beautiful lily' which despair rolls across the sky is a manifestly sexual symbol (he might have claimed support from the later line 'The promises of the nights were at last kept'); and that the swimming posture which the poem attributes to the girl 'foreknows' both the profession of his real-life beloved (she performs in swimming galas), and the place of their meeting (she is 'l'ondine' [water-nymph] of the café where 'l'on dîne' [one dines]!).

The problem with such proliferating correspondences is that they form an infinitely extensible, but ultimately tautologous, game. Even the single element of the poem which, so Breton declares, has resisted his interpretive patience – 'my dream this flask of smelling salts'– can be perfectly well integrated into the logic of Freudian prophecy. The flask of smelling-salts, contained in the – sexually symbolic – handbag, and which God's mother-in-law is said to be the only one to have sniffed, can very cogently be read as a burlesquely disguised and displaced dream of vertigo in sexual ecstasy! In this way, one ends up proving, not that a unique encounter is truly foreknown, but that the libidinal unconscious 'knows everything' –*providing* 'everything' comes down to 'one thing'...

Breton's 'veiled erotics' is, however, more than a matter of visiting the libidinal crypt. The other decipherments of the book offer a subtle and often cogent account of something akin to a 'feedback loop', linking what desire seeks and the circumstantial magic which the conscious mind discovers in the flow of events. The emphasis here is less on foreknowledge and prophecy, more on the transforming effect on the subject's encounter with certain objects such as the slipper-heeled wooden spoon, the mask or the Giacometti statue (II, 697–709). These offer hints, nudges, subliminal messages that actually inflect the course of events, not by modifying the external world – 'magically', but by alerting the subject of desire himself to his own deeper intentionality. The statue as interpreted by Breton, for instance, is a figuration of the desire to love and be loved – his own desire. It is unfinished and contradictory in its form. His discussion with Giacometti about it acts as dreams act: it liberates both the sculptor (from the affective scruples that had prevented him from harmonising the work), and the would-be lover (by enabling him to recognise the 'latent finality' by which his own desire solicits chance); it creates, in fact, the same empty space of invitation and invocation as the half-uplifted arms of the statue.

The spoon similarly fascinates Breton because it appears to emit obscure homophonic echoes of desire. It is recognised as a phallic object; but attention centres on its slipper-like 'heel' or grip-stop, which evokes in his mind the slipper of the Cinderella fairy-tale. This is analysed convincingly – indeed, with Lacanian prescience – as a tale of the 'lost object'. The Prince of the fairytale, like the narrator of *L'Amour fou*, attempts to recover the Object by a series of symbolic 'trial fittings'.

The veiled logic of desire does not, therefore – despite the mystico-poetic language of Surrealism – re-order the course of events magically; nor does it actually create its own object. What it does is to perform like a sonar system, emitting towards the world of the non-self echo-soundings that reflect back to the conscious mind the latent intentionality by which the unconscious solicits, selects and interprets the flow of experience presented to it.[9] If it is true, in Breton's memorable image that 'our chance [is] crumpled up like a poppy-flower in bud' (II, 705), then the self-scrutinising, presciently sonarised expectancy of Surrealism is perhaps, indeed, an efficacious way of promoting a *beautiful unfolding*.

***

The remarkable fifth chapter of the book brings a climax of poetic unfolding. Both the magic of circumstance and the veiled logic of desire are here raised to a point of exultant incandescence which justifies the attribution to surrealist beauty of the Breton's third qualifier, 'exploding-fixed'. The chapter presents the honeymooners' ascent to the summit of the volcanic peak dominating the island of Tenerife, the Teide. The poetic power of the writing derives from the way in which the expansive joy of ardently realised sexual union is reflected in the evocation of the external landscape. As in some immense, facetted, parabolic radar dish, illumination is projected back from the natural world towards the unseen *foyer* of volcanic fire deep in the human subject. Magically, every element of the natural décor enters into a play of correspondence with this vital centre. The two domains are thus fused in permanent exchange: nature is integrally eroticised, and, reciprocally, the inner *foyer* of exultant sexual energy is everywhere epiphanised in the external world.

The hidden centre, it will be clear, is for Breton the sexual unconscious, here solicited and rampant thanks to 'the physical goal attained' (II, 739). Its invisible presence, like the unseen heart of the volcano, is suggested throughout by imagery of incandescence and fire: in the glowing stone of the gothic arches ('flamboyants'), which are described as the cable-car rises above the Spanish town; in the white and black lava flows visible from halfway-up; and again in the apocalyptic eruption invoked by de Sade's hero of *La Nouvelle Justine*, recalled as the honeymooners approach the summit. In another image, the sexual unconscious is a multiply self-transforming and ever-renaissant fire-bird, an 'unheard of phoenix' (737). So it appears, with omnipresent allusiveness, in all the features of an eroticised landscape (the valley of the Oratava, the summit crater, the lava flows, the luxuriant vegetation) which exultantly assimilate mountainous and volcanic nature to a female body. The same erotic sensibilisation flickers or flares in the imagery. Cacti stoned by the town boys secrete a milk at once ejaculatory and lactational (they are 'displaced objects', mimicking the bull penetrated by the bullfighter's *banderillos*). In the climatological garden of the Oratava, the great dragon-tree, with its oozing red gum, belongs to the 'jurassic fauna that we rediscover when we scrutinise human libido' (739). The tree of giant girth, with its overhanging branches, fantastic shapes, and feline eyes peering through curtain-like foliage, is a strange and fascinating chamber of erotic intimacy, a 'vestibule of physical love' (744).

The quasi-hallucinatory presence of a libidinal imaginary thus irradiates through a fairytale universe. 'Mad' love belongs essentially to this environment in which it is defined. It is a 'delirium of absolute presence' (II, 744). By this, Breton means a trans-rational compulsion towards fusion; more properly (since the identities established by sexual alterity subsist), towards a co-fusion or con-fusion in which opposites are absorbed and transcended. In this respect, it of course models paradigmatically all Breton's attempts to define the surrealist 'point de l'esprit'.

The qualifier 'explosante-fixe' best describes the erotically energised, poetically illumined intelligence itself, as it expands to capture the irradiating consequences of the surreal fusion of inner and outer worlds. This movement tends to fix in lyrical theory the content of *l'amour fou* and, reciprocally, to answer 'the question of the future of love', posed at the outset of the chapter. Illumination is progressive, like the ascent itself towards the summit. A cable-car ride of several hours, 'launched into the shell-spiral of the island' (II, 738), rises to successive platforms of view (we are reminded of the ascendent dialectic of Péret's essay). Most notably, it discovers the luxuriant park or climatological garden of the Oratava valley, from which are visible the barren heights towards the summit and 'the most madly favoured point of the Island' (739). The summit itself remains unscaled: an ardent point of visionary imagination and an imagined focus for the eyes of a future generation of children. In one of the most sustained and memorable pieces of writing in the surrealist canon, Breton opens vibrantly to the reader's apprehension, 'with its abyssal flank, built in philosopher's stone', the starry castle of his Idea of Love (763).

The delirium of absolute presence attests in love – and attests *as* love – a desire which is not exhausted by physical and emotional possession. There is an elusive/

allusive *something else* which, slipping away, regenerates desire and redemands a return towards the elective Other. Breton is close here to Valéry's 'aesthetic infinite' (as he is in many of the other glimpses which will help give contour and substance to his conception). Later in the same chapter, he will denounce the 'appalling sophism' according to which 'love becomes worn out with the repetition of the sexual act' (II, 757), thus preparing the lovers' disaffection from, and eventual disloyalty to, each other. This widespread notion is dispiriting, he says, and shows the modern world in a truly pitiful light. The implication is that a love properly so-called is precisely that relationship which, thanks to the elusive 'X' just indicated, escapes or transcends reduction to positivist-functional definitions.

Lacan has made the point exactly in distinguishing between need and desire. If desire is considered as belonging to an exhaustible biological cycle and as tending to a finite satisfaction, it is negated by its very reduction to (sexual) need. On the other hand: 'If hallucinatory satisfaction is at stake, this means that there is another register. Desire is satisfied elsewhere than in effective satisfaction. It is the source, the introduction, of phantasm as such.'[10] Breton partially amends Lacan, however. He introduces (like Valéry) the further notion that reciprocated love is a 'a set-up of mirrors which send back, from the thousand angles that the unknown can take for me, the faithful image of the woman I love, ever more surprising in divination of my own desire and more golden with life' (II, 706). Here is indeed another register; yet Breton clearly does not mean, with Lacan, that love is an exchange of mutually supporting private phantasms. He exalts in the 'ever more' precisely because for him there is already, in a love worthy of the name, a 'real presence': that is, a non-phantasmatic satisfaction of desire itself, a true enhancement of being and well-being. That 'real presence' is just as *defining* for 'love' as is the ever-incomplete character of the satisfaction offered. It is what *rescues from phantasm* a dynamic of self-regeneration which, from a psychogenetic point of view, undoubtedly presents some of the characters of hallucination and potentially shares many of the same effects.

Yet the two images of 'presence' remain in his mind discrete; they are not reflectively co-ordinated. Breton's conception of *l'amour fou* is suspended on the all-sufficient, exemplary 'unit of reality' formed by the subject's discovery of reciprocity in amorous desire. He espouses, that is, the naturally ego-transcending movement of *excentration* in amorous feeling; to the point where, as Paule Plouvier shows,[11] the Other appears, jubilantly, as source of a completion of the subject's identity. Yet Breton gives little or no philosophic space in *L'Amour fou* to that Other. He seems more fascinated by the marvellous potency of the subject's own Desire than attentive to the Other-presence which alone rescues it from phantasm.

In this sense, Breton remains an Eros-centred idealist, ultimately in love with love itself. Revealingly, he will write to his daughter in the letter with which this book closes: 'what I have loved, whether I have kept it or not, I will always love it' (II, 780). The use of the impersonal 'ce que', in preference to 'celle(s) qui', implies a disjunction between subjective experience (seen as essence) and the personal Other (recognised as instrumental and occasional cause). This subject–object disjunction provides a major clue to what is phantasmatic still, and fragile still, in the starry castle of Surrealist love and desire.

**

Love so conceived is likely to be an exotic dream shot through with shadows of ambiguity and an anxious questioning of the god. Significantly, Breton's celebration continues:

> Delirium of absolute presence. How could one not catch oneself wanting to love thus, in the breast of reconciled nature? Yet here they are, the prohibitions, the alarm bells, they are ready to be activated, the snowy bells of the datura, in case we get it into our heads to erect these barriers between others and ourselves. Love, only love to exist, carnal love, I have never ceased to adore your poisonous shadow, your mortal shadow. A day will come when man will manage to recognise you as his only master and honour you even in the mysterious perversions with which you surround yourself. (II, 744)

Three pulsing and prophetic ideas of Bretonian 'desire to love' are interwoven here: the exemplary value of the self-sufficient couple; love as the gateway to a refound golden age; and the integral affirmation of love as morally and philosophically innocent in its single, physical basis. All three ideas irradiate out from his poetic 'delirium', all playing in polemical tension against some anti-thesis which alone supplies a genuine consistency.

Against the Second Communist International, Breton insists that the enchanted private world of the couple in love is not a 'selfish calculation' in contempt of the needs of the masses (the party line basely imposed on Bunuel in his retitling of *L'Age d'or*), but instead just what that film intentionally proclaims, namely an exemplary and embryonic realisation of human social possibility. Invoking support from Engels and Freud, Breton even goes so far as to affirm that monogamy is the highest form of sexual relationship and the greatest factor in moral and cultural progress generally. At all events, material – and materialist – necessity evaporates in the beatific Garden, in which the childlike myth of nature as infinitely bountiful holds sway and the severe adult moralities of work and effort yield to the pleasure principle: 'supposedly "gainful" life looks once more like "wasted life". Wasted for games, for love' (II, 748). In the perspective of a realised social utopia, only the inter-gender differential operating in love ('you the one ... always another' [749]) would subsist as a *raison d'être* for human existence; which is to say that it is what ultimately counts, even under present social conditions.

Breton is of course invoking a Rousseauesque *âge d'or*. This is assimilated, in a manner characteristic of the Romantic-Symbolist science of myth, to the Garden of Genesis. At the centre stands the Tree of Life; that is, for Breton, of Knowledge, not of divine Wisdom but of sexually-based human Eros. The myth irradiates from the limitless and magical meadow crossed by the lovers. It is apprehended orphically, in the music of the steps of the original couple:

For a woman and a man, who, until the end of time, must be you and me, will glide along in their turn without looking back, as far as the end of the path ...This saw-toothed grass made up of those thousand invisible, uncuttable, fibres, which have been united in your nervous system and mine in the dark night of knowledge [...]. The greatest hope, I say, that hope which subsumes all others, is that this should last. That the absolute gift of one being to another, which cannot exist with reciprocation, should be in the eyes of all the only natural and supernatural bridge thrown across life. (II, 749–50)

The only value, the one necessary source of human meaning, the one and only state of grace, are presented as comprehended in the Knowledge, immediate and surreal, that lovers psycho-physiologically have of each other. Like the grass known as 'la sensitive' (reactive grass), the contact of love commands the world of human subjectivity and is the key to a perpetually renewed poetry: 'I will re-invent you for myself, as I have the desire to see poetry and life perpetually recreated' (752).

No doubt lovers exist in a cloud of unknowing and incommunicability, like the turbulent whiteness which, falling over the highest reaches of the Oratava Reserve, briefly separates Breton and his bride. Yet the oracular visionary of the summits makes short work of converting the 'passivities' of love into its creative challenges, and of integrating them into the existential attitude of passive, desire-guided expectancy ('Desire, only spring of the world, desire, only rigour which man needs to know, where can I be more at ease to adore you than within a cloud?' [II, 755]). The Promise is simply to be disengaged from the – purely external and contingent – social and moral alienations that weigh upon it. It is enough to learn to 'expose oneself without defence to the devastating gaze of the god' (760). The cloud itself can become a tent, a 'bedroom filled with cygnet-down' (761).

The volcanic fire of the summit will be reserved, therefore, for the greatest of these external alienations. Implicitly, the whole of Breton's orphic hymn to love has been a contestatory remaking of Genesis, a subversive 'Serpent's sketch'. Now Breton's god thunders defiance against the God of Catholic moral regulation:

Such an enterprise cannot be carried out entirely as long as, on a universal scale, we have not yet done away with the infamous Christian idea of sin. There never was any forbidden fruit. Temptation alone is divine. Feeling the need to change the object of temptation shows one is about to demerit, and no doubt already has demerited, in respect of *innocence*. Of innocence in the sense of absolute non-guilt. (II, 760)

Breton does recognise both perversion and potential malignancy in sexual eros; yet he seeks to affirm Eros integrally, despite its poisonous and deadly shadow, rather in the manner of Nietzsche's *amor fati*. The logic of this delicate balancing act lies in his reading of the Fall myth in Genesis. The fruit tasted is identified – simply – as innocent erotic delight; the poisonous and deadly shadow falling across it that of Augustinian mistrust of libido (Freudian translation: 'taboo'). The sense and essence of the myth, on this view, lies in the idea, attributed (understandably, but, as we have seen, problematically) to Christianity, that sexuality itself is sinful. The counter-declaration of innocence, the defiant valorisation of 'temptation', the antithetical divinisation of liberated Eros are thus the ultimate keys to Breton's starry castle, just as they are in Péret's grand narrative of Eros in history.

The last word, consequently, is with revolt. This finds sanction in the 'sublime' collaboration between man and nature represented in de Sade's *La Nouvelle Justine*. In this work, the militant anarchist heroes, out of a hatred for nature and for man, invoke the fire of Etna by mingling their sperm with the lava flow. They set landmines to trigger its eruption, provoking a natural catastrophe, 'secret for unleashing an earthquake' (II, 761–2). Breton concedes that the only alliance of de Sade's anarchists with nature is 'in evil ... in crime' (761). Yet his admiration remains undeterred ('it remains to be seen whether this is not one more way, and the wildest, the most incontestable, of loving it' [761]). The 'sublime' example is thereby given of a magnetic interaction of mind and nature, fusing the volcanic potency without and within.

So in the matter of love and desire. The problem of evil, says Breton with transgressive bravado, 'is not worth raising before we have done away with the idea of transcendence and of any sort of good which might dictate his duties to man' (II, 762). Once the Sadean earthquake has destroyed in modern consciousness the otherworldly theistic love for Being, together with its this-worldly counterpart of a morality dictated by mistrust of fallen nature, the human horizon will be illuminated by 'the only love, the love of *a* being' (762). Breton's flames are – incongruously – gentler than de Sade's: they relieve inner devastation, illuminate and warm, as the brush-fire evoked in the epilogue to this section warms 'your enchanting hands, your transparent hands hovering above the fire of my life' (763). Nonetheless, the dream of Love restored to innocence, become harbinger of social utopia, is essentially a salvational counter-myth polemically directed at the Catholic Adversary. As such, the analogy with Sadean revolt is structurally crucial to it. Without this *repoussoir*, the immanent god has neither contour nor consistency, neither direction nor efficacy of conviction: 'Admirable Teide! Take my life! ... I wish only to be, with you, one being of your flesh, of the flesh of jellyfish, one being with the jellyfish of the seas of desire' (763).

*****

The oceans of desire have been known to engulf drifting jellyfish. The philosopher's stone sometimes fails, gold turning back to base metal. The locomotive of delirious love may well derail. What prospects are there that the poet's starry castle itself will survive the encounter with earth-bound time and chance?

The question is the more acute in that some aspect or other of failure is registered with ironic regularity as we follow Breton from *Nadja*, through *Les Vases communicants*, to *L'Amour fou* and beyond, to *Arcane 17*. In each book, we encounter the paradox of a hymn to passion written around a new *inspiratrix*; each more exalted than the last in declaring an unshakeable and exclusive Election – and each edified on the ruins of some previous elective love.[12] Aspiring to stand beyond Good and Evil, Breton is nevertheless haunted by an ill or malaise afflicting the immanent god. Nothing is more revealing of the starry castle than the way in which he faces the challenge of its 'abyssal flank', and manages still to organise the triumph of hope over experience.

Elementarily, the question of the 'vulnerability of Venus' is evoked by the poet of *L'Amour fou* in mythical terms. The goddess's 'passing mortification' is an allegory of the fated subjection of Passion to earthly struggles, the origin of this subjection lying outside herself, in the intervention of Eris or Discord (II, 765). Discord can slip in between lovers, aggravating small resentments, silences, stubborn withdrawals; and anguish edifies gigantic cardboard constructions of antagonism. But, says Breton, recalling his denial that love is ground down by contact with its own diamond-dust suspended in the flow of life, the absolutism of self-giving in love, its very generosity, tends to 'incriminate love when it is only life that is at fault' (768). Moreover, he declares, he has proof that what we might mistake for some natural risk inherent in life – a slippery ice-patch, a crevasse – is really in the nature of a trap: 'I mean that there seems to have presided over its making an ingeniousness and an assurance which are partly and provisionally beyond my understanding and which, by that very fact, had to make my fall inevitable' (768). More circumstantial magic in short; but this time, black magic, disculpating the fallen and protecting the splendid essence of love from its unhappy accidents by what amounts to a quasi-occultist conspiracy theory.

The theory is illustrated by the anecdote of the 'villa du Loch' (II, 737–7), site of an infamous and sordid sexual murder. During a walk on the beach in Brittany, the 'aura' of this sinister place, its 'deleterious emanations', are felt by Breton and his wife – before recognising its cause, and quite against their true feelings for each other – as driving between them a wedge of moral separation. Cézanne's rendition of just such an aura in his painting *La Maison du pendu*, reproduced photographically in the text (but without comment from Breton), exhibits a striking likeness to a fortified chateau 'with abyssal flank, of philosopher's stone'. The subliminal suggestion, unformulated in the text, would appear to be that the heavenly and infernal virtualities of sexual eros form a continuum, a single 'abyss' of height-and-depth: an insight of some moral and philosophic consequence, albeit uncongenial to Breton's declaration of aboriginal Innocence. Indeed, the great decipherer of interconnections carefully treads around this one by incriminating more local causes of the crime (neurotic heredity and loveless bourgeois marriage). It is *as if* he had glimpsed the potential for perversity and cruelty in human desire only to thrust it back from conscious awareness. As he revealingly states: 'there is no doubt that I harbour in relation to this picture a certain ambivalence of feeling' (775).

His ethico-philosophic distraction is reinforced by the mysterious underlying capillary tissue of interconnection between mind and world, surfacing once more in the guise of coincidence: the holiday reading of the couple 'prefigures' the murderer's hobby of fox-rearing, 'as if ... one were the victim of a hugely clever machination by powers which remain, for the moment, very obscure' (II, 776). This hypothesis has the effect of setting the Innocence of love apart from any possible contamination by morally ambiguous desires. Accordingly, the lovers will be spared any moral soul-searching. The disintegration of their relationship is not further analysed; nor does Breton ever tell us what went wrong with the assertion made earlier that true love is not subject to any appreciable alteration over time. This leaves the reader with the impression of a central moral unsightedness on Breton's part.

The psychodrama of unsightedness and moral malaise is staged in the opening sequence of *L'Amour fou*. Here we are introduced to the 'boys du sévère' who inhabit Breton's inner mental theatre: black-clad, waiter-like figures, all avatars of the narrator's identical and successive personae as lover, as they appear in Breton's own superego awareness. The scenario has a second scene which shows an equal number of the women whom he has loved or who have loved him, clad this time in 'light-coloured outfits', yet evoking the exclamation: 'How dark it is!' (II, 676).

Moral self-judgement is however shrugged off as mere gloom. The notion of love as having a single object derives, Breton here tells us, from a mystico-Romantic attitude, unsustainable in terms of current social practice which allows no true reciprocal election between lovers. The expectation of exclusivity has created a sense of malediction which has hung for a hundred years over modern man. Without prejudice to the social changes required (or, indeed, to the absolute meaning he himself attaches to the law of election and exclusivity), Breton immediately substitutes a dialectic 'resolution' in the Hegelian manner. There is no inconstancy, in that the last 'loved face' is to be seen as recapitulating and comprehending the whole series. In any personalist vision of love, this resolution must count as a revealing sophism; on this basis, Don Juan is a faithful lover!

How, we wonder, are *two* such desires ever to be reconciled in a stable, deepening, maturing relationship? How is the god regenerated in Other-centredness? How does the fitful volcano manage its accidents and avoid becoming extinct in mundane existence? Breton's answer seems to be in all cases: 'I invoke the obscure potency of the god; Desire will be enough to create love; or, at least to sustain a *dream* of Love... Perhaps we glimpse here the *intrinsic* reason why 'love' in Breton is defined in principle by delirious intensity; why it concentrates so exclusively on the initial phases of encounter and union – and why it is so vulnerable to the test of time. Does Breton not underestimate the discontinuity between desire and love? Has he not simply shrugged aside the *ars magna* of passing from the one to the other?

This suggestion recurs in his message to his daughter for the – still distant – occasion of her sixteenth birthday, which, as absent father, he will not see. The message is poetic, tender, laced with pathos and humour. It is also very public, and subtly shot through with self-justification. The 'point sublime' was an unrepeatable moment, he pleads. 'Always' is indeed the keyword of love; but he has chosen to express it as constancy to an Orphic vocation as seer and guide. The sophisms here trip poetically from his pen: he has never failed to link the being he loves (present tense, singular) to the vision of poetic splendour and the prophetic vocation (which has, however, 'always' commanded his supreme loyalty); so there is no 'demerit', only misfortune at the hands of life; at all events, love (or at least, its finest hour) must vanquish as Ideal; therefore it will do so, providing only its poetic intensity, as interpreted by its high-priest, dissolves all obstacles (apparently including previous love-ties). There is exorcism at work here: against all external reproach, all superego ghosts within, Breton is concerned to cling to the one chance he has identified of human self-transcendence, and to the carrying self-image it confers (780–3).

The madness of *l'amour fou*, its power of poetic bedazzlement and of moral unsightedness, is ultimately framed within a metaphysical pessimism. The starry castle is an antidote against Schopenhauerean disaffection with life: 'for a long time I thought that the worst folly was to give life. At least, I bore a grudge against those who had given it to me' (II, 779). 'This aspiration to the better would be enough to justify love as I conceive it, absolute love, as the only principle of physical and moral selection capable of answering for the non-vanity of human witness, human passage' (779). Referred to these ultimate axes, the wager of 'horizontal' transcendence ensures that *the less* the Promise is realised in experience, *the more* it will be lifted up onto the ideal plane, as salvational myth. Only in this mode will the object of desire be commensurate with the infinity of Desire as envisioned in poetic imagining.

This logic of mythogenesis is, esoterically, at work in Breton's later thought, in *Arcane 17* and beyond. As Breton struggles to compose Eros and Thanatos, and to re-invent a resurrection for war-torn Europe, so he assumes a solemn mission of exalting the feminine system of the world to the detriment of intelligence of the male type. So also, as Plouvier remarks: 'Fourier's utopia and the desirous generosity that passes through it act as backdrop to his making of the final love-myth, that of the child-woman on whom time has no purchase.'[13] We receive from Breton very little intimation that this grand Project, perhaps more than any other, is challenged by the concentration camps, the atomic bomb or the consumer society. Rather, Fourier and the Hopi Indians continue to persuade him that there is an untried alternative, the regeneration of Love through liberated Desire, and through both, a renewal of Western society.

***

The starry castle seems, in its poetic idealism, multiply fragile. As Alquié argues: 'One problem continually recurs: if the loved woman is not the sole and sufficient object of love, which reality does her image then signify to us? What does she refer us to? What sort of hope can be placed in love?'[14] The problem of desire is that of the 'lost object', and of the meaning and disposal of its 'excess'. Plato thought the allusive infinity of the *daimon* signified an essential Beauty beyond the world. In Christian thought, what is signified is a power of being which is properly divinisable, a potential for fellowship in the life of God for which the human Other is both the prefigure and the partner in apprenticeship. Dismissing the first hypothesis, and setting himself to extirpate the second, Breton does not see how the magic of amorous encounter can be more than a decrypting of ego-generated messages; yet he increasingly needs these messages to be the signs of a transcendent Promise, and to furnish the keys to the kingdom of the golden age. Failing which, the slippage in the gearing of human love onto the reality of things is fatal; there is merely love of love, and hope in hope ...

True, his starry castle recaptures something of the splendour of love, as perennially defined. It speaks with authority of its integrity, transcending inherited dualisms of flesh and spirit; and it rehabilitates woman. It lifts up a counter-proposal to the bourgeois reduction of marriage and to the predictability of hierarchical, pre-patterned gender-roles; and it rebukes a limited, deformed and prosaic sexuality which constrains human potential, allowing no transforming satisfaction of spirit. It is, in all these ways, a good poetry of love; even a prophetic Song.

Yet its limitations are, surely, grievous. 'It is not easy to replace human aspirations towards Being or the Absolute by woman,' comments Alquié profoundly. This is indeed the ultimate difficulty of Breton's bid for 'horizontal' transcendence. He is obliged to answer affirmatively to Nadja's question: 'Is it true that all the beyond is in this life?' And we have noted his embarrassment in making good his affirmative answer.

The starry castle, though sometimes glimpsed in splendour, is not without its swirling mists of ambiguity and obfuscation. Its 'flanc d'abîme' was perhaps deeper and steeper than the poet knew.

Notes

1   A. Breton, *L'Amour fou*, in *Œuvres complètes*, 3 vols, ed. M. Bonnet & E.-A. Hubert, Bibliothèque de la Pléiade (Paris: Gallimard, 1988–99), Vol. II, p. 763. References to Breton's works refer to this edition (Vol. II, 1992; Vol. III, 1999).

2   The first three of Freud's texts to be translated into French were *The Interpretation of Dreams* (1900), *Three Essays on the Theory of Sexuality* (1905), and *Introduction to Psychoanalysis* (1916). For the impact of Freud on the first Surrealist Manifesto of 1924, see A. Breton, *Manifeste du Surréalisme*, in A. Breton *Œuvres complètes*, 3 vols, Vol. 1 (1988), p. 316ff.

3   Schwaller de Lubicz's definition, quoted by R. Benyaoun, *L'Érotique du surréalisme* (Paris: Pauvert, 1965), p. 3.

4   A. Breton, 'Du Surréalisme dans ses œuvres vives', in *Manifestes du Surréalisme* (Paris: Gallimard, 1971), p. 165

5   In the second Manifesto, Breton denounces 'the specialists of pleasure, the collectors of adventures, the titillators of ecstasy' (I, 1021). 'Licentiousness is the worst enemy of elective love ... it makes sublimation impossible' (III, 518).

6   Cf. A. Breton, *Les Vases communicants*: 'The external world was not for me, as for Fichte, the non-self created by the self' (II, 180).

7   'Le hasard objectif' is, arguably, a misnomer: 'le hasard' signifies randomness, whereas what Breton has in mind is an obscure pattern of coincidence or convergence between independent causal series objectifying mind-generated figures of desire. See *L'Amour fou*, Chapter 2.

8   F. Alquié, *Philosophie du Surréalisme* (Paris: Flammarion, 1955), Chapter 3, 'L'attente et l'interprétation des signes'.

9   Cf. the 'cloud' of unknowing in Chapter 5, said to be like a screen on which 'everything a man wants to know is written in phosphorescent letters, in letters of *desire*' (754).

10   Lacan, 'Le moi dans la théorie de Freud et dans la technique de la psychanalyse', *Séminaire II* (Paris: Seuil, 1978), p. 249.

11   See P. Plouvier, *Poétique de l'amour chez André Breton* (Paris: Corti, 1983), chap. III 'Qui suis-je?'.

12   For a biographical listing of Breton's three wives and his dozen 'significant Others', see H. Pastoreau, 'André Breton, les femmes et l'amour', *Europe* (March 1991), pp. 81–94.

13   Plouvier, *Poétique de l'amour*, p. 11.

14   Alquié, *Philosophie du Surrealisme*, p. 120.

Chapter 10

Georges Bataille: The Erotic Abyss

...un besoin de désordre, de violence et d'indignité qui
est la racine de l'amour.

Where Breton places Eros under a resolutely ascendant sign, Bataille explores the
world of its nether deeps. He himself frequently uses the word *amour* in a loosely
generic sense; his exegetes mostly prefer the term *amour noir*. His true theme is
really *eroticism*. He aims at elucidating the awesome desirousness of sexuality itself:
something which transcends usefulness, pleasure and secure well-being because it
engages humankind's singular awareness of death and the sacred. 'Essentially, the
domain of eroticism is the domain of violence, the domain of violation.'[1] His
decipherment, we may say, is addressed to the archaic inner 'god' perceptible in
human sexual nature and re-expressed throughout human culture, prior to – but
Bataille will also say *beyond* – any civilising 'humanisation'.

True, his masterwork *L'Érotisme* (1957) distinguishes emotional as well as
physical and mystical levels of realisation. In principle, therefore, 'love' might be
said to be comprehended within a 'unitary field' theory of the erotic. Yet in practice,
we observe a conspicuously minimal recognition in Bataille of the tender, poetic,
life-enhancing bond of elective white magic which Breton (for instance) might have
acknowledged as 'love'. It is as if, questioning in his turn the forbidden fruit of the
tree of the Knowledge of good and evil, Bataille had chosen to specialise in the
decipherment of what Bretonian moral optimism registers only in passing; namely,
'your poisonous shadow, your mortal shadow'. Certainly, Bataille fulfils Breton's
prophecy: 'A day will come when humankind will manage to recognise you as its
only master and honour you even in the mysterious perversions with which you
surround love.'[2] This may imply, as one critic has suggested, a relationship of
dialectical complementarity between the two writers.[3] If we prefer Genesis to Hegel,
it may further suggest that each hears *one half* of the forked wisdom of 'knowing
good and evil'...

Breton mistrusted Bataille's attachment to de Sade, and, even more, the practical
exercises in 'debased' erotic excess practised by this marginal and dissident Surrealist.
(It is as leader of the disaffected, grouped around the review *Documents*, that Bataille
is savagely denounced in the Second Manifesto.)[4] Yet the common mindset is
unmistakeable too: in his defiant will to burst out of the rationalist and bourgeois
strait-jacket; in his radical social critique and his determination to re-invent a sense
of community; in the continuity he seeks between the modern world and mythical
modes of thinking; in his militant anti-Christianity (the more virulent since Bataille,
unlike Breton, displays a metaphysical and mystical sensibility that is shaken to the
core by the 'death of God'); in his anthropological intuition of the all-comprehending

centrality of Desire; in his need for a convulsive *telos*, and in his quest for an immanent absolute (Bataille will speak in para-mystical terms of 'ecstasy' and, in terms close to those of his supreme guide Nietzsche, of 'sovereignty').

Championed by the *Tel Quel* group in the post-1968 era, Bataille has often been read through a 'postmodern' prism: he is seen, that is, as a critical theorist of the same cloth as Derrida, Kristeva, Sollers, Barthes, Lyotard, Foucault and Baudrillart. Michael Richardson has shown, to the benefit of Bataille's reputation for originality as a sociological thinker, that a considerable distortion is involved in this perspective. Bataille's assumptions and mode of thinking, like his spiritual personality, are largely at odds, often fundamentally so, with the 'postmodern' relativists who claim him.[5] It blunts and banalises this very radical writer, as we shall see, to identify him as 'decentring' moral discourse or as putting an end to 'grand narratives'.

More to the radical point of Bataille is the admirable treatment of his 'secret' erotic fiction by Sarane Alexandrian devoted to *Histoire de l'œil, l'Abbé C., L'Anus solaire, Le Bleu du ciel, Madame Edwarda, Ma Mère* and *Le Mort*.[6] These private fictions of a quiet librarian, mostly published under pseudonyms some years after their composition, reflect Bataille's own determined forays into low-life debauchery and advanced pornotopia. Essentially, however, they are 'spiritual exercises': an imaginary and fictional apprenticeship in the quest that passes through all Bataillian eroticism. As such, they point to the later theorist who speaks with more-than-scholarly authority in the pages of *L'Érotisme*.

***

Bataille himself makes the same connection implicitly by including in this major treatise of 1957, *L'Érotisme*, his preface to *Madame Edwarda*. The reprinted preface of 1957 still refers to the author of *Mme Edwarda* pseudonymously, as 'Pierre Angélique'.[7] This clue is worth following. Bataille's theory finds its intuitive foundations in a psychodrama of the 'beast-angel'. Of course, the tension between spirit and flesh is perennially latent in the human experience of sexuality; but here we detect a singularly modern variant of it, a variant exacerbated not only by the crisis of dualism in Western thought, but also, biographically speaking, by Bataille's Oedipal relation to a monstrous and syphilitic father. We know also that the writer's youthful conversion to an extreme, puritanical Catholicism burned itself out, with a sense of having betrayed human love, after a year-long attempt in 1917–18 to espouse a monastic vocation.[8] Nor should we forget the 'extreme' climate of inter-war France, fraught with subterranean nihilisms and death-haunted ideological sacralisations.

Bataille's fiction displays a gnostic sense of scandal at the animality of the body and sexual function. So, for instance, the hero of *Madame Edwarda* reacts in panic horror at the libertine vision of sexually available female flesh; and the hero of *L'Impossible* flees 'as though this unintelligible world was communicating to me its damp secret of death'.[9] Never assimilating the flesh to 'sin', Bataille nevertheless exposes and exhibits relentlessly what is perhaps the real target of the twentieth-century's reaction against 'sin': the soiled and sullying character of the flesh. 'We surrender to our lower depths, spreading our legs, gaping open, as widely as possible, to what is no longer us but the impersonal, marshy existence of the flesh.'[10] Yielding to the obscene flesh, however, opens a secret door of being: 'I would put love (the indecent *corps-à-corps*) on a par with the unlimited quality of being – with nausea, with the sun, with death. Obscenity brings a moment of continuity to the delirium of the senses.'[11]

Not, however, without leaving a choked-back rage of disappointment against a life that cannot be lived and loved with the whole infinity of 'angelic' desire. In the first number of the review *Acéphale* (so called by way of denunciation of the rationalist and utilitarian head), Bataille writes: 'A world which cannot be loved absolutely ['à mort'], as a man loves a woman, represents merely self-interest and the obligation of work. If it is compared to worlds lost-and-gone, it is hideous and looks like the most failed of all worlds.'[12] Bataille here lets slip the implicitly framing truth of an amorous subject who haunts his own depths: an angel who expects to love integrally, with all the force of his being. We perhaps glimpse here the most intimate spring of disappointment and the deep-seated logic of displacement at work in his subversion of the inherited triangular figure of Eros. For want of an expected and adorable Other, the disappointed angel can only re-visit – and re-invest himself in – the carnal beast which appals him.

In this angelic revisitation, the cult of the 'common Aphrodite' stands revealed in its unacknowledged underside: as a death-haunted fascination and a violent exorcism. With what often seems like desperate spiritual courage, Bataille seems to wish to force the impasse of entrapped spirit by stripping human sexuality down to its most primitive and unavowable components, foregrounding in it everything that most disgusts him ('to face up to what frightens you' is the advice of the initiating Mother-figure of *Ma Mère*). All the carnal relations detailed in his fictions bear the dark halo of an 'obscene' reversion to animality, actively espoused as a kind of *acsesis-through-nausea* which strives ever harder to achieve an ecstasy *par le bas*. As Alexandrian notes: 'The erotic writings [of Bataille] are "terrifying" because they belong to a man who is meeting the terrorism of death with the terrorism of sex.'[13] The sexual act is linked consistently to excremental function, and to cruelty, violence and degradation. The act of stripping naked is already presented as a ritual or ceremony which, enacting the regressive passage from civilisation to animality, opens human beings in fear and trembling to the fundamental violence of what the later theorist will call 'the sacred'. Beauty itself is declared fascinating precisely in that it veils allusively the unavowable animal parts. Bataille's heroines typically reciprocate the hero's ascesis-in-nausea; they, too, display an inverse 'sanctity', outdoing in erotic martyrdom the degradations accepted by the most heroic of Catholic women saints. Woman, is not 'loved' in other-centred creaturely appreciation; she is sought and prized as a means necessary for a trial of the universal forces of primitive sacrality: 'What I love in the beloved – to the point of desiring to die of love— is not the particular being, but the portion of the universal which is in her.'[14]

Alexandrian is surely right also in diagnosing here an 'apology for debauchery which can be assimilated to the orgiastic rites of primitive religions, in which bestiality, far from being reproved, was a homage to "the gods".'[15] In an interesting *réplique* offered to the key image of *L'Amour fou*, the narrator of *L'Anus solaire* writes: 'Thus it is that love shouts in my throat: I am the Jesuvius, filthy parody of the torrid and blinding sun.'[16] The volcano-god (the French word telescopes the names 'Jésus' and 'Vésuve') is 'the image of the movement of eros, giving by effraction to the ideas contained in the mind a scandalous force of eruption'.[17] Where Breton's Sadean explosion merely blasts away the constraints of an inherited religious culture, Bataille, far more radically, espouses as a principle of subject-identity, transcendent and sacral, the scandal immanent in human sexual nature and in the nature of the world. It takes no great powers of divination to suspect in an eroticism conceived in these terms a dimension of vengeful provocation and profanation. We are in the realms, not simply of Freudian scientific curiosity about the mind's hidden obscenities, but of twentieth-century *ontological resentment*.

The metaphysical void will demand from the later theorist a Nietzschean 'transvaluation'. But the prior truth of angelic Disappointment commands first of all a 'Dionysian' sanctity passing through excess and abjection, rather than through abstinence and holiness. For Bataille, 'eroticism must be lived out religiously'.[18]

Nor does it require immense prescience to follow the inner syntax of a religious spirit whose anguished mysticity re-discovers, by displacement and compensation, the oldest and most immediate short-cut to divinity. As the brothel scenes of *Madame Edwarda* remind us luridly, the female genital opening was ever 'the narrow door to the infinite'.[19] That sex, rather than God, is the actual 'true referent' of Eros (as distinct from its ideal or imaginary 'projection'), is not, of course, an idea invented by Bataille. We have already encountered some cautious sketch of it in Zola, Valéry and Breton, not to mention de Sade himself. The reflexive suspicion which animates Western intelligence in the wake of the 'death of God' tends incoercibly to recompose some *inverse figure* of the collapsing Platonic-Christian triangle. Yet Bataille's singular 'religious' commitment is new and significant. He alone espouses with lucid consequentiality the 'low road' to the sacred as henceforth conceivable; that is, as a transcendence 'from below', rethought within the imaginative and logical space proper to 'decapitated' (or 'single-storey') twentieth-century Eros. Bataille, in fact, flips the Claudelian triangle right over, so that it comes to rest, disturbingly, on its obscene point of archaic and primitive emergence. 'God' becomes a metaphor or myth generated out of human erotic excess, the true referent of which must henceforth be entirely realised within the field of human possibility. It is, in *Madame Edwarda*, the common prostitute who is designated 'God'.

***

The theory of eroticism follows from these spiritual exercises. Bataille's introduction to *L'Érotisme* offers a pulsing series of vital, interlinked intuitions, which will be the articulating lineaments. The text as a whole will enrich and extend these intuitions, not by a movement of uniform or linear exposition, but by a patchwork which assembles overlapping thematic fragments (including, in Part II, essays written for other publications). Rather like a scrupulous roof-tiler, the essayist proceeds laboriously, warily, often repetitiously, working in circuitous patterns, to knit together themes and data drawn from natural history, ethnology, anthropology, sociology, sexology, literature and the history of religion. The aim is to compose a sufficiently cohesive roof-cone of theory, covering a collective dwelling-place of the modern spirit.

Against Kinsey, and other scientific sexologists, Bataille insists that the true nature of human sexuality is an *experience of the sacred*. It belongs to the human deeps that go unnamed and unrecognised in the workaday language we inherit from the 'profane' world; it must, he will say, be 'known from within' and 'communicated' in a 'silent awakening' (*E*, 182). He is concerned to evoke 'the *inner experience* – that is to say, to my way of thinking, the religious experience— outside defined religions' (*E*, 40). Despite the frequently contestable use of ethnological data, the essay's most striking formulations are for this reason strangely authoritative: this theorist, we sense, has 'been there' and found his own awakening.

Eroticism, Bataille tells us memorably, means *assenting to life up to the point of death*. It is specific to human beings in whom sexual activity implies not merely reproductive function, but also a psychic or spiritual quest focused and modelled on the violent, sensual pleasure of sex.

Its hallmark is that it engages our separate and discontinuous identities in a vertiginous moment of *continuity*, a *fusional vertigo together*. The profoundly disturbing *fascination* exercised on us by this experience derives from the depths apocalyptically stirred within us and from the contradictory tensions of desire called into play. The exuberance of all life passes through us ecstatically; but, at the same time, it intimates something antipodally different, namely the mortality to which we are condemned by the place of sexual reproduction in the life cycle ('the little death' of orgasm is interpreted as premonitory). We experience a blissful fusing which is, however, simultaneously, a fatal sign; a fleeting semblance of eternity, calling to a deep nostalgia within us for a primal continuity linking us with all things, but incoercibly promising us thereby to death. In the words of de Sade, whom Bataille cites three times in introduction, 'There is no better way of familiarising oneself with death than to associate it with some licentious image' (*E*, 18).

An *elemental violence*, consequently, kindles every manifestation of eroticism, whether physical, emotional or mystical. There is the immediate *violation* of our ordered, distinct and normal world of separate ('discontinuous') individuality; and there is an astonishing *turbulence of animal frenzy*. Both invoke a psychic shadow of nameless disquiet at the *fundamental violence done to us by death*. Stripping naked already heralds a dispossession of self, a transgressive and desirable uneasiness about bodies opening out to the invasive continuity of things. Here is Bataille's account of the 'All shook up' of erotic encounter. (Does it perhaps elucidate the abyssal subtext of the 'King' of Rock and Roll?)

This dispossession, this opening-up of our being to an invasive 'continuity', this enacted violence, all link the sexual act to crime and to ritual sacrifice. De Sade is again quoted, suggesting that murder is the pinnacle of erotic excitement; without some element of such excitement, would there, asks Bataille, be the necessary sexual climax? True, we are not destroyed by the erotic encounter, merely jolted, penetrated to the quick (the female literally and integrally, the male psychically), shaken in the foundations of our normal identity; yet this mitigation merely underscores the human meaning of eroticism. What we desire in erotic activity is to bring into a world founded on *discontinuity* all the *continuity* such a world can sustain. De Sade may exaggerate: his is a sphere of irrevocable acts and extreme practices. Yet for all of us, the stirrings of the inner god have their own *fearsome character of excess*. They signify that death, the ultimate breaking-open of those fenced-off individualities to which we cling, stands there, more real than life itself.

Romantic passion is, on this account, emotional eroticism, since it essentially retraces or prefigures the physical act at the level of affectivity. More than other forms, it reveals the negativity of all erotic experience as such. The fervour of *amour-passion* may even be more violently felt than physical desire, and, indeed, exist autonomously from any realised expression of it. Fulfilled, it is a violent agitation more like suffering than happiness; unfulfilled, it is an anguish of desire, an impotent, quivering yearning. It offers a glimpse of what human limitations deny to us: a total blending of two beings, a continuity between discontinuous creatures. Since this is intrinsically impossible, *amour-passion* must, in the ultimate, represent a fraudulent promise. Yet the idea of such a union takes shape with frenetic intensity in us, revitalised by separation and suffering, to the point of murder or suicide; this aura of death denotes *amour-passion* as such.

Only in the *violation* of human solitariness (in and through death, if needs be) can there appear that image of the Other which, in lovers' eyes, invests all being with significance. Through the instrumentality of the 'beloved', the world is made transparent, a place of full, limitless being (thus Bataille explains, implicitly, the nature of 'being in love with love'). Such a conception, he insists, is 'an absurdity, a horrible mix-up'; yet he is equally insistent that there is between lovers an authentic perception of 'the depth of being, the simplicity of being' (*E*, 28).

The name and nature of this erotically experienced ontological intuition is 'the sacred'. It is most dramatically observed in the experience which Bataille has given as consubstantial with physical eroticism, that of primitive ritual sacrifice. Here, the victim, divested of clothes and of life, is literally broken open, passing perceptibly from distinct identity into continuity with all things. The spectators, dissolved (like lovers) in communion, as waves in the sea, participate in what his death reveals: 'what subsists, and which, in the silence that falls, these anxious minds feel, is the continuity of being to which the victim is restored' (*E*, 29). The sex-act has a similar power to reveal the most fundamental quality of our being-in-the-world, the very form of our relationship to the ontologically real – mysterious, irreducible and terrifying – in which all else is embedded.

Religious (i.e., third-level) eroticism is the highest response to the sacred. Mysticism, its other name, derives, precisely, from primitive sacrifice; it constitutes an attempt to challenge death through indifference to death, achieved thanks to a heady nearness of approach to the unknown continuity itself, the brute mystery of being experienced in its ultimacy. Religious India shows us the succession and solidarity of eroticism's threefold form: physical in youth, emotional in advanced adulthood, mystical in old age. The challenge of erotic maturity is to 'tackle life face-to, and see in it, at length, the opening towards the unintelligible, unknowable continuity, which is the secret of eroticism, and of which only eroticism delivers the secret' (*E*, 31). The path revealed is the denial of our individual lives, the desire for the greater Thing that destroys us. Hence the spiritual and existential resonance of the question: 'Could we, without violence, assume a negation which leads us to the limit of all the possible?'(31). This question brings us to the point where the violent impulses at the heart of all things intersect – 'the cross-roads of all fundamental forms of violence' (32).

The elementary form of Bataille's thesis is now in place. Manifestly, it is a 'post-Christian' theory; specifically, a discourse about human Eros as it may be deciphered once the first chapter of Genesis, with its key themes of divine Creation, distinctiveness within the creaturely order, and divine blessing upon human sexuality as creative and good, has been relegated to the outer corridors of historical memory. Conspicuously, Bataille is dealing with the same themes as the Fall narrative in the third chapter of Genesis: erotic fascination, the vertigo of godlikeness, consciousness of death and nakedness, crime, violence. To these we will shortly see him add the further common themes of interdict, transgression and work. Yet the 'fallen' reality of the biblical narrative is here the *original and only* reality: the negativities of Desire in general, and of sexual passion in particular, are the *sole* characteristics of these things; blood-sacrifice, not praise of the transcendent Author and Giver of life, is the primordial and defining human action. There is no glimpse anywhere of a tree of Life (there is no Garden for it to grow in and no God to plant it); and the only relation founding man's being in the world is that linking him immediately to the awesome good-and-evil of undifferentiated being, experienced as ultimate and therefore as 'sacred'. Bataille's guiding thought, more consequently followed than Breton's or Valéry's, will be that only erotic Temptation is divine.

This subterranean intertextuality recalling the *excluded myth* of Judaeo-Christian tradition goes some way, it will be perceived, to explicating Bataille's assertion that eroticism is primarily a religious matter and that the present work is nearer to theology than to scientific or religious history (*E*, 31). As the work unfolds, it becomes clearer that, from a starting point in immediate experience (determinedly *not* in religious tradition), Bataille is attempting to construct a general theory of Desire which is at once a historical anthropology and an existential 'a-theology' (his own term for his atheistic and immanentist theorisation of human eros).

***

His treatment of *interdict and transgression* makes it clear that Bataille is interested both in the origins of these things in primitive religious consciousness and in their significance for contemporary secular man. If the term *interdict* is preferred to the Freudian 'taboo', it is because Bataille strenuously resists the view that the prohibitions imposed by human groupings on certain basic areas of life are superego restrictions arbitrarily imposed from without. On the contrary, they express a profound inner necessity relating to man's attempted management of the awesome god immanent in nature. The human animal is appalled at the sheer disruptive extravagance or 'excess' of life's energies which violently threaten both his individual and his social existence. The primary taboos, those fencing off the violence of death and the violence of untrammelled sexuality ('Thou shalt not kill', 'Thou shalt not perform the carnal act outside wedlock', 'The Act shall be private') equate to refusals to co-operate with nature's squandering orgy, its gratuitous and frightening outpouring of new life and annihilation. Man is the animal who stands abashed ('interdit', in French) before death and sexual union (*E*, 57); if we miss the real human anguish at the heart of the interdict, we will miss the complexity of the desire to transgress, hence the specificity of eroticism (45).

The main function of interdicts is to combat violence (*E*, 48). The interdict interposes a protective distance between normal life and the sacred, as manifest, for instance in its virulent effects upon a decomposing corpse, or in the frenzy of sexual union. Work, rationality, culture are only possible within the sphere of such protection:

> as if man had once intuitively grasped how impossible nature (what is given to us) truly is, requiring of the human beings it engenders that they participate in this frenzy of destruction which animates it and which nothing will satisfy … Human possibility depended on that moment when, caught up in an overwhelming vertigo, one creature attempted to answer *no*. (68–9)

At the crest of the convulsion which gives him shape, man attempts to say 'No' to the destructive and implacable frenzy which surrounds, traverses and grounds him ontologically. Bataille expresses surprise at being the first to enunciate clearly the general formula of all the multifarious particular prohibitions (on incest, on menstrual blood, on touching the corpse, etc.) which anthropologists have laboriously catalogued (58).

This founding refusal opens up the two contiguous spaces of the *sacred* and the *profane*. 'Human society is not just the world of work. Simultaneously – or successively – the profane world and the sacred world make it up, and are the complementary forms of it (*E*, 75). Respected absolutely, the protective set of self-imposed interdicts would confine man within a sphere of rational productivity, economic project and prudent consumption – the sphere of the profane. This would leave him without access to a union with that awesome vital energy which forms his own ground and origin in the natural world. Yet he yearns, not just for consumption, but for the unproductive and violent thrill of 'consummation'; he needs and wills to assent to life as *consuming him in the flame, to the point of death*. (The originality of Bataille's view of human desire, we notice, is that it explains the continuity between libidinal or erotic 'excess', the phenomenon registered in turn by each one of our writers, and the greater, primary excessiveness which pre-exists in the energies *of nature as a whole*: a less individualistic, even a less 'anthropocentric' perspective.)

Transgression is thus as necessary to man as interdict: it alone gives access to the world of the sacred, that is, of gratuitous and consuming self-expenditure, of consent to the overwhelming power of the immanent god. It suspends but does not negate the interdict. Specifically, it 'transcends' it in the Hegelian sense of *aufheben* ('exceeding while maintaining' [*E*, 42]). More than that: Bataille advances the paradox that 'The interdict is there to be violated' (72). The real *meaning* of interdict is that it calls to and enables a limited (less-than-annihilating) transgression. 'The sacred world opens up to limited transgressions. This is the world of festival, of kings and of the gods ' (76). Organising such transgression – rather than mere recoil from life, or the administering of restrictive prohibitions as such – is the business of 'religions'. It is a Freudian misunderstanding, in Bataille's view, to suggest that the basis of religion is taboo, when what is truly at stake is the management of man's approach to the sacred.

The swirling complexities of erotic desire are admirably analysed by Bataille within this conceptual frame. The effect of the interplay of interdict and transgression is that of compression and release, supercharging erotic energies. 'The essence of eroticism is given in the inextricable association of sexual pleasure and interdict' (*E*, 119). Prohibition of itself whips up desire ('Nothing holds licentiousness in check … The real way to extend and mutiply our desires is to attempt to impose boundaries upon them', writes de Sade in *Les 120 Journées de Sodome* [55]). Eroticism, moreover, like murder, is the conscious intention of a mind which has *resolved to trespass* into a forbidden field of behaviour. As such, it produces heady exhilaration at escaping the power of taboo: ecstasy begins where horror is sloughed off, the fear of pain and death transcended. Yet anguish transcended is not simply abolished. We do not escape the disgust of animality, the disordering violation, the wound in selfhood, the disappointed compulsion to transcend individual discontinuity, or the prefigured abyss of death; we merely yield to the divine power which abases, tears and terrifies in the same moment as it exhilarates and exalts. 'Mortal anguish does not conduce necessarily to sexual pleasure, but sexual pleasure is, within mortal anguish, more profound'(116).

Erotic experience, in short, is obscurely supercharged with the alternating current of ambiguity which characterises human experience of the archaic sacred in general: 'Men are at one and the same time subject to the two movements: of a repudiating terror and of attraction, commanding a fascinated respect'(*E*, 76).

Marriage is already, in this perspective, a limited and licensed transgression, hence a *rudimentary, permitted form* of eroticism. Bataille concedes that the full flowering of sexual life in marriage is not a negligible thing, since it favours the intimate understanding of two bodies that only grows with time (he mentions no other relational aspects than the physical). Yet this flowering is threatened by its very licit-ness, which makes the married state equivalent to a protective cocoon of habit-bound equilibrium, in other words, to a *reduced sacrality*. Of it he writes revealingly: 'Thus, would the profound love, which marriage does not in any way paralyse, be accessible without the contagion of illicit loves, which were alone able to give to love something stronger than law?' (*E*, 124). The more transgressive, wild or primitive love is, the greater the coefficient of sacrality, hence also the charge of excitement. This is seen in the ancient comparison of sacrifice and sexual intercourse, making 'love' implicitly synonymous with rape:

> The lover disaggregates the woman no less than the bloody sacrificer does the man or the animal sacrificed. Woman in the hands of the man who assails her is dispossessed of her being. She loses, with her *pudeur*, that firm barrier which, separating her from others, made her impenetrable: suddenly, she opens herself up to the violence of sexuality unleashed in her organs of reproduction, she opens up to the impersonal violence which overwhelms her from without. (104)

It is seen with exemplary clarity in the ancient ritual orgy, which was, Bataille insists

> from the beginning a religious effusion: in principle, a disorder of the being who surrendered and no longer resisted the wild proliferation of life. This immense unleashing appeared divine, so far did it lift man above the condition to which he himself had condemned himself. Disorder of cries, disorder of violent gestures, and of dances, disorder of embraces, disorder too of feelings energised by a measureless convulsion. The prospect of self-loss required this flight into indistinction, in which the human elements vanished, in which there was nothing that did not lose its footing. (126)

The orgy is a feast of licensed transgression and a ritually released paroxysm of 'divine' violence; it epitomises the Bataillian notions of consummation, sovereignty and the sacred. Yet even at its apex, the sacred does not cease to evoke a dynamics of the abyss, since it is conditioned always by man's anguished relation to what is ultimate in human experience. 'Anguish, it seems, constitutes humanity [yet] it is not anguish merely, but the outstripping of anguish.' For 'we want resolutely that which puts our lives at risk' (96).

As for Péret and Breton, the villain of the archaically desiring piece is Christianity. Christian theology and culture have rejected orgy, misunderstood transgression and lost the path of violence as a way of acceding to the sacred. True, Bataille concedes (by a curious hesitation of his own) a sublime and fascinating quality to the Christian vision of a violence transcended, transformed into its opposite: love of God and of humanity (*E*, 131–2). Yet his dominant theme is that of an alienating distortion introduced into man's religious life. The sacred is thereby split into pure and impure, good and evil principles: 'religion' is reduced to a purely gracious sacrality, the impure or evil aspect being thrust back into the profane world. Like many 'post-Christian' theorists, Bataille is struck by ecclesiastical responses to Medieval witchcraft: death by fire awaited anyone who rediscovered in erotic 'sin' a sacred power and an immediate sense of the divine. Transgression, as envisioned within a Christian framework, becomes the basis, not of man's divinity, but of his Fall.

Bataille thus presents Christianity as an inverted religious construct, at odds with humankind's deepest erotic memory. As even the devil is evacuated from religious consciousness, so modern secular man is left to inhabit an entirely profane world onto which has been projected all the impurity, uncleanness and guilt that have been evacuated from the sphere of the sacred.

Prostitution is an index of this inheritance. The erotic carvings incorporated in the temples of India exalt a sacred prostitution without scorn or shame. They remind us both of the obscenity buried deep within men's hearts and of an acknowledged need for the divine. By contrast, low or common prostitution appears as the inevitable counterpart of the Christian condemnation of eroticism as something evil, to be punished with despair, fallen creatures being left to wallow like pigs in their own animality and held up as counter-examples valorising a pure, transmundane spirituality. A dualistic falsification of sexuality, and with it of personal and social life, follows. Transgression condemned ushers in the rationalist denial of evil and the revolt against repressive morality. This reaction in turn heralds the purely profane world of contemporary society, emptied of the sacred, even at length of its last vestiges, of profanation itself. Where there is nothing to transgress and no transgression, there can be no encounter with the sacred. The Christian devalorisation of the dark side of the religious mystery prepares, in the history of Western culture, a loss of the erotic spring as such.

In our relation to Beauty, Bataille finds a pointer to the way back beyond the Christian aberration, a clue to eroticism rediscovered. Beauty offers a purity which appears to deny the animality of man, yet secretly it alludes to, and awakens a desire for, the animal act:

> If beauty, the perfection of which rejects animality, is passionately desired, this is because with beauty the possession of it calls to an animal soiling. It is desired so as to sully it. Not for itself, but for the joy tasted in the certainty of profaning it. (*E*, 160)

To despoil is the essence of eroticism: the greater the beauty, the greater the transgressive excitement of befouling it (so much for Plato, deprived of an undergirding Christian mediation!). In which dialectic, Bataille finds a confirmation that 'the final sense of eroticism is death' (*E*, 159); that is to say, 'nostalgia for lost continuity' (162).

De Sade counts as precursor of this path, albeit (as seen in 1957) a problematic one. His is the example of a sovereign liberty which denies the rights of the 'erotic Other' and makes victims of his sexual partners, upon whom he falls with the fury of a vicious hound. He allows free reign to the excess of elemental nature, regaining strength through the denial of pity, gratitude and love. He even sacrifices himself in the quest for an inflexible sovereignty, defined less as concern for mere 'power' than as an effort to rise above the bonds of necessity binding human existence. We are reminded of Malraux's formula: 'not power, but omnipotence'[20] – and recognise in Bataille's 'sovereignty' the 'being like gods' offered by the Serpent of Genesis.

Not that Bataille endorses de Sade as exemplary. He points out that none of his Surrealist colleagues is actually other than frightened of de Sade, and affirms that to admire him, as they lightly claim to do (he particularly has Breton in his sights), is really to diminish the force of his ideas. True violence, he suggests, is inarticulate and silent, whereas de Sade's verbalisations introduce us to something else: a rationalised will to violence, phantasmatically worked up, by way of vengeance and revolt under conditions of solitary imprisonment. For this very reason, his perversity is revelatory in a way it could not be prior to the era of psychoanalytical and ethnographic self-understanding. De Sade ushers our own inner violence into the field of conscious experience:

> If normal man today is entering profoundly into an awareness of what transgression signifies for him, this is because de Sade opened up the way. Now normal man knows that his consciousness should open itself to what had most violently revolted him: what revolts us most violently is within us. (*E*, 218)

***

The attempt to base upon this foundation of transgressive violence an existential attitude of higher (i.e. mystico-religious) eroticism constitutes the apex of Bataille's effort of theorisation. The word *attempt* is obligatory in this context: there is something tentative, unfinished and indeed unsatisfactory about this first sketch (destined for subsequent elaboration in the series of works composing the *Somme athéologique*).[21] The dialectic is curiously ambivalent: Bataille turns obsessionally around the Catholic edifice, seeking at once to understand it, to subvert it and to derive from it a rival and inverse construct of spirituality. His attitude is now sympathetic and respectful (in contrast to previous virulence), now sharply critical, finally profanatory (as he proclaims the fully divine status of the common prostitute of *Madame Edwarda*). Yet it is ever-fascinated, even in its imagery and language. It is as though the author of *L'Érotisme* were somehow wrestling with an adversary Angel, at once adored and loathed, for possession of the soul of Eros.

What is the connection between eroticism and mysticism, as practised in 'traditional' religious spirituality? Bataille will have nothing of post-Freudian reductionism in the tradition of Marie Bonaparte's reading of the 'transverberation' of Theresa of Avila: the ecstatic spear-thrust of divine union explained as a naive account of phantasmatic orgasm and classified as a transposed sexuality of neurotic status. He is fully persuaded against this view: not only by the openness to psychoanalysis of modern Catholic contemplatives, but also by the untroubled awareness of sexual *redundantia* in all the great Christian mystics and by the self-evident point that the same psycho-physiological apparatus is engaged in both experiences, founding a language of analogy thanks to which each experience may be evoked in terms of the other: 'There are flagrant similarities, even equivalences and exchanges, between the mystical and erotic systems of effusion' (*E,0* 250). Simply, clinical psychoanalysts lack the adequate experience of the two domains which, alone, would allow them to speak meaningfully of the relationship between them. We gather from this firm hermeneutical put-down that Bataille's business is more with religion than with psychoanalysis: at least, we are told, religion approaches the light (252).

Yet the Catholic version of the relationship between these two domains of experience will not do either for Bataille. If it is clearly premature to conclude that the nuptial symbolism of the mystics is to be reduced to a simple sexual signification, can we, on the other hand, admit that 'sexual union has a meaning which transcends it ... and which negates the horror of it, the muddy reality'(*E*, 248)? Catholics see God-orientation as written into 'the flesh': once, in the natural sexuality of the human creature, but also a second time, by express vocation of a grace 'which comes from Christ' (252). This understanding finds a twofold expression: in the sacramental sexuality of marriage ('a union ... all the more humanised in that it recognises the truth of an elective and exclusive love' [253]); and in the vocation of continence and contemplation. Each is predicated on an ethic of will, considered more central to love than physical gratification, and on 'the divine life', which is more threatened by mediocrity, prideful self-satisfaction and self-love than by any carnality. In practice, Catholic discourse proceeds as though morality – the morality of *death to self* – were the arbiter of the mystical life.

Yet the cult of God-willed, God-oriented, 'beneficent' sexuality reckons without '*la part maudite*': that element of excess which cannot be equated with the will of God, or domesticated or in any way accounted for, and which has to do with accursedness and death. 'Beneficent sexuality is close to animal sexuality, in opposition to eroticism which is specific to humankind and which is genital only in origin ... Eroticism is in principle sterile and represents evil and the diabolical' (*E*, 255). A dechristianised mysticism therefore starts here, with that 'diabolical' excess, belonging to us, known to us. The mystic life, when rethought in these terms, becomes, inversely to the Christian conception as Bataille reads it, the judge and guide of morality. It has already been defined as 'the inner experience of the distant horizons possible to being' (251).

Bataille's attempt to expound this definition is a discourse on Temptation. Obsessively, but in secret conformity with his own spiritual biography, he asks us to imagine the temptations of the dedicated religious. These are explained by analogy with the nuptial flight of the drone, nature's clearest example of the death to self involved in love, since the insect dies in mating with the queen. Sexuality can be sacrificed by the contemplative to the divine life he desires, or, on the contrary, succumbed to in that 'desired surrender', that 'effusion' which is the common experience of mystics and of passionate lovers. In neither form of temptation is there any such thing as 'pure' (i.e. merely sexual or merely spiritual) desire; all desire for Bataille is erotico-mystical in nature. In each form of temptation, this ambiguous composite is present:

> this is the desire to die, no doubt, but it is also the desire to live, at the limits of the possible and the impossible, with an ever greater intensity, the desire to live by ceasing to live or to die without ceasing to live, the desire for an extreme state which Saint Theresa, perhaps, alone has depicted strongly enough in the words: 'I die from not dying!' (265)

A common form, and a common spiritual content, designating the underlying unity of mystical experience and eroticism, emerges from the consideration of the two temptations:

> These trances, states of rapture and the theopathic states prolifically described by mystics of every religious discipline – Hindu, Buddhist, Muslim or Christian, not to mention the rarer ones who have no religion – all have the same significance: non-attachment to ordinary life, indifference to its needs, anguish felt in the midst of this until our being reels, and the way is left open to a spontaneous surge of life that is usually kept under control, but which now bursts forth in freedom and infinite bliss. The difference between this experience and that of sensuality is only a matter of confining these impulses to the domain of inner awareness, without the intervention of real and intentional physical activity. (*E*, 272)

Mystics and lovers are one in the nostalgia for such a moment of divine disequilibrium, the 'fulguration of an instant in which death is defied' (259).

This common form reduces Agape to Eros, within a 'one Love' perspective now re-read *erotically*. Mystical and sensual expressions of eroticism are seen as autonomously reciprocal: mystical movements of thought can trigger erotic reactions; and, in tantrism, we see the possibility of triggering a mystical ecstasy from an interrupted sexual embrace (*E*, 273). 'God' is superfluous in Bataille's equation. Catholic continence is seen as 'the condition of an unconditional moment'; yet the essential goal of the unconditioned – 'sovereign' – moment, touching the limits of human possibility, does not pass in any necessary or desirable way through it. Bataille therefore commends an attitude transcending what he regards as the calculating and parsimonious discipline of the monk, with his paralysed 'nuptial flight' towards carnal temptation (276).

The existential horizon opened up here is a Nietzschean one: *amor fati*; adherence, beyond good and evil, to chance; a consuming passion for extremes, lived out within a world whose fundamental indifference justifies laughter and transgressive play as well as tragic commitment. Man is not limited to the unavowable organ of sexual enjoyment, nor does Bataille wish to give to sexual love a pre-eminence that belongs to the whole of life. Yet the unavowable organ teaches a secret of excess, and the truth of a 'need for disorder, violence and indignity which is the root of love' (299). This is the truth of the 'lucid drone' (*E*, 260). A grim enough truth? If we did not carry the light to the very point where darkness falls, asks Bataille hauntingly, 'how should we know that we are, as we are, formed by the projection of being into horror?' (299).

***

Bataille's masterwork offers a challenging and deservedly influential 'general perspective'. Supposing Freud, it offers a non-Freudian mapping of the erotic abyss, an account of the dynamic shadow across all love and desire. Its essential merit is to sand-blast away from the henceforth interlocked domains of erotology and of theology much inherited roof-tiling – idealist, dualist, romantic, anthropocentric, rationalist and bourgeois. Reaching back beyond an increasingly secularised and 'profane' post-Enlightenment culture, Bataille directly exposes and confronts our Judaeo-Christian foundations. More specifically, his conception of 'la part maudite', like his discourse on the 'two temptations', situates this aspect of his thought in the long line of revolt against the traditional Catholic regulation of sexuality. (Is Bataille *imaginable*, one wonders, apart from Augustine's reading of Genesis, anathematising erotic excess? Where else would 'Pierre Angélique' find his *pierre angulaire*?).

One can hardly overstate the persuasion of the 'death of God' overshadowing Bataille's theory of the erotic. It plunges his ontological and relational sensibility, and with it his entire thought, into a negativity of the 'dark night'. Not only does it give him to hear the music of being as a heart-stopping, orgiastic beat of terror and exaltation; it persuades him that the need for disorder, violence and indignity is the 'root of love'; that the wound of ritual blood-sacrifice is the fundamental analogue for human sexuality; that the business of religion is the management of transgression (and at length, of morality); that beauty is the mask worn by obscenity; and that human life itself is a 'projection of being into horror'.

What dominates in Bataille's hymn-like Nietzschean finale is precisely the sense of transcendence ('dépassement'), deeply wounded by the 'death of God', yet defiantly – and *religiously* – regathered in affirmation of the need to make good, as best may be, an irremediable Absence:

> Being joins of its own accord the terrible, syncopated dance, whose rhythm governs ours, the dance we must accept for what it is, conscious of the horror it is in key with. If our hearts fail us, there is no torture like it. And the moment of torment will always be there: how would we overcome it if it were to be lacking? But all of being, ready and open – for death, joy or torment – unreservedly open and dying, painful and happy, appears then with its veiled light, and this light is divine: and the cry that being – vainly?– tries to utter from a twisted mouth is an immense *alleluia*, lost in endless silence. (*E*, 300)

In this dramatic hyperbole, are not deeper ambiguities inscribed? Bataille writes in a curious footnote an apology for not being able to give a philosophic account of his key concepts of 'being' and 'excess': 'excess is that by which being is first of all, before all things, outside all limits [...] excess is the exception, the marvellous, the miracle' (297). In the drifting of this sentence, it is suddenly as though excessiveness were, contrary to his own thesis, a positive founding value, a sort of grace, a transcending alpha and omega beyond our experience of mundane being —something perilously akin, in fact, to the good and transcendent Creator God! And of course, the disqualified Judaeo-Christian myth, in treating all Bataille's main themes, does indeed suggest something Bataillian about the Creator's prodigious and 'prodigal' love-energies (even if it insists, in a manifest refusal of 'fusional-effusional' religion, on their pattern of purposiveness, distinction, and alterity). Bataille himself half-recognises this in another footnote, yet sardonically, in a salute which reconverts itself into a movement of revolt:

> I might well point out moreover that excess is the very principle of sexual reproduction, for divine providence wished her secret to be plain in her work! Could humankind be spared nothing? The day it notices that the ground is snatched from beneath its feet, it is told that this is providential! But even if he produce a child from his blasphemy, it is by blaspheming and spitting upon his own limitations that the most miserable creature finds his climax, and it is by blaspheming that he is God. The fact is that creation is inextricable, irreducible to any other impulse of the mind than to the certitude, being exceeded, of exceeding. (298, note 2)

It is *as if* the theorist were haunted still, and still exorcising, obscure remembrances which his theory *cannot* accommodate: the nuptial splendour of the *Song of Songs*; the first word of the risen Christ ('Peace'), signifying the stilling of the horror of death predicated upon an 'endless silence' (hence, a deliverance from the anguished spring of archaic, i.e. *natural*, religion). Is he not haunted, even, by the most remarkable feature of Genesis itself – that it both *represents* in the figure of the Serpent the innate erotico-religious 'temptation', practised throughout history, and also *criticises* it as idolatry (an inauthentic 'being-like-gods')? Is Bataille, we wonder, secure in logical space from an alternative view of 'what Christianity signifies in relation to the entirety of these questions'? (289).

My own reading does not suggest, as does one commentator, 'a discreet return to Catholicism, which, it seems, has passed unnoticed'.[22] Yet, at the heterogeneous margins, we certainly do catch the harmonics of Bataille's *confidence* that 'nothing has attracted me more than the possibility of refinding in a general perspective the image with which my adolescence was obsessed, that of God' (*E*, 13). And, amid the ambiguities of this fascination, we glimpse the distinct possibility that *L'Érotisme* could be a prolegomenon to a modern re-reading of Genesis, and other biblical texts, rather than a footnote to their burial.

For Bataille's original and commanding intuition is surely this: that the very excessiveness of human Eros is, in origin and significance, *essentially religious*. Whatever his metaphysics or his theology, in ancient times as now, *homo eroticus* cannot help declaring – and is incomprehensible if we fail to notice – *homo religiosus*. The demolition of a received dogmatic superstructure points, not away from, but rather, more acutely towards, the primitive religious sacrality beneath. For Bataille, 'we receive being in an intolerable transcendence of being' (*E*, 297); and no less so love and desire. Anthropologically and a-theologically questioned, man is, more than ever, the *religious animal*.[23]

Bataille's dark and violent abyss registers, in the electric shock of horror-and-ecstasy, just as Breton's starry castle does in the thrill of poetic enchantment, an authentic mystery of being. We may, or may not, after reading *L'Érotisme*, 'go in fear of ourselves' (*E*, 11); but we can no longer underestimate the depth or density of the carrying enigma within.

Notes

1 G. Bataille, *L'Érotisme* édition illustrée (Paris: Minuit, 1957), p. 23. Further references will be given in the text as *E* followed by page number.
2 A. Breton, *Œuvres complètes*, Vol. II, ed. M. Bonnet & E.-A. Hubert, Bibliothèque de la Pléiade (Paris: Gallimard, 1988), p. 744.
3 M. Richardson, *Georges Bataille* (London: Routledge, 1994), p. 4.
4 A. Breton, *Œuvres complètes*, Vol. II, pp. 824–7.
5 See Richardson, *Georges Bataille*, pp. 4–14.
6 S. Alexandrian, *Les Libérateurs de l'amour* (Paris: Seuil, 1977), Chapter 9, 'Bataille et l'amour noir'.
7 These fictions are, within the meaning of the Obscene Publications Act, 'obscene'. Yet it would be misguided to score them from the record as 'dirty ... and unacceptable' (Richardson, *Georges Bataille*, p. 61): Bataille's theory is the product of its genesis.
8 See M. Surya, *Georges Bataille: An Intellectual Biography* (London & New York: Verso, 2002), pp. 23–38.
9 G. Bataille, *L'Impossible* in *Œuvres complètes*, Vol. 3 (Paris: Gallimard, 1970), pp. 211–12.
10 G. Bataille, *Sur Nietzsche*, quoted by Alexandrian in *Les Libérateurs*, p. 259.
11 G. Bataille, *La Scissiparité* in *Œuvres complètes*, Vol. 3, p. 228.
12 G. Bataille, 'La Conjuration sacrée', *Acéphale* 1 (1936).
13 Alexandrian, *Les Libérateurs*, p. 264.
14 Bataille, *Sur Nietzsche*, quoted by Alexandrian in *Les Libérateurs*, p. 262.
15 Alexandrian, *Les Libérateurs*, p. 260.
16 G. Bataille, *L'Anus solaire* in *Œuvres complètes*, Vol. 1 (Paris: Gallimard, 1970), p. 85.
17 Ibid.
18 Alexandrian, *Les Libérateurs*, p. 261.
19 See ibid., p. 273.
20 A. Malraux, *La Condition humaine* (Paris: Le Livre de poche, 1972), p. 186.
21 See G. Bataille, *Œuvres complètes* (Paris: Gallimard), in particular: *L'Expérience intérieure*, *Le Coupable* and *L'Allejuiah* (Vol. 5, 1973); *Sur Nietzsche* (Vol. 6, 1973); *Théorie de la religion* (Vol. 7, 1976).
22 J.-F. Fourny, *Introduction à la lecture de Bataille* (New York: Peter Lang, 1988), p. 126.
23 The true inheritor of Bataille, on this reading, is not postmodern critical theory, but René Girard, with his theory of 'Violence and the sacred'. Girard starts where Bataille ends: with the recognition that archaic or 'natural' religion is not a renounceable cultural accretion, but, seen and unseen, a constituting dimension of biologically desiring humanity, ancient and modern. Free of Bataille's freighted and weighted 'revolt', with its simplifying overbid, he elucidates (as Bataille does not, though he assuredly *exhibits* it) the *mimetic basis* of eroticism; and he offers a more diverse and supple reading of social and 'religious' violence (including 'transgressive' violence and 'sacrifice'). His more patient exegesis of ethnographic and cultural data consistently throws into relief the irreducible singularity of the Judaeo-Christian tradition (not least in relation to 'scapegoating' and to 'sacrifice'), while showing the historical 'anomalies' of Christianity itself as 'archaic' survivals. (For references, see the bibliography.)

Chapter 11

Marguerite Duras: The Haunting

Qui nous arrachera à la calamité du cœur?[1]

'The contemporary writer who has best understood love,' declared the weekly *Elle* in 1962 of Marguerite Duras.[2] This accolade from a glossy women's magazine of course predates the more *unreaderly* (or 'challenging') texts of the 'Lol V. Stein Cycle' and the apocalyptic social prophecy of the post-1968 novels, films and film scenarios; not to mention the deeper plunge into the nocturnal depths of eroticism marked by *L'Homme assis dans le couloir* (1980) or *La Maladie de la mort* (1982). It provides nevertheless a certificate of cultural conformity. Duras is seen to touch a pulse, and to render to her mid-late twentieth-century readership an entirely recognisable image and understanding of love.

To this attribute, this chapter seeks to join another, more remarkable and more challenging one. Marguerite Duras attends, in a problematising, modern art of writing, to the enigma of erotic excess and its ever-ambiguous decipherment. This places her, it will be seen, in direct line of descent, from the ancient question: 'Who is this who...?'

***

To all seeming, 'love' in the early Duras conforms effortlessly to a traditional erotico-romantic typology. It emerges within a state of inner torpor or confinement (by parental control, marriage or larger social structures). There is an awakening call to adventure: the scene of the dance or ball, omnipresent in her novels, is a metaphor for this promiscuous and venturesome stirring; and it prefigures the much vaster 'dance of desire' which unfolds throughout her work. Frequently, there is an electric surge of sexual attraction: a glance is enough to fix its object-choice; propagation of the spell within the psychic subject is near-instantaneous; and this *coup de foudre* leads directly to a sexual consummation. Amorous desire is (as Plato suggested) a visitation from the messenger of the gods. Duras ironically comments on this romantic stereotype in *Le Marin de Gibraltar*.[3] The narrator experiences *his* epiphany while contemplating a painting of the Annunciation, a reproduction of which had figured on his bedroom wall as a child and which he now discovers 'in the original' in a museum, amid the torrid heat of an Italian summer. (We note in passing the novelist's characteristically French *conflation* of culture-sources.) Yet while the Call is absolute, the message is, in this mid-twentieth-century text, very relative, and the spell quite temporary; so that the messenger is a frequent visitor, casting multiple spells and bringing serial loves.

Of this process of amorous-erotic *vagabondage*, the quest depicted in the last-mentioned of Duras' novels provides a fundamental metaphor. The elusive Gibraltarian sailor pursued across the oceans by the heroine figures the ideal or absolute of *Amour-Passion*, known only in its elusive promise; while the casual shipboard liaisons in which she engages in the meantime stand as proximate substitutes for the inaccessible ideal. The semi-mythic Sailor is, nevertheless, a crucial part of the game played out. It is from the Promise he represents that the heroine's *amours* derive their legitimacy (or at least their ironically justifying pretext). In turn, the erotic energies invested in these temporary loves re-consecrate his dubious standing as real entity and ultimate goal. Here is the fundamental statement of the *triangular relational figure* or 'love-trio' which critics have frequently discerned and sought to interpret in Duras. Before engaging with it in its more complex Durassian variations, it is worth noting that this *structure* reproduces in a modern, anthropocentric form the perennial pattern of Eros, and that it does so according to an inherited syntax of articulation of Western *amour-passion*.

A second characteristic figure of Durassian love-and-desire, however, emerges to view from behind the first (libertine/Romantic) one. The cruise is long, amorous dalliance palls; the Other-ideal condemns the imperfection of its proximate likenesses. The very differential between Promise and realisation generates the temptation to possess the haunting Third Term by proxy, in the only form available: namely, a self-administered death, erotic excess expending itself 'madly' in a consecration *à vide*, at the expense of life itself. This second (Wagnerian) figure, that of passion-unto-death or erotic love-suicide, is lightly sketched when the narrator of *Le Marin de Gibraltar* experiences the impulse to throw himself and his mistress under a bus in Tangiers. It is more fully realised in the 'crime passionnel' of *Moderato cantabile* (1958). Reconstructing the killing, the couple formed by Anne and Chauvin reproduces in amorous form the dynamic of separation-fusion-effusion, which is thus apprehended as the dynamic behind the murder. Reciprocally, the murder, occasion and focus of their rendezvous is seen to adumbrate the disturbing finality of the couple's *adultère blanc*.

Less immediately visible in Duras is the theoretical understanding of love, desire and transcendence – the erotology informing her fictional 'erotics'. Duras thinks, as many of her exegetes have subsequently also thought, in Bataillian terms.[4] 'Love', in this understanding, is always fundamentally equated with eroticism. The sexual act remains the defining reference. Love is the transgression of difference, the conscious acceptance of the experienced logic of pulsional or libidinal excess, overflowing barriers of prohibition and of individual identity, in an essentially fusional movement. Fusion and difference play against each other in dynamic polarity: prohibition reinforces desire, so that the charge will accumulate until it is *in extremis* powerful enough to overflow the last barrier, the interdict prohibiting the taking of life (the case of *crime passionnel*) or its surrender (as in love-suicide).

Short of this, 'any love is a degradation of Love'.[5] Here we have the basic formula of the related Durassian concepts of sexual *vagabondage* and amorous 'nomadism', as portrayed in *Le Marin de Gibraltar*. Marriage (originally and inevitably seen as 'bourgeois') is systematically depreciated in this framework (and in Duras' fiction generally). Indeed, impermanence strikes almost any form of faithful coupledom: not out of distaste or hedonism merely, but now ideologically, in the name of a higher ethic espousing, within Nietzschean horizons, the inherent logic of Eros (a logic already well identified by de Rougement as 'being in love with Love', but now re-legitimised in Bataillian terms as a transgressive, 'horizontal' transcendence, an experience of the archaic sacred in a bourgeois world). The Bataillian framework adds to the perennial dynamics of Eros a deliberate refusal to normalise or to moralise the erotic. Wherever it leads, whatever the perceived risks, there the subject will be right, in principle, to follow.

Moral judgements being suspended, the more radical question of subject-identity moves to the fore. This occurs as the autobiographical master-story of adolescent initiation and emancipation in Indo-China emerges in Duras' writing. 'That in love differences might be cancelled out to this point is something she would not forget.'[6] This authorial comment in *Barrage contre le Pacifique* summarises the heroine's 'new understanding of love'. Contextually, it refers to Suzanne's self-determined defloration by Agosti – an episode presented in the novel as an entirely unromantic rite of passage, marking her accession to the world of sexual adventure, social promotion and adult freedom already inhabited by her brother Joseph. What in retrospect is declared decisive ('elle ne l'oublierait plus') is a superordinate symbolic sense: in the sexual encounter is realised a proximity to the undifferentiated erotic life-current, an openness to being as such. The conditional tense engages a 'not-forgetting' proper to the writer herself: this is the latent intentionality *drawn out* in her own existential trajectory and *re-apprehended* in the very act of writing, as a thread of subject-identity. The proto-experience of erotic indifferentiation, experienced independently of and prior to 'love', becomes an obsessionally re-questioned key to the whole psychic Desire-world of the awakening feminine subject.

Four successive accounts of the story of adolescent sexual initiation are in fact given by Duras: in her own wartime diary, in *Barrage contre le Pacifique* (1952), in *L'Amant* (1984) and in *L'Amant de la Chine du Nord* (1991). All trace the growth of an essentialising 'memory-myth', that is a fiction drawn from life, but 'truer than life' in that it models and re-models the essential decipherment made by the author of a founding enigma, a perpetually present 'inner time'. If *Moderato cantabile* (1958) and *Hiroshima mon amour* (1960) already mark the advent of a major artist, this is because they are fully reflexive works which already look back to this *deeper psychic nerve-point*. The more subtle imaginary modelling made possible by a fully reflexive form attends to, and mirrors, the expressive emergence of 'the meta-sexual element of love' (Valéry's term); it captures, that is, the transcendent/transgressive 'something else' immanent within it, something normally unperceived and unsaid. Writing, for Duras, is increasingly the approach to what she, for her part, calls 'the inner shadow',[7] the dynamic *mouvance* in which are contained the unknown territories and secret springs of the psychic subject or 'self'.

That such a concept of writing runs parallel to psychoanalysis is clear; and Lacan's fascinating – and flawed – exegesis of her most central text confirms this ('Marguerite

Duras turns out to know without me what I teach').[8] Yet it is equally clear that the Durassian text pursues its own way to its own decipherment.

***

Le Ravissement de Lol V. Stein (1964)[9] marks the moment in the writer's itinerary where the knot of the enigma – and the shadow of Duras' own haunting – moves centre-stage, and is addressed in a fully adequate literary form. This knot has often been *exegetically cut* (not least, by Lacan, when – to the writer's understandable disconcertion – he congratulated her on having described 'a clinically perfect case of delirium').[10] Inversely, the hermeneutic knot has been *declared untieable* – a 'story of epistemological frustration' in which all major meanings 'are blocked by the text' itself.[11] Neither view quite does justice, I think, to the singular virtue of this particular exercise in fictional imagining and self-awareness – namely, its power of 'transferential haunting'. Duras' writing, it will be argued here, makes epistemological frustration into a resonantly configured hermeneutic obsession, referring the attentive reader back, in enlightened self-recognition, towards the entire enigma – or do we mean the mystery? – of love, desire and transcendence carried within the human subject.

The reader is invited to attend, along with the narrator who presents it, to the strange story of Lol V. Stein. (It is, indeed, crucial to *register accurately* the considerable data the text does give, and to observe its indubitable basic patterns). The case centres on a mysterious catastrophe, which erupts like some inner apocalypse. At the age of nineteen, Lol has seen her fiancé Michael Richardson stolen from her by an older woman during a ball at the Municipal Casino of T. Beach. In registering the *coup de foudre* which occurs between them and in observing the 'transgressive' couple dancing throughout the evening, she has appeared strangely passive, inexplicably wrapped or rapt in some 'elsewhere'. At the end of the night, when the new couple disappear together, she is said to have let out a cry and fallen prostrate. Victim of some trauma of passion which has unhinged her reason or dislocated her personality, she has been declared 'insane'.

Apparently recovering, she begins to make random nocturnal excursions in her home-town of S. Tahla. During one such outing, she picks up Jean Bedford, who subsequently proposes marriage. For ten years, Lol's condition is controlled, normalised. As bourgeois wife and mother living in another town, she leads an impeccably ordered existence, save only that she is obsessionally haunted, in her afternoon reveries or in solitary walks, by the memory of the ball: a scenario of rapture and of ravishing, of ecstasy and of loss, which is phantasmatically run and re-run in her head, albeit amputated of its ending. She tends therefore to invent what is lacking. The endgame scenario she imagines invariably takes the form of a voyeuristic phantasm of sexual encounter in which she always sees her lost fiancé beginning to undress her rival; yet this extended scenario in turn never reaches its consummation.

Following a move with her husband back to S. Tahla, the scenario running in Lol's head begins to emerge from its psychic latency and to inscribe itself into real life, prompted by a series of coincidences which give it foothold. Lol observes a passionate and furtive kiss between an illicit couple in front of her gate; later, she waits for the male protagonist, whom she catches emerging from 'the central cinema', and trails him to an assignation in the Hôtel des Bois. She proceeds to observe his illicit rendezvous voyeuristically, posted in a field of rye-grass behind the hotel. The female partner is her former friend, witness and *confidante* of the Ball scene at T. Beach, Tatiana Karl.

Lol becomes an increasingly active producer of her own scenario. Through Tatiana, she seeks out the latter's partner. At the point where he is formally presented to Lol, Jacques Hold reveals himself directly to the reader as the reconstructor of the story we have been following and as the narrator of its ongoing sequel. During a social occasion at her house, Lol is seen to seduce Jacques Hold into a fascinated complicity, semi-lucid and collaborating, with the voyeuristic scenario she is bent on enacting. Despite his declaration of love for her, she insists that he continue his erotic rendezvous with Tatiana, which she, for her part, continues to observe; she is now also able to hear about them directly from the male participant, who both acts out and recounts his rendezvous, increasingly in function of his amorous desire for the *voyeuse* herself.

A more radical enactment follows. During a dance recalling the ball, a switch of partners is seen to occur, leaving Tatiana as excluded third. Jacques becomes Lol's companion in the most extreme figure of variation, a figure tending to supply the ending which was lacking from the original programmatic phantasm. The new couple return to T. Beach, revisiting the biographical site and origin of the love-scenario in which they are both engaged – and a release from its haunting. They revisit the ballroom of the Municipal Casino at T. Beach, but Lol discovers there no traces, no ghosts and no exorcism.

The extreme figure of the enacted scenario produces a different climax. Transgressing the limit set in Lol's phantasm, the couple at last spend the night together in a hotel. Their love-making triggers in Lol a crisis of identity: as well as a surge of awakened erotic appetite, she shows symptoms of clinical schizophrenia. The couple then return to S. Tahla. Lol does not respond to an invitation to elope with Jacques. An ambiguous ending sees her positioned once more – albeit now sleeping – in front of the window of the hotel room within which Jacques Hold and Tatiana Karl have a last erotic assignation.

Clearly enough, the question of what haunts and drives Lol V. Stein is reborn, within the itinerary of quest, out of the attempted resolution itself (in this sense, the reverse of a *dénouement*). This gives the novel's key-signature: the 'case' of Lol, as shaped and patterned by Duras' fictional presentation, forms a kind of perfect hermeneutic circle. What the protagonist seeks existentially – her Quest – is consistently and finally reciprocal to the Question of the origin, nature and meaning of her questing movement; hence, to our decipherment of it. The more she advances in the enacted logic of her 'madness', the more fully this question is posed and re-posed in its principle. The more fully it is posed – and not answered – the more Lol advances in the logic of her 'madness'.

Moreover, this reciprocity of Quest and Question is hauntingly transmitted to the reader, thanks to Duras' admirable invention of having the partner-elect of Lol's scenario recount the ongoing story of that scenario as participant and as decipherer-in-chief. We have noted in passing the essential link between protagonist and narrator: Jacques emerges out of the 'cinéma du centre' (*R* 52) – as clear a *metatextual signal* (or 'clue') as we might hope to receive that both emerge from the same place and that what proceeds in him is the counterpart of what proceeds in her ... and in us. Jacques responds mimetically and by contagion to what he himself designates as 'le cinéma de Lol Valérie Stein' (49) (the French suggests inauthentic play-acting, as well an analogy between psychic process and cinema).

There are several capital implications here. The most fundamental concerns what we may call the 'hermeneutic standing' of the narrator. The only way he – or anybody else – can decipher Eros is *mimetically*, that is by entering into the scenario by which it is expressed, joining its movement, playing its game, enacting its tendency. Only thus can he validly re-trace any 'figure of sense' which the intelligence can take unto itself, apprehend or – Duras' name for this character – 'hold'. There is no other *comprehension* of Lol's 'madness' than that which Jacques Hold offers in self-definition: 'I know Lol V. Stein in the only way I can, through love' (*R*, 46).

This approach sets the narrator significantly apart in the world of the novel: at once from Tatiana-*la-bourgeoise*, who uses the the label 'madness' out of fear of the threat she instinctively apprehends in Lol; from her husband, the Consultant Pierre Beugner, who thinks, perhaps disingenuously, that Jacques' interest in Tatiana is purely a matter of clinical observation and medical concern (*R*, 90); from Jacques' own professional persona as clinician – and, indeed, from Jacques Lacan (who doubtless lends his first name to Duras' narrator). It is a central perspective of narrative form in this novel that the effort of deciphering Eros only ever emerges – precisely as does Jacques Hold – *from within* the 'central cinema' where desire-scenarios are mysteriously put together and projected: it does not belong to any autonomous rationality or science. Erotic excess is sovereign unto itself.

The same possibility condition determines, secondly, the narrator's power to engage the reader in the transferred or transmitted function of decipherment. In presenting Lol's proto-history (i.e., her 'case' as established prior to Jacques' own entry into the triangular game), the as-yet anonymous narrative voice is at conspicuous pains to underline the fragility of an act of understanding which is seen to combine all the hazards of documentary reconstruction ('Tatiana thinks that...') with all those of a mimetic re-invention or imaginative envisioning drawn from the narrator's own substance ('I see...' , 'I invent...'). Such indications, framing the data they interpret, act as a crucial *induction* into the hermeneutic function which the reader is invited to exercise: they prepare us to decipher the ongoing development of the scenario in a *second degree*, embracing the narrator's own discourse as a part of the game, proceeding and supplying the gaps in the causal tissue of his account by an act of mimetic identification analogous to that which Jacques himself continues to exercise in relation to Lol: 'Levelling the terrain, opening the tombs in which Lol is faking death, seems to me more legitimate when you have to invent the missing links in the chain of the story of Lol V. Stein' (*R*, 37).

So, for instance, at the moment when 'formal introductions' are effected, the text *repeats* sequences of information already given in describing Lol's case (*R*, 78ff., 102ff.). The effect is to *reposition the reader*, inviting the discovery that *data-interpetation* about amorous subjects is *relative to data-readers*, each having his or her own field of desire. More subtly still, the switch between the pronouns of self-reference, 'I' and 'he', in the narrator's discourse indicates the ambiguity of his status (at once interpreter of, and participant in, Lol's scenario); they mark the flickering shifts of his self-identification inflected by awareness of the desired Other; and they suggest the gravitational pull of *fascinated contagion* to which this entire version of events is subjected (cf. 124–5). In short, they induce the reader to stand imaginatively *in the place of the hermeneutic subject*, establishing, by dint of a perpetual word-by-word attention of decipherment, the fictional hypothesis explored under the name of Lol V. Stein.

We are thus drawn into deciphering an *alienation, malaise or illness* declared in the unknown subject of amorous desire ('If others come after me who also know that, I accept their coming,' says the narrator, by way of metatextual invitation [*R*, 166]). The novel's narrative form, in short, mirrors and inscribes its own condition of possibility: 'I try to understand, to contain what contains me': Valéry's splendid formula applies in respect of character, narrator, author and reader. There is no sure point of anchorage: deciphering our own haunting, we see 'as in a glass darkly', since the reading of it, like the writing of it, emerges out of the same scenario that it seeks to stage.

If we have accurately discerned the logic of the novel's signifying form, Duras enacts textually the questioning of an erotico-spiritual Quest. This novel first invites us to look back to an existential point of emergence: what is the logic of the paralysing-but-then-activating trauma that generates the strangely mad 'scenario' pursued by Lol V. Stein? Reciprocally, it invites us then to scan the obscure tendency or goal of the haunted subject, inscribed in the figures of contagion and recurrence engendered by her and around her. How do these things emerge from the 'primal scene' which seems to epitomise, as in a myth or a dream, the singular and enigmatic 'knot' of her haunting?

The novel engages us, in short, in a dialectical form of decipherment: it follows the river of amorous desire both upstream to its rising (in a movement of essentialist understanding), and downstream towards the universal sea (in existentialist exploration); it engages its reader in both a psychogenetics and a psychopoetics of the 'madness' presented.

***

Lol's case is strongly analogous – we have Lacan's word that it is *perfectly* so – to a case of schizophrenia, that is a psychic disorder implying extreme dislocation of the sense of personal identity. The traumatic experience of the Ball already displays a strange disjunction of two aspects of emotional experience suggested by the word 'ravissement': at once *rapture* (fascinated delight, euphoria, joy, excursion of being) and catastrophic *ravishing* (violating loss, devastation, abduction of the Object of desire in whom or in which one's own subject-identity is invested).

To this highly suggestive figure of sense, the novel offers the substantial – and haunting! – *caveat* already noted. If Lol is mad, then the madness appears to be strangely common, indeed universal. Her dance of desire is answered and replicated; her *collaborateur*-elect emerges from the (same?) 'central cinema', engaged by the question: 'but what is it of which I am so uninstructed in myself and which she puts me in a position to understand?' (*R*, 105). Indeed, conventional classifications being removed, are not the symptoms of schizophrenia disturbingly akin to those of amorous desire as such? Every conceivable case of falling love involves an agony and an ecstasy, a transfer of identity, an obsessional haunting, a 'traumatic' reconfiguration of the self compelled by the need for an intuited totality of being. In every experience of passion, there is a supra-individual 'absolute' blindly pursued. The specific difference of Lol's case would appear to be that Lol is, from the beginning, *pathologically* 'disjoined', *morbidly* locked or 'blocked' into a scenario which is *fundamentally unreal*; a scenario from which, crucially, the dream of Love flows away – the text says like the ocean from a broken vessel, the 'kingdom of the psyche' (55) – and which she yet follows compulsively, immersed in it as in some waking dream. Here, precisely, is the enigma-point.

The oneiric quality proper to her quest is strongly asserted in the 'primal scene' which Lol's own memory recycles and re-enacts in a manner of which the narrator's reconstruction and Duras' writing offer a suggestive account. As in a dreamsphere, the logic of events is both super-vivid and intellectually obscure; the 'ravishing' is registered as occurring in a world of displaced, condensed, fragmented and allusively symbolic meanings, of which the subject is the implied but strangely passive (impotent or absent) centre.

As key to the dreamsphere, the narrator himself retains 'the strange omission of her grief during the ball' (*R*, 24). Strange indeed: it is unclear why the nineteen-year-old girl, observing the seduction and abduction of her fiancé, should stand idly by, observing in seemingly euphoric fascination (particularly if, as is hinted at towards the end of the book, this reaction directly follows a 'love-vow', perhaps even a first sexual experience, at the Hôtel des Bois). And strangeness irradiates. Why does the twenty-five-year-old Richardson – even in a Duras novel! – experience such a devastating *coup de foudre* for a thin, black-clad woman who appears from nowhere, and who is old enough to be his mother? (As if to make this very point, Anne-Marie Stretter's *daughter* accompanies her entry, before slipping away unnoticed.) What is this fascinated complicity, defying the 'the ancient algebra of love's pains' (19)? Again: why is the dream-subject so removed physically from the dance-floor action, set apart with her friend Tatiana behind the screen of rubber-plants flanking the bar?

Why, when the suspended natural reaction does occur, does it begin so allusively, like a quasi-musical modulation of the dreamsphere itself ('a plaintive and tender modulation invades the empty room' [21]). Why is it triggered by the appearance of the intrusive and over-reacting mother (she later, we learn, attempts to summon the police); and why, when it does declare itself, does it erupt so apocalyptically, like some trump of the Last Day?

We have to supply the implicit *dream-syntax*. Here, the Durassian proto-text of adolescent initiation does offer some substantial clues. What happens at the Ball is *like* a scene in *Barrage:* the adolescent girl's discovery in the cinema of the kiss between screen lovers. The mystery of sexual attraction is discovered *at second-hand*, from the depths of a darkness in which many desires circulate; what is seen is the close-up of a 'clinch' in which lovers, fascinatingly if mysteriously, seek to devour each other and merge.[12] It is also *like* the phantasm of *L'Amant*, which shows the fifteen-year-old protagonist, excited by, and envious of, the physical beauty of her friend Hélène Lagonelle, proposing to offer her desirably beautiful friend to her Chinese lover as a substitute sexual partner, so that the circuit of male and female desire can be enjoyed, albeit by proxy, from a position as spectator, in the guise of an *imaginary spectacle of total Desire*.[13] Behind both these auto-fictional images is perhaps yet another reminiscence: the daydream, attributed to the even younger protagonist of *Le Boa* who, from her oppressive girls' boarding school, looks wistfully towards the nearby brothel, as an exotic haven of emancipation, where the curse of virginity might be shed and the Adventure of Life begun.[14]

All these 'reminiscences' haunt the 'primal scene' of *Le Ravissement*, offering clues to the roles of the protagonists and to the unspoken tenor of its affective impact. They establish 'the theme of the dream': the *fascination of the encounter with the erotic as such.* And, clearly, they attribute the dream to a *much younger subject* than the supposed 19-year old fiancé of our novel. The intervention of the reproving – and – '*so* embarrassing!'– Mother, come to collect an errant adolescent daughter in the wee small hours, begins at this point to be a little more transparent...

Yet the central key is still missing. First Love is *real* love, however embedded it may still be in adolescent fantasy. Logically, it must be the *betrayal* of a real love that produces, so late, the recognition of such woundedness. The novel invites us to seek a secret 'in the order of the heart'. The sealed drawer of autobiographical memory, declared such by Duras from 1981,[15] does indeed contain such a secret. There *was* historically a 'real' love: the unsayable and (potentially) incestuous passion of the adolescent Marguerite Duras for her brother Paulo. This biographical datum will impress any reader of *Barrage* as a cogent truth in the order of feeling. The Joseph of that novel (auto-fictional transposition of Paulo) is a handsome, virile adventurer, master of the jungle, as he is of his sister's phonograph, of her sexual 'coming out' and of her dreams of escape; he is Father-substitute and Hero. Three years older than Suzanne, he shares her aspirations and protects her with brusque masculine tenderness from everything that hurts: their abusive and maternally unjust mother, their thuggish older brother, the grimly unviable situation of the family itself, which his gifts of humorous burlesque dissolve into moments of euphoric hilarity.

Beside the admirable Joseph, Suzanne's first suitor in the novel, the significantly named M. Jo, cuts a reduced and sorry figure. It is Joseph's depreciatory glance upon the dancing couple of Suzanne and M. Jo that declares the latter's grotesque suit no more than a stunted caricature of 'the real thing'.

There is a further autobiographical datum that does *not* appear in *Barrage contre le Pacifique*. At a key point of Marguerite's adolescence in Vinh-Lhong, the adored brother Paulo was invited to play tennis at the country club run by a diplomat's wife, a certain Anne-Marie Stretter – the selfsame *femme fatale* featured, *under her own real-life name*, in the 'primal scene' of *Le Ravissement*. We have only to replace the fictional fiancé of *Le Ravissement*, Michael Richardson, by the true (but bracketed) Rival of this unavowable and denied passion to produce a figure of meaning that 'reads' the dream-syntax of the Ball at T. Beach exactly and transparently.

Armed with this 'key', we can decipher the cryptic sub-text of the primal scene and its power of expansive resonance. The dream Subject is hardly in the frame at all: she is the excluded Third, relegated behind the railings (implicitly: of the exclusive tennis club to which her [br]Other has miraculously acceded). She can do nothing but gaze intently, scrutinising the imminence of a *feared-and-desired coup de foudre* between this *femme fatale* and her own crypto love-partner elect. The Event at first thrills ('enraptures') her. (It is the sign of the sexual liberation, emancipation and social promotion of which brother and sister have tenderly co-dreamed and which represents for both the only Salvation. More than that: it is the – transgressive – encounter-by-procuration with the sacrality of Eros; there is a *delegation* of her own role.) 'She watched out for the event, broodily tended its immensity' (*R*, 18). The new 'couple' is at first envisaged without fear, almost maternally: 'a woman whose heart is free of all commitment, very old, watches the children move away, appeared to like them' (18). Yet there is also, *pianissimo*, a sense of helpless passivity (at the spell cast by the sexually experienced and sophisticated older woman); and an undertow of covert resentment ('that desiccated old Crow is ancient enough to be his mother!'). As the couple framed in the dream-subject's vision make to leave, a look is exchanged between the Subject and her [br]Other: Lol needs some 'sign of eternity'; but her brave smile of encouragement remains unseen, unanswered. 'They had silently contemplated each other, for a long time, not knowing what to do, how to emerge from the night' (21). The arrival of the intolerable Mother then triggers a dawning horror (an adolescent's parent is always an 'intrusive Third'; but, here uniquely, this superego figure alludes to an *incestuous* triangle, hence to a shameful *chagrin d'amour* deprived of its All).

The dream scenario, as we see, is that of an undeclared and thrilling Promise which is dashed in horror. It stages the shipwreck of a prior Expectancy which *cannot speak its name* (and is thus 'locked' to the subject's own self-understanding). To hold back the world of a frightful new Dawning, there can be only a cataclysmic Cry – as uttered by Lol V. Stein.

The exegesis of erotic dream-feeling helps us recognise in *what order of self-recognition*, in relation to *which subject*, the fictional Ball scene is to be situated. What emerges clearly here is that this 'primal scene', although 'delegated' to the author's fictional *alter ego*, lies within Duras herself. It is the writer of this text who is haunted by a deep-seated spiritual *malaise*, which, as writer, she is attempting to elucidate, confront and manage by staging it scripturally. The tenor of the cryptic figure of sense, as referred to the subject of writing, is that something was *dislocated* or *out-of-joint* in her own adolescent initiation to love and desire; and that this produced an *original trauma* of which she, the feminine subject-of-writing, is the ongoing victim. Accounting for subsequent sexual nomadism, the mythic dream-scene 'knows' that there was, underlying all the subsequent *folie d'érotisme*, somehow explaining all, an *unrealised and unsayable* 'Song of Songs'; and that this was taken away from her – '*ravi*'.

It follows that the venturesome nocturnal 'cruising' to come – like the transgressive night roamings of the Sulamite! – is a certain form of *imaginary and specular compensation*. The ersatz love is pursued, suggests the myth, because 'In the beginning' there was a loss, a fall, a mysterious Disappointment. This figure represents, in relation to Duras' earlier fictional decipherments, a newly authentic starting-point of genuine insight.

***

From this archaeology of inner feeling, we can derive a logic of Lol's strange 'voyeurism'. In its first (purely mental) variant, this shows the character replaying phantasmatically the scenario of the most erotically 'charged' relational moment between the transgressive couple – the scene in which her fiancé undresses the Rival who has replaced her. The phantasm seems bizarre – masochistic in its will to rehearse and develop the hurt sustained. Here, however, we must recall the Bataillian theory-matrix: there is no sacrality without a psychic tearing-open and a loss of personal identity; an agony of violation is part of the ecstasy. Lol is *not merely* seeking a perverse compensation for the lost fiancé and his love-making (she will later tell Jacques that she forgot Michael Richardson the moment the magnetic Third, delegated to fill her place as erotic 'partner-elect', entered the room! [*R*, 137]). Rather, her quest is for the *erotic 'sacred'*; and it tends, as the phantasm 'emerges' and proliferates in variant forms, to *rewrite and extend the dream-scenario in pursuance of that same sacrality*. Obsessionally, Lol will seek to reproduce her apocalyptic 'moment of truth' in variant patterns. The voyeuristic triangle, indefinitely re-enacted, enables her to participate 'by proxy' in the complete circuit of male-and-female desire, cultivating its total charge while preserving a vantage point of availability to its total figure of sense. The *figurants* will change, as in some invitation waltz of ritual erotic performance; but the scenario realised is also, in its compelled attentiveness to the extreme and sacred charge of Promise (and to the pre-programmed modality of 'triangulation'), obsessionally faithful.

Plus ça change, plus c'est la même chose… save that, in the scenario obsessionally re-played, there is also a logic of development. At first confined to the inner cinema of the de-personalised subject's devastated imagination, it then overflows these confines, projecting itself onto the screen of the real world in which it seeks enactment;

and in which its contagion engages and organises the complicity of others. Yet here, too, its logic is quest-driven, since it seeks also to *surmount the primordial trauma suffered* – either by a decisive act of witnessing presence, attaining the source of the psychic wound sustained and cancelling out in 'comprehension' its power to enrapture-and-hurt; or else in a submissive death of quietude achieved through a rubbing-away by repetition, as though 're-writing' the scenario could of itself erase the potency of the 'primal scene' that haunts it. In neither sense does the quest succeed. Lol's 'folie' never quite manages to *fulfil* the fascination that drives it, or to achieve a *therapy* of its woundedness – still less does it *resolve into simplicity* the alternating current of Rapture-and-Ravishment that exalts and calls it.

The novel's first hemeneuticist, its narrator, already directs our attention to the significance of Lol's obsessional 'return' to the critical moment of her Ravishing. The precise instant of separation and of dawning is, he says, a fragment of *Urzeit*, an instant of extreme tenuity, yet somehow infinitely 'graced' with the hope of self-understanding, hence also, perhaps, of healing the madness it commands: a trace, a clue, potentially a delivering Key. If some superordinate insight could have intervened at this point to help her, declares Lol's interpreter enigmatically, all would have been well, she could have faced the Day; but she was alone, annihilated before an essential Night. Implicitly: the 'Night' of ontological unknowing cast over her 'being-there' – hence, over the entire mystery of human sexuality and of life ('she isn't yet God, she is nobody').

What is missing from Lol's quest, Jacques Hold insists, is the total figure of sense; it is the unknown logic or 'Word' capable of explaining the bewildering excess of combined agony-and-ecstasy which, in amorous desire, 'ravishes' the human subject as such: 'It would have been an absence-word, a hole-word, hollowed out at its centre into a hole in which all other words would have been buried' (*R*, 48). All explanation would have been comprised in this all-encompassing Word; whereas what is actually experienced by Lol is an abyss of non-meaning, a *black hole* of Sense. From it, her obsessive memory-image, regurgitated like a dead dog washed up by the sea, overshadows and corrupts all experience; it is *not* understanding the amorous charge of the erotic psyche that is mankind's *original curse*… The narrator's analogy invoking the split, ocean-spewed 'hole in the flesh' (48) recalls both the genital opening and the wounded spiritual 'gaping' of the female subject. It conveys her underlying rage at the order of things: here is the most intimate nerve-centre of her 'soliloquy of an absolute passion, the sense of which was elusive' (34). It defines Lol's 'folie' itself as a kind of immediate *metaphysical despair* re-echoing and resonating without limit out of the first, adolescent intuition of Disappointment.

If there is no intrinsic Word explaining the 'excess' of amorous desire, and none to comprehend the Promise which leaves us cheated, the enigma can indeed only be sounded out empirically, by trial and error. This imperative is what will break the sphere of virtuality into which Lol's remembrance of *Urzeit* is locked. Remembering, she is *recaptured* by the compulsion of the lost Promise; and her dynamic of obscure expectancy is the 'ship of light' upon which her reverie daily embarks:

this ship of light on which, each afternoon, Lol embarks but which remains there, in the impossible port, for ever moored and ready to sail, with its three passengers, all this future in which Lol V. Stein now consists. Sometimes, it has for Lol the same impetus as on the first day, the same fabulous force. (55)

Yet the ship of remembrance and daydream will take her nowhere until she can 'see', beyond the point where the replayed film of the cheated first love flickers and runs out. The narrator's decipherment continues elliptically:

But Lol is not yet God nor anybody.
He would have undressed her slowly of her black dress and while he was doing so a great stage of the journey would have been accomplished.
I have seen Lol undressed, still inconsolable, inconsolable.
It isn't thinkable for Lol that she should be absent from the place where this gesture has occurred. This gesture would not have occurred without her: she is with him, form against form, her eyes fixed upon his corpse. She is born to see it. Others are born to die. This gesture, without her to see it, dies of thirst, it crumbles, it falls, Lol is in ashes.
The long, thin body of the other woman would have appeared little by little... (49)

The suggestion is that 'seeing' – Lol's voyeurism, at first phantasmal, then real – is an irresistible impulse, a destiny caught up in the 'force fabuleuse' of a primal erotic undertow that draws the subject of amorous desire (and without which all loves and all lovers fall into insignificance). Lol stands imaginatively in the place ('endroit') occupied by her Rival-and-Substitute (identified by the black dress). She is 'née pour le voir'; so persistently so that its thirst in her will command her ever-renewed actual presence.

In other words, Lol obeys a fascinated compulsion towards initiatory Knowledge: the need for a totality of apprehension and an immediacy of co-presence ('chair à chair, forme à forme'). It is an *élan* which transgresses the barriers both of decency and of knowability, seeking to make good the deficit of the missing Word. (If the decree excluding the subject from intelligence of her own mystery were lifted, Lol would be – as she is *not yet* – 'Dieu'.) We will discover later, in the novel's last sequence, *when* and *how* the narrator has seen a naked and inconsolable Lol, now occupying, but at last *without substitution*, the 'place' envisaged (*R*, 188–9). Describing the initial impulse behind Lol's compulsive scenario of voyeurism, the narrator, however, already knows that the quest-journey here indicated can only ever be a stage ('étape') or an approach ('geste') to the unveiling of the ontological enigma itself; and that Lol, even when she comes to write her phantasmal scenario into reality, with herself as would-be divine script-writer, will never be close enough in radical 'proximity' to the consummation sought: that swooning away, 'the velvety extinction of her own person' (50), transcending individuality and melting into the Source of her own ontological mystery.

Lol's 'madness', as we perceive, produces a 'mystical way' of the erotic sacred (just as Bataille produced its 'a-theology'). We know, too, that Duras read the great Catholic mystics, particularly Theresa of Avila and John of the Cross.[16] No doubt by mediation of the latter, her text weaves haunting variations on the *Song of Songs*: in its 'missing' nuptiality (recalled in Lol's – implicitly bridal – white dress, with its black counterpart worn by her transgressive *alter ego*); in her nocturnal street roamings (seeking not the Beloved but any eligible role-player); her 'rapture' (with its dark lining of malediction); and even in the more occasional imagery, such as the unlocked fountains of desire (*R*, 34). The purely carnal Tatiana will be described as experiencing in her post-coital body a cry, calling for 'the lost paradise of her unity' (79).

Lol's own 'Cry', by contrast, displays the 'sublimatory' case of this same call: her strange practice of specular proxy-sex is haunted and super-determined by a vaster and more imperative expectancy, strangely antecedent to sexuality – a larger, haunting *shadow of spirit* (cf. *R*, 80). Duras is here again reading from a Bataillian script; but this script is now presented from the viewpoint of the 'violated' or 'sacrificed' feminine subject, alerted to the orgasmic rapture promised her by the 'erotic sacred', yet unfulfilled by it and oneirically seeking her – or rather, *its* – completion. Lol V. Stein, we may say, is possessed by the fascination of 'la part maudite' and acting out its mysteriously *intrinsic* 'curse'.

As she does so, Lol the ravished becomes Lol the ravisher. The principle which haunts and drives her is seen to unfold all its consequences. These are principally *contagion* (erotic attraction between two individuals calls to and mimetically whips up desire in a third), and *transferential destabilisation* (it then reconfigures the relational triangle, devastating the established couple by creation of a new 'excluded Third'). These interlinked sub-figures are among the better-recognised dimensions of Duras' text and we may leave them largely to the reader's discovery: the scenes of the two *soirées* will repay particular attention.

The dance of desire is consistently presented as genuinely contagious, really destabilizing to subject-identity and to inter-personal relationships. Yet it remains even more centrally a spectral game which *de-realises* ('ravishes') love. Lol thus enjoins her new lover Jacques not to cease his rendezvous with Tatiana; for without the erotic energies which nourish her voyeurism, her solar Dream itself will wither and die. The cinematographic scenario she writes depends on the actors and the presences of life; but it thrusts away the test of actual incarnation. Suspended between dream and reality, Lol stages a counterfeit love – she is perpetually 'faking it'.

In respect of its inauthenticity, too, the specular and transferential dance is contagious. Even as he succumbs to her abducting spell, the narrator designates it as delusory, a lie ('a personal and crucial way of lying' [*R*, 106]). He can only play in Lol's scenario ('be a part of the lie lived out by her' [106]) by entering into her imaginary; which involves fictionalising his own relationship with Tatiana and perpetually exorcising the ghost of this intrusive Third Party. Yet even his best endeavours at counterfeiting are insufficient to effect the initiating proximity Lol seeks ('I'll never manage it. When you tell me about it, it's something else' [136]).

The text insists throughout on the insubstantiality that flows from the central void or absence that is Lol V. Stein. Semiotically, the heroine's name (Lol) itself is constructed as a redoubled, self-mirroring letter 'L' (French: 'les deux ailes'), lifting an empty subject (the intermediate letter 'o') in a dream of erotic flight, at odds with ('Vs') her auto-centred, depersonalised and stone-like human weight (Stein).

Lol's voyeuristic 'seeing', in short, signifies a *not* 'being there'; which is why the logic of quest ultimately demands a more radical scenario: a return to T. Beach, and an attempted re-incarnation at source. The pre-ordained journey opens with a Dawn music, a poetry of pristine Hope renewed. During the train journey itself, there is a fleeting communion of needs and a momentary closeness that the narrator will describe as their true 'night of love' (*R*, 177). Yet the scenario of the Ball, however authentically located in real space, however intensely re-imagined *à deux*, still brings no deliverance, since it offers no greater penetration into the essential Night. When the place of the *Urzeit* is revisited in person, its Promise finally retracts, escapes, vanishes:

> The vast dark meadow of dawn is coming. A monumental calm covers everything, swallows up everything. A trace subsists, one. A solitary, ineffaceable trace, but where, not known at first. What? Not known? No trace, none, everything has been swallowed up, Lol along with the whole. (181)

Even the slender clue to the ontological mystery, madly, impenitently, pursued by Lol through amorous desire itself, her tenuous thread in the quest for subject-identity and world-reason, remains present-absent – there and not there. Thus, in the following scene on the beach, the tide rises, drowning the blue salt-marshes, re-enacting the essential Loss of the Promise ('The death of the marshes fills Lol with an abominable sadness, she expects it, foresees it, sees it. She recognises it' [186]). Of the joining of river and sea, of essence and existence, nothing can be known: the initiatory quest rediscovers only the dead dog washed up from the ocean.

So, equally, with her attempt to escape the derealisation of love as projected by her own desire-driven imaginary: instead of making good the deficit of Reality, instead of healing the alienation of the driven subject, the act of love-making triggers a crisis splitting the subject from her Dream, from her lover and from herself (*R*, 188–9). It leaves Lol without awakening, haunted still, and locked even more firmly into the logic of her specular and spectral quest for Love.

Duras' text, accordingly, leaves the protagonist suspended within her own scenario of voyeurism. It is a haunting image of her Alienation – and, no doubt, of many twentieth-century loves.

***

Not *one* 'lock', we have suggested, but *two* stand in the way of deciphering the 'primal scene' of Durassian love and desire. One of them is contingent, and lies in the order of psychoanalysis (the 'denial' or 'denegation' of the incestuous passion for the [br]Other). This provides a 'point de capiton' (Lacan's 'tie-point': a point of psychic conncection offering a decipherable continuity between the imaginary and the symbolic), understood only much later by Duras herself; and it explains how Duras came by her own particular scenario of specular, triangulated eroticism. The second is essential and ontological: what is it, in the being of human desire, which, out of *erotic excess*, always projects a 'promise' or 'expectancy' of *love*? The emergence (at least) or the 'dawning' of the distinction just made would seem, hermeneutically, to be a possibility-condition of the writing of this novel.

This enigma, double-locked against understanding, is at all events, the nerve-point of the novel's recurring *triangular figure*, of which the Couple and the Dawn are said to be the eternal terms. 'She sees herself, and this is her true thought, in the same place, in this ending [i.e., the catastrophe with which the Ball scene finishes], always at the centre of a triangulation of which *the dawn and the two of them are the eternal terms*' (*R*, 47). Of the three terms identified, it is the 'dawn' which, hermeneutically speaking, must be seen as the key to the relational dynamics of the whole figure. Structurally, it marks the apex of the triangle, the point traditionally registering the function of 'transcendence'.

The Durassian triangle inherits from Bataille: subverting the upward-pointing Platonic-Christian figure, so that it now centres on the erotic promise of an 'absurd' sexuality. The 'voyeuse' herself may be seen as a diminished and deficient substitute for the world-containing *Divine Mind or Transcendental Spectator*, at least as conceived in Hellenic (idealist-essentialist) metaphysics. (The Christian God, himself a love-trio or 'Trinity', poses *another case* of 'triangulation', as we shall see in relation to Kristeva). Lol's fascination with initiatory 'seeing' makes her, in turn, a displaced and substituted spectator, watching and waiting for an absent 'Godot' who, sought in the accursed excess of human Eros, never 'appears' or 'comes'. Without access to the total figure of her own Eros – Lol only ever *half-sees* the scene she spies on - the subject at the centre of this triangulation bears the entire weight of erotic 'excess' and is herself *maudite* – visited by alienation, 'mad'.

'I have never written anything, thinking I was writing, I have never loved, thinking I was loving, I have never done anything except wait in front of the closed door,'[17] says Duras. No doubt the autobiographical key of her incestuous first-love opens up a chink through which to peer; it contributes at least something to our understanding of the circumstantial origin in her work of the destabilising dance of nomadic desire, with its recurrent triangular figures and temporary loves. Yet, even in this respect, it is perhaps less significant than the Bataillian decision to equate 'love' with 'eroticism'. The 'scenario' of *Le Ravissement* is most 'haunting', not as a curiosity of the creative writer's psycho-biography, but precisely because it explores with such troubling resonance a deep-seated and very modern *alienation* of the human potential for loving. Duras' full decipherment, from 1980, of the *circumstantial* key did not, of course, cause this writer to *cease* waiting before the closed door. On the contrary, the later work is even more anxiously attentive to the alienating shadow identified within amorous desire: the 'death-sickness', as she now calls it, by which eroticism fails to answer the dawn music of communion, enhancement of life, and the call to an excess of Reality ('ecstasy', 'rapture') – and so is '*not*-Love'. It registers, on-goingly, her *fundamental* 'calamity of the heart'.[18]

'Mysterious is that which is out in the open without unveiling itself,' says Blanchot.[19] For Duras, reader of Nietzsche and Bataille, the mystery declared in Eros signifies above all the 'closed door', eliciting her desolate faithfulness as a writer to an indecipherable enigma: that the erotic spring of human loves should, by obscure decree of the order of things, be denied the decipherable meaning of its own mystery.

In which respect, she confirms the culturally excluded text of Genesis:[20] initiatory 'seeing' and 'tasting' is a counterfeit transcendence, born of mimetic rivalry, bringing the knowledge of good and evil, but not the fruits of the tree of Life. It is eminently thinkable that the remarkable textual haunting of Duras' works by the empty and 'shifting' verbal signifier 'Dieu' constitutes a dream-reminiscence of just this 'blocked' answer; and that it registers, at some level, the writer's residual malaise at pushing ever further into the Night, towards the closed door.[21]

Is this perhaps the measure of the Durassian 'calamity of the heart' – and of the dignity of its Haunting?

Notes

1 M. Duras, letter of 1942, Archive Dionys Mascolo, quoted by L. Adler, *Marguerite Duras* (Paris: Gallimard, 1998), p. 226.

2 See Adler, ibid., p. 374.

3 M. Duras, *Le Marin de Gibraltar* (Paris: Gallimard, 1952).

4 See Adler, *Marguerite Duras*: 'Bataille and Blanchot are her masters. Their influence on his literary work, though never declared by her explicitly, was considerable' (p. 332). Bataille was a member of the same Communist cell after the war, subsequently of Marguerite's 'gang of the rue St Benoît' and, with her, of the 'Committee of revolutionary intellectuals'.

5 M. Duras, *Les Petits chevaux de Tarquinia* Folio (Paris: Gallimard, 1953), p. 88.

6 M. Duras, *Barrage contre le Paciqfiue* Folio (Paris: Gallimard, 1952), p. 343.

7 See Adler, *Marguerite Duras*, pp. 302, 366.

8 Lacan, 'Hommage fait à Marguerite Duras', in Duras, Lacan, Blanchot, Mascolo & Gauthier (eds), *Marguerite Duras* (Paris: Albatros, 1975), p. 130.

9 M. Duras, *Le Ravissement de Lol V. Stein* Folio (Paris: Gallimard, 1964). Further references will be given in the text as *R* followed by page number.

10 Lacan, 'Hommage fait à Marguerite Duras', quoted by Duras in 'Entretien avec J. Rivette', *Cahiers de cinéma* 217 (1969), p. 56.

11 L. Hill, *Marguerite Duras, Apocalyptic Desires* (London: Routledge, 1993), pp. 73–4.

12 *Barrage*, p. 259.

13 M. Duras, *L'Amant* (Paris: Minuit, 1984), pp. 91–2.

14 In *Duras. Romans, cinéma, théâtre: un parcours 1943–1999* Quarto (Paris: Gallimard, 1994), pp. 387–99.

15 To Luce Perrot, Duras confided that she had sexually initiated her younger brother by cunnilingus. See Adler, *Marguerite Duras*, p. 162.

16 Adler evokes her familiarity with the mystical tradition 'which Duras never claimed to inherit from, even if her friends knew she was an attentive reader of the writings of Theresa of Avila and saint John of the Cross' (*Marguerite Duras*, p. 389).

17 Duras, *L'Amant*, p. 35.

18 Marcelle Marini suggests that Duras is caught in the unhappy endgame alternative: either an erotics of death or the death of the erotic as such. See M. Marini, 'La mort d'une érotique', *Cahiers Renaud Barrault* 106 (Dec. 1965), p. 49.

19 Blanchot, in *L'Attente, l'oubli*, quoted by Adler (*Marguerite Duras*, p. 370).

20 See *Le Marin de Gibraltar* (p. 96): the Serpent indicates by way of temptation a *fallen* apple which is fermenting; Adam, 'the first true traitor to God, and father to all of us', makes the mouldering, worm-eaten fruit into Calvados. Adler (*Marguerite Duras*, p. 481) points to the link between Duras' alcoholism and a sense of metaphysical void: 'Nobody can replace God/Nothing can replace alcohol/So God remains unreplaced.'

21 Cf. 'All my books speak of God and nobody notices' (quoted by Adler, *Marguerite Duras*, p. 371). On the many questions raised by this essential recognition, see A. Vircondelet (ed.), *Duras, Dieu et l'écrit* (Paris: Éditions du Rocher, 1998).

The Postmodern Symposium

Eros 'Post-Everything'

The last three decades of the twentieth century in France were first designated 'post-1968'– then 'post-structuralist', then 'post-modern'; more recently, 'post-feminist'. They were of course already 'post-critical' and 'post-Enlightenment', which in turn made them 'post-Christian' (in France, this term is often used indistinctly to mean both 'post-Christendom' and 'beyond Christianity'). The compulsive scattering of the qualifier 'post-', prefixed to every new impulse of the proliferating genre of critical theory, points to a certain endgame being played out: that of the twentieth-century adventure in reflexivity and self-suspicion, pursued within the horizons of a now declared cultural crisis.

The 'post-everything' syndrome marks the natural terminus of a century-long, mirror-like return-in-consciousness towards the collective subject of our own Western history: deconstructing this subject's own psychic constitution, his own societal and cultural creations, his own foundations of knowledge and sense-making, value and identity, the primary focus of attack being the hitherto persuasive and sustaining Enlightenment project: that of a rationally mastered, humane self-emancipation, to be achieved without 'religion'. Rather than a period or a historical era, 'postmodernism' seems to be a condition, a mood, an ethos associated with this endgame.[1]

The endgame scenario is admirably caught in Michel Tournier's novel *Vendredi ou les limbes du Pacifique* (1969). Symptomatically, this has no place for love:[2] the island upon which his latter-day Crusoe is shipwrecked contains no feminine other (this very lack giving rise to the creative invention of maternal and erotic substitutes). It is, on the other hand, very much about polymorphous post-Freudian Eros: its religious repressions, its patriarchal sublimation in the service of an erstwhile culture of mastery, its dualist discourses of sense-making, its cosmic loves and its impulses of 'new age' spirituality.

In the form of an initiatory adventure re-writing Defoe's eighteenth-century tale of self-reliance and virile Protestant fortitude, Tournier offers a brilliantly conceived deconstructionist's model of the twentieth-century culture-shipwreck and its aftermath. The Western subject-hero's contemporary emergence from his traditional *habitus* is seen as reciprocal to his search for a new dwelling-place of the eroticised flesh: psychically self-aware, post-colonially other-inclusive, sexually androgynous, cosmically related, spiritually self-regenerating. The search is pursued via a perpetual subversion of Judaeo-Christian tradition, conducted through a series of – invariably 'unreliable' or 'diverted' – biblical exegeses.[3] Predicted by the Tarot cards, this island experiment finally 'elevates' a solar sexuality, sublimated and self-enfolded, into a perfect figure of the Ouroboros (Gnostic tail-biting serpent).

Post-1968 'love-ethics' also close back upon the experimental and perversely polymorphous erotic ego. Michel Onfray's *Théorie du corps amoureux: Pour une érotique solaire* (2000) is characteristic:

> Against life mutilated, this book invites us to a solar erotics entirely indexed upon the life-drives and radically refuses all death-drives. It proposes to answer the question: how can one remain free in amorous relationships? To this end, it proposes to dechristianise ethics, to realise a licentious feminism, to promote a light and playful eros and to formulate a physiology of the passions, thus allowing us to develop an art of remaining oneself in other-relations.[4]

We recognise here a collage of late-twentieth-century (mainly masculinist) ideas, values and attitudes. There is a reactive inversion of idealist–spiritualist metaphysics, now recentred on what Foucault calls 'le souci de soi' [care for the self]. Loving is henceforth the body's business; indeed, it follows the male sex organ (the cover design of this book is a cartoon in the style of a Greek vase-painting: a naked woman carries, dildo-like, a personified and very cheery-looking phallus!). Human amorous practice is referred in deliberately 'playful' mode to animal antecedents (the 'masturbatory fish', the 'gregarious bee' and the 'bachelor hedgehog', etc). The 'excess' still recognised in human sexuality is annexed purely and simply to the pleasure principle, warrant for which is found in the materialist and sensualist philosophers of Graeco-Roman antiquity. The driving inspiration, here and unfailingly, is the resentful conviction, derived from Nietzsche's genealogy of morals, that the Judaeo-Christian inheritance equates to a world-denying spiritualist puritanism, true inheritor of Plato's 'lack', the frowning Superego of an entire civilisation. 'In the first dawn of the new millennium, dechristianisation remains very much on the agenda.'[5]

In the making of this *fin-de-siècle* ethos, Surrealism and its culture-narrative are relayed by the more radical theories of the later prophets of Eros unlimited who fuelled the revolt of May 1968. Wilhelm Reich and Herbert Marcuse indicted a society which, defining man as the libidinal animal, confined him within a social order geared to a repletion of human *need*, but leaving unacknowledged the immaterial, the numinous or the transcendent in human *desire*. Reich's crusade had been directed at revolutionising society and emancipating the entire range and reach of sexual energies.[6] Marcuse's heterodox Freudo-Marxian prophecy of the imagination in the service of a bio-electric and cosmic Eros had sought to disrupt the dead logocentric structures and ideologies of bourgeois capitalism.[7]

Among the latter-day prophets interpreting post-factum the oracle of 1968, G. Deleuze and F. Guattari denounced Freud's theorisation of the Oedipus complex as complicit with capitalist structures, and repudiated all theoretical models predicated on desire as lack.[8] Desire was affirmed, on the contrary, as an intensely productive socio-cultural energy, an unstoppable flow, incessantly multiplying, fragmenting, reconfiguring, impersonally connecting one 'desiring machine' with another and inventing new circuits through which to swirl. J.-F. Lyotard echoes this indictment of a Freudian order imposed upon creative libidinal anarchy; he delivers his own anti-humanist repudiation of the 'wanting' Freudo-Lacanian subject and develops the image of the 'immense membrane of the libidinal body' in the form of a 'Mœbius strip' representing the ever-diverse, continuously fluctuating and involuted weave of individual and societal desire.[9] For J. Baudrillart the same all-pervasive and unforeseeable pulse-and-flicker points to the ruin of all theoretical systematisations, inaugurating within the communications society the rule of play and the strategies of simulacrum and appearance.[10] The 'time of desire' (Denis Vasse's phrase) belongs to Libido unlimited.

It also marks, contrariwise, the apogee of desire logocentrically dissected, defined and codified. Though much contested, the hugely influential master-code of Freudo-Lacanian psychoanalysis provided an axis for the would-be scientificity of much 'critical theory'. For Lacan, the unconscious itself is structured 'like a language'; his thinking therefore looked towards language science and assumed epistemologically the omni-competent paradigm of Saussure's broken and arbitrary verbal sign.[11] Discursivity, its codes and rhetorical figures, provided a certain – albeit partial and unstable – mediation towards an unseizable 'real'. With this mediation in view, post-structuralist theory 'textualised' or 'discursified' everything: history, philosophy, jurisprudence, sociology, religion – and, as we shall see, amorous feeling itself. It also promoted the idea that 'reality' as such is a purely discursive phenomenon, a product of the various codes, conventions, language games or signifying practices which provide the only means of interpreting experience.

Freudo-Lacanian hermeneutics, while it had much that was worthwhile to say about sexuality in relation to philosophy, or the structures of knowledge and power, had little interest in, or cognisance of, the phenomenon of love. Within the specular erotosphere which it conceived, love finds no real subject to belong to, no real 'other' to relate to, no real transcendence of its own negativity, and no appeal beyond the mirror of imaginary/symbolic representation which refers it back indefinitely to its own lack and to the forces that speak through it. It has no reality or consistency of its own. It is, literally, deconstructed into nothing (Lacan's 'désêtre'); more exactly, into an insatiable and groundless *desire for* love; that is, for the recognition constituted by the Other's desire. Plato read backwards, in other words, gives an entirely virtual and/or specular image of love; at most, a psychopoetics of phantasmal amorous need.

Reviewing the fruits of the post-1968 sexual revolution and of its logocentric theorisations, many voices began at century's end to speak with concern of the 'loss' or 'silence' of love as concept and as value. Almost single-handedly, feminism, in the persons of Hélène Cixous, Luce Irigaray, Julia Kristeva and others, brought to the postmodern symposium the oxygen of real sexual difference (as opposed to masculine theorisations of it). Together with that existential speaking point, came the sense of a holistic relationality irreducible to third-person (masculine) science. The dilemma of feminism has been to know how much, in pursuing these intuitions, it needs to admit, or can afford to accommodate, the reductive masculine hermeneutics in which it finds itself historically embedded. What new sources and resources, and which more subtle languages can it find? How far will they take us in the recognition and rehabilitation of love?

'Postmodern' love thus speaks paradoxically: against the grain, against the times. Roland Barthes and Luce Irigaray, speaking of love nevertheless, illustrate these two cases.

Notes

1   Ricœur comments: 'As to the use of the term "postmodern" as describing a new era, I take it as a dubious "philosophy of history:"', in P. Gifford et al. (eds.), *2000 Years and Beyond: Faith, Identity and the Common Era* (London: Routledge, 2002), p. 168.
2   The same ambiguous recognition and the same marginal status given to 'love' are recognisable in other male writers, such as Phillippe Sollers and Michel Houellebecq. I have preferred for this reason to follow the 'other' line that of the 'rediscovery' of love.
3   See D. Gascoigne, '(Mis)reading the Bible' in: *Michel Tournier* (Oxford: Berg, 1996), pp. 98–124.
4   Book-jacket text for M. Onfray, *Théorie du corps amoureux: Pour une érotique solaire* (Paris: Grasset, 2000).
5   Onfray, *Théorie du corps amoureux,* p. 304.
6   W. Reich, *La Révolution sexuelle* 10/18 (Paris: Minuit, 1970).
7   H. Marcuse, *Éros et civilisation* 10/18 (Paris: Minuit, 1963).
8   See G. Deleuze & F. Guattari, *Anti-Oedipus: Capitalism and Schizophrenia* (New York: Viking, 1977).
9   See J.-F. Lyotard, *The Postmodern Condition: A Report on Knowledge* (Manchester: Manchester University Press, 1984).
10 See 'The Ecstasy of Communication', in H. Foster (ed.), *Postmodern Culture* (London: Pluto, 1985), pp. 129–47.
11 Ricœur comments: 'I am perpetually astonished by the misuse of the so-called Saussurian model. It concerns only the realm of lexical signs (*langue*) and not at all that of discourse (*parole*). Nobody can ignore this more accurate reading if they read the whole of Saussure' (*2000 Years*, p. 168).

Chapter 12

Roland Barthes:
Amorous Discourse and its Subject

Pour un intellectuel aujourd'hui, être amoureux, c'est être vraiment plongé dans la dernière des solitudes.[1]

A seemingly all-sufficing love of exploring the world as constructed in language informs the 'mind of theory' Roland Barthes shares with friends and intellectual contemporaries in the orbit of *Tel Quel*. His is a world viewed as discourse, text and sign, a world lightened of intrinsic meaningfulness, divorced from nature and Origin – indefinitely deconstructible as mind-made artifice:

> He feels himself in solidarity with all writings which affirm as a principle that the subject is merely an effect of language [...] he imagines a very vast science of the effects of language, in the enunciation of which the scientist would at length include himself.[2]

In any such third-person, logocentric hyperscience, 'love' itself would seem to represent a relic, a limit case or an anomaly. As Valéry presciently foresaw, 'the last lover will be classified an erotomaniac'. Barthes's 'solitariness' as lover looks at this point very much like the obverse of his intellectual 'solidarity'.

From *L'Empire des signes* (1970) to *Le Plaisir du Texte* (1973) and *Roland Barthes* (1975), however, the mind of theory encounters the pleasure principle vitally and is transformed by it. In the post-1968 climate of sexual liberation, what Barthes calls 'happy sexuality' (*RB*, 138) overflows jubilantly, with irradiating intellectual consequences, progressively assumed: a theory of the text invoking the notions of 'pleasure' and 'ecstasy', a theory of writing linked to the 'unknown body', even an *art de vivre* metaphorising a more or less explicitly sexual erotics: 'a multiple and mobile flirtation links the subject to what passes ... this very changing landscape is traversed by some sudden immobilisation: love' (65).

Yet there is a qualitative step from the paradigm of the gay 'cruiser' who surfaces in *L'Empire des signes* to the isolated 'subject-in-love' of the *Fagments d'un discours amoureux*. What distinguishes the state of being in love ('être amoureux') is precisely the *distancing* of sexuality which it creates. The 'transcendence' (Barthes's own term) or added-value in respect of feeling ('plus-value sentimental') is no doubt prefigured in the purely erotic relationship; but love is distinguishable from hedonistic quest as concentration is distinct from dispersion. Barthes agrees with his interviewer that his *Fragments* are, in respect of the post-1968 sexual revolution, *anti-libertarian* (III, 785).

The isolation of the subject-in-love is precisely a function of this perceived 'transcendence', which appears now deprived of all social credit. 'Passion-love is no longer well-considered; it is viewed as an illness to be cured; it is not credited with any power of enrichment' (III, 781). By a strange reversal, quite unforeseen by de Sade or Bataille, it is amorous feeling, not depersonalised, transgressive sexuality, that has become, at the latter end of the twentieth century, 'obscene'.[3] Here is a *theoretical* solitude, a nudity *of language* experienced *by the human subject as such*.

Published in 1977, *Fragments d'un discours amoureux* took shape during a seminar for doctoral students at the École des Hautes Études in 1974–75 and 1975–76. The 'teacher's report' states that this seminar proposed to tackle a problem of enunciation: amorous discourse. At the same time, Barthes insists that his *Fragments* are intensely personal. Behind the work lies a 'crystallising episode' of his private life which had found a painful 'dialectical resolution'. He recognises that the book was conceived 'as a way of not collapsing into despair', and acknowledges the 'marvellous power of writing' as having effected a pacifying sublimation. The act of writing is also seen as communicating a problem of intense contemporary resonance. Within the unfriendly environments of eroticised mass culture and of theory-bound intellectuality, it projects a hard-won ethic of affirmation.

The new-found sense of the lover's 'difference' introduces these unwontedly personalist harmonics into a text initially conceived as a third-person academic exercise in discursivity. With them comes a heightened tension between the Barthes of theory, and a deeper, more fruitful engagement with the unstable and evolving paradox that is the enunciating subject of Barthes's work. To this tension we may attend in turn. 'Is not the most erotic spot of the body the place where the clothing bulges open?' (II, 1489).

***

'So this is an amorous subject speaking, who says...' Rather than a 'lover', the speaking subject staged by the text is a 'subject-in-love' (we might say an 'in-lover'): someone defined by his speaking position in relation to a loved 'other', who is evoked only allusively and has no textual presence or voice. The choice of first-person enunciatory standpoint is deliberate. The subject-in-love is not to be reduced simply to a collection of classifiable symptoms; prior to any theorisation, we must first hear, in its quasi-Nietzschean untimeliness and intractability, the voice of this strange first-person singular.

The resulting portrait, says Barthes, is structural rather than figurative in a psychological sense. The person speaking is not X or Y, but anybody occupying this speaking position. How do the disconnected fragments of discourse we encounter compose even a structural portrait? Etymologically, 'discourse' implies a running hither and thither, which accurately reflects the psychological movements of amorous passion. Analogously to the movements of the body in action, the 'bursts of utterance' generated by the subject-in-love allow us to recognise these inner movements which are partly culture-coded (less so today than in the times of courtly love or of the 'map of the heart'), partly uncoded and unknown (they 'project' or 'express' a sense to be explicated, in which respect they invite the reader's collaboration). In this way, they mirror the functioning of the amorous psyche. They offer discursively developed snapshots of passion 'at work'; the analogue given is that of gymnastic or choreographical 'figures'.

Textual presentation of each figure obeys certain conventions. Each is identified by a memorable proto-utterance (e.g. 'What am I to do?', 'I want to understand') corresponding to a recognisable *topos* of amorous affectivity, summarised in the liminal 'argument'. This is then developed, explored and commented upon in a series of paragraphs articulated as a numbered sequence (usually between three and eight per 'figure'). The textual ordering of the book's eighty 'figures' follows no obvious pattern of psychogenesis or of narrativisation; they are meant to be discrete episodes, without syntagmatic continuity. They do not make up the story of any particular love-affair, nor any kind of love-story (Julia Kristeva's *Histoires d'amour*, written six years later, marks, in this respect, as in others, a deliberate reaction against Barthes's synchronic and structural perspective). Nor do they (overtly at least) offer any dialectical pattern; no philosophy of love is being presented (more exactly: no *overarching* or *declared* philosophy), merely an 'assertion' of love. As ever, Barthes is tilting at the conventional attribution of sense he refers to as *doxa*; particularly, at the monological, authoritative, metadiscursive meaning-making he is wont to think of as 'theological' (this label, in Barthes, as in Lacan and Derrida, enacts a founding postulate of a-theism).

The non-integrative, distributional staging of the amorous subject-who-speaks is given broader resonance by reference to two forms of intertext: the first is personal (insights, observations and case-histories of friends, identified in the margins of Barthes's text by their initials); the second is cultural (a wide-ranging network of philosophers, psychologists, novelists, poets and mystics, also named marginally and often quoted in footnotes). On the one hand, this wider reference generalises the structural portrait presented; on the other, it defines the special sensibility of the speaking subject and the intellectual orientations which inform the act of staging and reading it.

Nothing, in fact, specifies the supposedly 'structural' subject of enunciation more than his tone of voice and his developing pattern of reference; and the corpus of fragments as a whole tends willy-nilly towards a form of undeclared interpretative theory situating a personal subject. So in the first figure ('Surrendering, succumbing'): the register of amorous passion is established as 'that abyssal feeling'; its lines of decipherment adumbrated; its sphere of experience, sensibility and intellectual reference are pencilled in (*Werther*, *Tristan*, Sartre); its ethic of affirmation is discreetly announced. The ambiguous status of the speaking subject is displayed ('the author invests the speaking subject with his own culture, and the speaking subject lends the author the innocence of his imaginary'). The art of development in this figure defines the ambiguous subject of enunciation as an *undeclared hermeneuticist* wrestling consequently and profoundly with self-adresssed questions of existential resonance and weight. If we take a sufficiently strategic view, Barthes's 'guide-text' (Goethe's *The Sufferings of the young Werther*) already epitomises the preferred sense of the word 'love' actually retained by the class of '68, its favourite 'other' of cultural memory.

Here and throughout, Barthes is turning around his own enigma as amorous subject in an enfolding movement of reflexive consciousness: very much the same movement by which Valéry's Serpent, in the much-reproduced symbolic badge of the *Cahiers*, entwines questingly upwards around the key of Knowledge. From Valéry to Barthes, the difference, perhaps, lies in a deeper plunge into the mirror of representation. In Barthes, the methodological and conceptual apparatus of *logos* is, accordingly, more obtrusive, more heavily deconstructive, whereas his *eros* is more dispersed and elusive.

***

Barthes's text enacts vividly the claim that love is, at least and indeed, a 'discourse': a matter both of actual utterance, and of pre-verbal, language-like psychic and bodily processes, to be grasped and deciphered by the specialised conceptual tools of language science – an analogically conceived 'linguistics of love'.

The figure entitled 'I-love-you' focuses his approach. This message-bearing *declaration* is singular, outside normal signification. Any attempt at comparative parsing breaks down comically. Subject and complement, in this case, are no longer separate referents logically conjoined by the verb. There can be no infinitive form; and no possibility of structural transformation (this cry can never, within the logic of amorous identification, become 'I love him/her'). It cannot be expanded, save by the addition of one proper name. Nor can it, within the context of utterance, be anything other than true – it is a pure performative. Does it even admit any relativising situation of reference, any magazine-clip of alternative ritual formulae? On the contrary: it is the irreducible utterance of the original mother–child dyad, an uncloven sign, a metaphor for nothing else. It seeks only the functionally reciprocal, but formally a-symmetrical, response 'So do I'. This utterance belongs neither to the order of the enunciated, nor to that of enunciation. Its nearest classification, suggests Barthes, is the order of song or of music.

The account Barthes gives of this singular linguistic practice in its fuller development invokes a twofold movement of analysis, reminiscent of the semiotics of cultural myth pursued in his *Mythologies*. He is, he says, joining two forms of linguistics: amplifying a traditional structural analysis of message by an 'active philology' of the forces which generate, drive or attract the message. Practised in disciplined and methodic retrospect, the subject's spontaneous scanning of message, conjugated with an 'etymology' or a 'philology' of its underlying pschyogenetic forces, can become a mode of theory. The *Symposium* itself, Barthes elsewhere recalls, arises from an exchange between travellers who recount Agathon's party for lovers. Love-theory in the West arises from … 'a three-kilometre-long gossip' (*FDA*, 218).

An instance of what Barthes means by the 'philology of active forces' (*FDA*, 218) is supplied by the 'figure' of 'The ravishing' (which 'remembers' Duras' novel).

This explores the supposedly initial episode – in fact reconstituted (as Marguerite Duras would agree) – *retrospectively* – in which the subject is –'ravished' (captured and enchanted); in short, the episode of the 'coup de foudre', or what psychology calls 'enamoration'. There is a buried etymology here, a memory of archaic cultural practice retained in language. This links love and war: loving is conquering, snatching, capturing. When we 'fall' in love, we are re-enacting the times when men kidnapped women to ensure exogamy (cf. the 'rape' of the Sabine women). The modern myth of *amour-passion* however registers a curious role-reversal: the ravisher or subject no longer wants or does anything; he is motionless (like an image). It is the ravished object who is now the true subject of the ravishing: the object of capture and conquest has become the subject of love (even if a trace of the former structure survives in the common perception of the 'in-lover' as implicitly feminised). This singular reversal derives, suggests Barthes, from the fact that, since Christianity, the subject has been perceived as 'the one who suffers': where there is a wound, there is a subject; the more gaping and intimate the wound, the more the subject is a subject (marginal references: *Parsifal*, Ruysbroek, Ruysbroek). The love-wound is a radical gaping (at the 'roots' of being) which cannot be closed and through which the subject, escaping, is constituted as subject by this very outflowing (186).

Elsewhere, the philology of active forces involves not merely an etymological decipherment, but an entire semeiology. Barthes's subject-in-love is essentially a reader of signs. If I am entangled in futilities (why has the other not telephoned? why no message about the holidays? what should I do about this?), this is because I am a prisoner of the hyper-productive machine of the desiring imaginary which makes the entire sphere of experience fraught with meaning-bearing indications (signs), subjecting me to an obsessive play of signification. I am drawn into endeavouring to decipher causality and intention. 'For me, as amorous subject, everything that is new, everything that disturbs me, is received, not as a fact, but as a sign to be interpreted … Everything signifies' (*FDA*, 76).

I am also a manipulator and manager of signs. To what extent should I hide the turbulence of my passion or my hurt? A subtle figure entitled 'Shades' explores this second-order anguish. My discourse is divided, fatally schizophrenic. Perhaps I should signal my feelings: maybe the other expects, wants, needs this excess which is my madness and my strength? But then perhaps my signals of passion risk stifling the other's interest and goodwill: should I not, then, conceal my amorous feelings precisely for the sake of love? I hesitate, decide to show my passion 'just a bit'. But then I cannot help indicating this reservation and the remainder it conceals ('the fact of hiding must be seen'); so that I advance wearing the mask, while pointing to it as mask with a discreet and crooked finger. There is no amorous oblation without theatre, says Barthes: the sign is always in the end triumphant (*FDA*, 51).

The philology of active forces can just as well start from an identification and decipherment of structural relationships. The triangle of lover, beloved and rival interests Barthes. Ever alert to a good paradox, he asks: with whom can I speak of my love, to whom confide, if not to the person who shares the same Image and confirms its worth, namely, my rival? This *connivence* (etymology: to blink, wink, close one's eyes) can extend to the point where the beloved can seem the intrusive and superfluous third party. My speaking position, and my situation as subject-in-love, is thereby defined. Structurally speaking, I occupy the same place as my rival. What is jealousy if not an equation with three permutable (and inseparable) terms: I am jealous of the beloved and of the rival Other (Italian: *odiosamato*); the latter is indeed also loved by me, since he interests, intrigues, calls to me (*FDA*, 79).

Elsewhere, decipherment leads from sign to structure. The figure 'When my finger inadvertently...' evokes furtive bodily contact (touching, stroking, hand-pressure) – the 'the paradisal region of subtle and stealthy signs' (*FDA*, 81). Such signs, he suggests, are a festival, not of the senses, but of meaning. So Charlus, taking the chin of Proust's narrator and prolonging the caress, is making a bid for love which obliges the other to enter into the game of meaning-making. Love is governed by the system (paradigm) of Demand-Response (Barthes borrows this model from Valéry). When I am troubled by some 'incident', which summons all my language towards it, I am responding fundamentally to this structure as such. For this reason, Barthes claims that the 'incident' is a sign rather than a clue ('indice'): one element of a system, rather than the burgeoning of a causality (84).

The singularity of love is often expressed, as this last figure already implies, as a tension between sign and structure. If the subject-in-love is a supercharged maker and reader of signs, this is because he secretes meanings and demands meaningfulness within a highly specialised and singular structure of other-relatedness. He wants to concentrate all meanings within this sphere; reciprocally, a sense of de-reality, alienation and exclusion strikes the rest of the world which cannot be so included. Moping in a café (like Sartre's Roquentin), he asks: why are *they* laying down the law, arguing, showing off? 'I experience the world – the other world – as a generalised case of hysteria.' On the one hand, therefore, the subject-in-love is the only one who, so it seems subjectively, perceives 'the other' in his or her true light (a truth-sensation which leaves the lover characteristically intractable). But, inversely, this meaning-rich and intractable amorous subject is, structurally speaking, and in relation to the world at large, displaced, out of place or place-less (*atopos*) (*FDA*, 271).

The structural difficulty of the 'in-lover' runs beyond loneliness or marginality. The discursive episode 'I want to understand' shows the amorous subject displaced in relation to the very phenomenon he discourses about, separated from the intelligence of himself as amorous subject – *atopos* in respect of love itself. Certainly, I can reflect, theorise; yet my theorising is caught up in the image-flux of the amorous psyche and is never truly reflexive. It is excluded from logic, which supposes an externality of language. It catches the concept of love only 'by the tail' in flashes, images, adventitious formulations dispersed throughout the great streaming flood of the Imaginary. As amorous subject, I stand in the 'blind spot' of love, its zone of bedazzlement (*FDA*, 71).

Zeus, when ordering Apollo to split the primitive androgynes in half, ordered him to turn their heads around to face the 'other', severed, belly-face. As self-theorising subject-in-love, I, too, discover, and set myself to confront, my separated other self. 'Understanding, isn't this to split the image, undo the "I", display it as the proud organ of misrecognition?' (*FDA*, 71). The amorous subject, in so far as he undertakes to discourse delocutively on his own condition, is playing Apollo and Zeus in respect of his own rivenness. (If his name is Roland Barthes, he is also, implicitly, making an anthropological symbol out of Saussure's cloven and arbitrary verbal sign!)

The *atopicality* of the reflexive self-enunciating subject-in-love precisely defines the paradox of the 'discourse' whose fragments we are currently reading. As reflexive theorist, the subject-in-love is structurally excluded from any ultimate intelligence of his own enigma. To recover from this exclusion, he would have to be or to become the divine third-person *Noûs* who conceived and commanded his rivenness (Barthes' ascendant spiral, for all its fragmentary presentation, remembers and obeys in turn just this structural logic of all Eros theory). Discursivity, objectifying the amorous subject, loses the singularity of love itself, which is experienced only immediately, within a relational structure of allocution or address. This is an ultimate irony. 'The atopicality of love, the specific quality which makes it elusive to all discoursing, might be that, *in the last resort*, it isn't possible to speak of it except from a *specifically allocutory position* ... Nobody wants to speak about love except *for* somebody' (*FDA*, 88).

The language-like nature of love, its openness to linguistics-referred analysis and theorisation, finds here its limit ('love inexpressible' [*FDA*, 113]). At the same time, the supposedly 'functional' discursive subject displays and discreetly confesses his own ambiguous and paradoxical speaking position as writer of the discourse we are reading.

***

What most defies representation in articulate language is the semi-articulate and heterogeneous inner monologue of the amorous subject. This flood of words running in my head, supercharged with all the energies of desire and the whole power of the libidinal imaginary is designated, in a term borrowed from Loyola, as the *loquela*. Barthes's philology of active forces is centrally concerned to give a psychogenetic and functional account of this phenomenon, and to theorise it in the explicative code of Freudo-Lacanian psychoanalysis.

My mental volubility corresponds to the impossibility of anchoring usefully or purposefully the signs I emit in the real world: I am freewheeling within a self-generated language-sphere; mad within language, delirious for and from language (*FDA*, 192). Yet 'language', in its psychogenetic reality, implies image as well as word. Barthes suggests this by offering us the – Durassian – metaphor of the inner cinema: there is no director to control or edit my inner image-production, my scenario-sketching, my role-playing – no-one to say 'Cut!' The further back one traces the genesis of the *loquela*, and the more extensively one pursues its irradiations through the entire set of enacted language 'episodes', the more this excitable and excessive inner 'talkativity' becomes, in fact, the metonymic sign and symptom of something much larger: the immersion of my whole amorous discourse in the order of the Imaginary; hence, its openness to the unconscious, structured 'like a language' (Lacan). A clear indication of this metonymy is the fact that I experience a demon of language – or rather a plurality of such demons – who inflect my inner speech to my harm and hurt, 'busying me with the business of engendering images (of jealousy, abandonment, humiliation, etc.)' (96–7).

At this point, Barthes enters a territory much explored by other twentieth-century deconstructors of *amour-passion*: the psychogenesis of amorous feeling and relationality viewed as a function of the Imaginary. His analysis of the 'coup de foudre' is a case in point. This is a form of image-fascination ('since nothing distinguishes the way of enamoration from the Damascus road' [*FDA*, 224]) and a form of hypnosis, which has an occasional trigger, but also a deep structure of anticipation. It involves a complex psychic framing or haloing and a 'consecration' of the love-object. The specifically Barthesian note comes at the end: I can fall in love with a sentence spoken to me; or be precipitated towards the lure by a novel about love.

The enigmatic fixation on the One-and-only object is a similarly revisited *topos*: 'Mega-enigma to which I shall never have the key: why do I desire X?' (*FDA*, 27). Barthes's originality here lies in both his references to psychoanalysis and his linguistic subtlety. This phenomenon is like the psychoanalytic 'transference' (i.e. the emotional identification of analysand with analyst, the former projecting onto the latter unconscious desires and repressed affects). Yet whereas transference-love is potentially universal, amorous identification is person-specific; the difference has to do with the strange *ipse*-feeling which designates the other as the exactly symmetrical complement of my own desiring structure; of which genuinely unsayable mystery, the word 'adorable' is the only discursive trace (25).

The Imaginary itself is not exhausted, however, by this specialisation. The amorous subject posits obstinately the possibility and the desire of a total and flawless success in amorous relationality, its eternal fulfilment; he pursues the paradisal *image* of this sovereign good given and received. Barthes's illustrative references and quotations are drawn here – revealingly – not from the guide-text – *Werther*, but from the Christian mystic Ruysbroek: 'my soul is not only filled and overflowing: ecstasy outstrips the possibilities glimpsed by desire' (*FDA*, 65). Barthes comments that what characterises the imaginary of fulfilment is its excess, its fullness beyond sufficiency: 'the *too much* belongs to the regime of the imaginary' (65). If I adhere to the Image as excessive, therefore, I experience a coincidence with my own measure; hence 'the definitive assumption of the Imaginary, its triumph' (66). Barthes neglects to tell us whether he thinks that either the lover or the Christian mystic, or both, have in fact, throughout the ages, managed this feat without any real, relational Other to support their image-making; whether, in fact, they are, in the ultimate, hallucinating. He writes instead:

Really, I don't much care about my chances of being genuinely fulfilled (I admit that they are nil). Only the will to fulfilment, indestructible, shines brightly. In that determination, I drift: I form within myself the utopia of a subject abstracted from repression; I am already that subject. (66)

***

We catch here the note of dejected philosophical idealism which informs the whole of Barthes's psychopoetics of the amorous imaginary. The subject-in-love is, in fact, the creative *artist* of a back-to-front mirror-world 'since every image is its own end (nothing beyond the image)' (*FDA*, 159). If we enquire more philosophically what makes Barthes so depressed about love, the answer would seem to be that his theoretical discourse is nourished, shaped and inflected by the hermeneutic code which dominates the cultural milieu within which he speaks: that of Freudo-Lacanian psychoanalysis.[4] He may lament the result as lover; but as decipherer of love, he first interiorises unquestioningly this self-same 'hermeneutics of suspicion' (Ricœur's term).His progress in psychoanalytical deconstruction may be expressed as a twofold movement: an ascent in third-person knowledge achieved at the price of a descending and depressive self-comprehension as first-person amorous subject; the more I know about myself, the less I understand myself and my own loving.

Lacan is a constant reference for Barthes's persuasion of never touching the real. 'Irreality' is central to the experience of the amorous subject, 'because he fantasises, delivers himself up to the Image, in relation to which all reality is a disturbance' (*FDA*, 106). 'Dereality' overcomes him because he is enclosed within the order of a tyrannical, monological Imaginary (129). Every gesture, every incident, every episode of the love relation is 'caught up in the devouring metonymy which governs imaginary life, I am transported into it entirely' (89). Plato's fable of the Androgyne now stands corrected by its Lacanian commentary: the two halves seeking their re-union are subject to his 'story of the egg, the vanishing blade and the little-man/omelette [l'homelette]'.[5] Desire now means lacking what one has and giving what one does not have – 'which is a matter of supplement, not of complement' (268). Barthes appends in a footnote a quotation from Lacan's *Séminaire* on which he comments revealingly: 'Psychoanalysis seeks the missing organ (libido) and not the missing other half. (What a pity!)' (267).

Behind Lacan stands Father Freud. When I dream of a tranquil embrace 'in the loving serenity of your arms', I am really forming an incestuous phantasm of return to the Mother, suspending time, law and the Interdict. Yet genitality rears up from my infantile longing, the adult superimposes himself on the inner child: I want both maternal affection and genitality. 'The in-lover could be defined as a child with an erection: young Eros was like that' (*FDA*, 121). The amorous crisis, so Freud said, is to be understood from the standpoint of the psychoanalytic therapy-session. Love is indeed a matter of identification and transference. The languor of love, for instance, is 'this exhausting transition from narcissistic libido to object-libido' (205). I resolve to quit it as a patient de-identifies with his analyst ('I wind up my transference' [125]); unless, like Freud's patients, I cling to the lost object in a hallucinatory psychosis of desire (126). If there is any hope at all for love, it is figured in Freud's reading of Jensen's *Gradiva*: the loved object might consent to enter into a simulated relationship in order to help me quit. One cannot quite, says Barthes, discount the curative power of love within the delirium of my transferential mis-identifications (186).

One is unsurprised that the Freudo-Lacanian code subscribed to by Barthes as theorist depresses him deeply as in-lover. This hermeneutic code offers an introspective and retrospective *reduction* of the amorous project as such. Love as other-relatedness is referred, without compensation, to its imprisonment within the Imaginary, to its constitutional illusionism, to the entire weight of its narcissistic disabilities. It proclaims at every turn that love is 'nothing but' libidinal Eros; and libido is 'nothing but' the logic of its infantile antecedents. To discover that 'the language of the Imaginary is reckoned to be nothing other than the utopia of language' (*FDA*, 115), or that 'it is love the subject loves, not the object' (39) may temporarily gratify my curiosity; but it also excludes me from myself. If amorous feeling is merely the *loquela* of my imaginary, and my imaginary is merely the agitation of my irretrievably lost Object of desire, with its delirious and deluded transferences, my condition as amorous subject must indeed be truly tragic: a destiny of woundedness, unfulfilment and humiliation.

Moreover, if I am 'gay', the Freudo-Lacanian hermeneutic space is even more unfriendly, since it basically views this sexual orientation as the product of an arrested (mother-fixated) libidinal development. Barthes's anxious attention to the third man of the psychoanalytical trio, the child psychologist Winnicott, corresponds, perhaps, to the recognition, very clearly expressed in the present work (*FDA*, 231, 252, 265) and confirmed in *La Chambre claire*, that Barthes' own amorousness is indeed shaped and patterned by his attachment to his mother. The figure 'Agony', devoted to the amorous subject's fear of danger, hurt and abandonment, suggests just this point of engagement. Winnicott is cited on 'primitive agony', the recurrent fear of collapse in the psychotic patient, whose need is to be re-assured that his collapse has already happened (in the trauma of weaning). 'The same goes, it seems to me, for the anguish of love: this is the fear of a grief which has already happened, at the origins of love, from the moment in which I was snatched away. What is needful is that someone should say to me: Don't be anguished any more, you have already lost him or her' (38).

By putting the Phallus in the place of the Mother (*FDA*, 205), Lacan leaves the amorous subject, at this point, with the full anguish of his reversionary, incestuous and fetishising responsibility for the failure of amorous relationships. Winnicott, by contrast, offers a paradoxical reassurance within, and on account of, loss. The person I am waiting for was never real: 'Like the breast of the mother for the suckling child, I create and recreate the other out of my capacity for loving, out of the need that I have for the other: the other comes where he or she is expected by me, at the point where I have already created him or her' (49). This enables Barthes to decode without secondary anguish the two key ideograms of amorous feeling (again, derived from Ruysbroek): 'there are the *Upraised arms of Desire*; and there are the *Outstretched arms of Need*. I oscillate, I vacillate, between the phallic image of the upraised arms and the doll-like image of the outstretched arms of need' (72). Winnicott is, in this sense, at least half-merciful to the in-lover's need. (Neither modern thinker, we note in passing, recalls the open and welcoming arms of the Prodigal's Father.)

***

From *Roland Barthes par Roland Barthes*, we know that a 'discourse on homosexuality' figured among the author's projects (*RB*, 132). A good deal of what might have gone into it emerges discreetly from *Fragments d'un discours amoureux*. This text is very substantially a treatise on homosexual Eros, standing within a tradition of theory referred to its source in the *Symposium*, and invoking the important lateral intertext it finds in Proust and Gide: a fact somewhat veiled by the book's gesture of gender-neutral formalisation, ostensibly offering the 'structural profile' under the signs of 'the subject' and 'the loved object'. The effect of this enunciatory mode is to infiltrate the truth of a sexual orientation in fact pertaining to the *authorial subject*, while at the same time maximising the universality of the *subject of textual enunciation*.

Barthes justifies this textual practice by invoking the – undoubted – commonality of psychic and discursive substance between different sexual orientations. Yet the game of gender neutrality is, as he recognises, difficult to play in French (III, 782). In practice, despite some 'il/elle' formulations, the textual predominance of masculine subject and object pronouns is very perceptible. Barthes's practice of enunciation here raises in a new and acute way the age-old hermeneutic question of the identity of the speaking subject as such: *Who is this who* speaks? How far are we persuaded that the substance of amorous feeling is genuinely interchangeable between subjects of different gender and/or sexual orientation? Is love, in fact, as *detachable* from psycho-biological and psychosexual 'nature' (including the structure of the Imaginary) as is posited by Barthes's strategy of enunciation?

Characteristically, Barthes insists that it is the placing of the subject within the structural relation lover/beloved, with its relativities of investment, dependency and power, rather than any complementarity in the natural order, that shapes and determines love; it is all a matter of roles, not of 'natures'. Both gender and sexual orientation, on this view, are permutable elements within the structure. So for instance, the passivity induced by the *coup de foudre*, or the dependency induced by waiting, are seen to feminise the masculine 'in-lover', not only in public perception (*FDA*, 223), but also in fact (18). Achilles and Patrocles, rather than Orpheus and Eurydice, offer Barthes the image of the perfect couple, since the feeling differential which already exists within the same-sex couple encounters less resistance than in the heterosexual case. The stereotypical notion itself of the perfect couple, as inscribed in folk wisdom and myth, is, he further suggests, an imaginary construct deriving union out of division; sexual and emotional roles being mistakenly equated for this purpose with masculine and feminine gender (269).

His argument goes beyond a formalist questioning of over-simple culture-stereotypes. Love's fusional dream *as such* is felt by Barthes to depend *strategically* on the indifferent permutability of amorous roles. Amorous reciprocity, he declares, finds its centre and its value-weighting in 'the consistency of the Same' (*FDA*, 269). This notion implies that transference of identity between subjects-in-love can be total *only* where there is *no difference* of essence or nature to obstruct it (sex-and-gender differentiation being, of course, the most fundamental of these, apart from the ontological distinctiveness establishing individuality itself). For 'if *everything* isn't contained in two, why struggle?'; that is, why struggle for *love*, why not drift from one object of pleasure to another? Barthes the theorist is really wishing here to lay down a philosophic 'possibility condition' of his own. This outstrips observation and reasonable epistemological credit at least as objectionably as the stereotypes he denounces; it is clearly open, moreover, to the charge of being a *pro domo* requirement ('everyone defends his own sexuality' [*RB*, 138]).

Barthes might perhaps respond here that he is simply retracing Plato. Is not the intuition that *consistency in sameness* represents a *condition of amorous fusion* the radicalised form of a postulate native to all Eros theory? However, he also undermines any such defence by describing the Platonic Androgyne – figuration of the desired consistency of the Same, hence of the fully permutable psychosexual human subject– – as *in practice* unrepresentable, grotesque and improbable: a mythical monster projected by the amorous psyche (*FDA*, 268). Hermeneutically speaking, this latter insight is surely the more insightful element of his paradox. It suggests that Plato's myth is, indeed, a mind-generated fable attempting to express amorous transcendence in terms of a purely *individual* mindspace; an attempt to map a three-dimensional truth of amorous relationality onto a two-dimensional surface supplied by the mind's own experienced psychosexual bi-valence or ambivalence.

A subtle test of the general validity of Barthes' theoretical position might be to apply it, say, to a ' bisexual' *feminine* text, such as Cixous's *Le Livre de Promethea* (1983). Here, too, the dream of Eros is very clearly drawn on androgynous lines: both partners encompass both genders and markedly interchange their feelings and roles; the consistency of Same with Same is thus powerfully realised. Yet no reader of Cixous will be for a moment tempted to confuse the passionate and pulsing lyricism of her 'écriture féminine' with the fevered, sombre, recessive, hyper-intellectualised discourse of imaginary desire in Barthes; nor to detect the same organising philosophic postulate – that gender is insignificant and sexual alterity an obstacle to love. The language of divinity, of paradise reconstituted, of cosmic expansiveness, invokes an entirely different libidinal economy, predicated unmistakeably on a 'feminine' gifting and birthing.

Moreover, this is a *non-fusional,* even a *personalist* economy, homophonous still, for all its 'transgressive' character, with the culture-source which Barthes singularly evacuates. Of the two 'androgynous' writers, one has retained no echo whatever of the Hebrew Bible, while the other is entirely permeated by it:

> Never am I you. That's what surprises me. That's what reassures me. That's what exasperates my passion. I lick your soul, to the bone, I know the taste of each millimetre of your nerves, but I do not know you, you I do not know.[6]

> I am frightened of the gods. I'm frightened they may exist. I'm also frightened they don't exist. For if they don't exist, who, if I venture too high, will check me? Who, if I cry out too loudly, will stifle me? Who, if I love too burningly, will apply the ice? Who will keep me from the Too Much to which I must yield, which I must avoid? [7]

and even, *mutatis mutandis,* by the New Testament:

> You are the Child whose business is to capture all love, and to give herself entirely to loving. Whoever gives without counting is loved without counting. As we know: whoever loves God is divinely loved.[8]

The subject voice and its utterance appear to proclaim that there is, beyond psychosexual androgyny, an objectively real truth of gender (and of non-fusional individuality) which is not to be discounted *even* within a relational practice of 'same with same', nor, *a fortiori*, within a fully gender-differentiated economy of heterosexual complementarity ('same and other'). Whatever our modern recognition of the complexities of human psychosexual make-up, hence also of amorous relationalities, it is difficult, at this point, to follow Barthes in seeing any general theoretical validity in the postulate of indifferent permutability of sex-and-gender roles. This appears to be, rather, an unstable paradox relative to its time, its place and its formalist enunciator.

As Michael Moriarty has noted: 'Love in Barthes is solipsistic: it is not an interpersonal relation but an investment in a necessarily fallacious image.'[9] The investment, as we have seen, is indeed condemned to the disappointment of infinite metonymy, to psychotic and neurotic instability, and to a self-diagnosis of psychic infantilism; all of which exacerbate the imprisonment of the amorous subject within the order of the Imaginary. To which we must now add, more fundamentally, that it struggles to surmount an original *deficit of reality*. Barthes's 'other Same', with his unseizable surface of personal identity, and in his lack of presence or voice within this text, suggests that a complementarity normally supplied by nature is simply missing from the reckoning. 'Gayness' reinforces, and perhaps in some measure explains, the idealist pessimism underlying the vision of love explored in these *Fragments.*

Barthes is, of course, used to dismissing the order of nature, in order to benefit just this space of free-play in relation to the Law ('norm', 'doxa') which oppressively 'places' him as transgressive. 'We cannot have the opposition of sexes as a law of nature; one must therefore dissolve the contrastive oppositions and paradigms, pluralise both meanings and sexes' (*RB*, 70). The *topos* of love, however, makes the cost of this defence strategy painfully apparent. Philosophically speaking, Barthesian love-theory fails to show any adequate ground or basis *as relationality*. The only credible other-reciprocity it indicates is with oneself. By way of a sublimating compensation similar, we may think, to Proust's, the writer's amorous investment is displaced: towards self-awareness, sensitivity to language and writing itself.

***

For all that, the – far better – paradox remains: love is for Barthes an immediately experienced value, resisting external discouragement, empirical failure, the theoretical conviction of impossibility. It asserts 'the reality of value'(*FDA*, 29). 'Against all comers. The subject affirms love as a value' (30).

The least deniable form of reality is, of course, one's own energy. 'What love lays bare in me is energy' (*FDA*, 30). Not only so: against the conventional wisdom labelling the 'in-lover' as madman, a being alienated from himself, Barthes presents him as entering into an enhanced, more truly constituting subjectivity: 'it is not being able to prevent this which sends me wild' (142). The promise of becoming a subject, even when qualified as metonymic and disappointed, exists irreducibly: 'fulfilment exists, and I will have no rest except I bring it back' (122).

The word 'adorable' witnesses to Barthes's sharpest insight into this singularity:

> Adorable means: this is my desire, in so far as it is unique. 'That's it! That's it exactly (exactly what I love)'! Yet the more I experience the specialised nature of my desire, the less I can name it; precision of aim brings an instability of name; the proper quality of desire can only produce and improperness in the enunciation of it. Of this failure of language, there remains a single trace: the word 'adorable' (the right translation of adorable would be the Latin *ipse*: it's him, the very one in person). (*FDA*, 27)

The distinction between *idem* and *ipse*, as forming two distinct modes of other-recognition, is precisely the departure point of the influential theory of 'self and other' developed in 1990 by Paul Ricœur in *Soi-même comme un autre*. Ricœur's essay rejects both Western metaphysical idealism and the postmodern deconstruction of it as two sides of the single, deficient logic of sameness.[10] For Barthes too, 'the other can never be a referent: you are only ever you' (219). Having once known this strange alternative economy of amorous relationality, the subject can only rebegin the venture, however extenuating and absurd, of passing beyond the sphere of narcissistic self-enclosure. Oddly, but indubitably, 'the other founds me in truth' (271).

Barthes's ethic of affirmation, answering this perception, will be a baseless yet incoercible will to transcend language, mind and theory. The strangely transcendent movement of affirmation finds no comfort in the received codes and discourses of late-twentieth-century theory. Marxism, says Barthes, has nothing at all to say about love. Psychoanalysis, as we have seen, takes note of the amorous subject, but gives him back a devalued subjectivity and a deficit of hope; it invites him merely to part with his Imaginary (*FDA*, 250). Barthes is, obliquely, concerned with Christianity, at least as a metaphor for psychic desire in its ultimate reaches; even though his dismissal of it as a matrix or model of theory is confrontational and immediate. 'Christian discourse, if it still exists, [...] exhorts us to repress and suppress [desire]' (250). It represents, in other words, a merely moral code imprinted with culpabilising Augustinian mistrust of sexuality (implicitly: of homosexual eros, in particular). It offers no valorisation of the immanent absolute of love, and it brooks no rival priesthood (31, 162). As for 'compassion', Barthes's intertext, remarkably enough, reads: Schopenhauer, Nietzsche, Michelet, Plato... (69). Zen certainly provides a refuge for the in-lover's agitation, but no real home for his singular sense of transcendence (77).

There is, Barthes concludes, no welcoming theory. The Androgyne itself, as a 'figure of the former unity, the desire and pursuit of which constitute what we call love', cannot be redrawn by modern understanding (*FDA*, 268). Our modernity does not even offer any equivalent of the uncensored, system-free space of discursive exchange represented in the *Symposium*. Love is 'a doctrine which nobody shares with me' (249–50).

Nietzsche alone is seen as fellow-traveller: not, assuredly, in amorousness, but as the prophet of an 'absurd', second-order life-affirmation. The ethic of *Fragments d'un discours amoureux* is placed, gingerly and precariously, under his patronage (cf. *RB*, 129). Nietzsche, for Barthes, teaches the 'amen' which follows the loss of all sacrality, all belief in an other-related transcendence of self – all grounded hope. He models the possibility of affirming a *form* of value that is *pure creation* (*FDA*, 181).

Could one not sustain an 'I-love-you' outside both the *loquela* and its theorisation – outside and beyond language? Is there not a difference between being 'in love' ('être amoureux') and 'loving' ('aimer')? (*FDA*, 149). Could one not break the hypnotic fascination of the first in acceding to the purifying virtue of the second (III, 783)? This would be to stand on the side of Dionysos: a transcending Subject capable of referring back to a deaf-and-glum world of signs an utterance of pure expenditure; it would be to join the elect company of those poets and acrobats who, at the extremes of language, above the abyss of the real with which language cannot cope, operate without a safety net (*FDA*, 180–3).

This ultimate ethico-spiritual paradox developed by Roland Barthes points towards an art of loving designed for a world beyond theory, beyond language. The 'place' of being it refers to is not really open to delocutive discourse; and Barthes' texts offer only the most fragmentary glimpses of it. Central to it is the determination to allow the tender, non-possessive, even oblative, components of love to emerge in a construct of deferred satisfaction, keeping alive at least the imaginative possibility of an other-presence, and its vitalising energies:

It isn't merely a need for tenderness. It's also a need to be tender towards the other: we enfold each other in mutual goodness, we mother each other reciprocally; we return to the root of all relationality, where need and desire coincide. (*FDA*, 265)

Like Zen, it practises a 'not-wanting-to-grasp' (275): a difficult and morally ambiguous ascesis breaking with the system of the Imaginary (276). It even consents in self-denial to the infidelity ('le pluriel') of its Other (266). Werther-like passion thus generates its purified antithesis, like some postmodern echo of *La Nouvelle Héloïse*.

Yet Barthes's ultimate metaphoric comparators are still, remarkably, the Christian mystics: St John of the Cross[11] distinguishes being in the dark (*estar a oscuras*: the condition of being, without personal fault, deprived of the knowledge of causes and ends) and being in darkness (*estar en tinieblas*: the state of disorder occasioned by excessive attachment to things desired). While acknowledging the habitual dominance of the latter condition, Barthes finds a model in the former:

But sometimes, also, there is a different night, [...] I suspend all interpretation; I enter into the night of non-meaning; desire continues to vibrate (the darkness is transluminous), but I do not want to possess anything; this is the night of non-profit, of subtle, invisible self-expenditure: *estoy a oscuras*. (*FDA*, 203)

Barthes's mystical intertext is here, as ever, misleadingly partial and appropriative: it takes no account of the 'passivity' of the Dark Night (which, even in the privation of its divine Other, obeys by faith a given love, a communicated 'grace'); and it entirely sets aside the Christian mystic's 'Dawn'. Yet this chosen analogy provides a suggestive and necessary homophony for a mystical vibration authentically present in Barthes' textual voice. The book's last 'figure', accordingly, fuses the Nietzschean register ('No longer pray, just bless!') with a mysticity referred (again, problematically) to Ruysbroek: the most delectable wine is the self-sufficient intoxication of a desire that thirsts but will never drink (276).

***

In his 'autobiography', Barthes speaks of his long game of 'upper-hand' played out, as theorist, against Nature, and of his recessive Derridian quest to deconstruct the notion of Origin (*RB*, 124). The complication apparent in *Fragments d'un discours amoureux* is that 'nature' has returned in force by the back door, in the guise of an unsuspected depth of value constitutive of the amorous subject as such. His discourse of theory, in the last analysis, *obeys* this experienced depth, at the risk of registering the subject's deepest contradictions and opening up his native 'woundedness'.

The 'dialectical resolution' projected by Barthes's love ethic marks for this reason a turning-point. If nature is not to be undone by theory, perhaps it is theory that needs to close its discrepancy with nature? Is it possible – after the structuralist and poststructuralist interludes spent denouncing naive realism (something Barthes the theorist finally sees as modish)[12] – to re-anchor the newly 'heavy' subject to a non-naive realism, transcending the simple alternative of mimetic analogy or semiotic code?

Barthes's ascendant spiral, prior to his untimely death in 1980, does indeed register a last twist of this type. *La Chambre claire* has the double character of hermeneutic re-evaluation and of existential quest for the figure subtending Barthesian love. The resurrecting photograph of Barthes's mother at the Winter Gardens here provides an Ariadne's thread, which the theorist follows through a number of clearings or crossways (*CC*, 114). Most crucial of these is the decipherment of the 'noème'– the fundamental unit of knowledge. The photo is 'connatural with its referent': different, therefore, from other systems of representation, notably the verbal sign. It bears witness to the past in the mode of re-actualised *attestation* – something Barthes, remarkably, calls 'proof-according-to-Thomas-wanting-to-touch-the-risen-Christ' (*CC*, 125).[13] This unwonted comparison refers implicitly to his central insight about the amorous subject: that the Other of love cannot be known as object of identifying reference, but only as singular relational *ipse*.

We cannot say where or how far this insight might have taken Barthes. What hermeneutical horizons are there, precisely, for a postmodern opponent of 'coming the heavy', when, encountering value in love, he resolves to 'get real'?

It is a discovery of some weight, at least, to find that – even for this arch-exponent of logocentric, twentieth-century reflexivity – love in the end commands theory more intimately and more ultimately than theory commands love. 'We mustn't be impressed by the depreciations of which amorous feeling has been the butt. We have to affirm. We must dare to. Dare to love…' (III, 706).

Notes

1   R. Barthes, *Œuvres*, 3 vols, ed. E. Marty (Paris: Seuil, 1993–95), Vol. III (1995), p. 796. Further references will be given in the text as volume followed by page number. See also Volumes I (1993) and II (1994).

2   R. Barthes, *Roland Barthes par Roland Barthes* (Paris: Seuil, 1995), p. 77. Further references will be given in the text as *RB* followed by page number.

3   See R. Barthes, *Fragments d'un discours amoureux* (Paris: Seuil, 1977), pp. 207–9. Further references will be given in the text as *FDA* followed by page number.

4   See III, 757, 775.

5   The 'little man/omelette' is Lacan's punning characteristion of the earliest phase of subjectivity: an amorphous state in which there are no boundaries to the infant's experience or sense of need (*The Four Fundamental Concepts of Pshycho-Analysis,* London: Hogarth Press, 1977, p. 197.

6   H. Cixous, *Le livre de Promethea* (Paris: Gallimard, 1983), p. 80.

7   Ibid., p. 95.

8   Ibid., p. 224.

9   M. Moriarty, *Roland Barthes* (Cambridge: Polity Press, 1991), p. 184.

10 See my study of this text, 'The Resonance of Ricœur: Soi-même comme un autre', in P. Gifford and J. Gratton (eds.), *Subject Matters: Subject and Self in French Literature from Descartes to the Present* (Amsterdam: Rodopi, 2000), pp. 200–25.

11 This writer was known to Barthes exclusively through the sceptical, criticist study of Jean Baruzi: *Saint Jean de la Croix et le problème de l'expérience mystique* (Paris: Alcan, 1925; 2nd edn 1931), a work influential among French intellectuals (Valéry corresponded with this author); cf. *FDA*, 130 (note), 203, 204 etc.

12 See R. Barthes, *La Chambre claire: Note sur la photographie* (Paris: Seuil, 1980): 'la mode aujourd'hui … est à la relativité sémantique' (p. 136). Further references will be given in the text as *CC* followed by page number.

13 The reference is to St John's Gospel (20: 24–9). Barthes may or may not be aware that that the episode he quotes represents a hermeneutic 'crux': in Ricœurean terms, it offers a paradigmatic example of 'identifying reference', or *idem*-recognition, applied to a situation actually calling for *ipse*-recognition.

Chapter 13

Luce Irigaray: Lifting the Curse of Genesis

Rien de plus spirituel... que la sexualité féminine.[1]

Luce Irigaray scatters to the four winds loosely metaphorised fragments of Judaeo-Christian theology: we hear much of 'word', 'covenant', 'promise', 'incarnation', 'resurrection', 'pentecost', 'communion' and 'parousia', not to mention intermediary angels. Yet her writings refer in practice to an Eros that is recognisably Platonic: sexually-based, naturally mysterious, cosmic, upward-reaching, quasi-divine, belonging to 'being'. Save that, counter-platonically, the lost homeland of spiritual ascent will be relocated by Irigaray in the space-time of historical becoming, and re-rooted firmly in the human psyche, viewed in its unseen continuity with the body.

This thinker stands ever-ready to make the male subject and hero of Western philosophic tradition re-address the body and confess to past errors of idealist misrecognition and spiritualist contempt. In the last decades of the twentieth century, the subject-hero's covert masculinist bias, his cultural privilege, his social power-status are also, for the first time, directly challenged. As dissident young colleague of Lacan at Vincennes, Irigaray famously turned the 'law of the Father' against its patriarchal Lawyers.[2] Her own subsequent remodelling of the libidinal economy has recourse to a conceptual language woven out of metaphors highlighting female sexual morphology ('lips', 'mucous membrane', 'womb'...). This riposte-in-kind, countering the ascendancy of the 'Phallus' in Freudo-Lacanian discourse, blossoms in her work into fugue-like developments of ever-widening symbolic import, giving birth at length to gender typologies, a culture critique, an ethics, and even a quasi-theology of sexual difference.

Irigaray matters to us here in a threefold sense: as a reader of the culture-story; as postmodern rediscoverer of a sense of 'love' irreducible to third-person (masculine) rationality; and as would-be prophet of a human genesis-in-love still to be. Her power of insight in all these roles is often impressive. Yet, more than most, she is caught in cross-currents of ambiguity perennially associated with the 'Bermuda triangle'.[3] Many of these centre on her postmodern relationship – allusive, fragmentary and deeply paradoxical – with the biblical Book of Genesis.

***

It is of some importance to attend to this feminist thinker's narrativisation of Western culture, as mapped from a distinctive speaking position within her own socio-cultural time-and-place. Despite her very sharp critique of the Oedipal paradigm, as re-enacted to the detriment of women by Freudo-Lacanians, Irigaray does not contest the pertinence of psychoanalysis as such for scanning human phenomena of love, desire and transcendence. Nor does she entertain any significant hermeneutical doubts about the competence of psychoanalytically based 'critical theory'– at least as re-written by feminists – to decipher the imaginary and symbolic orders informing an entire historical culture of the West. Above all – and this conviction conditions her entire style of thinking – she endorses (albeit with feminist amendments addressed to each) the intuitions of an upward-reaching 'transcendence from below' inherited from her most frequently quoted (male) masters of postmodernity: Hegel, Nietzsche and Heidegger. Together with that endorsement goes a repudiation of all pre-knowable 'absolutes' and a corresponding acceptance of the temporal rhythms of becoming in the 'here-and-now' (a much-repeated phrase).

In all these respects (perhaps not excluding the tendency to elliptical and implicit metanarratives), Luce Irigaray belongs at the table of the postmodern symposium. Her originality, in this company, lies in her intuitions of, and concern for, 'love' as a value; and in her attempts to draw from 'the feminine' a sketch of how this value may be rethought and re-assumed, within post-Freudian horizons, as a function of fully recognised sexual difference.

Her *Ethique de la différence sexuelle* (1984) starts from a lament at the contemporary state of Western societies, and of the symptomatic status of love within them. Psychoanalysis, she declares, for all its vastly deployed problematics of 'desire', has not yet brought about any worthwhile sexual revolution (*EDS*, 16), by which she understands any humane, value-positive revolution, concretely enhancing amorous relationships. Of Freudian sublimation – perhaps the single most important notion borrowed by critical theorists from the toolkit of psychoanalysis – she will say that it needs completing positively, so as to give full play to a double polarity of desire, masculine *and* feminine, each pole becoming genuinely constitutive of a sexuate personal identity, thus allowing a 'field' of mutual attraction, discovery and exchange (she uses the biblical words 'parole', 'promesse', 'alliance') to exist and subsist between the genders (17).

Irigaray, we perceive, is no gender warrior. Her intention in foregrounding 'the feminine' is to tap into a culturally repressed 'reserve' of human potential; her real topos is the possible efflorescence of the spirit in and through the socio-culturally situated flesh. Though she rarely evokes directly the experience of loving, and never attempts to define love conceptually, her whole effort is directed at sketching the conditions of possibility which enable amorous relationships to flourish and endure. In an age amputated from any enlarging transcendence, much given to multiple, superficial relationships and to sexual indifferentism, the question is crucial and urgent

> From the micro- to the macro-scale, from the most intimate to the most political sphere, a genesis of love between the sexes should be there for the making. A world to be created or recreated so that man and woman may once again or at last co-habit, encounter the other and sometimes dwell in the same place. (*EDS*, 23)

The bi-polar desire-field, insofar as it is seen to regather all the energies of sex-and-gender into the service of a re-spiritualisation of love, represents a reservoir of untapped creative potential. Irigaray speaks of a 'remainder' not consumable by the human other and hitherto invested in 'God' (*EDS*, 20–1). This potential, as she envisions it, forms the entire basis of her proposal, just as the de-alienation of it represents the single underlying theme of her culture-critique. Following Nietzsche – she refers us back to the concluding essay 'Epistle to the last Christians' in her keynote work *L'Amante marine: Sur Friedrich Nietzsche*' (1980) – she suspects, moreover, that she knows the main source of the alienating shadow lying over the hidden wellsprings of amorous possibility:

> Destiny of love, still split and spreadeagled between here and elsewhere. Work of love, originally sinful since the first garden, the lost earthly paradise? This destiny of the flesh being, into the bargain, imputed to God! (22)

The destiny of love in the West is – is it not? – to have been historically mortgaged to a world-denying theistic transcendentalism bearing the name of Christianity.

For Irigaray, the contemporary disorders of love are those of a 'post-religious' age, suffering the symptoms of the crash of a symbolic culture-construct of the type which Freud takes to be the formula of all 'religion'. Yet it remains no less true that – under pain of being dispersed by the multiple winds of desire, or tied into knots of psychosexual pathology, or traduced into an oppressive relationship of power – i.e. into a caricature of itself – love cannot develop as a merely one-dimensional ('horizontal') transaction between individuals:

> The bond uniting or re-uniting masculine and feminine must be horizontal and vertical, terrestrial and heavenly. As Heidegger – among others – writes, it must effect the alliance between gods and mortals. Sexual encounter being a festival, a celebration, and not, masked or polemical, a master–slave relationship. Nor a rendezvous in the shadow or the ambit of a Father-God, who would lay down the law unilaterally, or be the immutable spokesman of one sex only. (*EDS*, 23–4)

To become itself, to be open to its own calling, it does require a dimension of *depth*, by which it sends its roots deep down into the anthropological 'flesh', and of *height*, engaging a human potential of 'spirit'. Failing which, the 'envelopes' which the lovers constitute for each other will be merely imprisoning; and the 'interval' between the partners will shrink, so that desire no longer dynamises and 'transports' the lovers. Amorous relationality will then be reduced to a quasi-digestive need-circuit: 'The envelope ... becomes a danger if a third term does not exist' (16).

Love, in short, needs a vector of verticality, and a horizon of transcendence; both predicated on a third-party Other (real or ideal: hitherto understood as 'the child', 'society' or 'God'). We encounter here the structuring 'conditions of possibility' to which Irigaray is always attentive, very much as Kant is attentive to the categories of space and time which condition the human act of knowing. Like Kant, she will refer to such structuring conditions as 'transcendentals', adding in respect of the transcendental of amorous desire that it is *perceptible* to the subject ('transcendental sensible') (*EDS*, 38).

The other thing that love is said by Irigaray to require is, symmetrically, a threshold: a point of passage delimiting a space or place of being and marking out individual identity as such. Such a threshold marks out the relational possibilities between two sexually differentiated, complementary (non-permutable) 'others'. It is at this point that acceptance of the amorous 'other' is given or refused; here that amorous election-in-difference intervenes, and the accession-in-novelty of the lovers to a greater wholeness of being becomes possible. Irigaray's founding intuition is that this threshold is, in fact, that of sexual difference itself, written into the flesh, male and female. She thinks correspondingly that sexual indifferentism of all kinds, like the temptation of embracing both genders within a single androgynous subject-identity, is always, in relation to the full and proper potential of love, a deficiency, a loss or an evasion. Difference *matters*; so much so that even the important goal of social equality for women, if bought at the cost of a mimetic absorption into the 'envelope' of masculine identity, is a misguided option for feminists.

Is Irigaray's projected 'love-genesis', we might wonder, derived from some revisionist re-reading of Genesis? Her fundamental speaking point coincides remarkably with the anthropological vision which all competent, hermeneutically aware modern exegetes derive from this text. This would seem true in respect of the complementarity-in-difference of the sexes, given in the biblical text as the finishing touch of the 'good creation' ('male and female he created them'), and of the energy-reserve of admiration and wonder which operates at this identity-threshold (*EDS*, 19–20), but also of the sense of 'the divine' generated out of that differential, and of the pathological disorders which are seen in Genesis to follow from the human appropriation of divine transcendence and from the human distortion of godlikeness. ('Thy desire shall be unto thy husband and he shall rule over thee', we have suggested, be read as a proto-feminist text, 'patriarchy' being seen to characterise human 'fallenness'). The convergence on points of such centrality might, quite reasonably, lead us to identify Genesis as the probable matrix of Irigaray's entire construction.

This supposition, however, reckons without the distorting force-field of cultural mis-recognitions and cross-purposes which we have come to discover within the 'Bermuda triangle' of Eros. Though allusively insistent, Irigaray's re-appropriation of a very large slice of the anthropology of Genesis will go unacknowledged in her writings, like some undeciphered or forbidden dream-encounter. Over this text (metonymically standing for the Judaeo-Christian culture-matrix as such), lies a long shadow of Oedipian repudiation: something co-resonant with the wider identity-narrative of secularist French thought (itself perhaps the last remaining strand, still unrevised, in the classic 'nation-state story' as formulated and propagated by the Third Republic).[4] We have noted in passing its recognisable leitmotif: 'love originally sinful from the first garden'. Like de Sade, Valéry, Proust, Péret, Breton, Bataille, Cixous, Foucault and many another French thinker, Irigaray, simply by virtue of this shared *tradition of cultural memory*, has introjected the 'curse' of Genesis according to the letter of its mythical expression: as a divine anathema, patriarchally punishing all transgressions of natural eros, sexual or intellectual, by the pains of fallenness and exile; not least, the disorder which sets inter-gender relations under the determining sign of masculinist power and domination.

We owe to Paul Ricœur (whom Irigaray does not quote) the patient, steely and cogent demonstration that the Oedipal paradigm, as deployed by Freudo-Lacanian deconstructors, most notably in respect of the symbolic life of religious myth, constitutes a flawed, suspicion-led hermeneutics, snatching (for instance) at the sense of Genesis and misconstruing it antipodally.[5] Where the 'hermeneutic moment' is short-circuited, Genesis is necessarily seen by deconstructors as *instituting* within Western culture the one-sided, unjust Law-of-the-father, and thus as *sanctioning* the entire historico-cultural order of patriarchy. In Irigarayan terms, it represents a first and founding 'rendezvous in the shadow or the ambit of a Father-God' (*EDS*, 23).

As the warning displayed at unguarded railway crossings in France has it: 'one train may hide another.' The intervening Freudo-Lacanian train seems to have concealed from Irigaray's view – in part, or perhaps indeed wholly – the older and more radical anthropology of sexual difference transmitted by Genesis: the very ground she rediscovers as her own and which she elects to expound as her own starting point. Misconstrued as the fountainhead of patriarchal essentialism, Genesis itself, meanwhile, remains the occluded source-text: repudiated, unthought (i.e. all-too-easily thought)[6] – and, for both reasons, unavowable as such.

Some qualification is no doubt possible. It is noticeable that apart from a mild jab or two at 'spare-ribbery',[7] Irigaray does not (unlike many new-wave feminists) especially indict or scapegoat this text, nor, indeed, the Judaeo-Christian scriptures as a whole, whereas she can be fiercely critical of the institutional Catholic church.[8] This pattern of critical sensibilisation bears the hallmarks of French secularism generally, which 'reads' the institutions of power more clearly than the logic of doctrine, being itself a form of socio-political emancipation from a particular institutional structure. Its understanding of 'religion' commonly espouses the modalities of this viewpoint, with both the tolerances and the blindspots thereby implied. The recognisably secularist gesture of 'taking back from religion what is ours' (Mallarmé's phrase) is clear enough when Irigaray writes that the element in human love which is not reducible to a form of mutual consumption (i.e. its spiritual or 'divine' part) has 'traditionally' (i.e. in the cultural tradition *of Catholic France*) been invested in God and in the child (*EDS*, 14). Against this same tradition, she will insist that sexuality is not limited to, or solely defined by, reproductive function; it is to be taken as subject-intrinsic (i.e. as a matter of regenerating the lovers themselves). This is indeed an important perspective, progressively foregrounded by post-Renaissance individuation. English-speaking readers may have the sense that it has long since been integrated by large provinces of Christian thinking and practice.

Nor can we overstate the secularist persuasion of the loss of any logically possible antecedent foundation for human love: Irigaray is integrally (i.e. literally) persuaded by the Nietzschean 'death of God'. This motif is explicitly cited in her own account of start-point and context: 'the question of sexual difference is a question to be asked more especially after and with the 'death of God' (*EDS*, 88). If no prior ontological foundation exists for amorous relationality, if no *telos* traverses it, if no pattern for real loving illumines it from above, no prevenient divine grace creates, redeems or calls it, then human love is reduced to its vulnerable phenomenological reality, and to its own intrinsic powers of self-recognition and invention. Conversely, there is – at least in logical space – a blank page on which to re-write amorous relationality anew. All projected essences having been cleared from the intelligible heavens, all oppressive distortions, real or symbolic, might – in thinkable principle – be lifted. Could not all inherited flaws and alienations be analysed as contingent defects of the inherited imaginary-symbolic construct-in-culture *and hence, perhaps, rectified*?

In a sense, the 'liberation' of love in France has, in its successive moments and phases, always travelled the road of this intuition. Irigaray, speaks from the secularist *terminus ad quem*. Yet, remarkably, she speaks at this point to insist that it is the 'divine' term of the triangle which is, no less than before, the key to any and all hold on the very notion of love. More so, indeed, than before, since 'If no third term exists in and for the encompassing lover, he or she becomes almighty' (*EDS*, 19); again, we might think, a fair gist-translation of the serpent-led scenario of Genesis...

Irigaray has, in short, the pertinent intuition that the key to amorous relationality between the sexes is indeed the invisible Third; and that this key itself is to be retrieved from its bankrupt theistic matrix and reinterpreted anthropocentrically, as a transcendence 'from below'.

A further contextual marker specified by Irigaray is worth noticing here, since it explains a characteristically relativistic 'double-take' or 'double-talk' on 'the divine' that has often perplexed her readers. The cultural moment she inhabits is, she says, characterised as that of 'the ontico-ontological difference' (*EDS*, 88). The term 'ontological', as Irigaray uses it, connotes a metaphysical and masculine discourse of speculative reason claiming (vainly) to explain the nature and origins, the causes and ends of being – that is, the erstwhile foundation from which the event of the 'death of God' has shorn the modern mind loose. The term 'ontic', by contrast, is used to designate her own energising concern, guided by Heidegger, for a qualitative depth of personal identity, and for a value-enhanced existence which she conceives as an inner duration enfolded within historical space-time – such is the 'first dwelling in which nobody any longer abides today' (176). This dwelling-place is still, she thinks, open to reflective pursuit by the lover of wisdom (the philosopher), at least as an experiential reality, to be approached with rationally developed intuition, 'from the side of the feminine'; and its pursuit is all the more urgent given the 'perils' of banalisation, mediocrity, failure and despair run by human loves within a cultural mindspace which – for the first time in European history, and perhaps in human history – has no structure of verticality, no agreed and accepted mapping of 'transcendence'.

To follow Irigaray as she navigates these tricky and turbulent twentieth-century waters, we may again recall the inherited culture-matrix. Here and throughout, this writer speaks as someone emerging from, and reacting to, a pre-programmed, highly structured, onto-theological form of religious 'verticality'. Within her own living memory, the religious establishment of the French church was still presenting Aquinas' 'five ways' of theistic proof as an *étape obligée* of a normative religious belief. For her part, Irigaray has the intuitive acuity to understand that where the 'certainties' of metaphysical reason are seen to have broken down, no longer pre-insuring or re-insuring the 'God-hypothesis', the mystery of being still remains entire, indeed re-emerges anew; and so, in the end, does the chance *a posteriori* of a Wholly Other to be encountered in and through the deepening of that very mystery. Simply, we do not dispose of any such assurance *as a given*, that is, as foundational for our philosophising or for our lives. One must add: this is decisively true if (and only if) the faith tradition of Judaeo-Christian revelation as such is *also and consequently* repudiated *along with rationalist-idealist metaphysics*, as an inferior or objectionable symbolic construct forged solely by a process of mythic psycho-partheno-genesis.

The same perspectives of context help explain, finally, the prodigious – but perhaps also 'prodigal'? – theological metaphoricity of this thinker. What remains of a religious 'tradition' that has been 'deconstructed' in this way is a powerfully remembered and in-dwelling set of imaginative structures (patterns, pictures, iconic figures, parables). These – rather than any – *truth-content* are seen to form the real stuff and substance of the repudiated edifice of metaphysico-religious belief. Irigaray's psychopoetics of religion here bears a characteristically 'postmodern' imprint of reflexivity and relativism. Moved by the directing suspicion that our intuitions of *divine* love are sublimated, symbolically transformed projections of the same psychic forces which govern the experience of *human* love, desire and transcendence, it wishes to demystify these projected 'figures' of the desiring human imaginary, so as to re-assign them to their 'real' psychic source, thus making them available once more to describe our own 'perceptible transcendental'.

Re-appropriated, such figures constitute a metaphoric treasure: a map of poetic-intuitional dreamthought still to be deciphered, an energising resource enabling the thinker to gesture imaginatively towards the 'first dwelling' divined and intended by its philosophic lover. Thus for Irigaray: 'Certain figures of gods made men, of the God made man, and of the twice-born, point to a way for love to travel, (*EDS*, 25). Not, it must be said, without distinct risks and perils. To take a single example: Irigaray throws out, by way of aside, the claim that the two sets of lips of the female body, when superimposed, represent a cruciform figure analogous to the Christian cross (*EDS*, 24). What are we to make of this statement? True, the two patterns are formally isomorphic; and both can be seen as embracing 'horizontal' and 'vertical' dimensions of human being. The anatomical 'crucifix' (if we may so call it) does point towards the resource which love finds in the sexuate female body, just as its theological 'counterpart' (also, as we recall, referring to a fully incarnate bodily experience) manifests the nature of Christian Agape. The analogy, as far as it goes, has a certain suggestiveness.

Yet how far does it go? Is not the subversive *frisson* of the analogy the real – provocative – point of it? Or is the 'covenant in the flesh' (of which the Judaeo-Christian scriptures indeed speak) being understood here in all anatomical literalness?

Perhaps appropriatively, by way of gesturing towards a transferred sacrality? Is there – or not? – an attempted *mise en équivalence* between the Christian icon of the Third Term (specified as Love), and the feminist icon which sacralises one of the two contingent partners situated at the horizontal (human) base of the amorous triangle? A replacement of the former icon by the latter? Or its attempted re-casting in the image of the former?[9]

Metaphoricity of this boldness, playing between religious and sexual fields of reference, is temptingly lively: a destabilising, yet also inherently unstable, form of philosophic sense-making (is it perhaps more profitable to read Irigaray as a lyrico-intuitive theorist rather than as a philosopher?); and the risk of uncontrolled suggestion increases with the proliferation of metaphors which are in this writer often unglossed, gnomic in affirmation and piled up in sequence. Irigaray the writer offers many such hostages to fortune.[10]

***

None of which prevents her chosen starting point from offering a highly suggestive approach to the contemporary problem of rehabilitating love. She herself points directly to the seminal insight when she questions why Western religion, unlike certain religions of the East, has not made the sexuate body the basis of its approach to the mystery of being and of the regeneration-in-being of the lovers (*EDS*, 21). Her predictable answer lies in 'Western dualism', which has for so long separated *soma* and *psyche*, sexuality and spirituality.

As we might expect from her implied culture narrative and from her speaking position within it, it is Irigaray's dialogue with Plato's *Symposium* that charts her larger response. Diotima represents for Irigaray the 'reserve' which the 'feminine' is seen to constitute in our patriarchal culture. This character is marginalised in Plato's masculinist text, her insights mediated for the company and the reader by the male writer's spokesman and *alter ego*, Socrates – perhaps unreliably so (this circumstance is invoked by Irigaray in explaining what she sees as the fatal 'wobble' and final deficiency of Plato's theory). Diotima it is who formulates the decisive insight into the business and nature of Eros. Love is 'a bringing to birth in beauty both according to the body and to the soul', by which male–female unions discover the 'presence of the immortal in every living mortal' (*EDS*, 205, 206). Not procreation alone therefore, but the 'divine' recreation of the lovers, is glimpsed as intrinsic finality. The incessant movement of transvaluation of subject-relationality, its own transfiguring ascent, is the essential 'inner motive', the 'intrinsic' *telos*. Eros, on this account, is the way, the truth and the prophetic life of an 'immanent efflorescence of the divine in the flesh' (36).

Yet Plato's spokesman, and Plato's text, so Irigaray claims, fall away from this seminal insight, causing Diotima herself to lose the thread also. Plato's theorisation develops – inconsistently, on this account – according to a logic of external *telos*. On the one hand, the theory drifts towards the extrinsic goal of reproductive function, taking the animal world as model, and the immortality achieved through the generation of offspring as a justifying *telos*. On the other, the daimonic, medium-like quality of Eros and its virtue of perpetually transfiguring the present is sublimated into a logic of transcendent, teleological quest – 'an act foundational for metaphyics' (*EDS*, 33). Within the framing 'teleological triangle' of Platonic ascent, the child, rather than love itself, becomes the justifying focus of lower loves. Amorous desire of and towards women – fruitful according to the body, but reputedly incapable of creativity according to the soul – is downgraded. In respect of the higher philosophic love, meanwhile, (homo)sexual attachments are invoked as a favourable 'auxiliary circumstance'. Eros is thus fragmented, disintegrated; its intermediary (daimonic and creative) potential is decentred, redistributed – dualistically lost.

'Love might be said to split here into eros and agape?' (*EDS*, 36). No doubt this is Irigaray's explanatory genetic formula of the malaise of love in the West, albeit gnomically and interrogatively asserted. But the terms of the formulation are curious. 'Eros' is used, in post-Freudian shorthand, as a synonym for 'libidinal' or 'sexual' love, while 'Agape' connotes here – as for Tournier, and again following Hegel and Nietzsche – an ascetic and transcendent *human* love of a spiritual order, which Irigaray attributes almost casually, and by association, to *Christianity*. Her own analysis has, however, been addressed directly and solely to *Platonism*, which, of and by itself, has been shown to generate the entire logic of mis-sublimation which leaves Eros alienated.

If this is true, the real force and cogency of Irigaray's debate with Plato might well seem to lie in the way it *relocates* the origin of the alienation; perhaps even to the extent of *discharging* Christianity as historic 'culture-villain' (save to the extent that it is indeed, historico-culturally, 'guilty by association'). This major corollary of her dialogue with Plato goes unexamined and, to all seeming, unobserved – a tribute, perhaps, to the immense sway over the postmodern French mind exercised by Hegel, Nietzsche and Freud.

Her broader response to Western dualism follows. Irigaray will turn around the 'alchemical place of the sublimation of genitality' (*EDS*, 21), questioning sexual difference ever more closely at the level of anatomical morphology and psychosexual functioning; irradiating always outwards from the 'act of love' itself, but always seeking to recognise the higher psychosexual prolongations and the deeper spiritual resonances of the way we are 'made male and female' (hence the meaning of 'gender', as observably written in the human flesh, and *consequently also* in the order of culture).

Her most interesting forays in this order concern the way in which our differently sexuated bodies inform different perceptions of time and space, different responses of spirituality, different approaches to refinding or constructing 'the dwelling-place of being'. Men have no intuitive apprehension of the spiritual promise of their own sexuality, just as they have no direct, intimate access to their own genital pleasure (they need an intermediary hand or a mediating Other). Imaginatively and symbolically, they are programmed by the space-time of the schema 'seduction, caress, build-up, expenditure, falling back into formlessness or regression to the foetal position' (*EDS*, 49). The temptation of regression is strong, since the haunting-pattern, always implicitly present in male sexuality and masculine relationality, is that of reversion to the womb, which forms for this post-Freudian writer the informing and programmed memory of the 'place of being'. According to Irigaray's psychopoetics of transcending desire, metaphysics and religion are, or can become in a masculinist culture, a form of projected womb-memory, either short-circuiting the encounter with the real sexual other or overshadowing and distorting it. The sexual desire which 'remembers' the matrix, but now without being able to rejoin it, passes through its proximate 'envelope' (the female Other) towards the infinite, since it no longer encounters a sufficiently enveloping limit. It thereby loses itself either in a sublimated form, that of a transcendent 'Other', or else in horizontal series of multiple Other-liaisons (64).

Woman, by contrast, has immediate access, by virtue of her own biologically programmed psychosexual constitution, to the mucous membrane and its symbolic referents. *She* is, morphologically and at all levels, a matrix or container for the Other: the child, the lover, the transcending creation or the god. *Her* danger is that, programmed for other-relationality, she may lose the taste, the fluid enjoyment or the identity-defining aptitude for the 'place' itself in which intimacy is fostered:

> This place, productive of intimacy, is in some way a transmutation of earth into heaven, in the here-and-now. On condition that she [woman] is mindful of it. Alchemist of the sexual, attempting to rescue it from repetition, from degradation. Trying to conserve and yet sublimate it. In-between. In the intervals of time, of forms of time. Weaving time... with space, in space. (*EDS*, 56–7)

The vast horizons of the cultural renewal Irigaray envisages commence with the individual relationship: what a woman can do for a man is to bring him at all levels a containing place for sublimation and spiritual growth, a place both limited against his inherent infinitism and porous to a larger cosmic being. What a man can bring in authentic love to a woman is to re-enfold her own irradiating grace of other-centredness into the place of its own growth, re-implicating her in the 'mucous' space-time of being which she herself, at the risk of her own loss of identity, generates or creates:

> The sexual act would be the thing by which the other gives me form, birth, incarnation... No other act is like it in this sense. The most divine act. The man makes the woman feel her body as dwelling-place. Not only her genitals and her womb, but her body. He situates her in her body and in a macrocosm, withdrawing her from a possible allegiance to the cosmos through participation in a micro-society. (55)

What is true at the level of the sexual act remains true at all levels of psychic and spiritual realisation, and true again as irradiated from the individual to the socio-cultural sphere.

The irradiating centrality of sexuality is, certainly, an acquired insight of the century and liable to pass unchallenged by most readers. What is more subtly problematic is the untheorised treatise we discover here of psychosexual *analogy*. One wonders how the insistent Irigarayan extrapolation from female (and male) physiology to feminine (and masculine) psyche and to 'maternal-feminine' Spirit (in both genders) might 'work' at all, if sexual difference is *not* in fact written into the order of created nature, as a covenant programmed into the created flesh. How, otherwise, could this solidarity prove to be so consistent, its levels mirror each other so faithfully, yet so plastically? How could the recognition of this vital continuum be as potentially life-enhancing to human beings as the prophetic Irigaray will proclaim it to be if there is no joined-up, purposive writing of the analogy in the first place, 'always-already-there', for the feminist philosopher to decipher? Equally, how could this continuum avoid invariance and statism unless the writing of it were also an *unfinished* 'manuscript', to be collaboratively completed? (This would seem to be the most adequate formulation of a debate often pursued, unhelpfully, within frameworks of thought borrowed exclusively from the rationalist-idealist tradition: 'ontology', 'essentialism' etc.).[11]

Without saying so, Irigaray is in fact positing anthropologically exactly what is meant in the Judaeo-Christian scriptures by the term 'the flesh'; that is, the 'natural human being', continuing created nature, but as a self-aware composite of *soma* and *psyche*; or, better, as spirit in process, written continuously through the psychosomatic continuum, like the lettering in the seaside stick of rock. Characteristically, Irigaray shows that love and desire display pre-eminently the 'signs' of an ongoingly creative writing hand, only then to dismiss these signs as 'not-proofs', a gesture which leaves her free to metaphorise her own deciphered 'transcendentals' in Judaeo-Christian language while re-projecting them freely as signifiers of a purely human space and time. Thus she writes of the necessary 'interval' of desire:

> For desire to subsist, it takes a twofold place, a double envelope. Or God as subsistence of the interval, set within and tending towards the infinite. Unfolding his being, his beyond. Irreducible. In this sense, the interval would produce the place. The interval, as it changes, seems to be something: sexuality perhaps encounters this aporia or this question, in which it becomes the rival to the question of God? (*EDS*, 53)

Irigaray tends to 'freeze' at just this extreme point of interrogative assertion, caught between the persuasion of her own insistently felt 'transcendentals' on the one hand and, on the other, a fear of transgressing the post-Kantian sphere of representation and of claiming to know things as they are in themselves – perceiving no alternative to 'rivalry' with onto-theism. How can one lift the curse of Genesis without repudiating Genesis in all its supposed works? This characteristic 'aporia' is perhaps the last residual imprint in Irigaray herself of the Western dualism she denounces.

***

On the criticist and deconstructionist wing of her thought, her search posits love of the Other as being rooted in a love of the Same. The Other, she asserts, can only exist in so far as it draws its matter, its texture, its horizon, from the Same – otherwise there would be no reciprocity and no recognition between 'others' or between lovers: 'love of the same, sub-soil of every other' (*EDS*, 97). Her insistence on the Same as governing Other-relations again recalls Plato and Plotinus (rather than Genesis). But Irigaray has in mind what the *pre-Socratic* Greek philosophers called 'being' (*to on*) – something common to both sexes prior to sexual differentiation. She, however, gives this notion a distinctive psychologistic and feminist twist: 'being' is thought of as the sense of what has originally and necessarily conceived, nourished, carried, warmed us; as what constitutes us through the neglected body; as the memory of non-difference with mother earth as first, living dwelling; in sum, our archaic and primary relation to 'the maternal feminine'.

This relation is for Irigaray, at all events, the leading thread of all developmental stories, whether of individuals (as in psychotherapy) or of cultures (as in critical theory). It is also the criterion of the health of both masculine and feminine 'envelopes' and of the human loves which they, in turn, determine or enable. Dialectically, this relation is crucial to her thought, since without some prior ground of resource, to which women relate in a privileged way, and of which inter-gender relations are the shared locus, there can be no reservoir of human possibility to emancipate – hence no Irigarayan prophecy.

What is asserted by her deconstructionist culture-critique is that the love of the Same occurs in two sexually differentiated patterns. There is a masculine nostalgia for a return to the originating matrix of the One. This typically masters the world through war, work and systems of symbolic exchange: all expressing ultimately a pursuit of the 'place of being', and all tending at length to substitute for the body a metaphysical edifice with 'God' as its cornerstone and guarantor. The masculine variant thereby arrives at an accountancy of *what is*, but at the price of *discounting* the cost of its own birth and growth; it fails to decipher its own moving *telos* and neglects man's own ground-of-possibility, namely his indebtedness to the maternal feminine, in both concrete and cosmic senses. Given that cultures and culture-stories are written in this dominant masculinist code, the contrasting feminine response – asserting that there is no love of Other without love of Same – is of course made relationally; but it is 'lost' to women's self-understanding and to public awareness for want of a cultural counter-history in which its particularity is recognised and transmitted as value. So, for instance, in religion: women can be mothers or servants of God, but not spouses or incarnations of the divinity. Unrecognised and repressed by a series of hostile male phantasms (witch, demoniac, devouring monster, etc.), woman as value-creator is like Antigone, rejected and buried alive (*EDS*, 105). In the culture-regime of the masculinist imaginary, verticality is always taken away from her (106).

Yet *she* is, Irigaray insists, centrally, immediately, intimate with the shared matrix of human being as such. Her physiology – porous, half-open, in touch with itself, continuously seeking its renewed consummation, as in the sexual encounter – remembers this cosmic filiation with Earth-Mother. Her psychosexual constitution is called by the 'mucosity' of the dwelling place of which she has in her own flesh immediate apprehension. Women, as in birthing, have the quasi-divine gift of assisting, without constraint, the threshold emergence in the world of the other. As subjects in nurturing, they are open to the becoming of the other. Why should they not *also* define the threshold of human spirituality, the emergence of humankind to awareness and realisation of its divine otherness? 'As stranger to the perceptible transcendental, the dimension of the divine *par excellence*, and of its grace, man would find himself somewhat external to the religious world, unless he were initiated into it by women' (*EDS*, 111).

Even 'our tradition' covertly admits this, so Irigaray asserts in a noticeably rapid aside accounting for the historical genesis of Christianity ('a sedimentation, at the right moment, of previous traditions'). We only have to scan the Song of Songs, the New Testament, the mystics... (*EDS*, 111). Yet *She* is now the One-who-comes to prepare the feast of being, the 'nuptials' towards which the Nietzschean 'death of God', acknowledging the bankruptcy of masculinist transcendentalism, truly summons us' (133).

The prophetic wing of Irigaray's thought develops these perspectives affirmatively, as an ethics of difference in which amorous relationality is seen as the locus par excellence of the discovery of the place of being, and of the construction of its dwelling – the growing-point of all humane, value-informed action. The essay 'On the fruitfulness of the caress', which is a meditation around Emmanuel Levinas' *Totalité et infini*, best illustrates this dialectical moment. It is likely that the encounter with the Jewish philosopher develops her Judaeo-Christian sensibility, and places her own intuitions in fuller (but still unacknowledged) resonance with a biblical intertext. Irigaray's writing is, at all events, powerfully co-resonant with this source.

Woman, in the physical act of love, is said to revert to a formless chaos and a submarine darkness, awaiting the light, and to be reborn from cosmic immersion, in harmony with the rhythm of earth and stars. The act of love and of living form a single participation in the ongoing movement of divine creation, 'a mystery still to be deciphered' (*EDS*, 181). Her own divinity, which the male lover so often profanes – rationalising it and measuring it with the tables of the law, or reducing her to childishness or to animality, or to mere need for the male or for him – is said to be a co-creation with God, pursued in fruitfulness, inspired by the most absolute confidence in the transcendence of life still-to-be, ever-renascent. So Irigaray's imagination moves over the waters of the first page of Genesis.

Then it re-discovers the second. Is she not, truly, First-created? Before the peopling of earth and heaven, before any organising and ordering of the world, contemplation before all seeing, contact by touching with the originating mystery, openness to the No-thing which is 'not-nothing' – the light itself. The light here (but also in Genesis) is the hopeful emergence from chaos and formlessness, the grace of regeneration and transfiguration – the divine breath itself. Irigaray may also have in mind the Old

Testament texts which speak of the feminine 'Wisdom' of God in creation. She may be writing in directly contemporaneous echo to Pierre Emmanuel;[12] or she may be thinking of Claudel, who did most to give this idea currency in twentieth-century French Catholic thinking.[13]

As lover ('amante') – and not merely as 'beloved' ('aimée') – *she* is called to cultivate her given and privileged intimacy with this original passage from the night of (mystic) unknowing to daytime efflorescence of all life. The most obvious categorical imperative of Irigayan ethics lies here: in the creative understanding and purposeful cultivation of this difference. So she must resist the temptation of allowing herself to be snatched away from her fundamental *habitus* by masculinist misunderstanding or contempt. Otherwise, she too will fail to participate in the construction of a world mindful of natural generation and gestation, and the conditions of human flourishing. She too will subscribe to *his* disastrous belief in a right of exploitation absolute, *his* proprietorial cultivation of a 'closed garden'.

What are the chances that the Feminine can be redemptive of love in our libido-liberated, erotically obsessed, horizontally flattened (and 'depressed') cultural mindspace? Irigaray notes the simultaneous emergence of transcendence and concupiscence as characteristic of human eros in 'our tradition'. She refers this emergence to the symbolism of the angel, 'messenger of the divine' (rather than referring it to the human 'flesh' more concretely envisaged by Genesis): this angel looks very much like a Christianised avatar of Plato's *daimon*. Is the angel's transcendence to be mortgaged to the destiny of a 'irremissible fault' (the anti-Catholic culture narrative re-appears)? Will the masculine lover turn back from the serial infinity, the restlessness, the discontinuity, of the god Eros? Will the feminine lover, faithful to her calling, touch and awaken also in him a sense of intimacy with the more central, mucous-like place of being, preparing a new dawn before and beyond the spoiling, the sacrilege?

Perhaps in oblique recollection of (Judaeo-Christian) prodigal sons, even of cruciform redemptive sacrifices, Irigaray here dances allusively with the theme of 'a return in forgiveness'. The return supposes a sacrifice which is demanded of women and justified in the name of the Promise. 'The lover asks of the beloved that she rub out an original complaint she is said to have against him' (*EDS*, 185). Is the context of reference contemporary relationships in general (autobiographical ones in particular, perhaps?), or is it, more symbolically, the age-old, historico-cultural grievance of women against patriarchal men? No doubt all of the above: love forgives and restores for the sake of its transcendence, out of its very divinity. *She* will not refuse herself to the returning Prodigal: the rose-petal flesh has the scent of mucosity regenerated; the caress which calls also redeems and heals.

With forgiveness and reconciliation comes the time of the Promise. The latter may short-circuit and fail if *she* is instrumentalised as a tool of masculine self-touching, or used as a reproductive bridge between father and son. (The reader has to supply the likely context of reference: bourgeois marriage.) But it can also become the matrix which gives to each partner identity and intimacy with being – access to the Other which is the divinity they share. And durably so. Whereas erotic hedonism is subject to a permanent 'drifting away', an eros which crosses the threshold towards a properly ethical love (Irigaray means: something undreamed of by Freud or Lacan) can permit and nurture the shared flowering of a true communion in being.

If the author of *Éthique de la différence sexuelle* has chosen to centre her culminating reflection on the 'caress', this is because the caress stands as a metonymy for all the tenuous signs of invitation and possibility which our culture drowns out in its vain fury of sexual emancipation and perpetual coitus. This deeply-held ethical counter-persuasion finds in Irigaray a fully-fledged millennarian prophet who reaches out – true to her tacit transposition of the forms of Judaeo-Christian revelation – towards a lyrico-poetic eschatology. There will be a new Pentecost for which (as the Gospels enjoin) we should watch and wait. Women, once excluded from the Last Supper, yet first witnesses to the Resurrection and now invited to the banquet of the Kingdom,[14] will receive the charism of tongues of fire and the quickening wind of the spirit. They will prophesy the parousia – the coming of God, or at least (the bet is characteristically hedged) of the newly discerned Other of Love:

> The third age of the West would be, finally, that of the couple: the spirit and the spouse
> [...].
> – The Father invites, alone, and he disappears with Moses and the written law.
> – The son (and his mother) invite; but the son remains tied to the Father, to whom he
> returns, ascends.
> – The spirit and the spouse invite, beyond genealogical destiny, in the time of nuptials
> and of the feast of this world. In the time of the theology of the spirit-breath, in its
> horizontal and vertical becoming, without murder. (*EDS*, 140)

***

Many of Irigaray's readers will warm to her sense of the prodigious potential of sexual difference. Yet few are likely to feel quite comfortable with this – entirely characteristic – metaphoric excursion, sketching in borrowed 'theological' clothing a historical dialectic of the ages of the Spirit. For radical (atheistic-revolutionary) feminists, there will be the unhappy sense that the mimetic rivalry of feminism with the West's founding gospel of religious salvation is here being enacted all too transparently, without the required atheistic killer-instinct. In the ears of a genuine Christian theologian (such as Jürgen Moltmann), this eschatological projection of an ethical message will sound like the ancient overbid of theosophy.[15] (The 'third age of the Spirit', Moltmann points out, is a centuries-old millennarian sketch already signed by Joachim of Fiore at the threshold of the modern era.)[16] A historian of French thought might add that this particular secularising and postmodern version of it would appear to owe something to Auguste Comte: his narrativisation of the 'three ages of history', filtered through Hegel, Nietzsche and Heidegger, is here being reworked by Comte's erstwhile pupil in 'catechism', now come of age and become oracular in feminist advocacy. Philosophers may wonder if this is indeed what the *ultima verba* of the two last-named masters of modernity, reputedly harbingers of the 'death of God', point to by way of a 'return' of the divine (*EDS*, 133).

Rather than claiming to 'evaluate' Irigarayan prophecy, I would prefer to place this thinker's urgent sense of renewal in dialogue with its symmetrical counterpart. In his series of philosophic meditations on *Le Phénomène érotique* (2003),[17] another academic philosopher, Jean-Luc Marion (one of Ricœur's successors at the Sorbonne and at Chicago) responds to a similar challenge, from very much the same diagnostic starting-point. Advisedly, none of Marion's sources and interlocutors is named (one lesson of the 'Bermuda triangle' has been learned: in order to render all insights non-polemically rediscoverable-in-common at the table of the postmodern symposium, one had better *anonymise* them...). We recognise nonetheless a distinct *reprise* of Irigarayan motifs ('the eroticisation of the flesh', 'the caress', 'the same, 'the Third', etc.), together with many shared movements of thought.

Yet, in respect of the love of wisdom ('philosophy'), Marion is decidedly Irigaray's masculine Other. His precision of analysis is 'Cartesian', even if with 'masculine' boldness – he finds his leading thread in the entirely non-Cartesian notion of 'the erotic reduction', that is the strategic and fully consequent form of hermeneutic simplification which specifies the *identity of human persons*. Purely and simply, they are – we are – needy subjects *of loving*.

Descartes, says Marion, has misled us: he inaugurates the time of an ego predicated on auto-centred certifiability ('am I re-insured against doubt?', in particular, against the ultimate doubt of the 'what's the use?'). Such questions have been superimposed on, and made to do duty for, the primary, existentially authentic question of human eros, which is 'am I loved *from elsewhere*'? Western scientific and technical mastery, coinciding with the flowering of speculative ontologies, is thus achieved at the expense of a falsification and diminishment of the identity-constituting dynamic of eros. The modern fragmentation of the very concept of love, the loss of any holistic recognition of this most centrally constituting human phenomenon, and the diminishment of the actual capacity for loving result, suggests Marion, from the false persuasion which leads us to seek the locus, origin and cause of love in the auto-centred individual ego.

Thus far, Irigaray's culture critique is specified by Marion in its rationalist–idealist reference and its historico-cultural time-frame: it is seen here to correspond principally to the ascendancy of modern anthropocentric humanism. Yet it is specified in a manner broadly supportive of her analysis; at least, in so far as we agree to recognise her masculine gender-typology as accounting for the series: anthropocentrism, rationalism, individualism, capitalism, culture of mastery, etc.

Moreover, the two approaches, though very different, are arguably not in competition, but, rather, are complementary in principle. Irigaray rediscovers the constituting virtue of sexual difference; Marion speaks of the subject of love according to the one category recognised by Irigaray as more fundamental than her own – that of a *'sameness' shared* by the differentiated *him* and *her*. Marion too invokes the category, rooted in being, of distinct personal identity (*ego* and *alter ego*). For Marion, 'being' is not especially connoted as cosmic hinterland or womb-land (he might agree to it as mytho-poetry); it certainly does engage an observable and dynamic *ontogenesis* within love (as Irigaray might well agree).

More challenging to Irigaray, however, is Marion's central thesis. Eros, phenomenologically described, is seen to display an entirely rigorous logic of its own: invariably and always, love is first 'given' *from elsewhere* ('love does not derive from the ego, but precedes it and gives the ego to itself').[18] This sense is examined and verified by Marion in a number of 'figures' retracing the structural development of the love-encounter. These are: my radical incapacity as solitary ego to 'love' myself, save in a diminished sense ('self-love can be proclaimed, but not performed'),[19] and my consequent need to be loved from elsewhere; my unilateral advance in the role of lover; the lovers' vows which give rise to the erotic phenomenon as such, at once unique and shared; the paradox by which each gives to the other an eroticised flesh, which neither possesses as self-related individual ego; the unending yet always finite act of interpenetration and mutual enfolding, which enhances personhood and is ontogentically transforming. Thus is verified 'The same sense for all. God included. For love unfolds as rigorously as the most rigorous of concepts.'[20]

Is there, indeed, a *logic of love*: a discernable order and pattern of functioning, empirically recognisable (if we look hard enough and long enough), describing all cases (not excluding God), missing which, we fall short of ourselves? Irigaray undoubtedly has her own unitary sense of love; yet it is a sense so oceanic, so intuitively assumed-as-known (at least to women) and so little conceptualised that she leaves us frequently 'all at sea'. Is not Marion, however, right in claiming that the 'silence of love' in our culture is in large part due to sheer mental confusion; and that the contemporary philosopher, in particular, can best serve the times by a renewed attempt at a clarifying and unifying conceptuality?

And what of Marion's insistence that love properly so-called is always sought and given *from elsewhere*? At its 'horizontal' base, Irigaray's erotic triangle indeed mirrors this crucial insight; yet when the same 'law' is re-applied in the vertical dimension, her figure of sense appears, from Marion's viewpoint, as a distinctly unstable paradox. It conforms, certainly, to Marion's 'advance' of the genuine lover, initially assuming the risk of non-reciprocity, 'assured' only in respect of *his or her own identity as lover*. But what ongoing and transforming 'eroticisation' is possible if the amorous advance is *in principle* confined to a sphere of unilateral idealism – a pure immanence deprived of all 'vertical' reciprocity? Can an impersonal 'interval' create an inter-personally transforming dynamic? Can an abstract principle ('the Feminine'), however intuitively touched-and-felt and cosmically grounded, contrive to *love first?* By whose quickening Spirit will tongues of fire *descend* for a new Pentecost?

In short: if God is not the first, best and most real lover, is *any* 'way of love' truly thinkable, concretely sustainable, actually viable? Irigaray's *La Voie de l'amour* (1993) might be read as having prompted this very question. It is acutely posed: by the structure of Irigaray's book, progressive only in oceanic utopian aspiration; by its quality of soporific abstraction; by its very reliance on formulations of the type 'love requires…'. Perhaps it does. But still we ask: by what mysterious alchemy will the formal condition specified pass into incarnate human reality? ('A love ethic can do nothing about that,' insists Marion)?[21]

His own final suggestion is more radical. Might we not instead try understanding God as first Lover?

> For, in fact, God reveals himself to us not only out of love and as love, he reveals himself also by the means, the figures, the moments, the acts and the stages of love – of the one and only love which we also practice... Save for one infinite difference... [...] God transcends us, as a better Lover...[22]

All masculine transcendentalism of Hellenic inspiration, considered as re-insuring Judaeo-Christian revelation, has here passed away. The question of love, then, remains entire; likewise that of God. All Oedipean fever of deconstruction spent, an entirely consequent erotic anthropology beckons still to its natural complement – an energetically stripped-down Christian theology.

Both these French philosophers, in inversely symmetrical ways, suggest the wisdom of lifting the 'curse' *culturally introjected* by the Western intelligence out of Genesis. Their different intuitions of transcendence send us back to this text, which, crucially summoned up by both, is not truly studied by either. This is why, as prophet, each voice is better heard stereophonically with the other.

How hard, we wonder, is each listening? And are we ourselves listening with both ears?

Notes

1 L. Irigary, *Éthique de la différence sexuelle* (Paris: Minuit, 1984), p. 57. Further references will be given in the text as *EDS* followed by page number.
2 See L. Irigaray, 'The Poverty of Psychoanalysis', *Critique* 365 (1977), and *Speculum de l'autre femme* (Paris: Minuit, 1974).
3 See chap. 3, p. 64.
4 See S. Citron, *Le Mythe national: L'Histoire de France en question* (Paris: Éditions Ouvrières, 1991).
5 See P. Ricœur, *De l'Interprétation: Essai sur Freud* (Paris: Seuil, 1965) and *Le Conflit des interprétations: Essais d'herméneutique* (Paris: Seuil, 1969). See also Ricœur's view expressed in 1999: 'the Oedipus complex is going out of fashion now as a model, having dominated intellectual debate in three or four decades of the middle-late twentieth century ... our current neurosis is one of depression, abandonment,' quoted in P. Gifford et al. (eds.), *2000 Years and Beyond* (London: Routledge, 2002), p. 170.
6 See *EDS*, 154, where 'what is at issue in the first sin' is explicated dualistically, as a 'transgression of the limits of the flesh, of its visible character'.
7 See *EDS*, 94: 'the feminine in Genesis lacks a concept. It is figured as having been brought to birth out of the envelope of the male, by God.' Biblical exegetes point out rather that the primary sense, read in non-literalist and non-sequential terms, is that of

the sexually differentiated 'female other' being of the *same human substance* as her husband. On the concept of the feminine suggested to Pierre Emmanuel by Genesis, see chapter 14.

8 This is seen as a masculinist authoritarian structure where the 'Phallus is alive and well'; quoted by Whitford, *The Irigaray Reader* (Cambridge, MA & Oxford: Blackwell, 1991), pp. 35–6.

9 For the background to this image, see the chapter 'Veiled lips' in *L'Amante marine de Friedrich Nieztsche*, trans. G. C. Gill (Columbia: Columbia University Press, 1991), pp. 77–119.

10 For a contrary view of Irigaray – as a controlled and 'cunning' stylist, 'jamming the machinery of ontotheology' – see E. Weed, 'The Question of style', in C. Burke, N. Schor & M. Whitford (eds.), *Engaging with Irigaray* (New York: Columbia University Press, 1994), pp. 79–109.

11 As suspected by Naomi Schor, though without my suggested resolution. See her 'This essentialism which is not one: coming to grips with Irigaray', in *Engaging with Irigaray*, pp. 55–78.

12 See chapter 14.

13 See E. Beaumont, *Le Sens de l'amour dans le théâtre de Paul Claudel* (Paris: Les Lettres Modernes, 1958).

14 Irigaray elsewhere complains that Catholic commentators have neglected the attentiveness of the Gospels to women (*EDS*, 70–1).

15 Irigaray herself lays claim to this title. See the Introduction to *The Way of Love* (London, & New York: Continuum, 2002).

16 See J. Moltmann, 'Progress and Abyss', in P. Gifford et al. (eds.), *2000 Years and Beyond*, p. 20ff. See also Moltmann's highly significant *The Coming of God: Christian eschatology*, trans. M. Kohl (London: SCM, 1996).

17 J.-L. Marion, *Le Phénomène érotique: Six méditations* (Paris: Grasset, 2003).

18 Ibid., author's book-jacket summary.

19 Ibid., p. 76.

20 Ibid., author's book-jacket summary.

21 Ibid., p. 81.

22 Ibid., pp. 341–2.

Agape Remembered?

'Post-Christian' Memory of Agape

What, in the century of the 'death of God' and of 'libido unlimited', of the *other* motif? Whatever happened to Agape?

It no doubt takes the Nietzschean – and ethnocentric – prevention of a *fin-de-siècle* Parisian intellectual to pen an 'Epistle to the last Christians'; or to question whether such a thing as a Christian love-discourse still exists. In fact, the 'lost tribe', though rare enough in the rue d'Ulm, the location of France's elite École normale supérieure, are more numerous worldwide than at any time in their history; while the quiet revolution of twentieth-century Christian theology, when discerned amid more visible upheavals, will be seen by those who have followed it – how numerous *they* are is an altogether shrewder question – to have tended solely towards disengaging this discourse from its cultural accretions, often using the paradigm shifts taken from the natural and human sciences to return more surely to its own energising sources.

Postmodern *contemptus* is really a further sign of what we have come to recognise as the 'Bermuda triangle' of Eros, distorting all compasses. It betokens a culturally naturalised aversion, crucially determining contemporary French *mis*recognitions of the Judaeo-Christian tradition as such. Characteristically, as we have observed in passing, this has been identified with a Hellenic ontology, a world-denying idealism, a spiritualistic asceticism, a puritan moralism, an imperialist ideology, a romantic poem of Eros, an archaic insurance policy, an outgrown growing-myth, a monotheism, a fundamentalism, a Law of the Father, a logocentric Word – anything and everything, in short, *but* the received faith of Agape.[1] Nietzsche himself was shrewder in alerting us to the sheer relativity of such (mis)identifications: 'Christianity is still possible at any moment. It does not need any of the shameless dogmas which have adorned themselves with its name.'

A love-discourse of French Catholic writers exists, in accelerating evolution throughout the twentieth century, though it does not itself escape the ambiguities and perils of the Bermuda triangle. We might follow it in Teilhard de Chardin, who envisions the Love divine as the energy diaphanous in the heart of matter, writing the script of cosmogenesis, and within it, of cultural anthropogenesis; in Simone Weil, who writes memorably of a Love that is at once utterly gracious (i.e. gratuitous) yet also purely necessary and mathematically rigorous in its operation, to be awaited in motionless attention, therefore, since it infallibly knows its hour; in Emmanuel Mounier or François Mauriac, supreme decipherers of the contemporary 'desert of love'. Yet, crucially, none of these addresses the most intimate knot of what 'spirituality' (Christian or not) owes to sexuality, and what both have to do with Grace. Still less do they attempt a fundamental decipherment of the relations between Eros and Agape.

Bernanos, grappling with the already widespread 'dechristianisation' of Third-Republic France in the 1930s, writes best, perhaps, of love as belonging to the order of Grace: 'It is not we who have invented love. It has its order, its law... If you wish to love, do not put yourself outside love!'[2] Such is the bold word-to-power of his humanly timid and self-doubting country priest. Yet even this writer does little to untie the knot of the sacred-and-erotic enigma at the heart of twentieth-century subjectivity. He is content to denounce instead the banal reduction of 'love' to 'sex' within a materialistic and secularised society, hinting darkly (as Claudel also does) at sexual perversion as fount-and-paradigm of all spiritual evil. The traditional Catholic imagination, focusing on the metasexual 'conversion' promised to human Eros, has not infrequently inclined to classify sexual 'transgression' summarily as a merely culpable backsliding towards paganism – not always, indeed, with the moral consternation of ex-Protestant cultures, but equally without any great 'Freudian' prescience as to the extent and thickness of its enigma.

What seems to have escaped French Catholic writers for a surprisingly long time is the positive potential of sexuality, as erotic *vector for divinisation*. Missing in the first half-century, and belated in relation to the secularised, libido-liberated century, is the confident, hopeful, genuinely Christian account of its baffling 'excess' as recognised and valorised through the faith-dialogue of Agape. There is something constrained and oblique, for instance, about Mauriac's decipherments of this theme ('Le christianisme ne fait pas sa part à la chair').[3] Claudel, as we have seen, does register with rare stubbornness the first reflective questionings of the sealed fountains of psychosexual desire. Yet he does so within still traditional parameters.

A fuller and more imaginatively vital scrutiny comes with Pierre-Jean Jouve and Pierre Emmanuel. The significance in context of the latter's mid-to-late twentieth-century itinerary may be judged from the name given to the hero of his early autofiction about sexual transgression: Emmanuel's 'Déodat' refers us revealingly to Deodatus, only son of St Augustine;[4] a certain historic knot is here identified and untied. This poet's remarkable – and almost unnoticed – decipherment of Eros is among the most suggestive of the century; and yet (as he himself might have agreed) it is still close to an onto-theological frame of thought, pre-sketching only from afar the vaster adventure of deciphering in revealed Agape the true 'Other' of natural Eros.

The margins, more than the centre, have been innovative. I have not hesitated, for this reason, to include in this section a study of the contemporary culture theorist, Julia Kristeva, who has sometimes appeared to her contemporaries as a 'Christian atheist'. She herself glosses 'atheism' in the following way: 'If atheism existed – which is not certain – it would not be of any religion, but rather of the exhaustion of all of them, as good old Hegel saw, not forgetting the universal one, the Christian one.'[5] As to her 'Christianity', it consists, as we shall see, in a certain remembrance of Agape which is worth reading alongside that of Emmanuel.

Modern critical reflexivity resembles cosmic space-time in Einstein's theory: it is subject to relativity, yet enfolded back upon itself in a dimly apprehended unity.

Those who set out to traverse it in one direction, under one name, may find themselves converging at their antipodes with those who set out in the opposite direction, under a quite different banner. On arrival, no doubt, *Dieu reconnaîtra les siens.*

Notes

1 See chap. 5, p. 97.
2 J. Bernanos, *Journal d'un curé de campagne*, in *Œuvres romanesques* Bibliothèque de la Pléaide, ed. G. Picon (Paris: Gallimard, 1961), p. 1158.
3 See F. Mauriac, 'Souffrances et bonheur du chrétien' in *Dieu et Mammon* (Paris: Grasset, 1958), p. 97. 'La crise de Mauriac' is well treated in M. Scott, *Mauriac et Gide, La recherche du Moi* (Paris: L'Esprit du temps, 2004), pp. 81-93. See also ibid. pp. 183-212 ('Le Moi et ses masques').
4 See St Augustine, *Confessions*, trans. H. Chadwick (Oxford & New York: Oxford University Press, 1998).
5 J. Kristeva, *Le Féminin et le sacré* (Paris: Stock, 1998), p. 183.

Chapter 14

Pierre Emmanuel: 'Car enfin je vous aime'

L'amour à la double racine, sexuelle et divine.[1]

Pierre Emmanuel describes himself as a 'diviner of the wellsprings at the centre' (*VT*, 14). The sources he intuits are those perceptibly watering our own corporeal-and-psychic being; at the centre is something entirely non-apparent – the form of a relationship to Being as such.

Unless we happen to be also readers of Heidegger (or Irigaray), we may not immediately respond to the 'ontic sensibility' that is so powerfully native to this poet.[2] Yet his poetry itself, with its dynamic weave of myth and image, is a great stirrer and communicator of this same central sense. Even his most reticent readers may come to agree with Emmanuel that sensitivity to 'being' is latent in even the modern psyche, albeit unvisited by our hermeneutically deficient human sciences.

Poetry, like love and religious faith – and, in general, all essential things which share the defining property that they invariably elude the grimly straining grasp of the abstractive intellect ('l'*ahan* de la pensée') – are for Emmanuel just such wellsprings and sources; they make us attentive to being; they bring us to birth in being; they irrigate and nourish our growth in being; and they open us to the spirit-winds of Being:

> Comment étreindre autrement
> La raison de toutes choses
> Et devenir autrement
> Son parfait entendement.
> Qu'en mourant à la raison
> Pour que raison nous vienne...[3]

> How do we embrace/The reason of all things/And become/Its perfect understanding/ Save by dying to reason/So that reason may come to us...

From this standpoint, our themes of love, desire and transcendence are woven in a single tress into the fabric of a mystery so central and so source-like as to require for its decipherment a lifelong itinerary, and a veritable genesis: the coming-to-be of an 'I' capable of understanding that which can be spoken only from within.

***

Like the rest of his century, Emmanuel starts by exploring the spiritual erotics of liberated sexuality. *Car enfin je vous aime* is, in fact, the title of his one and only novel, written in 1949: a transparently biographical autofiction, transposing the author's early experiences of erotic love;[4] the story of a seismic love-affair which is seen to problematise the discrepancy between 'libido liberation' and the *ability to love*.[5]

Like Gide's *L'Immoraliste*, this novel stages a failed experiment. Where Gide's narrrator seeks liberation from the dead hand of culture and from a religion of moral prohibition, Emmanuel's diarist-hero Déodat – although he is also, as we come to discover, in reaction against an unloving and sexually repressive religious background – engages in a quest for meaning which always remains deeply religious in character. It is directed, albeit in a tangle of relational failures, psycho-spiritual knots and theological ambiguities, to 'being' and the discernment of 'God'.

The 'problem' staged is the hero's failure to decipher adequately or to manage existentially the exultant 'transcendence' experienced in sexual love itself. The mastermotif of erotic divinisation is given in the sustained, valorising use of a religious register: the awakening rhythm of the dance for two is 'a peaceful and almost religious certainty of the senses' confirming that 'our encounter was a gift' (*JVA*, 26); the serenity, the gravity of the lovers, with their mixture of tenderness and absolute attention, is concentrated in a 'a gaze without shadow, like that of the saints' (24). The sense of personal opacity becoming transparent as the lovers recognise and respond to each other is a form of 'grace' (24). In the physical act of love, with its complex and accorded crescendo, each lover becomes for the other a source of identity, in a death and gifting of self. 'To want what the other wants, absolutely and in a reciprocal way, is to lose oneself and be refound in that other, die to oneself and relive' (26). The 'Cahier gris' (as the narrator's journal is premonitorily known) has its indubitable starting point in a 'religion of the senses' (26), restoring an immediately present mystery that has been culturally depreciated or despoiled. *Voluptas ab opprobriis vindicata...*

Significantly, the writing of this high place of the magic energies of being mirrors recapitulatively intuitions scattered throughout the French literature of its century: those of 'arch-libber' Gide; Valéry's ardent intelligence of the body and of the fusion of *eros* and *mystis* (*La Jeune Parque*, we recall, was the shock that first awakened Emmanuel to the vocation of poetry);[6] Claudel's cosmic consciousness and his symbolic imagination; the Surrealists' sense of the mysterious depths, imaginary landscapes and ideal distances of the amorous psyche. A further intertextual reference, invoked as counter-example by the diarist himself, provides a clue to the novel sense of Emmanuel's lyrical starburst. A certain writer, referred to as 'G', author of a recently published 'great work', is presented as a sensualist mystic, seeker after the Absolute, who pursues a malefic sexual career fundamentally determined by ontological disappointment and pride. G explores 'the abyss of evil' in a series of cruel and humiliating seductions, without however finding the sexual partner-in-evil he craves: 'he puts into it a tragic obscenity, which he is the only one to enjoy. He's doing evil all by himself, and doing it badly, which is a bit much' (*JVA*, 28–9). The reference to Georges Bataille, in 1949, seems transparent.

True, sexual love knows the 'high ill' of the mystics: a climactic apex in which life touches its human limits and consciousness is engulfed in a delight too acute to be contained or retained except as a vertiginous and haunting trace: 'there is no memory of the absolute' (*JVA*, 31). Yet it is still to a particular and non-interchangeable other ('tu') that the lover returns in his quest for the rootedness of his life, for a therapeutic re-immersion in the physical sources of his mental powers, and for an unforgettable sign of the mind's holistic re-integration in Being. G's 'disappointment' appears at this point as a reductive misreading: 'One has to admit the effect of grace, the prior purpose which united us and preceded our conscious encounter: that countryside before dawn which the day, by degrees, lives upon exploring' (32).

Love is not to be shorn of its cosmic resonance or of the obscure waking dream of the Promise that passes through it: the dream of a regenerating return to a universal life in which the body ceases to be the prison of the psyche and becomes its true extent and form; of the airy tree of a rooted cosmic wholeness; of the miracle of a presence that is two-in-one; of the inner music that re-echoes beyond the act; of the expansive and enchanted starry spaces that call to the nocturnal psyche; of the 'return to the mother-identity, to unlimited existence'. Such an experience is regenerative, salvational: 'plunged into this total dream, saturated with latent analogies, we would emerge from it awakened to the correspondences of the universe. Our love unlocked the embrace by which Babel imprisons humankind' (*JVA*, 39–40).

Sexual love is thus seen as a dynamic initiation into the mystery of personal being and of Being. Out of this magic intimacy, existence can begin again. Such, at least, is the persuasion of the amorous narrator. A shadow is, indeed, fleetingly glimpsed in his paradise. One key image of the 'Cahier gris' likens the high-furling dream of the narrator's 'I love you' to a hollowed ocean wave: 'the joy of loving furls up into a tearing need, and nothingness is hollowed out beneath: I am alone' (*JVA*, 43). Yet, premonitory glimpses apart, the narrator's magic idealism and his unconscious solipsism are first discovered by the reader in the very brusqueness with which reality breaks in upon the dream: 'When we parted...' (46).

Paradoxically, however, separation and absence bring a more decisive initiation into the form of poetry, love and religious relationality:

> From the day when your absence made me know the true nature of my desire – this thirstiness for love which would draw water from the heart of stones – I knew that it would take me beyond any limit: that it was of God and went to God. (*JVA*, 66)

The rest of Emmanuel's novel of 1949 is a *critique*, or at least a trial by purification, of this conception. The narrator-hero's subsequent career is recounted in a relativising play of different viewpoints. His lover Laurence, to whom he submits his journal of their love, makes a sharp rejoinder. His was no love at all, merely an egotistical parody. He has gloried in ignoring the person of his lover in her human and feminine specificity, just as he has falsified in narrating it the real circumstances of their sexual adventure. She brings him back from his literary glory-clouds to his physical and moral failings as a lover, and to his basic need for a salvation myth exorcising inner demons. His is a fundamental failure of incarnation, witnessed by the fact that she has felt unable to declare to him the news of her pregnancy and miscarriage. He has falsified their love irrevocably, misunderstanding even her genuine love for him: 'For, after all, Déodat, I do love you' (83).

A masculine friend (later identified as Fabien) adds his own damning commentary. Déodat has been busy 'discovering America' (this derisive French expression for the rediscovery of primary truths also alludes to an actual excursion to the United States, where, as we later learn, this adulterous relationship has taken place). It represents a departure from the hero's 'normal' Parisian pattern of casual and exploitative affairs. Fabien hints at a Freudian explanation: 'his powerful yet barred sensuality fomented in him energies which he "sublimated", not without suffering and unhappiness, as psychoanalysts would say.' He contests the philosophic validity of the hero's guiding ontological intuition which seems, conveniently, to reverse into delight a prior viscous horror of the senses (Sartre, we suspect, is implicitly in the frame). Pascal, too, is turned against the hero in mocking reversal: 'whoever would play the beast plays the angel – the fallen angel.'[7] Déodat's spiritual rebirth is presented, in short, as that of a 'liberated' but self-deceiving modern Jansenist who has conveniently forgotten about sin. He is a confused dreamer, without shape or centre (*JVA*, 92).

Can Déodat sustain and validate his guiding intuition that sexual love experienced in its depth offers, however ambivalently, a figure of the true relationship to being and to God? Emmanuel's hero, whose voice we hear once again through his journal, is shaken and admits criticisms of bad faith, hidden confusion, Romantic myth-building and exploitative hedonism. Yet he clings to a sense of an authentic grace vouchsafed to him: 'the errors of the night have brought me within sight of home' (*JVA*, 118). He is in a transitional stage of a long journey. A genuine illumination has set him in motion and framed a human destiny which is, obscurely, 'addressed'; a divine image is in him, lacking incarnational efficacy. It remains to 'develop my conversion to love' (*JVA*, 124).

The novel's *dénouement* of 1949 turns around a 'second chance' offered by another woman, Eve, a talented concert artist who also loves him with a pure and unswerving devotion. His response is, initially, to reject and humiliate her love, accentuating his sexual adventurism. A second illuminative moment, at the level this time of moral self-awareness however comes to him as she interprets the role of Elvire in Mozart's *Don Giovanni*, and, immediately afterwards, a celebration by Schumann of the faithful couple. Rebounding out of deepest despair, Déodat chases Eve to Normandy, catching up with her just before she disappears with her manager to America. As the Angelus rings from the village church, he proposes a marriage of the eleventh hour, and their love is consummated.

Suffering a kind of nuclear fission, the Promise of liberated Eros generates in this novel the dynamic of a quest that is simultaneously sexual and spiritual in character, and is pursued along parallel – but as yet unrelated – twin-tracks; it is rescued from its own schizophrenia only by a banally novelistic *deus ex machina*. We are unsurprised that Emmanuel neither re-published this work for thirty years, nor tried his hand again at fiction. Yet the problematising 'case' of spiritual erotics it presents is deeply revealing of the poet's own hidden genesis.

The case envisaged re-echoes, moreover, with the whole magnetic enigma of Eros in twentieth-century French literature. What does Eros liberated say about human possibility and the nature of the 'divinity' immanent in humankind? Is its Promise merely an enchanted Romantic dream-wish; or is it, obscurely, a clue to lost Being? Is the hero's dark night the first step towards an authentic genesis in faith, or merely a night of confusion awaiting the deliverance of an atheistic and Freudo-Nietzschean dawn?

***

The second – 'divine' – root of love is discerned by Emmanuel more progressively and more painfully, through the mediation of poetry, as he learns to decipher the essentially ambiguous character of erotic 'transcendence'; something he does – very much against the tide of the century – in a perspective increasingly open to, and convergent with, Christian faith.

Emmanuel speaks of poetry as the theatre in which the forces of the obscure psyche play out their essential drama, in terms both personal and universal, in so far as they are grasped and mastered by a symbolic language (*GU*, 79–81). Poets, he suggests, are the exiles of Desire, always seeking an identity-in-being which cannot be merely a quest for the Same; in which respect they are exemplary speakers of the human psyche as such. Sexual differentiation offers them (and us) an 'other' which is always felt as the mediating analogue of some transcending Third sought through and beyond the immediate object-elect. 'Every erotic relationship is a triangular relation in which the absolute is one of the partners' (133). This triangulation, with its essential ambiguity of sense, involves a management of the deepest knots and most 'transcending' energies of the psyche. For this reason, the erotic and the religious are entwined throughout the length and breadth of poetic utterance; they constitute the source and end of poetry (133).

Among the precursor poets, in whose work his decipherment of erotic 'transcendence' is first pursued, Emmanuel identifies Éluard, negatively, as having domesticated the enigma and neglected the challenge of the 'absolute Third'. The erotic here connotes nothing of guilt, suffering or danger; the feminine 'other' is a magic being who acts as an automaton within the poet's idealising dream, the tenor of which is not fundamentally different from that of popular romance. He sees Éluard's line 'If we wished, there would be only marvels' ('Si on voulait, il n'y aurait que des merveilles') as characteristic: the lover's wonder is purified of its inhabiting shadow. It remains innocent –'provided one wants that dream and lives by it' – of any conflictual tension with the Interdict or any vital consciousness of death. His is a song *in love* (like the early Déodat's) with its own enchanted infinity (*GU*, 134–6).

Emmanuel's great counter-reference, as we know, is Baudelaire. The alternating current of attraction and repulsion for the feminine Object in this poet marks an authentic – and profoundly revealing – encounter with the ambiguous transcendence of Eros. Baudelaire's misogyny invests Woman with the entire charge and aura of value projected by the archaic religious psyche: magic powers of seduction and exclusion; control of access to the forbidden gate of matricial Nature; awakening to prohibition, transgression, sin and the consciousness of death; dominion over heaven and hell. His poetic destiny unfolds within the space of this diabolising and fatal aura; it is fundamentally a 'refusal of the Other, of the infinitely desired' (*GU*, 139).

Psychoanalysis offers some purchase on the logic of this paradox (it elucidates, for instance, the relation to the Mother); but it leaves unexplained the sense of irremediable lack and the hollow of an infinite reaching-out or 'appel'. The nature of the case is, however, precisely, that the ambivalence of Eros is lived out by Baudelaire in the mode of torment-and-salvation, as a mystically accepted suffering. There is no eluding this ultimate dimension, which is that of relationality to being. At least negatively – in so far as sickness can show us the meaning of health or wholeness in the life of the spirit – Baudelaire points Emmanuel towards the nature of love as a transcendence common to co-subjects; and towards an alternative form of transcendence that is *affirmation of being* –'praise' (*GU, 139*).

Claudel, by contrast, does know that love is a relation between equal and interactive co-subjects recognising each other as complementary players in a drama of transcendence. What is explored in *Partage de Midi* is the conflictual play of the two *rival forms* of transcendence: one, exasperated and destructive, since it is essentially a defiance of the interdict which seeks to realise an absolute identity transgressively, in the here-and-now; the other, accepting creaturely status and admitting that there is no unitary love save in God. The interdict is seen in this perspective as the nerve-point of the dynamic ambivalence of Eros, since it compels human moral choice between these two possible realisations of the energies and movements of erotic transcendence. For Claudel, the interdict is a sharp blade dividing the up-reaching current of Eros: a symbol of the sacred nature of being, therefore, rather than an arbitrary and external limit placed upon the erotic spring in man (*GU*, 145).

Pierre-Jean Jouve, Emmanuel's closest mentor, brings this battle of the Interdict into sharpest focus. He makes it a crucial axis and vector in the growth of an authentic spirituality. Like Claudel, Jouve presents a transgressive erotic drive, undoubtedly biographical in origin. The fruit of his victory over the Interdict is to discover the unity of desire in its total range from the most earthily sexual to the most soaringly spiritual. Yet in the retrospect of his poetry, he also reintegrates and transfigures the limit, showing how the sexual and the spiritual mirror each other *en abyme*. Just as our sexuality invents figures which initiate the movement of spiritual transcendence, so the act of the spirit bears witness to its incarnation at source, out of an energy of the sexual type. Jouve's poetry, rather than stitching together these two terms and series, intimately fuses them in a single poetic act, so that everything is sayable and communicates the whole of our personal-and-cosmic being. It offers 'a symbolic orchestration with hierarchically arranged levels of incarnation and spiritualisation' (*GU*, 147).

The limit, revalorised in the perspective of its transgression, presents in all these cases one major virtue: it re-collects, re-animates and re-verticalises the sub-jet of erotic energy which, without it, threatens to turn into a spreading plain of donjuanesque sexual adventure; all three poets display 'an utterance or word [*verbe*] substituted for physical possession, yet as much and more creative than it is' (*GU*, 150). Emmanuel's retrospective decipherment of his own early poetry may be seen as predicated on his readings of other poets and as deepening his understanding of the figure of sense discerned in their work. The mythic images of his own to which he refers are the ones which give their titles to his first poetic works: the 'myths' of Christ Entombed and of Orpheus in the Underworld. Both stage a psychodrama, at once personal and universal, of sexuality, revolt and spiritual quest.

At a first level of decipherment, these myths give rise to an exercise in existential psychonalysis, firmly executed in Freudian categories: 'a drama in which woman, God and myself ... would rehearse the Oedipus story in the shadow cast by mine' (*GU*, 151). This basic frame of self-decipherment is all the more cogent since it integrates important biographical data cited by Emmanuel: a childhood spent in separation from his parents; a father perceived as standing between him and his mother; an institutional religious upbringing saturated with mistrust of sexuality and moral prohibition (151). The Freudian key is, however, used to test and purge the religious motif of Eros, rather than to reduce Eros to a merely libidinal function emptied of transcendent intentionality and reference.

It enables Emmanuel to decipher, above all, the 'promethean aggressiveness' (*GU*, 161) of his youthful poetic myths. The Law of the Father places a symbolic interdiction on any and every woman, who can only be conquered transgressively, by a revolt against the Keeper of the Law ('God'), and this implies an 'atheistic' liberation. The hero, his desire exacerbated by interdiction, descends into the underworld impelled by an incestuous love-hate relation to the Mother. Yet Orpheus not only needs to transgress the interdict; he needs the interdict which he transgresses. The rivalry with the tyrannical Father is something he clings to, as to the one thing that confers identity, albeit at the cost of deepening his self-division and alienation from the Whole. It is, however, self-defeating: it involves a devouring impotence to be as God is, and a boulimic multiplication of desire, escaping all form and derisorily aping the eternal by the instantaneous in ever-renewed sexual conquest (162).

Emmanuel finds here the deep-seated root of the moral impotence, intellectual confusion and sense of spiritual impasse affecting all his poetic alter egos who have been nourished by the same twentieth-century 'growing-myth'. It follows that the promise of Eros has to be liberated, not just from the Law of the Father, but also from the imaginary dynamics of edipal rivalry with the Interdict personified and divinised under the name of 'God'; for, as his own triangular model of Eros suggests, 'love-hatred for God is the corollary of terror-love for woman' (*GU*, 155).

Freud thus helps Emmanuel decipher a neurosis ('névrose') latent in the unfolding of his own youthful myth of Eros, and to exorcise the demons of 'the sacred and erotic triangle' of his century. It provides a key to the motif of Rivalry running subterraneously through the entire Romantic-Symbolist tradition of poetic myth-making which finds its centre and recapitulative symbol in the figure of Orpheus. In this tradition, some form of descent into the underworld effects an imaginary catharsis by staging a symbolic 'sacred action' in which the hero of the Word is initiated and consecrated. Emmanuel thus comes to see this entire tradition of mytho-poetic figuration as a failed attempt to master the 'accursed portion' ('la part maudite') (*GU*, 165) of the psyche, and to repossess the erotic-sacred mainspring of transcendence. From Nerval to Nietzsche – but Baudelaire, Rimbaud, Valéry, Proust, Gide, Malraux, Apollinaire and Cocteau might also have been cited (and what of Bataille and Lacan himself?) – the Temptation of the artist has been the anthropocentric hope of mastering the dark forces of the psyche and of one day saving humankind from its own interdicts and monsters, thus substituting art for religion (83).

Yet, Emmanuel objects fundamentally, 'man cannot be his own mediator' (*GU*, 83). This philosophic conclusion follows, if not in Freud or for Freud, then very cogently *from* Freud. Psychoanalysis, for this diviner of the centre, is, in the last resort, only ever a reduction of the unknown to the known. 'I would like to invert the illuminating insight, for the explanation of the known by the unknown seems to me far more fundamental' (196).

An important part of the Unknown becomes known through the experienced analogy between poetic creation and love. In both orders, the principal mistake is the attempt to effect or engender unity by a possessive objectification. The 'Other' of our unitive tendency is always, on the contrary, another 'subject', to be comprehended in a mysterious and inexhaustible alterity. The erotic instinct of artist and of lover thus has to die and live again in a 'conversion to the other'. This is the *form* of an indispensable evolution, rectifying our inherent narcissism, transforming our erotic energies, exorcising their vampiristic and promethean virtualities, and thereby preparing an 'oblative opening-up' to the equal and complementary *alter ego* (*GU*, 165).

The Oedipal knot untied, the *form* of an authentic transcendence discerned, the way towards *another* determination of the religious function of Eros is open. Emmanuel insists that his evolution towards a clearly understood and deeply held Christian faith is not simply the product of this movement of self-decipherment, a revisiting of the spiritual erotics of poetry and love. In his language, the process of decipherment is the 'matrix', and not the 'Word', of his own genesis. Equally significant in relation to his intellectual confusion was Emmanuel's reading of the Swiss protestant theologian Karl Barth, particularly of the latter's *Parole de Dieu et Parole humaine* (*VT*, 20). This is considered one of the seminal works of twentieth-century Christian theology precisely because it disengages the particularity of Judaeo-Christian revelation from the proliferating undergrowth of doctrines of 'immanent transcendence' or 'the divinity within man' generated by the idealist and spiritualist nineteenth century.

The initiative, for Barth, lies once-and-for-all with divine Love (the 'Wholly-Other'); divine self-utterance is humanly received and is narrativised in salvation history as a dialogue of call and response; it is a sequence of mediated true signs, traversing vertically mankind's self-generated myths of Eros, which are human speech merely and inadequate to their Object; the Incarnation is a decisive divine self-communication, crucial for the knowledge of grace and the response of faith. Salvation here is unambiguously 'from above'. Emmanuel, following Barth, will always refer to 'le Tout-Autre' and insist that the gospels are not to be understood *at all* except 'vertically', within the frame of reference set by their 'ontological' preface: 'In the beginning was the Word' (*GU*, 180).

He himself read the gospels over a two-year period, prompted by the *commande* which resulted in *Evangéliaires*. They produced a revision of his purely aesthetic response to Christian symbolism, and a profound ethico-spiritual recognition. Emmanuel speaks of the power of the gospel story to symbolise radically the drama the contemporary world of Hitler and Stalin, with its legions of 'volunteers of torture and abjectness' (*GU*, 188); a world in which the divine image-and-likeness of man is continually defaced, rejected and done to death (*VT*, 23).

Most intimately – but here his words leave only re-echoing traces – there is his own experience of resurrection from the abyss, from the dereliction, extinction and spiritual death reflected in the 'matricial images' of his Orpheus myth and of his novel. There is perhaps a clue to his inner movement in his insistence that only the absence of God, experienced in it fullest extent and intensity, can bring a true sense of the relational form of being as creative deficiency or lack. 'The silence of Being is for me the most impressive of its manifestations among men' (*GU*, 186). In a world of much sound and fury, signifying nothing, the silence of Being is the sign both of a truly divine Transcendence and of a genuine human freedom, lovingly respected, which calls forth man's own coming-to-be (201–36).

This thought connects vitally with further insights. The crucified Jesus is, strictly to the extent of his self-emptying, his 'abandonment' and 'atheistic death', 'capable of God'; that is, capable of being raised to a life before-and-beyond death (*VT*, 132–3). Here is the prototype of divine action, grounding his own fragile intuition: the abyss, hollowed to its ultimate extent, becomes an indubitable 'sustaining hand' by which being is graciously restored to the subject, albeit remade anew (*VT*, 27, 132; cf. *T*, 32–3, 127, etc.). 'This being-made-as-nothing discloses to me that the Object of my desire is situated always beyond the object of my desire' (*GU*, 151–2). The central Christian mystery thus draws Orpheus towards a spiritually cogent, if ever-unfinished, Dawn.

The overall tenor of Emmanuel's intense hermeneutic 'battle for transcendence' is mirrored for him in Delacroix's painting of Jacob's struggle with the angel in the Book of Genesis: a quasi-erotic encounter in which sexuality pre-traces spirituality (even down to the 'feminine' opening of the wound it leaves). The Sense retained is that the Orphic hero must, in conclusion to his necessary struggle, allow God to be God, and that, in truth, such a 'defeat' is reality, blessing and grace (*VT*, 37).

Mediated through decipherment of the erotics of poetry, the second – divine – 'root' of love thus stands disclosed: *second*, that is, in the order of knowing, yet clearly *first* in the order of being. Henceforth, 'the myth which is growing in me' is raised to a knowledge of its own finality: 'a word whose mysterious end is the dialogue of the One – between Eros and Agape' (*GU*, 169).

***

His finally Christian decipherment of erotic transcendence sets Emmanuel apart from – and often at odds with – all forms and currents of 'death-of-God' thought. His discourse as essayist and commentator on the contemporary crisis of love and desire is distinctive – on occasion, vehemently so – because it has a different root and centre.

Gide's Immoralist had spoken of liberating oneself as a minor challenge in comparison to the problems of knowing how to be free. Emmanuel, for his part, points to what he sees as the darkly unresolved nerve-points of twentieth-century 'liberated' *unfreedom*. For the essayist of *La Vie terrestre*, all the ramified manifestations of the century's promethianism have not yet exorcised the edipean shadow: in particular, the obsessional need to challenge and transgress, with its unquiet and haunted sexual hedonism, which spreads out ever shallower the overflowing waters of erotic desire. They are still obscurely subject to 'the image of a totalitarian and jealous God ... which rises up out of our vast ancestral mythology' (*GU*, 161). An even more fundamental disability is that contemporary 'death-of-God' thinking does not allow an 'honest confrontation with death', reconciling the thinker with human finitude – a reconciliation which the essayist declares 'impossible as long as the child in him [humankind] remains crushed by the presence or absence of the mythical Mother or Father' (*VT*, 38).

Contemporary culture is characterised, on this view, by one master-paradox. It advances in a waking dream of rational, scientific and technological mastery, while driven and haunted by the archaic demons which its third-person science prides itself on deciphering, but which it is always, in the final analysis, impotent to diagnose adequately, and, particularly, to cure. Its 'freedom' is thus for Emmanuel a matter of half-finished, pseudo-liberation. Seen from his 'centre', it is not merely emancipation from moral prohibition that the archaic psyche requires, still less reduction to scientific rationality; and, least of all, the former solicited in the name of the latter. It is a transfiguring redemption that recognises the psyche in its archaic depths, but also elevates it towards its own potential and vocation of coming-to-be. Thus, centrally: 'My time is living out a headlong flight forwards; I believe in the great return' (*GU*, 191).

The disorders of contemporary sexual liberation are all analysed by Emmanuel in the perspective of this unitary return to centre: the perspective of desire holistically recognised and re-sourced ontogenetically, in being. The paradigm is, here again, Baudelaire, whom Emmanuel perpetually questions, as avatar of modernity, since he reveals 'the sacred dimension of erotics, linked in reciprocity to moral failing or fault and to the divine' (*VT*, 44).

His cross-questioning of Baudelaire's 'mystique of the fall' offers Emmanuel many of his leading intuitions. The first is to recognise the 'the darker, sacred part' of the amorous psyche, its mysterious wound which can open up in the erotic frenzy of the body and a desire for fusional extinction in the psyche. Yet the limit can equally be taken, he suggests, as the conditioning occasion of a slow and difficult enterprise of total dialogue, within which the contradictions of Eros may seek a re-integrating transfiguration of their terms. Such a dialogue demands a disciplining of instinct, hence a permanent choice of committed partners in favour of a shared effort of elevation. 'Sexual energy taken by itself is, in relation to our other powers, discharged too violently, too exclusively for the mind not to bend to its law of incarnation.' 'It does not seem,' adds the essayist, conscious of delivering a message almost irreceivable in its time, 'that our contemporary world is aware of this requirement for sublimation, proceeding from a unifying and sober confidence, rather than from a dispersed and frivolous one, of the sexual instinct within the totality of human being' (VT, 51).

In reconfiguring a stabilised amorous relationality, Emmanuel invokes the contribution and role of women and 'the Feminine'. Whereas the masculine principle, in the male of the species and in humankind at large, is readily subject to regression and dispersal, the Feminine is seen by Emmanuel as 'more collected, more integrating, more symbolic of natural unity' (VT, 51). Hence the importance – 'underestimated by women themselves' – of women's understanding of love and their indispensable role in the task of working out an 'ontology born of the Feminine'. 'Men and women will soon no longer be able to avoid re-examining together, in the tragic light of black Eros, the sexual pseudo-liberation, which our mediocre psychology self-deludingly champions' (51).

The agenda for this dialogue as set by the permissive society is a long one. Much of it is summarised by the programmatic intention announced in Emmanuel's essay 'Putting an end to woman as object' (VT, 75-86). The proliferation of pornography and its widespread acceptance or toleration are seen as emblematic of a culture of dissociated eros which compulsively objectifies women, just as it mechanises sex and makes a consumer commodity out of sexual pleasure. 'Our society is sick from its objectifying voyeurism' (VT, 59). In a quasi-Baudelairean sense, it contrives both to degrade the person of women and to idolise their Image. The very existence of the porn industry is an affront (61); we hypocritically admit both the sex-shop and the – often eager – human sacrifices of the continuous celluloid sex-show; perhaps in function of our phantasmal struggle with the Law of the Father (since it is 'censorship', rather than the degrading of human persons, that appears to many the more heinous offence). Equally symptomatic is the aggressive banalisation of sexuality in media speech and image (so that no car can be sold without its sub-text of erotic allurement or its prostituted female image). Thus far, Emmanuel has much common ground with secularist feminists.

More distinctive is his mistrust of other aspects of the post-1968 waking dream of liberated eros. He is deeply unpersuaded by the rationalist-progressive programme of extending 'social justice' to the equitable distribution of sexual pleasure (VT, 55). 'Almost nobody any more challenges the perception that sexual satisfaction belongs among human rights and that it constitutes happiness' (66). He denounces the dream entertained by sexologists and psychologists of mastering sexual energies so that ever greater erotic appetite is supplied with ever greater sexual satisfaction (not the least of his objections to such boulimic sexual self-stimulation is that it *de*-eroticises and dries up the wellspring of sexual energy' [51, 55]). He mistrusts the 'unisex' cult; it invokes an androgynous model tending to neutralise the vital role of sexual differentiation within the erotic economy; and, in practice, it usually signifies the sacrifice of feminine difference ('the difference which is really irreducible is that the mother will always be a mother' [63]). Above all, he indicts the bio-medical dream of indefinitely manipulating sexual function (e.g. by accelerated pregnancy) so as to 'relieve' women ever more of the 'burden' of their biological nature. Fleeing our own gnostic shadow, we risk limiting the intimate dialogue of the sexes to the anonymous reproductive interview between sperm and ovary ('why not artificial wombs ... a substitute maternal psyche?' [65]).

His critique of 'liberation', it will be seen, has many facets; but all refer back to the central intuition of a dissociated and stunted Eros, in which the interwoven strands of sexuality and spirituality are torn apart, the archaic sacred ignored or indulged stealthily, the potential for transcendence neglected – all aspects of a single process by which the human person is disintegrated, mutilated. His constant procedure is to question contemporary disorders of Eros to the point where they reveal their hidden– 'black-erotic' or 'sacred' intentionality. Thus, the essayist will show that the new (post-1968) sexual ideology is indeed that of revolt against a capitalist obsession with production and consumption; then he goes on to show that the explosion of sexual revolt in the generation of May 1968 represents, reactively, a reaching back towards a more immediate contact with cosmic nature and a deeper sacrality (*VT*, 79). That we are caught in the vicious circle of consumption and production in the first place is because the only shared mysticism conceivable within our culture is that of the orgasm produced and consumed (66).

Love, however, is to be understood precisely as the *inverse* of sexual liberation. Characteristic and defining is its 'unifying heart' (*VT*, 68). Rather than dividing instinctual and spiritual levels of Eros, it subordinates both to the relational 'feeling' and 'form' which integrates them. This subordination unifies the erotic lovers, making each the revealer of the oneness or wholeness of the other: 'a unique encounter, the frequency of which does not alter its absoluteness.' When two beings 'know' each other in this mode, at a depth which each aids the other to attain, 'the sexual act becomes the tangible sign of their mutual penetration, their mutual enveloping.' Rather than the fear of exhaustion through habit, what is *created* within this form of love is an eternal beginning, pursued in time, across successive thresholds, by means of the very obstacles it encounters (68).

This counter-proposal is explicated from Genesis: 'the two shall become one flesh.' The flesh they become engages the whole existential content of the relationship; for the 'work' of the flesh is to give this same relational form to everything the couple experience together 'from the trivial daily incidents to the *élan* of a shared ideal'. Whereas erotic satisfaction touches its peak in the instant of its imminent evaporation, 'love is a form which is being made, a living duration'. It demands a common conception of human time, and a project 'lived out in two modes wedded together'. It takes its root in a projected eternity which, although humanly unrealisable, is, potentially, the supreme transparency of the lovers, and the perfected identity of each thanks to the other, within an economy of their reciprocal flowering. 'Anti-modern idea: a whole which is in process of becoming, an identity progressively unfolding towards being' (*VT*, 70).

This counter-proposal is offered – with due humility – as witnessing to a truth drawn from the author's errors as much as from his aspiring. It is intentionally addressed to all contemporaries 'of goodwill' who will recognise it as making holistic sense of a central human experience and showing how 'the human person … emerges from his or her night by a continuous act of attention' (*VT*, 73). It is rarely presented in specifically Christian terms, save for a few references:

> For love is a step, a progress, which is measured by the emergence and perfecting of our inward being, what Soloviev calls the 'visible reconstitution of the divine image' through the action, twofold and yet one, of the lovers. The spiritual complementarity of the sexes is not a myth, as modern minds suppose: it is the shared mystery, the discovery, through reciprocal attention, of ever vaster correspondences, born of the difference of sensual, affective and intellectual viewpoints, drawn together by the heart and by erotic warmth. Complementarity is an attempt at mutual completion, and not at all an attempt to reconstitute a primitive androgyne.[8] It is the hope of a common procreation, in all senses of the word. (71)

As transpires from this striking passage, Emmanuel's originality is to illustrate the *form* of a dialogue of *Eros* and *Agape* in a way cavernously absent from a vast swathe of Western Christian discourse, at least in its traditional forms: absent alike from the unidimensional Catholic stress on the procreational finality of marriage, and from Protestant tendency to humanise ethically (but also to domesticate and make respectable) the 'beast' of erotic instinct. Emmanuel, refreshingly, valorises the *surplus-for-divinisation* immanent in the erotic energies and amorous virtualities of 'the flesh'.

***

Emmanuel's last word is a mytho-poetic ontology, holistically defining masculine and feminine. Such an enterprise is by no means unfamiliar at the latter end of the twentieth century. Cixous, Kristeva and particularly Irigaray attempt it variously – and precariously; frequently at the price of being taxed with 'essentialism'.

Emmanuel, however, is distinctive: he is not an inheritor of Plato falling out with masculinist Western logocentrism, but a poet imaginatively re-reading Genesis. To think mytho-poetically is to begin to comprehend sexual difference according to the ontic nature of the case. There would, moreover, be no 'magic' in love, white or black, if sexual instinct did not engage lovers in a mythopoeic drama which passes through them: each partner is invested with symbolic significance and each in turn responds to archetypes which re-echo in an archaic psyche common to both.

> Océan de soleil
> Petite fille
> La femme que tu es
> M'attend dans tes yeux
> [...]
> Entre nous que de mondes
> Ont ricoché
> Car tu es très ancienne
> Si lisse et si bleu
> Ton ventre a pour centre
> L'ombilic des cieux
> Grande mère impubère
> Dont je suis non né
> C'est ton blanc noisetier
> Ecorché à la fourche
> Qui m'enseigne le gué
> De la voie lactée. ('Ylem', *T*, 83)

Ocean of sun/Little girl/The woman that you are/Awaits me in your eyes/[...]/Between us how many worlds/Have ricocheted/For you are very ancient./So smooth and so blue/Your belly has as its centre/The birth-chord of the heavens/Great pre-nubile mother/Of whom I am not born/It is your white hazel tree/Lightning-struck at its fork/Which teaches me/The crossing-place/Of the milky way.

Without knowledge of this cosmic and mythopoeic interaction, in which the 'masculine' and 'feminine' principles are the *players* and of which the dialectic of Same and Other is the *form*, we are blind to escape the negative dynamics of involution, and the downward spiral which can devastate human loves. Equally, we are impotent to recognise the immense potential of our amorous energies. To decipher – better than 'our mediocre psychology' – this antecedent depth of our everyday loves is the best hope of ensuring 'liberation' for both men and women.

The whole of the late trilogy *Le Livre de l'homme et de la femme* explores this 'ontology born of the Feminine'; and the final volume, *L'Autre* (1980),[9] offers its most cogent recapitulative decipherment. The first part of the poem, entitled 'Eden', evokes the mythopoeic drama of creation and fall in its universality *as known to all lovers*; the second, entitled 'Perdu', follows the drama in its contemporary resonance for the poet. Rather than using Genesis as an external commentary on the dynamics of love, Emmanuel brilliantly unfolds the myth itself from within the original couple's human experience of sexual differentiation and erotic encounter. The myth thus discloses the deeper sense of the lover's experience and of gendered existence in general; and, reciprocally, the experience of erotic love is seen to illuminate the genesis of the myth – and to point to the nature of human spiritual growth or 'genesis'.

To traditionalist readers anxious to assert that Genesis is not 'about' erotic relations at all but about the abstract universal of human choice as between good and evil, this poem will suggest that it is about the second *to the extent that it has already known the first*, at close quarters, in the depth of 'the flesh'. Herein, equally, lies its response to contemporary atheistic or secularist readers keen to say, on the other hand, that the Genesis myth is reducible to a hidden sexual key, a mere projection of the unrecognised shadows of Freudian libido and of patriarchal oppression.

The depth of 'the flesh' is the story of its making. Adam (Hebrew: 'humankind') is made in two sexually differentiated exemplars ('male and female he created them'). Woman is drawn from the side of man, leaving a gap or wound which is the archaic symbol of a dynamising nostalgia for a lost integrity of being, a quest for the One (*A*, 1). Yet who is truly first in the order of created being?

> Qui fut créé le premier du néant?
> Si la matière est tout au féminin[10]
> Eve avant Eve a recelé l'argile
> Dont fut pétri le premier mâle humain
> C'est l'Eve originelle et cependant son autre
> Tirée d'Adam dormeur avant qu'il ne se vît
> Qui du fond du sommeil éternisé en lui
> Le contemple et de son nadir lève l'étoile
> Imposant à l'esprit naissant sa verticale. (80)

Who was first created out of nothingness?/If matter is entirely of the feminine /Eve before Eve concealed the clay/From which the first human male was shaped./This is the original Eve, and yet her other/Drawn from sleeping Adam before he saw himself/Who from the depths of sleep eternalised in him/Contemplates him and from his lowest point lifts the star/Stamping on the birth-sprung spirit its verticality.

Before Eve, there was in Eve-in-Adam – Ylem/Sophia, already present in matter, and in living things.[11] What Genesis represents is sexually differentiated human individuation; that is, that which creates in human beings the play of alterity and which permits human awakening to the life of the spirit, without which there would be no intuition of the depth and mystery of being, no aspiring Eros (1). The spasm that joins sexual lovers already contains a nostalgia for the cosmic Night from which they come (3), while the eyes of each, opening to the other (but it is Eve who sees first the sleeping Other from whom she is drawn), know the Promise that sets them in movement: a call to novelty, a creative new birth which each will mediate to the other (4). The male is awakened out of the sleep of matter, the female endowed with a constituting gaze and focus, an enlivening jet (8): 'And each of them is the dawn of the Garden' (5).

What, then, of guilt, transgression and the Fall? The intuition of these things is also born out of human erotic experience:

> Aimer creuse entre nous l'abîme à tout instant
> Et nos accouplements ne sont que leur contraire
> A chaque fois ce vide entre nous est plus grand
> Où l'univers en son néant doit se parfaire. (*A*, 10)

> Loving hollows out between us the abyss at each instant/And our couplings are but their opposite/Each time this void between us is greater/In which the universe in its nothingness has to reach perfection.

The disappointment of *not* attaining the Promise towards which erotic love entirely strains – at its most acute in the fleeting instant of imminent gnosis, which spends itself in erotic death, and vanishes, serpent-like – is ontological proof enough, proof *par le vide*, of the absent One, 'inexistent outside of his inconceivable centre' (11). Within the very commotion of Eros, this *trace* of the inconceivable epicentre-in-being is discernible; a trace sufficient to throw the brazier of the human nerve-system high up towards the stars (15), yet leaving it still with the evidence of its own mortal non-divinity, its *ontological* otherness (18).

Fallenness is thus, first of all, a matter of the awareness of a difference or separation from the engendering Other. The original couple

> Sentent la Main ou l'eau qui se retire
> Très lentement comme pour les lisser. (*A*, 17)

> Feel the hand or the slowly retreating water/As though to smooth them down.

The drying clay is left unfinished, without direct access to its own memory of origin in the One. This is for Emmanuel the primary – that is *ontological and pre-moral* – reality of 'fallenness'; a perspective which profoundly anticipates what he sees as the *theological* intention of Genesis. What determines the human aptitude for the life of the spirit is, on the one hand, the freedom allowed to it and, on the other, the excentrating and excursive potential for other-relatedness, which imparts a perceptible dynamic in both horizontal and vertical planes. 'Humankind cannot economise upon its deification' (*VT*, 230). We cannot dispense with or spare ourselves the *coming-to-be* into which we are initiated by the delight and the peril of sexual difference.

The original 'crime', as sought by rationalist detectives in the Genesis myth, never happened:

> Il n'y eut d'autre faute originelle
> Que le double appétit de ce vertige en eux
> Mais le Serpent [...]
> ...guidait le désir de l'homme vers la mort. (*A*, 18)

There was no original fault/Save the twofold appetite of vertigo in them/But the Serpent ... guided the desire of man towards death.

The Serpent expresses mytho-poetically the transcendent spring of human Eros, seen in its *ethico-spiritual ambivalence*, that is as subject to a principle of illusion about Being, hence also of moral corruption. As in Valéry's 'Ébauche', he is a figuration of the power of reflexively-directed self-pleasing or narcissism lodged in the up-reaching tree of sexual and spiritual energy. He insinuates an alternative Dream of Transcendence – a 'mystery' skin-deep and circular, entirely enclosed within the immanence of the Same:

Ici est tout ce qui est: tout est peau de la nuit
Ou ma peau, c'est même texture et monde clos. (23)

Here is everything that is: all is night-skin/Or my skin, of one weave and a closed world.

As Eve listens to the Seducer, so the Tree becomes alive with the cruel and fascinating gaze of the perilous ophidian *voyeur* (24). She is now her own Other-in-desire, her own repository of the mystery of Being, her own forbidden fruit; her temptation is to close back upon herself the dream of immense and magic contemplation, instrumentalising her masculine other and excluding the absent One (28).

The poet's mytho-genetic suggestion (here echoing Valéry's *La Jeune Parque*) is that Eve is 'first tempted' because adolescent sexuality develops earlier in girls, and because she is more precocious than he is in grasping the *spiritual* potential and peril of sexuality. *Her* temptation of self-enfoldment is, however, presented as directly symmetrical to *his* temptation of piercing the mystery of being appropriatively and violently (sexuality again pre-tracing spirituality). Moreover, each temptation is seen to exist in both sexes, by virtue of an alterity *within* each psychosexual identity. When Eve takes the fruit, therefore, Eve-in-Adam eats and, by intimate contagion, awakens Serpent-like (*A*, 30).

The serpent's promise – the inherent dream of Eros, 'ardent rival of Paradise' – is essentially modelled and pre-figured by the passion which empties the universe of all save the two self-regarding lovers (*A*, 29). The serpent here sketches an alternative figure of the erotic triangle: a figure bracketing off its transcendent Other, and seeking to engender, from within its own resources, and for its own pleasing, its own self-divinisation, 'each for self twice over' (33). The result is a caricature of the lost Paradise: *her* self-enfoldment feeding on *his* violence, the teeth that have together eaten the fruit clash and tear at the other, and enter into a cannibal-feast of blood and death.

Devouring its own, Eros returns to the chaos. Its regressive spiral is driven by a rivalry which seeks to outrun the shadow of nothingness cast by the couple's own separation from Being. Two nocturnal and transgressive dreams of divinisation are then played out: *hers*, of an immaculate conception of the mirror, producing magic offspring and an absolute beginning in Being; *his*, a nostalgia for gnosis, restoring him to the womb of the archaic Earth-Mother. The Serpent's promise is thus the involuted and infernal figure of the paradise of Being – and the negation of Love.

The motif of the banishment, exile and errancy of the couple develops this inverse figure. Having embraced the malefic realisation of the couple's 'divine' potential, they are by definition in exile from the Other. Backs turned to Paradise, they are driven out by their own 'desirous despair' (*A*, 50). The Serpent will later teach them to call this expulsion the curse of the jealous Father. The poet-narrator's own voice, however, while commenting on the propensity of poets to at least half-share the Serpent's transgressive viewpoint (61; cf. 64), sees their exile and errancy as a development of their own misconceived and self-wounding rivalry with the ontological order which founds their being (58).

Human existence at large is thus set under the sign of Eros, of human Desire henceforth knowing its own ambivalent virtuality for good and evil. Scorched, driven and carried forward by the angel of Interdiction, the human couple do not know 'If the wing-span at their shoulders/Is the measure of their void or of their life' (*A*, 50). The Serpent's science causes Eve to give birth in pain and grief: her children are not, after all, the sons of Light; and life in its fallenness is condemned to an eternal return of the same (67). Their two offspring divide and dispute the Promise; as do the couple themselves. Masculine and Feminine no longer have intelligence of each other: she resents the fact that, in her, he loves Beauty (54); he resents her larger love, instrumentalising him, for the Poem of Creation (55). With each sex pursuing a self-related dream of transcendence by means of the other, the matrix of their common existence produces only a spectral dream of growth-in-being, a Babelian war of languages and of worlds (68).

Yet Exile, felt as such, remains for this poet a sign of the Kingdom. Eve, the recapitulative figure of the mythopoeic Feminine and mother of humankind, is still the matrix of an obscured-but-indelible divine filiation. The downward spiral of Eros, bringing the phase-change which exposes the erotic 'nudity' of the human psyche and of all life, cannot efface the inward lining of mythopoeic memory, with its subsistent potential for transparency to Being. Fallen nature retains its obscure memory of origin; just as – in good theological orthodoxy – the actual corruption of nature defaces, but does not obliterate, its divine *capacity* or *potential*. Like J. R. R. Tolkien, C. S. Lewis and Simone Weil, this poet believes that, to this extent, myth can and does prefigure religious (i.e. relational) *truth*.

What Eve knows is 'always already' present and given in the Feminine. *She* sees that love is the relational form uniting two halves of one vase; which is the eminent sign, indelibly written 'in the flesh', of the wholeness of Being. The two halves are disjoined so that, out of the experience of alterity and the work of learning to love, the human animal may come to a transfiguring rebirth, redeeming the ambiguous transcendence of natural Eros (*A*, 76).

Within this singular logic of unfinished anthropogenesis, human love may indeed prefigure the Love that is before all worlds, its own wounded disjunction pointing upward, beyond the visible spiral of being, to what only the eyes opened in faith and hope can see and answer: the antecedent mystery of its own divine vocation of Being. Between the two halves of humankind, Masculine and Feminine, as Emmanuel finally imagines them, are thus, 'always already there', 'the Virgin and child, mysterious signs' (A, 76).

***

Some discouragement at his own this-worldly and still all-to-human immanentism causes Pierre Emmanuel, in his preface to L'Autre, to apologise for not taking us closer to the ardent heart of the mystery of divine Love, where the mystics have been (A, vi). As late as 1980, the subterranean epic of Rivalry, with its Oedipean shadow is cited as the reason why this 'labourer of the eleventh hour' always felt a deficit of intimacy with the addressing Other of his faith and refused to allow his poetry to be labelled Christian (A, 192).

Yet it is no small harvest to have shown that Eros, consequently deciphered, points us still to the mystery of human transcendence written, integrally and psychosomatically, 'in the flesh'; or to have tackled directly the 'ambiguity' of the transcendence recognisable in the structure of human Eros; or to have suggested to this Freudo-Nietzschean century that myth can be the harbinger of religious truth'– that there is, after all, 'something in what we say';[12] or to have brought, in his own poetic saying, the persuasion that the sense of things, the centre in which they cohere, is the wellspring of Joy everlasting, of which our human loves are the indigent but ever-haunting sign.

Whatever the hour of his coming, the labourer, we may feel, was not unworthy of his hire.

Notes

1   P. Emmanuel, *La Vie terrestre* (Paris: Seuil, 1976), p. 59. Further references will be given in the text as *VT* followed by page number.
2   *Le Goût de l'Un* (Paris: Seuil, 1963) gives an important gloss on Emmanuel's use of the words 'Etre', 'âme' and 'esprit'; see 'Avant-propos', pp. 13–17. Further references to *Le Goût de l'Un* will be given in the text as *GU* followed by page number.
3   *Tu* (Paris: Seuil, 1982), p. 53. Further references will be given in the text as *T* followed by page number.
4   *Car enfin je vous aime* (Paris: Seuil, 1982). Further references will be given in the text as *JVA* followed by page number.
5   That the novel fails to achieve this goal to the writer's own satisfaction is attested by the fact that he refused for more than 30 years to republish it, despite its prize-winning reception, yielding to pressing solicitations only in 1982, and then only with the addition of a 150-page sequel re-narrativising the early work in the perspective of his mature poetic trilogy *Le Livre de l'homme et de la femme* (1978–80).
6   See *VT*, 16.
7   Pascal writes: 'Man is neither angel nor beast and, unfortunately, whoever plays the angel plays the beast', *Pensées*, ed. Lafuma (Paris, 1952), frag. 678, p. 391.

8   Emmanuel recognises in the paradigm of the Androgyne a psychosomatic pertinence, but objects that it is an inert and regressive dream of re-combining the sundered halves: 'a variant of the return to the womb' (*GU*, 157).

9   The trilogy comprises *Una: La mort, la vie* (Paris: Seuil, 1978), *Duel* (Paris: Seuil, 1979) and *L'Autre* (Paris: Seuil, 1980); further references to *L'Autre* will be given in the text as *A* followed by poem number.

10 For an explicitation of this gnomic utterance, see 'La matière mère' (*VT*, 87–103).

11 Ylem is the Hebrew word for the Wisdom which constitutes the feminine element of the thought of the Creator, the Sophia of some (mainly Eastern) Christian theologies. See P. Emmanuel, *Sophia* (Paris: Seuil, 1973).

12 See G. Steiner, *Real Presences: Is There Anything in What we Say?* (London: Faber, 1989).

Chapter 15

Julia Kristeva: Re-Telling the Love-Story

Je ... me ferai l'avocate de ce diable qu'est en passe de devenir aujourd' hui le monothéisme. Lequel affirme que le sacré n'est autre, tout bêtement, que l'amour.[1]

Counter-culturally (in the climate of post-1968 France), Julia Kristeva is prepared to recognise that Western civilisation has emerged from, and still owes a great deal to, its nurturing Judaeo-Christian faith-matrix. Where Irigaray reads Christianity solely in a Freudo-Lacanian schematisation, presenting it as the religion of the ('phallogocentric') Word, Kristeva enters into this religion's own proclaimed distinctiveness as the faith of self-revealing Agape. Her variation on the contemporary malaise at the 'loss of love' centres on the question: what is lost to 'advanced' Western humankind when *this* faith is relegated to the cultural margins? What bridges to the future are still imaginable?

Her characteristic approach derives most obviously from the academic research project which underlies her major study retracing the history of amorous subjectivity in the West, *Histoires d'amour* (1983).[2] For this project, she read widely in (among other source texts) the Jewish Bible, the New Testament, and many of the theologians and mystics of the – pre-modern – Catholic tradition. This distinctive anchorage point in sensibilisation, knowledge and understanding is the basis of what she will call her 'analyst's complicity with believers' (*FS*, 264). More distantly, her approach perhaps retraces something of her attachment to her own father,[3] a believer in the faith of the Orthodox Church. He it was who first exposed the child Julia to the language and culture of France, as taught by French Dominican sisters, in the hope of inoculating her against the 'virus' of Enlightenment rationalism (163).

In relation to Kristeva's intellectual background, complicity with the sacred in its Judaeo-Christian form otherwise represents an unlikely excursus. Of French culture, her later schooling in Communist Bulgaria communicated only the progressivist and secularising current.[4] Her involvement in the Young Communist Pioneers, her university career in Bulgaria, and her later doctoral studies at the Sorbonne under Lucien Goldmann left the imprint of a basically Hegelian-Marxist model of history and culture. Onto this model was grafted the product of her own brilliant advance in linguistics, semiotics and psychoanalysis. Her progress towards a state-of-the-art scientificity in the analysis of cultural phenomena was completed by her integration into the – Paris-based, post-structuralist and Freudo-Nietzschean – *avant-garde* revolving around the review *Tel Quel*.

We shall be concerned here both with her recognitions of Agape and with the ambiguities of her act of re-telling and remembrance.

***

What does Julia Kristeva understand by the word 'love'? She points to the inevitable discrepancy between an immediate subjective certainty that dispenses with definitions and the cognitively valid, third-person conceptuality required by her present project of sketching 'a sort of love philosophy' (*HA*, 9). Subjectively, it is clear enough that love is an exaltation transcending eroticism, an exorbitant happiness as well as a form of purest suffering. Cognitively, we can say that it is a complex intertwining of sexuality and ideals (9) which, as Barthes pointed out, challenges the univocity of language, its referential and communicative powers.

Central to this human phenomenon is a crisis of subject-identity, involving a momentous and regenerating acceptance of loss in the other for the sake of the other ('accepter de se perdre dans l'autre, pour l'autre'), but also the sense of a higher realisation of selfhood ('Je suis un autre ... au zénith de ma subjectivité'). In this 'identity transfer' lies the immanent transcendence of love, a character anthropologically intrinsic to it – or, in Kristeva's favourite formula (derived from phenomenology and naturalised within psychoanalysis), 'always already there' ('toujours déjà là'). In love I experience my incompleteness, at once desirous and fearful of transgressing social prohibitions; more fundamentally, of transcending the very boundaries of selfhood – but towards what end ('Tout ... ou rien?')? (*HA*, 11–15).

The contemporary temptation is to bury this elusive specificity, like some indefinable-unavowable Unknown, beneath anything and everything else ('to the benefit of pleasure, desire, if not revolution, evolution, management, that is, of politics'): so many 'over-bold or timid attempts to satisfy a thirst for love' (*HA*, 14). As the title of her subsequent essay, *Au Commencement était l'amour* (1985), will re-affirm, Kristeva insists unswervingly on the anthropological centrality of love, its foundational reality (however problematic philosophically) for human being. Here, immediately, we glimpse the – unexpectedly personalist and 'unscientific' – persuasion at the heart of Kristeva's discourse.

More immediately obvious, however, is the 'guarantee' of scientific rationality displayed in Kristeva's constant reference to psychoanalysis. This shapes her discourse in three decisive ways: firstly, as a speaking position or 'point of view' from which the entire field of amorous discourse is envisaged unitarily; secondly, as a conceptual instrument deployed in forming a model of the 'amorous subject' and in analysing not only the discourses of her 'analysands' or patients in psychotherapy, but also the love-discourses she finds in literature, religion, theology and philosophy. Implicit in both of the foregoing is a third dimension to which we shall attend progressively: a 'metapsychology' of anthropological and more broadly philosophic import, determining for her understanding of culture, for her view of love and religion, and for her own 'atheistic' frame of reference.

Kristeva starts from the Freudian inheritance; that is to say, on her own account, from a spectacularly gloomy view of the nature and chances of love. For Freud, 'love' is a perverse and paradoxical symptom of the libidinal economy; it is originally and irredeemably narcissistic ('narcissism' being an investment of libidinal energy in the ego rather than in its objects). If love connects the ego to an external other, this is purely and simply as a source of pleasure, signifying an incorporation of the object, via imaginary identifications, into an enlarged ego. Freud's view is well summarised by Kristeva: 'in the beginning was the love of self' (*HA*, 155). Always, moreover, 'love' is borne and determined by the older and deeper passion of hatred, indissolubly interwoven with it. From *Beyond the pleasure principle* onwards, amorous passion is even viewed by Freud as secretly inhabited by the death-drive: the amorous Narcissus is fundamentally suicidal.

Is Freud, then, an unpropitious starting point for a discourse on love? Not so, maintains Kristeva. For Freud's original mission, as she expounds it, was to *rehabilitate* Narcissus thanks to the invention of psychotherapy, which she views – not unproblematically, as we shall see – as an *exemplary form of love* transcending the Narcissan definition:

> Inheriting through his humanist culture both Christian spirituality and symbolism, Freud attempted a to take over from this salvation-religion by borrowing its 'talking cure'. (*HA*, 156)

> Freudian love – the transference – maintains the wager lucidly projected beyond hatred and death: it is the amorous transference that produces the dynamic effects of the cure. (*HA*, 158)

The relational bond of 'transference' and 'counter-transference' between therapist and analysand becomes the very model of optimal amorous functioning: an other-connected 'open system', capable of disentangling the confusions of the real, symbolic and imaginary orders out of which our alienated love-lives are woven, hence able to liberate, re-order and restore our capacity for loving. Psychotherapy represents for Kristeva the only explicitly authorised culture-space in which the quest for love *can* today be expressed and explored (*HA*, 15).

In her role as post-Freudian culture theorist and love-philosopher also, she speaks 'from behind the couch'. *Histoires d'amour* reminds us of this by interspersing its literary or philosophical analyses with anonymised case-histories from her psychotherapist's casebook, in which the concepts and models deployed in the service of critical theory are exhibited in their context of origin: 'such a scanning of meaning applies to any discourse, even if the transference actualises it in the strongest and most observable way' (*ACA*, 17). Psychoanalysis is thus seen as a 'micro-anthropology of our depths' (*FS*, 41), providing an adequate basis for culture-theory. The ambitious project of *Histoires d'amour* takes shape at just this point. It is offered as a contribution to a history of Western subjectivity, in which the formative ideas of the West, its great myths and the variations of discursive or rhetorical manner in its great writers are 'read' (more exactly: *deciphered*) as revealing the psychic make-up of love, and as exploring the genesis of a contemporary crisis of the amorous subject (*HA*, 27–8).

***

'French Freud' is, however, always 're-fried' Freud. The theorisation of the subject of desire which Kristeva deploys in the service of her wider project significantly *modifies* the master. Grasping firmly the nettle of Freudo-Lacanian gloom in relation to love, she states that narcissism rather than libido is actually the dominant fact of psychic life as described by both thinkers, since both install illusionism ('le chimère') as the basis of the ego's relation to the real world. Both, however, explain narcissism, not as originating, but as something super-added to auto-eroticism: in their work, it has the status of a formation occurring in the symbolic order, but depending, in some unspecified modality reaching back to before the Oedipal crisis, on a Third Term, or Other. Is there some way of specifying this foundation? (*HA*, 32–3.)

Kristeva sees an 'originally amorous' state of the subject as preceding all identification with any actual object of desire – a *blank love-potential* 'for an object to come, later or never' (*HA*, 36). Freud himself had glimpsed something of the sort: a sense of 'the Other' formed by the imaginary interiorisation of the mother's relation to the father. He had referred to this most archaic form of unspecified affective attachment as 'the father of personal pre-history'. Kristevan psychic archeology makes this neglected glimpse a significant new cornerstone. Following Melanie Klein, she interprets it as a response of primordial 'gratitude', that is to the bi-parental function of the gifting of enjoyment, fullness, life; something for which the maternal breast is the occasion and the metaphoric trigger – something pre-known ('always already') prior to the child's entry into the symbolic order (38–41). Hegel and Heidegger are invoked as witnesses to the pre-reflective immediacy of this ontic perception (53–6).

The key to Kristeva's position is thus a rethought version of the *triadic structure* of Freudo-Lacanian narcissism. She posits the informing psychic presence, alongside the subject and its concretely given other (originally the mother), of the imaginary-symbolic Third Party (or 'Tiers'), seen as 'the condition of psychic life in so far as it is amorous life' (*HA*, 48). When we accept that the informing triadic pattern already contains 'the hysterical beginnings of an object of identification', says Kristeva, then we understand much better the dynamics of amorous idealisation, as a projective, metaphorising movement. The ego comes to exist only by virtue of identifying with an 'Other-ideal' – not as libidinal object, desiring what the Other *has*, but for what the Other *is*. The Other-ideal is of course imaginary, a symbolic formation 'beyond the mirror'. Yet this ideal includes the ego by virtue of the love that the ego invests in it; and the 'phantom' is genuinely operative in unifying the subject – that is, in containing its drives and calling forth its sense of *ipse*. The subject, in fact, exists, consists and subsists in belonging to the indeterminate Other as to the 'place' from which he or she is seen and heard. This is what makes the ego 'subject to' – and, potentially, 'a subject of'– loving:

> Always already there, this shaping presence, which satisfies no need of my auto-eroticism, draws me into imaginary exchange, into specular seduction. It or me, who is the agent? And again: is it him, is it her? The immanence of its transcendence, like the instability of

our limits prior to the fixing of my own image as my own, make this source of disturbance, from which narcissism will emerge, a dynamics of confusion and delight. Secrets of our loves. (58)

Conversely, we also understand on this model the *inability* to love. This is really an auto-eroticism deprived of, or insufficiently endowed with, an enhancing ego-reflection; the deprived ego then redemands a mother substitute and finds objects of identification only in hatred (49).

Defined in purely Freudo-Lacanian terms, Narcissus is, or logically should be, incapable of loving; yet thanks to the structure of alterity-formation which Kristeva sees as 're-lining' the Freudo-Lacanian psyche, he is in fact a potentially viable lover. He becomes, at least, a compromise between the pole of a deficient (merely specular) primary identification, eternally giving him back his own image as lack or loss, and the beneficent 'hysteria' of amorous identification, whereby the ideal Other he structurally anticipates acts as a metaphoric bridge to the objectively existent other of real encounter.

This mediation remains, of course, ever-precarious. The triadic structure of the archaic psyche is never without a shadow side of terror and rage (at the mother, at the Other, at the ego's own emergent self-image); psychic life is still always (as for Lacan) a conjuration of the void; and the enabling triad always threatens to collapse into the original dyad. The Oedipal drama introduces further hazards, since our own genitality becomes an integral part of the signifying or symbolic system, barring a daughter from mother's having and a son from having mother (both forms of symbolic castration) (*HA*, 56–61). Yet the *open relationality of the triadic form* as interpreted by Kristeva does, in principle, allow an interchange in which my imaginary and that of my partner elect become mutually supporting and enhance subject-identity. 'The in-lover is a narcissist who has an *object*' (47).

Contrasting Lacan's notion of 'the metonymic object of desire' with her own conception of 'the metaphoric object of love', Kristeva writes: 'The former governs the phantasmal scenario. The second pre-sketches the crystallisation of phantasm and gives poeticity to amorous discourse' (*HA*, 44). Lacanian metonymy, that is, promises only *more of the lack* which Plato already considered to be the essence of desire and which Lacan himself registers as 'désêtre' (want-of-being). Metaphor, by contrast, prefigures by analogy some real Other which exists or may come to exist. Claudel would here have said: metonymy connotes 'illusion', metaphoricity 'allusion'. Kristeva, for her part, carefully brackets off any 'ontologico-theological' implications raised by the 'innateness' of the human capacity for loving. She speaks of the 'impossible quest for the absolute origin of this psychological and symbolic capacity' (41). If we read very carefully her account of Freud's inhibited, puzzled and finally Oedipean relation to Christianity, we may sense, too, that Kristeva feels that, where Freud 'failed', she, for her part, now has the rational measure of the 'dazzling effect' of the human (Christic) face of the self-revealing God (61–5). Nonetheless, she is strategically clear that 'the capacity for loving' constitutes 'the primordial activity of the self' (40). The human subject as such is, originally and always-already, an amorous subject: 'In the beginning was Love' – *psychoanalytically speaking*.

As a reader of the thought-forms and the writings of her culture, Kristeva attends fundamentally to the ways in which the prevalent or dominant symbolic system – the discourse of ideas of self, other, love, meaning, 'God' etc., as realised at any given moment of personal or collective history – favour, or on the contrary diminish, disorder and disable, the 'Narcissan' project (as she terms it) of transcending our self-relatedness and of instituting, through a process of healing sublimation, an economy of relationality and amorous bonding.

***

When plotted onto this master-axis of signification, Kristeva's various studies show a consistent and very striking pattern: Western tradition owes the near-entirety of its enabling transcendence of Narcissism to the inheritance of Judaeo-Christian Agape; conversely, every form of disability, disorder and diminishment is seen to derive from the Hellenic (Platonic, Plotinian – and, we must surely add, Freudian) tradition of Eros.

This general figure of interpretation is, to be sure, lightly sketched, and very deliberately kept as relativistic and ideologically neutral as possible. It receives no decisive final formulation. Instead, Kristeva orders the discrete studies of the work so as to avoid consistent comparison or systematised contrast. The minor theme is given major development; while the major theme receives discreetly minor treatment. The author usually positions herself in relation to her own culture-narrative with a kind of dancing obliqueness. She manipulates the heuristic focus of the study in a way she herself acknowledges to be arbitrary (*HA*, 238–9): informing belief-and-value systems are followed exclusively in the pre-modern period, whereas the expressive potency of myth and the rhetoric of metaphoricity form the primary focus of her treatment of modern and contemporary periods.

Kristeva is aware, in short, of making delicately hedged bets of interpretation: she speaks of psychoanalysis as travelling 'alongside' religious faith, only to discharge its affinity in literary discourse (*HA*, 53). The price she pays for this flirtatious, semi-declared 'fellow-travelling' is an ultimate ambiguity of affirmation with which she herself – and her readers after her – will subsequently wish to come to terms.

***

The metaphorising homology that unites Kristeva's discourse on love with Judaeo-Christian Agape is the more remarkable for being set in counterpoint to a consistently negative and – when stripped to essentials – deeply unflattering view of the tradition of Hellenic Eros. Plato is seen to offer the first apology of Western love under the dualist sign of manic/sublime Desire. He inaugurates in reality a sado-masochistic psychodrama set in the shadow of the Phallus. The Platonic subject, thanks to its hidden feminine principle, does indeed dream of a sublimation ennobling the erotic drive and lifting it to the perfection of the Good, the True and the Beautiful. Yet his Eros is Other-deficient. The Platonic androgyne is read in this perspective as a homosexual phantasm which uses the names of the two sexes in order the better to deny their difference: a 'hypocritical masquerade' in fact liquidating femininity ('without love as he is, which love will save him?' [*HA*, 91]).

Ovid's Narcissus sets the seal on this masculinist and auto-erotic perversion. His is an exaltation before a non-object, a mirage or soul-error born of ignorance of his imprisonment in a world of signs. This same mistake about the Other is hypostasised by Plotinus who sublimates the specular auto-eroticism of Ovid's persona into a quest for the ultimate One. Metaphysically idealising the interiorised mirage, the neo-Platonic mystic leaves the subject in solo self-contemplation (*monos pros monon*: 'the same with the same'). The modern Narcissus, his legatee, will attempt painfully to cancel the deficit of alterity by seeking the Other as a creation of his own seeing. Indeed, he wishes to cancel all distance and all difference by a still-mystical dream of fusion with the Other; yet he reaps in return only an alienated self-image. 'Is it an accident – muses Kristeva allusively – that psychological or aesthetic avatars of Narcissus accompany the crisis of salvation-religions, or that they are asserting themselves in our contemporary world shaken by the death of God/the One?' (*HA*, 153).

The question derives acutest resonance from Kristeva's review of the 'maux d'amour' (troubles or dysfunctions of love), illustrated alike by modern love-myths and by the metaphorical function as displayed in the work of modern writers. Don Juan, for instance, figures Narcissus in love with his own power to seduce, loving himself through the desirable phantoms he conquers but is incapable of holding. As 'monotheism' falters, so the secret spring of Don Juan is seen to reside no longer in the need for punishment by the Father; yet modern – Nietzschean or Bataillian – readings, which champion the libidinous nobleman as an exemplary practitioner of the unfettered pleasure principle and of the 'open work' in matters amorous, reckon without the death-drive implicit in Juan's fascination with the Phallus; just as they neglect the regressive mother-fixation supposed by his indefinite quest for Beauty.

Romeo and Juliet, too, for all their prestige as figurations of 'the West's finest love-dream' (*HA*, 274), embody for Kristeva a mutilating and regressive idealisation. Shakespeare's star-crossed lovers defy the Name of the Father only to the benefit of a fusional self-loss experienced in the flood of imagined pleasure; they are driven by the secret hatred of each partner for the other ('my only love sprung from my only hate') and they are drawn by a secret death-wish. Truly figured in the West's finest love-dream is the narcissistic haven dreamed of by the eternal children the lovers have succeeded in remaining.

Writers fare no better; on the contrary, their metaphorical gift writes large – no doubt to the aesthetic benefit of their work, through the sublimatory grace of metaphor itself – the confession of grievous human inadequacies in the order of idealisation. Thus, Baudelairean 'love' rests upon death, the abject, and narcissistic disappointment. The poet exemplifies the 'other' Western tradition: the one which reveals 'a wounded, holed, haemorrhaging self, attempting to staunch his losses by eroticising his private parts or his rage' (*HA*, 421). Thus, under the desired-and-hated shadow of 'l'Idéal', a horror of being works itself out in fetishism, voyeurism, exhibitionism and perversion.

Stendhal, for his part, is the politician of love – *in love* with calculation, masks and power. What he 'crystallises' are alienating phantasms ('seldom has anyone got closer to the elusive, metonymic logic of the object of desire illustrated in the phantasm') (*HA*, 431). The Stendhalian 'fiasco' reveals the politician as a Werther-figure and an aesthete of sado-masochistic propensities, whose virile mistresses are the projections of an adored Phallus. This makes the Stendhalian lover 'a secret lesbian' (unless, suggests Kristeva mischievously, he be an – unlikely– secret feminist?). But perhaps he is just 'a man seeking in love a refuge-value against his own anguish' (252).

Bataille marks the endgame of Platonic Eros deprived of its metaphoric power of reference to a hinterworld and to any founding meaningfulness. The sublime is now a self-divinisation resting only on sexual energy, as fuelled by abjection and self-disgust. Bataille's jubilant and guilty obscenities accumulate all imaginable disorders: 'Perverse? Paranoid? Obstinate and obsessional believer in an almighty feminine libido? ...Oedipean enemy of the father, condemned henceforth to imagining homosexual partners for his mother, and to himself undergoing feminisation, passive and quasi-victimised?' And this vigorous diagnosis (or charge-sheet?) still neglects the main feature of his case: Eros has become, as Freud warned it might, 'a coding for Thanatos' (*HA*, 460).

All is not well, we gather, in the house of Western Eros. The common denominator of all these disorders of love is that they represent defective idealisations which develop the triadic structure of the amorous subject abortively – either because they hypostasise a deficient or distorted version of the 'imaginary Third', or because they collapse the structuring triad regressively into its original mother-child dyad. Freud was right in asserting what all Kristeva's analysands also confirm: that there is a deep malaise in our civilisation. It is expressed in this: that the symbolic order of our culture of Eros allows no viable psychic space to the amorous subject as such. Here is Kristeva's minor theme, textually foregrounded as major.

***

More exactly stated, the West *did* have a viable amorous space for as long as it adhered to the vision and faith of the Judaeo-Christian religious tradition. The function of the major theme of the counterpoint realised in *Histoires d'amour*, albeit in minor mode, is to enter this vital qualification. It is, moreover, remarkably entered: with an ardent sympathy of rediscovery, a glowing, celebratory lyricism, which frequently overflows the precautionary bounds self-imposed by Kristeva as 'scientific' Freudo-Hegelian culture theorist writing for readers of *Tel Quel*.

We have already noted this thinker's originality in analysing Judaeo-Christianity: it turns on her willingness *not* to interpret the God of faith simply as the phallic

Father (connoting Law, prohibition and patriarchy). Against Freud and the whole of secularist 'postmodernism', she reads this 'God' as the symbolic representative of the originating, pre-genital Third Party, modelling and reflecting subject-identity as prevenient love, affirmation and acceptance. These, she declares, are the connotations already attaching to the biblical (Jewish) notion of 'ahav', even where it qualifies a God conceived as Law-giver. 'The immediate love of God for his people, a love which neither demands nor deserves justification, which is purely by preference and election, *constitutes* the beloved (who is also a subject of loving) in the strongest sense of this term' (*HA*, 107).

'Never will oriental eroticism equal the joyous and quivering passion of the *Song*' (*HA*, 78). The keynote is given in Kristeva's treatment of the Old Testament love song, which, she insists, is no anomaly in its religious context of emergence. The implicit but omnipresent symbolic Third is seen here as crucial in establishing a viable amorous subject in a favourable amorous space, something 'impossible' within the strict logic of narcissism. It sustains an absolute tension of desire, in which the ultimate addressee is, ambiguously, both specified and concrete and unspecified and transcendent.[5] It creates a non-fusional reciprocity, accepting the distance of the Other confidently, being assured that distance is not inexistence or unreality, and that present incompleteness is a suffering to be borne for love's sake. It unites the sexually differentiated lovers in a real and symbolic communion, materialised by the dialogic structure of the poem: 'the fragile, precocious, marvellously unlikely triumph of heterosexuality' (78).

The *Song* in fact recapitulates every positive value we might wish to signify by 'love'. Indeed, it establishes the concept as such in a novel meeting of opposites: 'The term love enshrines their meeting: a love both sensual and deferred; engaging body and power; a present passion and an ideal' (*HA*, 122). It is, additionally, foundational for the conjugal couple, just as it represents a prototype of Western subjectivity and the very first movement of 'liberation' to touch the speaking feminine subject. As if these virtues were not sufficient, the miraculous *Song* displays love as the source of an astonishing metaphoricity; it generates 'self-similar' rhetorical patterns, transcending all uncertainties as to the poem's provenance, structure and meaning. Within its open textuality, the 'semiotic' unconscious plays and blossoms exuberantly.

It would be difficult to imagine a higher Kristevan endorsement than is given to the superlative *Song of Songs*. Yet the celebration continues at much the same level in her treatment of New Testament Agape, seen as heralded by the 'incarnational potential' of the *Song*. True, Kristeva draws here on Anders Nygren, whose *topoi*, perspectives of judgement and choice of texts she follows more extensively than the few, bare footnotes acknowledging *Eros and Agape* might suggest. This debt, however, signals a mediated but personalised enthusiasm, rather than a merely derivative second-hand one. Kristeva's procedure is to (re)state in three points the original figure of 'Christian love' as discerned by this acknowledged theologian: (i) the identification of God with Love (implying both the unmerited gratuity proper to this Love and its descent 'from above' as acceptance, gift and grace, anticipating human need and inverting the dynamic of Eros); (ii) its scandalous expression in the divine 'madness' of the Cross (and the consequent 'homologation' of the believer by immersion into this paradigmatic death-and-resurrection); (iii) its issue in love of neighbour, within a renewed symbolic space of subjectivity and other-relatedness. Her originality is to retrace this figure, showing how it operates psychoanalytically, and valorising the efficacy of a construct perfectly matching the need-structures of the idealising and amorous human Narcissus.

The immediate effect of this dialectic is to justify the figure of Agape against Nietzschean contempt and the grosser forms of Freudian reductionism, with both of which Kristeva takes issue. Only at the end of this careful and admiring dialectic does she – systematising Nygren's hint of a discrepancy of language between the principal theorists St Paul and St John – call attention to what she takes to be a fissure of inspiration, distantly preluding a decline of the towering influence exercised by this New Testament conception.

Essentially, Kristeva sees Christian Agape as effecting a successful identificatory sublimation, maximising the 'triadic' potential of the psyche and so inaugurating a psycho-social space of reconstituted 'open' subjectivity. She speaks (in a Hegelian formula which, revealingly, conflates her own psychic triad and the ternary structure of the latter's historical dialectic) of the movement of reconciliation with the Father-God: it starts from 'love posited from eternity', integrates its negation (narcissism, Thanatos) and culminates in the 'synthesis' (the Resurrection, as understood by Kristeva) (HA, 178). The God who is homologous to men becomes mortal so that mortal man may become analogous to God. Any idealising identification supposes the 'murder' of the loved object; and the Cross asserts this pattern. Yet there is no sado-masochism: 'the passion of Agape traverses this economy with the assurance of passing beyond it' (182). The death of the Son which I read in gospel narrative and re-enact in baptism and in the eucharist also short-circuits phantasm and promotes my leap towards the symbolic Name of the Father: 'a subtle machine – for idealisation, more than for repression' (182). Nor is there any encouragement to the death-drive, save in the case of pseudo-'mystics' such as de Sade or Artaud 'proclaiming themselves Jesus Christ in a rage which is amorous as well as destructive' (182) – Kristeva does not say whether Nietzsche also qualifies under this formula. 'For the believer, the putting to death of one's own body as the condition of ideal identification is in some sense suspended by the gospel story' (183).

In short, what Nietzsche called the 'horrible paradox' of God crucified 'turns out to be more profoundly a sublimatory transcendence of the masochistic position as conditioning idealisation' (HA, 185). Indeed, says Kristeva – echoing René Girard[6] and countering Freud – as a triumph of idealisation, based on the sublimatory development of suffering and the destruction of 'the my-body', the Cross actually signifies the *end* of sacrifice (i.e., in its traditional 'archaic religious' acceptance) (179, 185). Perhaps even the end of the omnipotence in human affairs of the Interdict (178). Equally, the eucharistic remembrance of this death sublimates and transmutes our sadism directed towards the archaic, maternal, body. Interposing a (paternal) Third between the ego and its destructive hunger, creating a distance between the

Self and its (maternal) Nurse, the Christian faith 'pacifies our destructive avidity with the satisfaction of ... a Word' (189).

The novelty of Agape is, for Kristeva, that of an 'adopting' love; one capable of defying narcissistic anguish, and re-ordering Narcissus 'as subject-for-the-Other'. What completes this 'ideal take-over from narcissism' (*HA*, 185) is the third movement of Agape, opening the regenerated believer to the love of neighbour, now universal and unconditional (since it includes both the undeserving and the stranger). In glorifying a Self lodged with the adoptive Father, Agape constructs a psychological space transmuting the erotic ego-body: a space for the amorous, other-oriented Subject. It even deculpabilises residual self-love, claims Kristeva, in making 'as oneself' the yardstick of the injunction to 'love one's neighbour'. 'The re-absorbtion of narcissism in the figuration of the self, now understood as extended to all neighbours, strangers and sinners, will have been the final touch of this construct within which the dynamics of inner life will now be able to work themselves out' (186). Narcissus as amorous subject is thus saved from himself: saved by and for the Other. Holding together the symbolic representation of the Father as Loving Law-giver and the representation of the archaic mother as purely loving Virgin Mother, Christianity sustains the triadic foundation of relational subjectivity, as though made to measure.

***

What, then, happened? And why is the good news of our capacity for amorous self-transcendence restored no longer receivable? Kristeva's narrativisation of cultural history is concerned to trace how this miraculously well-crafted, psycho-social symbolic space, after delivering its fruits in the admirable love mysticism of Saint Bernard (and the Troubadours), hesitates with Saint Thomas and thereafter collapses in the period of post-Renaissance reflexivity and anthropocentrism. A particular tension animates this movement of Kristeva's thought: she wishes *both* to invoke the splendid 'sublimations' of Christian Agape (thus correcting Freud and accrediting her own 'take-over') *and* to sacrifice Christianity to a Freudian *metapsychological* diagnosis of 'illusionism' (thus declaring a post-Christian 'take-over' necessary). This tension constitutes the most awkward and questionable part of her dialectic, and we shall return to it. But first: how does the narrative run and where does it lead the culture-theorist herself?

Bernard of Clairvaux is still a major Kristevan hero. New Testament relationality informs his distinctive representation of a self conceived as amorous passion ('*ego affectus est*') directed to God as 'loving Beloved'; and the Sermons on the *Song of Songs* provide for the psychoanalyst and culture theorist a wealth of insight into the themes of love, desire and transcendence. Essentially, St Bernard retraces the transferential sublimation of bodily 'affections' in an astonishingly modern way, since he envisages, within these affections, and ideally inscribing their own potential and movement, the immanence of a signified 'transcendence'. Bernardian desire – *rerum absentium concupiscientia* – is at bottom an animal appetite, a 'voracity', yet informed, directed and ordered by 'God', despite and beyond fallen nature. What is 'lacking' is also, apparently, 'fulfilling', since the lover-in-faith accepts that God desires us first, to the extent of creating us in his own image (*HA*, 202).

This belief, Kristeva gives us to understand, is a matter of Christian specularity: 'this specularity of Christian love and the sublimatory reworking of narcissism it produces are frequent: we shall find them again in Saint Thomas.' Yet without some such postulate, she muses, do we not fall back into primary narcissism, 'not otherwise to be transcended than through the supposition of an Other prior to ourselves, who is also aware of our tendency to auto-satisfaction and to total satisfaction' (*HA,* 202)? Hence, perhaps, at the point of her own farewell to fellow-travelling, this quivering salute:

> No philosophy will match this psychological success-story, which offers satisfaction to pulsional narcissism while lifting it above its native region and conferring on it an irradiation towards the other, and towards others; a divine irradiation, certainly, and accessorily, a social one. (212)

> [W]e are dealing with an alchemy of idealisation whose ins-and-outs we secularists fail to grasp. If we have trouble loving, this is because we have trouble idealising: trouble in investing our narcissism in an other held to represent an incommensurable value, and guaranteeing us against our own propensity to excess [...].

> A museum page: let us once more admire the exceptional balance between a voracious and tyrannical ideal, a desire unfulfilled and a possession nevertheless assured. This peace shot through with tension, this painful harmony, this narcissism of the my-body infinitely extended so as to be emptied out in favour of a violent alter ego identification: *that* is love. (214)

If we follow the Kristevan narrativisation, the fall from grace appears to emanate from within the Judaeo-Christian tradition itself. It is to be situated, she claims, in a disastrous admission or concession, bearing the name of Saint Thomas Aquinas. 'Thomist theology rehabilitates narcissism as *amor sui*, the pivot-point of salvation-love, thus consolidating the reconciliation of the Western soul with itself for 2000 years' (*HA*, 78–9). What Kristeva means by this dense formulation, with its somewhat awkward expression of time-frame and its obscure telescoping of praise and blame, is that the thirteenth-century Doctor of the Church inadvertently fuses the pure tradition of revealed Agape with elements of Plotinian narcissism. In synthesising Hellenic Eros and Christian Agape, he consolidates the symbolic space, nurturing to love, of religious faith; but in *re-insuring* it, he also *adulterates* it, preparing its ultimate collapse.

The Thomist subject 'asserts himself by loving his own ontological consistency'; as I desire being for myself, and its absolute presence, which is beatitude, so I similarly desire it for the other. It is at least arguable, therefore, that 'this apology for what belongs to us ... subsumes what the modern mind will call narcissism in an ontology of love' (*HA*, 222). Lacan's phantasmatic metonymies, accordingly, will be seen as those of a 'Thomist without God': 'If there is no Creator, where would the good *appetibilis* come from that causes us to love?' (235).

We might express this crucial mind-shift more neutrally than Kristeva does by saying that Aquinas' retracing in ontological categories of the content of scriptural revelation powerfully consolidates the European psycho-social space (Valéry speaks in very much this sense of the 'extraordinary marriage' of Greek reason and Hebrew scriptures that was 'so important for Europe');[7] but that it does so at the cost of a secret displacement, enfolding the motif of Agape within the sphere of Reason. *Paradoxically*, then, against the intention of its author, this move does indeed provide a *point of emergence* for the *growth over four centuries* of an increasingly sceptical and subjectivist secular anthropocentrism.

This development occurs as the reflexive character of European thought is progressively affirmed, and as philosophical and scientific reason is emancipated from its ontologist matrix. Henceforth, any thought of an originating Love from elsewhere is subject to a logic of self-reflection and self-contemplation. The loved/loving subjectivity of the New Testament is reconfigured in the image of a self-knowing, self-concerned human subjectivity, finding its modern prototype in the *cogito ergo sum* of Descartes. The triadic structure of the Judaeo-Christian subject thereafter collapses into its original dyad.

The coming of modernity, on this account, has a dark and terrible shadow-side which defines our own contemporary crisis of culture: the grievous weakening of the 'open' subject, the subject of otherness. *Amor sui* in its modern mode and practice produces knowledge as subjugation of otherness and difference: Galileo for the physical world, and de Sade for the erotic, exemplify, in Kristeva's view, this same 'Narcissan' retreat from triadic 'psycho-space' (*HA*, 469). The enlightened – but unloved – postmodern Narcissus, though he speaks ever more compulsively, with codified 'correctness', of 'the Other', speaks fatally from a position of self-enclosure. His rage at the void plays itself out as depersonalisation and domination of the Other. He can cope neither with the Law of the Father ('réparer le père'), nor with the rejected Mother ('apaiser la mère'). He has no home-space of subject-identity. He is a perverse child who loves nothing, because – spiritually – he is nothing (467).

Our myths, our writers, confess their malaise and mirror ours. Leading thinkers (Freud's 'death-drive', Lacan's 'désêtre') confirm it. Kristeva's analysands cry out from it. In the absence of any other sustaining discourse of triadic subject-identity, we are living out – badly – the 'death of God', synonymous with the breakdown of a culture-wide, historic project for the restructuring of symbolic psycho-space. We are, in Kristeva's final estimation, extra-terrestrials wanting for love ('Des extra-terrestres en mal d'amour').[8]

***

Two consequences follow in Kristeva's work: first, a perceptible need to revisit the figure of sense produced by *Histoires d'amour* so as to clarify and revise its author's speaking position; second, the attempt to replace the 'lost salvation' by appeal to a feminine principle of re-sacralisation.

Kristeva's obscurely-clear dialectic, with its harmonics of admiration and its subterranean nostalgia for the lost splendour of Judaeo-Christian Agape, throws into relief the paradox of the 'Christian atheist' herself.[9] Challengingly, in *Histoires d'amour* the adjective is more transparent and cogent than the noun. On this showing, we might almost imagine Kristeva about to declare the 'Law of the Father' the obsessional master-motif of an adolescent growth-crisis of Western intelligence. Judaeo-Christianity was (historically), and still (in principle) bids fair to be the exactly matching, exactly missing, complement of the amorous Narcissus – *were it not that* ...? It is Kristeva's 'atheism' that is the elusive and muted term.

A more deliberate philosophic retrenchment, delimiting her 'complicity' with Christianity, seems, at all events, to have been felt necessary. *Au Commencement était l'amour*, subtitled *Psychanalyse et foi*, brings a distinct ideological hardening and foreclosure. Here, in a series of lectures delivered to Catholic sixth-formers at the École Ste Geneviève, the Freudo–Nietzschean–Hegelian law is sternly laid down. Freud's *The Future of an Illusion* is explicated in strictest orthodoxy: religion has a great future precisely as a pre-scientific construct of little reality; the reality it has consisting in the difficulty men experience in seeing their phantasms collapse; our distress is our own, and not negotiable.

For the first time, the Freudian 'father of personal pre-history' is explicitly related by Kristeva to the Christian God: 'a form, a pattern, an instance ... whose permanence ensures the founding stabilisation of the subject, *and whose oblative character... is perhaps what Christianity celebrates in the love divine*' (*ACA*, 44; my italics). 'Faith' is expounded as an 'accrediting belief' ('croyance-créance') gratifying and consoling infantile needs (St Augustine's relational image of the soul as a child suckling is adduced as epitomising a primary identification displaced into the symbolic order). Christianity is declared the best appeaser-consoler, since it offers: (i) a pre-existent guarantee of divine generosity; (ii) a mother-oriented account of virgin birth ('that secret dream of every childhood'); and (iii) a magical conversion of Deficit into Gain: 'the torment of the flesh at Golgotha ... gives a new life in glory to the essential melancholy of a humanity which aspires to reintegrate the body and the name of the father from whom it is irremediably separated' (44).

The last item is particularly interesting. Here Kristeva develops integrally the figure of psychoanalytical decipherment which George Steiner calls 'Freud's revenge': the subversive appropriation, to the benefit of psychoanalysis, of the most central Christian theme of the redeeming descent of the Word into the flesh.[10] Her re-statement of this figure re-asserts psychoanalysis as master-discourse and commands a renewed urgency of Suspicion: the *better* a religion is seen to match the needs of the human subject, the *more suspect* the illusion it represents and the *greater* its probable illegitimate future.[11]

Kristeva does not hesitate, accordingly, to 'deconstruct' the Apostle's Creed. The articles of the Creed are reviewed in the guise of a symbolic support system, created by imaginary credit-transfer: a *psycho-trellis* of admirable logical coherence into which are intervowen 'the most fundamental phantasms which I encounter daily in the psychic realities of my patients' (*ACA*, 62). On this basis, the Creed appears to Kristeva to say about Christian believers very much what their phantasms say about her patients. Usually, it is something Freudian ('murderous desires against the father', sublimated homosexuality, 'melancholic anguish to the point of suicide' etc.), or something Nietzschean: 'on this point, Christianity carries the allegiance of the masses – here is a discourse which traverses us secretly and fundamentally: how could one not believe it?' (65). It signally offers nothing conciliatory to faith ('but who these days believes all these items?'). The Kristevan 'semiotic' subtext is: 'All Boats Burned. No Way Back.'

A second consequence follows: the need to substitute for a salvation which has first been declared adorable-but-lost, and then more deliberately burned. Kristeva's interest in the 'feminine sacred' declares its logic within her atheistic project of *replacing* the faith of Agape. As in the case of Irigaray,[12] her sense of the sacred as love and as feminine has a visible point of emergence within Christianity: the feminist Eve is drawn from the flank of the Catholic Adam.

Her constant reference to the 'myth of the Virgin' is well known (and notoriously irritating to many secularising feminists). For Kristeva, this icon of the Feminine marks a correction to an inadequately 'idealised', mono-gendered symbolisation of the divine 'Tiers'. Historically, this myth has allowed women (and men) to 'subsume the maternal abject', hence to transcend their own rejection of the 'archaic mother' (*HA*, 320–3) and to establish a real community-in-difference of the sexes, as no modern symbolic code allows (289, 464–5). The nerve-point of the Kristevan decipherment is, however, the insight that the 'bowed head' of the Virgin Mother connotes principally, not submission to patriarchy, but gratification, enjoyment, pride. Beside the love which links Mary to her Son – or any woman to hers –'the rest of human relations is conspicuously declared as a flagrant counterfeit' (310). For Kristeva, joyous maternal *amour-tendresse*, such as overflows 'semiotically' in the parallel prose poems accompanying her treatment of the theme in *Histoires d'amour* (written shortly after the birth of her son David), is the true gold-standard in the matter of loving. Indeed, it is the psycho-matrix of all real loving: 'It is upon maternal love that … the caritas of Christians and the human rights of secularists have been built' (*FS*, 94). Ultimately, this is the concealed principle – occluded by the patriarchal Word in *both* religion *and* Freudian psychoanalysis – of which 'divine love will be merely the not-always-convincing derivative' (*HA*, 315).

Retrieving from religion its own, 'the sacred', now identified as love, begins from the maternal Feminine. What is 'the sacred', exactly? Most clearly, it is the religious sense stripped of everything Freud identifies with 'religion': narcissistic compensation, imaginary consolation, the magic of sacrifice and taboo, the Law of the Father, a repressive social organisation. The sacred is *not* 'monotheism' (the generic Freudian term prevails revealingly in Kristeva, as in Irigaray). Positively, the notion embraces a vast range of experienced epiphanies: the cry of a trance-struck African woman during Mass; Georgia O'Keefe's painting of the sex-flower/cow's head, said to evoke life-death-the-cosmos-and-being; the decorous ceremonial of British academic life ('le sacré anglais'); the Marseillaise ('le sacré républicain'); the music of Mozart. The dark fervour of Hitler's rallies may or may not belong to this series (there is debate between Clément and Kristeva). The sacred is 'another time' sprung from the dark continent to which Freud compared femininity in general – in Kristevan terms, the maternal 'chora' or archaic, pre-Oedipal reservoir of the deep unconscious (*ACA*, 16; *HA*, 107). It *emanates* from the point of intersection of body and psyche, sexuality and thought, a hidden crossroads most intimately present in, and apprehended by, women. It *emerges* as a linkage of life and meaningfulness: within desire, it creates a dynamic of value-positive sense-making (*FS*, 65). 'Suppose what we call the sacred were the celebration of this mystery, which is the emergence of meaningfulness?' (*FS*, 26).

Does this immanentist redefinition put an end to Kristeva's transgressive Judaeo-Christian love-affair? Not quite, not yet, given that the emergence of what makes for the greatest and highest value-oriented meaningfulness is still consistently prefigured within this religious tradition. In distinct tension with her interlocutor, Kristeva rehearses the same admiration, scanning the same semi-declared reference programme for a 'feminine sacred'. There is the matter of 'life, as a Judaeo-Christian value' (*FS* 134): not simply *zoe* (biological life), she insists, following Hanna Arendt and Greek usage,[13] but *bios* (life determined by its gift-like quality [25]) –'meaning-bearing life, to the formulation of which women are called to bring their desire and their utterance' (26). After 2,000 years of world history dominated by sacralisations of the child Jesus, are not women in a position to give another 'coloration' ('colour', 'slant') to the ultimate sacred, which is the miracle of human life (26)? They *can* speak of and from a maternal 'amour-tendresse' which defers eroticism, turning it into tenderness and making its object into an Other of myself (94). All of which takes Kristeva back at length to the Virgin Mary, oblative maternity and the conversion of the 'abject'(99–102; 119–33). They could and should speak for the life of the male-female couple in its liberated fullness; which again relaunches Kristeva, at fervent length, into the themes of the biblical valorisation of woman and of 'the love of the Sulamite, manifestation *par excellence* of the sacred' (157–69).

In this dialogue between atheistic and secularising feminists, the Judaeo-Christian religious tradition – or at least a feeling for 'the sacred' conceived and carried within it – is, it seems, a strangely persistent ghost, albeit now re-specified as an immanent *feminine* principle of transcendence.

***

How, and how well, we may still reasonably enquire, has Kristeva remembered Agape?

A precautionary disclaimer is appended in conclusion to *Psychanalyse et foi*: the psychoanalyst's reading has been an X-ray of essential human desires and phantasms, and, as such, has nothing to do with 'dogma'; the lecturer has simply been offering 'another meaning' (*ACA*, 8). This is, at best, misleadingly 'diplomatic'. Kristevan 'decipherment' of the texts, rituals, theological structures and meaning of the faith of Agape is at bottom a deconstructive and (in its second phase) advisedly subversive psychopoetics of religion. It obeys a declared philosophical postulate: all religious phenomena are reducible to forms of artistic creation, of which the sexual and semiotic unconscious is the only origin, and psychoanalysis the all-sufficient key. As applied to the religion of revealed Agape, this procedure can only equate to reading such phenomena upside-down and back-to-front, as if they were products of a primary ego-identification.[14] It means extrapolating from the libidinal 'microphantasms' deciphered to the figure of a theological 'macrophantasm' which is then held to constitute the entire sense of the 'construct' – and cannot do otherwise, until and unless some 'hermeneutic moment' intervenes.

In Kristeva's deconstruction of the Apostles' Creed, we wait in vain for such a moment. Kristeva does not give us so much as a basic recognition that a *symbolum* (recapitulative formulary, symbol) is something to be read in the meaning *towards which* it 'projects' its readers, rather than as a screen on which are projected various figures of libidinal emergence and identity-exchange. Her sixth-form audience is simply left to understand, as best it may, any or all of four equally-plausible messages: (i) the projection of libidinally determined phantasms is a factor of distortion which even the believer cannot entirely avoid, being human, but ought to be aware of in him/herself; (ii) the presence in the believer of libidinal energies and imaginary phantasms sufficiently explains the theological sense realised, and its historic effects, thus disqualifying the entire credit-transfer operation of faith; (iii) the psychotherapist's extrapolation from microphantasm to macrophantasm is a distortion which tells us *only* how the *unbeliever* goes about decoding a notion of 'faith' which (s)he *always already rejects*; (iv) this type of psychogenetic reading is a confused and confusing account of the relation between psychoanalysis and faith.

More centrally still, the question-begging principle of Kristeva's entire 'metapsychology' remains quite unformulated: how would we begin to *differentiate* between a 'prevenient' Love answering the primary needs of the human subject, and a delusional phantasm of Love projected by the narcissistic subject in order to satisfy primary needs? Does the libidinal sub-text of which the psychotherapist becomes the confessor displace and replace the overtly projected theological meaning? Is it in fact being asserted that Christian *Agape* is a phantasm whose true signified is post-Freudian *Eros*? This type of question has in fact been very well addressed by contemporary hermeneutic philosophers (including the 'luminous' Paul Ricœur) (*HA*, 333, note 3), whose challenge for Kristeva's own practice, however, passes entirely unmet.

The basic working assumption – that there is 'no problem' with a Freudian metapsychology of religion – is itself problematic. Though enacted at the end of the twentieth century, it really reflects much earlier persuasions: the ex-theologian Hegel's dissolution of Christian doctrine into an idealism of Absolute Mind;[15] the post-Kantian collapse of referentiality; the entire narrativisation of culture-history which urges that the Enlightenment project has the *historic destiny* of displacing and replacing 'religion'. Within these horizons, Freud signifies to Kristeva (just as his very different functionalist psychology signified to the youthful Valéry) that 'the science of the forms of the mind contains all knowledge'.[16]

More than a theory of knowledge, however, Kristeva's atheism appears here as a dynamic postulate of the will, tending to reconfigure the human subject and its spring of transcendence. Here lies the final *theosophic* sense realised by her title 'In the beginning was love'. The 'beginning' invoked is ultimately her own spiritual start-point: the gesture of metaphorising, relocating *and appropriating*, no longer just the 'talking cure' of the old religion, but now also its theological mainspring and master-motif of Agape. This design extends to an explicitly 'Christic' assumption of the role of mediator, effecting from behind the psychoanalyst's couch a redemptive dying and living again. This bonding transference-love, 'synonymous with love *and faith*' (*ACA*, 85; my italics) has become the model and ground plan of her own project of a post-Christian salvation – a project completing the work of the Father Sigmund Freud,[17] and (perhaps) effecting a reconciliation with Kristeva's own father (to 'repair' the father is also to *make reparation* to him [cf. *HA*, 37]).

One perceives here what is 'slightly odd' about Kristeva's proposal to the girls of the École Ste Geneviève. Kristeva is in effect offering her own psychotherapist's transference-love as a post-Christian paradigm for Love *as such*. The text does not say how convincing her audience found this equivalence; and the jury is still out on its subsequent translation into 'the feminine sacred'.

Moreover, we can see in retrospect how this ideologically-directed *value-project* already inflects Kristeva's narrative of cultural history. Discussing the problematics of incarnation in the *Song of Songs*, for instance, where she is concerned to show bodily passion interacting with idealisation to produce metaphors, the author slips, in one remarkable sentence, from literary psychogenetics into the psychopoetics of religion:

> Unless the incarnation is a metaphor which slipped into reality, and was taken for reality? An hallucination having acquired the weight of the real in the violence of amorous passion, which is in fact the normal form of alienation, telescoping the registers of representation (real, imaginary, symbolic). (*HA*, 121)

One takes a moment to understand that 'incarnation' here has an undeclared capital letter. In a 'semiotic' flicker, Kristeva has just discovered her own 'orphic' formula for the genesis of Christianity... Of which Suspicion, we hear nothing more (since the section *ends* with this pirouette), unless it be by *abstention*, in the chapter 'Dieu est agape', where no reference *at all* is made to the founder of Christianity, but only to Paul and John, presumptively and by default viewed as the true inventors of a 2,000-year metaphoric Hallucination. The question of Christian origins has flickered across Kristeva's textual screen, to be immediately resolved by the formula of a religious partheno-psycho-genesis – the 'true virgin birth' as deciphered by Freudian psychoanalysis.[18]

The case is surely this: psychoanalytic deconstruction irresistibly converts *every* love into an exemplar of idealist metaphoricity; that is, into a mirror-image of its own form of decipherment, its own hermeutical 'figure'. Kristeva tries conspicuously hard to remember that, for her Christian subjects, the 'ideal Object' of human love is, precisely, *more real* than the desire which explores it; and that such love is *not at all* a 'fusional identification with the ideal, *ad unum*', but a communion-in-difference with an *actual-genuine-real* Other. Yet the quoted words are the very ones she uses in (mis-)construing the sense of 'unfulfilment of desire' in Bernard of Clairvaux.[19] Again, in explicating Bernard's degrees or steps of love (which trace the progressive transmutation of natural, pulsional eros into appreciative and other-centred love under the influence of Grace), Kristeva reminds her reader and herself not to interpret this progress within a dualistic framework 'which would take no account of the precedence of the Christian One' (*HA*, 209). Yet this whole section, including the very terms of this reminder, suggest her own difficulty in doing so; indeed, in remembering that the Agape-God – quite *unlike* the Plotinian 'One'– is *always already* a loving inter-personal communion.

This hermeneutical difficulty is quite fundamental. In the end, one of two things must, philosophically speaking, be the case. *Either* Bernard's Other is more real than Bernard, and human loving is then indeed founded, called and graced. (In that case, we might begin to understand what makes the model exemplary; and, at the same time, why its exemplariness might be expected to survive all vicissitudes of cultural disaffection). *Or else* it is a 'mere metaphor' projecting heavenwards an immanently human mechanism of identification (in which case, Kristeva's own enterprise of re-building the exemplary triadic structure from below also lies under the same dynamic shadow she has herself so vividly shown us at work within the rationalist-idealist tradition of Hellenic Eros; and the question then remains open as to whether her derived metaphor, even as re-specified in the feminine, amounts to more than a 'first-aid' of goodwill). Kristeva simply ducks this hermeneutic crux because the idealist option is the only one Hegel and Freud will allow her. Warning us that her Judaeo-Christian fellow-travelling will dissolve into metaphoricity, she simply leaves us to suppose that the development of modern reflexivity *of itself* resolves the question of whether or not human loving is grounded and called 'from elsewhere'.

She indeed discusses the cognitive status of metaphor in her introduction of the 'literary' part of her analysis, where she declares her disagreement with Ricœur's theory of *La Métaphore vive* postulating an 'ontological liveliness of metaphor in action' (*HA*, 339). She declines, that is, to envisage that metaphor carries within it the prescience of an 'Unknown', antecedent in the order of things, which our conceptuality is called to catch up with. Metaphors, she says, announce nothing *other*, nothing *new* to be named; they just present differently what we already know, with some relational effects. This is indeed consistent with her culture narrative and its Suspicion. By the same token, human loving – even where directed to a 'divine object'– is still only a human love expending its hysteria and compensating *à vide* for its lack. (Yet does this view not sit oddly together with her own 'metaphoric' project of a 'feminine sacred' attached to the emergence of meaningfulness? Is its status, in turn, that of literary rhetoric?)

And what of Kristeva's contention that the collapse of the privileged psychospace of the Narcissan subject finds its roots in the secretly flawed Judaeo-Christian metaphorisation of love itself? Kristeva's thesis here revolves around a point first raised in relation to the injunction of the gospels to 'love one's neighbour as oneself'. Which, after all, then, is primary: self-love or other-love? She has already suggested that St John contaminates the pure Pauline doctrine of gratuitous or unmotivated Agape by attributing to Jesus the words: 'The Father loves you [the disciples] *because you love me and believe I am come from the Father*' (John 16: 27). Is not this causative co-ordination the first sign of narcissism, inviting the suspicion that this religion is, after all, cast in the likeness of humankind and beckoning to the entire modern primacy of a purely idealising self-love?

Kristeva's objection provides here a second, even more revealing, hermeneutic crux. Clearly enough, her own title 'In the beginning was love' refers intertextually to the prologue of the fourth gospel. However, it ignores a fact of some importance: this gospel – uniquely – represents, inscribed in the heart of the Godhead, Kristeva's own 'triadic structure'. The Johannine Christ is presented as showing forth and imparting 'horizontally' (i.e. in human terms) whatever is shown and imparted to him 'vertically' (i.e. within the intimate relational circuit of divine Agape). Kristeva's own triangular figure of the amorous Narcissus is reproduced *recognisably* (since whatever the Subject of this gospel is and does reproduces exactly and solely what *his* 'Father of personal prehistory' *always-already is and does*), yet in *inverse configuration* (since Love is antecedently given, 'from above'). The Narcissan triangle is reprised, but 'stood on its head'. The difference of affirmed meaning is momentous. The *Other* of Narcissistic idealisation is thereby declared: no longer in function of the needs, demands, and desires of the idealising Narcissus, but now 'in his own likeness', 'authoritatively', 'in person', as *Ipse*; here is given the measure, the name and the nature of the 'blank love potential' which, for Kristeva, defines the amorous Narcissus.

This richly-charged isomorphism might, in principle, have provided for Kristeva a metaphoric bridge from her own model of psychic functioning towards the distinctive sense and original claims of Judaeo-Christian 'revelation'. Conspicuously, it does not do so: this figure of sense is formed in the blind-spot of her backward-and-downward – *narcissistic* – scanning. It therefore remains unperceived, invisible. As Emmanuel saw, however, the axis of vertical 'descent' remains crucial if *any sense at all* is to be made of the gospels. There is no eluding the key-signature given to the entire score: the gospel-writer's claim that this *loving* 'Word' is the purposive principle in whom the created world exists, consists and, creatively, subsists.

In 'vertical' logic, what is actually expressed by the 'causal' predication on which Kristevan Suspicion rests? It cannot, within this framing, be an external motive, connoting arbitrary divine preference (as a Mafia boss might look favourably on the docility of his son's associates!). Rather: it expresses an entirely rigorous law of reciprocity *always already there* in Love itself. Love is the more given (is more 'gracious') where it is the more enabled; and it is the more enabled where it finds answering recognition and response in the 'other' addressed (cf. 'to them that have shall be given'). The disciples are more loving as they learn, receive and reproduce the likeness of Love; this is the exact sense of their being 'more loved'. The 'causal' predication to which Kristeva objects actually states something close to a 'possibility condition' of the type: 'this television-set works *because* it is plugged in and switched on': a meaning fully consistent with the Pauline logic of Agape.

The original 'tear in the fabric', in short, may be construed as nothing of the kind. It appears so only if one *begins* (as Kristeva always fundamentally does begin) by *re-writing* the logic of Agape into the thought-forms of Hegelian idealism, and thence into the perspectives and categories of neo-Freudian libido-decipherment.

∗∗∗

We may perhaps conclude that 'discerning Agape' is not the same thing as 'deciphering Eros', even if the second may supply metaphoric bridges towards the first. Arguably, the epigraph quotation of the present chapter already illustrates the two basic Kristevan (and Western) *mis*-remembrances: the first reducing Christianity to 'monotheism', the second reducing Agape-faith to the sacralisation of an *already-known* value called 'love'.

And yet Kristeva is indispensable. Which other contemporary theorist has seen the problem of love, desire and transcendence implanted so intimately within the human subject? 'If it is alive, your psyche is amorous. If it not amorous, it is dead.' For our transitional times, at any rate, her post-Freudian variations as 'Christian atheist' are richly instructive. This postmodern Sulamite leaves a remarkable love discourse, re-telling the Western love-story, pre-tracing a transitional way of love and, perhaps, within reach of metaphorical understanding, prefiguring the greatest of Love-affairs.

Notes

1 J. Kristeva, *Le Féminin et le sacré* (Paris: Stock, 1998), p. 148. Further references will be given in the text as *FS* followed by page number.
2 J. Kristeva, *Histoires d'amour* (Paris: Denoel, 1983). Edition used: Folio 'Essais' (Paris: Gallimard, 1990). Further references will be given in the text as *HA* followed by page number.
3 Kristeva spoke in 1998 of 'the archaeologies of faith towards which my father pushed me' (*FS*, 65).
4 See J. Kristeva, *Au Commencement était l'amour: Psychanalyse et foi* Livre de poche (Paris, 1997), pp. 41–2 (first published Paris: Hachette, 1985). Further references will be given in the text as *ACA* followed by page number.

5 Exegesis of this key point is complicated by the fact that Kristeva still thinks, traditionally, of Solomon as the real or fictional 'author' – hence the 'addressed Other' – of the text (even though she does mention the epithalamic tradition among possible other sources). See my chapter 1.

6 See *HA*, 179, note 3, referring to *Des Choses cachées depuis la fondation du monde* (Paris: Grasset, 1978).

7 P. Valéry, *Cahiers* Vol. XI (Paris: CNRS), p. 110.

8 This image, which lends its title to Kristeva's conclusion, is suggested by Stephen Spielberg's much-discussed film *E.T.* (1982).

9 Catherine Clément's term for Kristeva; see *FS*, 170.

10 By virtue of this 'deciphered' analogy, the descent of the psychoanalytic Word (ordering rationality) into the (psychoanalysed) 'flesh' is seen to displace and replace the divine Logos – a 'revenge' (as Steiner, himself Jewish, points out) in that it 'gets back at Christianity' for historically displacing or replacing the Chosen People. See 'The God-shaped hole', Channel Four Television, broadcast in UK 27 May 1992.

11 Cf. *HA* 79 where Kristeva evokes the Image of the Virgin and child: 'The basis for the most cherished element of love, Christian love itself feeds on all manner of individual deficiencies and offers, perhaps, the richest mosaic of words that the human being, this precocious, driven-and-haunted subject, this in-lover, wants to hear.'

12 See 'When the Gods are born' in *L'Amante marine: De Friedrich Nietzsche*, trans. G. C. Gill (Columbia: Columbia University Press, 1991), pp. 123–42.

13 This view does not acknowledge New Testament usage. See e.g. John 1: 4: 'in Him was life'. The Greek word for the *divine* life, said to be with the Logos 'in the beginning', is not *bios* (ordinary biological life), nor even *psykhe* (pyschic, sense-bearing energy), but a 'Third Party' – *Zoe*. This latter is the Life 'from above' seen to address the 'blank love-potential' of the psyche, understood as aptitude for the relationality and meaningfulness into which the human psyche is called, and for the Love in which it is regenerated.

14 Cf. *HA* 67: 'I will here be using the term Agape *as a synonym for primary identification*' (my italics).

15 Cf. *FS* 266: 'I am persuaded, as a reader of Hegel, that it is by passing through Christianity that the free subjectivity of men and women arrives at its flowering.'

16 P. Valéry, *Cahiers* Vol. I (Paris: CNRS, 1957), p. 825

17 Kristeva speaks of Freud's anxiety in relation to Christianity, and of his circumspection in discussing Zoroaster where he really means the figure of Christ (*HA*, 61–2); she also puts back into the appropriated figure its content of Love.

18 The Oxford biblical scholar and exegete C. H. Dodd gives a careful refutation of this influential nineteenth-century thesis in *The Founder of Christianity* (London: Collins-Fontana, 1971). Readers of Kristeva's *Étrangers à nous-mêmes* will be aware that the selfsame 'gap' exists in the culture-narrative of that book.

19 See *HA*, 204, note 2. The theologian will certainly object here that Kristeva misconstrues her author significantly: this is no reluctant admission on Bernard's part of a destiny of unfulfilment in desire; it is, on the contrary, the jubilant claim that the pre-tasted joy of heaven is not satiety, but indefinitely regenerated delight.

Conclusion

Remembering the Past,
Negotiating the Future

We have followed some of the greatest French writers at their fullest intellectual and artistic stretch, resplendent with a subject matter which most intimately and ultimately engages them as human subjects. The most tangible result, I hope, is to have suggested, enjoyably, how central to contemporary consciousness and self-understanding has been the motif of deciphering Eros.

In a sense, all explorations of love and desire in Western culture form a single development of the same fugue-like sense of enigma registered by the emergent question of the *Song of Songs* 'Who is this who...?' One of the advantages of consenting *not* to reduce cultural pre-history to some slim antecedence of our own 'present-of-theory' is to retain the possibility of seeing ourselves comparatively, in the perspective of a perennial problematics. Conversely, the same thread of variation-in-continuity enables us to recognise the singularity of the century just closed. Crucial to the reflexive awakening of that century has been the dislocation of our thematic triad in its 'vertical function' ('transcendence'), registering a culture-wide breakdown of confidence in the foundational Christian–Platonic framing of Western cultures and destabilising in turn the functions of 'love' and 'desire'. We are still observing the irradiations of that – itself ambiguous – event-in-culture known as the 'death of God'. Many of the parameters of decipherment we have observed follow more or less directly from it.

Most conspicuously, these include the progressively affirmed sense of a self-enclosed hermeneutic circle centred on the individual ego ('I try to understand, to contain what contains me'); concomitantly, also, the sense of a required deconstruction of inherited forms and models, and of a necessary re-beginning ('Love is to be re-invented like all the rest'). We have observed, too, a modulation in the co-ordinates of desire-writing and of questionings of love. The creative writer's employment of more subtle languages of decoding, often based on, or else paralleling, phenomenology or psychoanalysis, constitutes one such shift; as do the richer, more authentic and closely textured accounts of love and desire thus produced – but also, by century's end, the tendency of imaginative writing to become infused by theory, and even displaced by it. Authorised by the century's newly adopted mastercode of psychoanalysis, there has been a hope, recycled from the nineteenth century (often enough from Hegel): that of a complete coming-to-awareness of the occult intentionality of Desire itself and of an existential *prise en charge* of this carrying inner enigma, surmounting its own deficiencies and contradictions. Out of this matrix comes a more secretly dynamising hope: that of recovering some form of lost transcendence 'from below', and with it, of a refound consistency and viability for 'love'.

Conversely, too, we have followed a growing shadow: the de-realisation and loss of identity which are implied in such specular reflexivity. From Proust to Kristeva, the hermeneutic circle is seen to close back upon the individual subject of desire, increasingly understood as bearing a narcissistic imprint of amorous need, disability and frustration. This movement tends to form a 'vicious' circle in which self-love is often enshrined as the defining measure of all love because it represents, in the amorous phenomenon, that part which *can* be rationally decoded and pinned down.

No doubt the more empirical of our writers and the more venturesome of our theorists still give us memorable bursts of moral sunshine. In Valéry and Breton, in Irigaray, Emmanuel and Kristeva, we get celebratory moments in which love as life-enhancing value is glimpsed, celebrated, championed. But, in the problematising and problematic confines of the century's hermeneutic circle, and, more particularly, within the often anguished horizons of its deconstructionist palace of mirrors, this is a minor tonality. Overall, the picture is sombre. 'Love' figures as a strange and fractured proposal of uncertain sense – a plot substantially lost. The growing semantic imprecision which attends the linguistic usage of this term reflects a deeper uncertainty. By century's end, the question becomes: if the erotico-romantic model of love is all too suspect, and too suspect to define for today a receivable concept of love – still less an art of loving – then what is 'love'? And is it anything?

At the centre of the sphere of self-reflecting twentieth-century Eros is, often enough, the diminished subject of a formidably diminished practice of human loving. Duras, perhaps, gives this impasse its most radical formulation. In a structural sense, the lover's 'other-image' *always* has a psychic 'haunting' which is *destabilising*, since the very fact that erotic excess projects a 'haunted image' threatens to subvert the love-partner, transforming her or him into a partial and metonymic actualisation of 'the real Thing'; that is, a contingent, replaceable and provisional cipher for 'the lost Object of Desire'. Lacan's most central insight about the allusive and metonymic specularity of all human desiring is centrally relevant here; it suggests that some such process is declarable within everybody's 'central cinema' of amorous desire.

What also typifies the Durassian inner cinema – and is true of the century – is, however, that an *anti-bonding virus* is at work *unrecognised*: once, because the subject cannot decipher her own psychodrama; but also a second time, and here irreparably, in that she cannot discern in the order of things any fundamental script supportive of human love, still less any invitation to loving; merely a sub-text of Other-deficient erotic excess. Subject to both these secret 'locks', the psychic subject's inner cinema cannot invent any awakening from the logic of 'excess', now at work destructively – displaced and transferential, contagious and relationally destabilising. It can only replicate its own devastated and devastating 'triangulation'. As Kristeva sees acutely, it is a far cry from the 'peace' of the biblical Sulamite to the haunted and driven schizophrenia of Lol V. Stein.

Twentieth-century writers thus often reproduce the 'shadow' of Genesis. They more rarely see the 'splendour' against which the shadow is profiled; and they give little account, if any, of the *expectation* of splendour. It is to a Dawn of fearsomely reduced hope that Lol herself awakens. Yet the erotic-specular 'love' *is* known to be a counterfeit of some *other* Love, which it vainly mimics to the point of madness – a real solar flight and a true Dawn, the obscure loss of which alone explains the persistence-in-devastation of the Durrassian protagonist; the impossible is obscurely expected, as well as impotently pursued. *Why* this should be so is the 'excessive' question Duras does *not* answer.

In all this, France emerges, not indeed as a unique case, but as privileged locus and examplar of European, or more broadly Western, cultural transition. Often enough, the country of the Revolution, of Surrealism and of May 1968 – sometimes more locally, its capital city or its Latin Quarter – has been the epicentre of the culture-crisis more diffusely registered elsewhere; hence also the laboratory of precocious experimentation in cultural change. And this has been true in the matter of love and desire, as in other fields. Erotic sensibilisation and eroticised intelligence are recognised as leading elements in everyone's culture-stereotype of 'Frenchness'; and this study of the second of these characteristics as re-applied to the first cannot be said to have dispelled this image. Just as importantly, the 'intellectual sensibility' (Valéry's term) of French writers confers on them the virtues of a particularly 'fast processor', accelerating and radicalising the treatment of common themes that are to be encountered elsewhere within a shared European (and, with due adjustments, Western) mindspace ('Rapid minds', notes Valéry acutely 'exposed to verification by slower ones').

My hope is that this book has provided at least some basis for a more informed and discriminating reading of the realities behind the cliché. We have recurrently encountered features of cultural identity which are suggestive in this respect. To recall merely a few: the mental subsoil represented by the 'caritas synthesis' of the Medieval church (with its ambiguous reflections in the troubadour tradition); the ever-latent form of the oppositional dynamic by which France emerged from the Middle Ages; the centrality to the French outlook of the Revolution and the Enlightenment project; its models of *galanterie* and *libertinage*; its peculiarly erotic fascination with the ambiguous frontiers of transgression/transcendence; the tension between its repudiated onto-theological certainties and its lively, forward-leaning (but unstable) flair for radical experimentation, always programmed (from Descartes onwards) in rationalist-dualist categories (and, in the century just finished, by a latent Hegelianism); its (erotic) delight in the *tabula rasa,* answering its own propensity for a deeply *unerotic* bourgeois conservatism; its superego rationality, and its singular and inevitable fixation with the Oedipal paradigm. These (among many others) are factors of cultural identity which, often subterraneously, form the (inter-)texture of present-day French thought and writing.

Perhaps we can even see why another of the more haunting constants we have encountered is most sharply characteristic of modern French mindspace: the omnipresent sense of uncertainty and ambiguity, with its eddying persuasions, its swirling difficulties of recognition of provenance and origin, its gaps in memory, its dislocations of philosophic and moral judgement – the entire set of symptoms making up the 'Bermuda triangle' of the era of reflexive Eros. Despite these caveats, the chapters presented here do, I hope, give a sense of acute and insightful French intelligence enjoyably, profitably – and often *transposably* – at work. As readers of these writers, we ourselves become more alert and intelligent decipherers.

What bridges to the future of the decipherment and discernment of Eros can our authors be said to offer? What indications towards a renewed self-understanding, perhaps even towards a re-finding of the lost thread of the 'plot' of love? Every reader will wish to discern for him or herself the most 'prophetic' patterns. My own version of this exercise is set in dialogue with that of Jean-Luc Marion, whose *Le Phénomène érotique* appearing just as this book is completed, confirms beyond expectation many of my own intuitions and certifies the echo they find in current French thinking.

Post-1968 'critical theory' in France, inheriting from Hegel in a newly reflexive and objectivising mode, has undoubtedly nourished, somewhere within its own erotic *telos*, a dream of mastery: that of a unitary-field theory of all phenomena of desire, posited as including 'love'. Yet its generic disabilities have been deeply disqualifying: an incomplete and suspicion-led hermeneutics, misconstruing the thickness of Eros; a propensity to ideological antipathies and reactive anti-metaphysical stances; a hyperbolic third-person scientificity; an anti-humanism nevertheless cultivating the 'self' or 'ego'; a post-structuralist de-connection from incarnate cultural history, and an ever-partial acknowledgement of cultural sources; the ideological and agenda-driven excesses of its 'liberationist' wing; its very difficulty in integrating the destabilising novelty fruitfully wrought by feminism, its companion of circumstance and increasingly reactive partner. In terms of current brain-theory, it has been (until feminism) a well-nigh exclusively 'left-hemisphere' exercise. Is it possible to apply both hemispheres, hearing both genders?

Another still unrealised condition would appear to be a willingness to gather patiently together from all disciplinary horizons the dispersed, and still unrelated, anthropological data already extant; and our ability to adopt a practice of phenomenological 'reduction' of the data adequate to the *whole* phenomenon attested. It may be that, in this gathering, creative writers have their eminent place: they are primary witnesses, prior to any third-person codification, of the living emergence, unfolding and human resonance of Eros; conscious subjects seeking to contain in a mastered language what contains them; authentic witnesses precisely because understanding operates imaginatively, through the narrativising, modelling, experimental decipherment which is purposefully at play in creative form.

As every patient reader of the arduous, but uniquely indispensable, Paul Ricœur is – or will be – persuaded, we then need an *adequate hermeneutics*,[1] as distinct from an indecently summary and self-confirming *deconstruction*. How would this *not* apply to the decipherment of love, desire and transcendence? Emmanuel's 'sacred and erotic triangle' represents, at the heart of the anthropological subject, an enigma no less extraordinary, challenging or universal than the more basic encoding of the human genome – more so, indeed, since what is here envisaged is the universe of human liberty. An adequate art of decipherment would seem to be the most obvious bridge to the future, opening up vistas beyond the late twentieth-century epic of 'French Freud'.

The 'sacred-erotic triangle' itself provides a worthy object. We have re-found at every turn some *triangular figure of articulation* (involving a dynamic relation of self, other and Third Party) – in ancient myth, in cultural paradigms of every age, and at the centre of the spiritual dialectics of every modern writer treated here (without prejudice to further readings within a clearly extendable series). Psychoanalytical archaeologies of the desirous ego (Lacan, Kristeva) give their own (various) accounts of it. Girardian desire theory sets it at the heart of mythic consciousness and social interaction, as the signature of the archaic psyche and of the socio-cultural regulation of violence. The theological myth of Genesis, at the sources of our own culture, is memorably addressed to it. The trinitarian Agape-God of Christian theology (as distinct from the Platonic-Plotinian One of Hellenic essentialism) offers a suggestively *reversed* figure of it.

This triangle is undoubtedly one of the most central of 'anthropological structures'. (If it were not, could it provide the literary critic with such a sensitive index of cultural change?) At the same time, it is steeped in enigma and ambiguity. It does not of itself allow its decipherers to determine what the mysterious 'excessiveness' of desire *is*, or *tends towards* or *signifies* in its own right; nor does it 'explain' the total relational figure. Interpretation is always something to be added to it, in the very act by which it attains concrete relational embodiment. It is thus a 'carrying enigma'. As we interpret the triangle, so, knowingly or unknowingly, we construct our loves and lives; and as we construct our loves and our lives, so we interpret Eros. This is relativity theory.

As well as the interest of a hermeneutics that is adequate to its object, and well-focused in respect of it, we have observed the pertinence of the interplay between two motifs and organising logics of Eros and Agape. This binome, re-discoverable at both micro and macro levels, establishes a polarity which best measures the field of the phenomena of love and desire; and, perhaps, it allows us to elucidate best the relation between these terms. Of course, it comes with its own baggage of difficulties (of definition, of usage, of provenance and association, of application, of interpretation); and it is not entirely surprising that the century of 'the death of God', of rebeginnings 'from below' and of hermeneutic scientificity should have bracketed it – and so largely lost the use of it. This is, indeed, one more sign of the age of self-reflecting Eros. Yet we have also observed both the well-founded need for this structure of interpretation and its actual, if often covert and ambiguous, 'return' in French writing.

Partly, this return has to do with a larger recovery from an amnesia of aversion, which, for large parts of the twentieth century, struck out from memory and all genuine cognisance the Judaeo-Christian culture-matrix as such. Partly, it is linked to the resurgence from within our adventures of decipherment of the gap left by the excluded term: a phenomenon sometimes recognised by contemporary philosophers (such as Levinas) as 'the trace'. Valéry, consenting at the last to envisage an order of reality that alone makes sense of the positive potential of human loving, already points towards it. Emmanuel calls attention to one of the more considerable philosophic issues raised by it: is sexuality the sole root of all love; or is Agape not, rather, the antecedent condition and *telos* of all sexuality? Kristeva, at century's end, perhaps identifies the largest stake for the future of our culture and civilisation when she defines the entire positive potential of human loving as having been, historically, enfolded within the motif of Agape.

For an uprooted age – alienated from its own tradition, technically masterful, but marvellously equipped for nihilism and sure only of psychosomatic Desire – might not the 'maternal-feminine' be a *chemin de traverse* running not away from, but round the mountain and back up towards its summit; perhaps even up to the rediscovery of the doctrine of spirit-written 'flesh', and thence to the whole faith of 'new creation' and of 'Grace'? Could this bridge be a prolegomenon to a full and coherent theology of the divine Third, obscurely known to prophets of the sexuate body?

A similarly radical train of intuition is, I think, at work in the thought of Jean-Luc Marion. From the evidence offered in the present book, I see no objection to Marion's twenty-first century proposal of a *phenomenological reduction* presenting the human animal as 'subject of loving'. From Proust to Kristeva, all the voices studied here seem to say in the end something akin to this, or tributary to it (not excluding Roland Barthes: 'I write in order to be loved').[2]

Nor am I surprised at Marion's concluding articulation of anthropology to theology. That a French academic philosopher from the Sorbonne should, in 2003, suggest in his conclusion that the most rigorous phenomenological reduction of the human subject directly raises the question of whether God is not also the first subject of loving, and a *transcendently better Lover*, may have startled many and perhaps alarmed some. I read it, rather, as a hopeful sign that the 'Bermuda triangle' of twentieth-century Eros has been and will be crossed, its mines cleared, its spells dispelled, its memory restored and its taboos lifted ...

The liberated unfreedom which 'the time of Desire' leaves in its wake, together with its subsistent shadow of 'calamity' (Duras) and of the intrinsic accursedness still attaching to 'la part maudite'(Bataille), may certainly be thought to call for a renewed attentiveness to the logic and credentials of the 'other love', all but forgotten as model and as resource.

On this model, it is *given* to us to dispose of our own erotic 'excess' in creatively self-determining freedom: not within a logic of Eros alone, but within the transforming relational field of Agape, from which Eros derives its sense and its dignity in the order of things. *How* we love is seen here as the primary implication and the perennial point of human 'transcendence'.

'In contrast to erotic love, freedom, not desire, is at the heart of the matter', writes Robert Wagoner of Agape. 'Love in this sense is a gift of what the self is – freedom. To stand in a loving relation with another person is to give what I have been given. In a paradoxical way, the most unique act of the self is to be self*less*.'[3] So St Paul speaks of the love that escapes the gravitational field of that narcissism which is ever present in all psychosomatic Desire: a self-bestowal which is giving and forgiving (transcending the need to possess or to be right); which allows faithful commitment (transcending the pulse and flicker of libido, the variability of emotional states and attitudes, the drives of biological nature); and which (transcending the logic of self-concern) recognises and seeks the good of the other. This love 'endures': both in the sense that it 'bears all things' with resilience, in ever-renewed hope; and in the more fundamental, enabling, sense that it partakes of the Love divine which 'never ends' (1 Cor. 13: 1-13).

Will the amorously dysfunctional postmodern Narcissus (Kristeva's 'extra-terrestrial wanting for love') come to perfect the arts of analysis and transference, thereby learning to do without any transcendence other than the emergent meaningfulness of the 'maternal sacred'? Then, perhaps, the strangely haunting 'womb memory' of lost splendour will come to fade before its true Hegeliano-Freudo-Nietzschean Dawn. But will this effort of exhaustion not, rather, exhaust itself (rather as *Tel Quel* has now become *l'Infini*), showing the psychotherapeutic 'talking-cure' to have something less than the measure of the amorous Narcissus whose dysfunctionality it would heal?

St Paul (we recall, against Kristeva) did not *invent* the splendour of Agape outlined above; it came upon him, dazzlingly and despite himself, 'from elsewhere'... Nor is his hymn to Love a form of erotic striving. It offers no love ethic, no moral code; not one word in it addresses the question of how we *ought* to be loving or living. Rather, it celebrates what in fact happens when faith, receiving a first Love 'from elsewhere', discovers in this recreating gift the whole transcendent potential of the human subject of loving.

The ultimate question, addressed to all, is then perhaps that of knowing which we recognise better as an image of human potential: 'love within the bounds of self-reflecting Eros' or 'Eros re-informed by Agape'? If we wish the love-story to continue recognisably, and with creative energy, within our culture, our third millennium may well have to choose.

Perhaps this book contributes some sense of this larger ferment at work. The reactive suspicion of onto-theological metaphysics and re-insured religion, having done its work and spent its vigour, is passing away. A certain Oedipal rivalry with a superego representation of an archaic deity has, in the century of psychoanalysis, doubled back on itself and cracked its own code; it is becoming yesterday's demonology. The cultural matrix in which the Western notion of love has arisen and received its successive forms of cultural currency is seen to be a mixed inheritance, formed of an interweaving of fundamental motifs which we are now learning more adequately to decode and to recombine. The possible – and impossible – senses of the essentially ambiguous notion of 'the death of God' have been largely disentangled; their real consequences registered. Today's love-philosopher can simply take the amorous Narcissus at the point where the twentieth century has left him – and ask him who he is *now*...

Fortunately, it does not belong to the mere literary critic to call bets, prescribe choices or predict the future. I hope, simply, to have made some, perhaps stimulating, contribution to 'discerning the now'.

Notes

1 Defined as 'the examination of modes of understanding involved in knowledges with a vocation of objectivity'. See P. Ricœur, *La Mémoire, l'histoire, l'oubli* (Paris: Seuil, 2002), p. 373.
2 *Roland Barthes par Roland Barthes* (Paris: Seuil, 1975), p. 97.
3 R. E. Wagoner, *The Meanings of Love: An Introduction to the Philosophy of Love* (Westport, CT & London: Praeger, 1997), p. 36.

Select Bibliography

Full bibliographical references for all sources used can be found in the endnotes to the chapters of this study. The bibliography is devoted to those works which are related most closely to the themes and authors dealt with in this book or which have contributed in a fundamental way to shaping its arguments.

Principal texts studied, with English translations (where available)

Barthes, Roland, *Fragments d'un discours amoureux* (Paris: Seuil, 1977). Trans. Richard Howard, *A Lover's Discourse* (New York: Hill and Wang, 1978; London: Cape, 1979).

———, *La Chambre claire: Note sur la photographie* (Paris: Seuil, 1980). Trans. Richard Howard, *Camera Lucida: Reflections on Photography* (London: Flamingo, 1984).

———, *Roland Barthes par Roland Barthes* (Paris: Seuil, 1995). Trans. Richard Howard, *Roland Barthes by Roland Barthes* (Berkley: University of California Press, 1994).

Bataille, Georges, *L'Érotisme* (Paris: Minuit, édn illustrée, 1957). Trans. Mary Dalwood, *Eroticism* (Marion Boyars: London & New York, 1990).

Breton, André, *L'Amour fou* (Paris: Gallimard, 1976). Trans. Mary Ann Caws, *Mad Love* (Lincoln: University of Nebraska Press, 1987).

Claudel, Paul, *Partage de Midi* and *Le Soulier de Satin*, in *Théâtre*, 2 vols, eds. J. Madaule & J. Petit (Paris: Bibliothèque de la Pléiade, Gallimard, 1965–67).

Duras, Marguerite, *Barrage contre le Pacifique* (Paris: Folio, Gallimard, 1950). Trans. Herma Briffault, *The Sea Wall* (London: Faber and Faber, 1986).

———, *Le Marin de Gibraltar* (Paris: Gallimard, 1952). Trans. Barbara Bray, *The Sailor from Gibraltar* (London: Calder & Boyars, 1966).

———, *Le Ravissement de Lol V. Stein* (Folio, Gallimard, 1964). Trans. Richard Seaver, *The Ravishing of Lol Stein* (New York: Grove Press, 1966).

Emmanuel, Pierre, *Le Goût de l'Un* (Paris: Seuil, 1963).

———, *Sophia* (Paris: Seuil, 1973).

———, *La Vie terrestre* (Paris: Seuil, 1976).

———, *L'Autre* (Paris: Seuil, 1980).

———, *Tu* (Paris: Seuil, 1982).

———, *Car enfin je vous aime* (Paris: Seuil, 1983).

Falk, Marcia, *Love Lyrics from the Bible: A Translation and Literary Study of the Song of Songs* (Sheffield: The Almond Press, 1982).

Irigaray, Luce, *Éthique de la différence sexuelle* (Paris: Minuit, 1984). Trans. Carolyn Burke & Gillian C. Gill, *An Ethics of Sexual Difference* (London: Athlone, 1993).

———, *L'Amante marine: De Friedrich Nietzsche* (Paris: Minuit, 1982). Trans. Gillian C. Gill, *Marine Lover of Friedrich Nietzsche* (New York, Columbia, 1991).

Kristeva, Julia, *Histoires d'amour* (Paris: Denoël, 1983). Trans. Leon Roudiez, *Tales of Love* (New York, Guildford: Columbia University Press, 1987).

———, *Le Féminin et le sacré* (Paris: Stock, 1998).

———, *Au Commencement était l'amour: Psychanalyse et foi* (Paris: Hachette, 1985; Le Livre de poche, 1997). Trans. Arthur Goldhammer, *In the Beginning was Love: Psychoanalysis and Faith* (New York: Columbia University Press, 1987).

Plato, *The Symposium*, trans. W. Hamilton (London: Penguin, 1951).

Proust, Marcel, *A la recherché du temps perdu*, 4 vols, ed. Jean-Yves Tadié (Paris: Bibliothèque de la Pléiade, Gallimard, 1987–89). Trans. C. Scott Moncrieff (with Stephen Hudson for vol. 12), *Remembrance of Things Past*, 12 vols (London: Chatto and Windus, 1957).

Valéry, Paul, *La Jeune Parque* in J. Hytier (ed.), *Œuvres*, Bibliothèque de la Pléiade, Vol. 1 (Paris: Gallimard, 1957). Trans. Alistair Elliott, *Paul Valéry: 'La Jeune Parque' French–English bi-lingual edition* (Newcastle: Bloodaxe Books, 1997).

———, *Mon Faust*. Trans. in Jackson Matthews (ed.), *The Collected Works of Paul Valéry*, Bollingen series 45 (New York: Pantheon Books, 1956).

———, *Cahiers*, 2 vols, ed. J. Robinson (Paris: Bibliothèque de la Pléiade, Gallimard, 1972–74). Trans. Paul Gifford, Sían Miles, Robert Pickering & Brian Stimpson, *Paul Valéry Cahiers/Notebooks*, ed. Brian Stimpson, with Paul Gifford & Robert Pickering, 5 vols (New York: Peter Lang, Vols 1 and 2, 2000).

Other works and authors cited

Balzac, Honoré de, *Le Lys dans la vallée* (Paris: Garnier, 1966).

Barthes, Roland, *Œuvres*, ed. Eric Marty, 3 vols (Paris: Seuil, 1993–95).

Bataille, Georges, *Œuvres complètes*, 12 vols (Paris: Gallimard, 1970–88).

Baudelaire, Charles, *Œuvres complètes*, ed. Y.-G. Le Dantec (Paris: Bibliothèque de la Pléiade, Gallimard, 1961).

Bernanos, Georges, *Œuvres romanesques suivies de 'Dialogue des Carmélites'* (Paris: Bibliothèque de la Pléaide, Gallimard, 1962).

Breton, André, *Œuvres complètes*, ed. M. Bonnet & E.-A. Hubert, 3 vols (Paris: Bibliothèque de la Pléiade, Gallimard, Vol, 1. 1988; Vol. II, 1992; Vol. III, 1999).

Chateaubriand, Alphonse de, *René* (Paris: Bordas, 1976).

Cixous, Hélène, *Le Livre de Promethea* (Paris: Gallimard, 1983).

Claudel, Paul, *Mémoires improvisés recueillis par Jean Amrouche* (Paris: Gallimard, 1954).

———, *Œuvres en prose*, eds. J. Petit & Ch. Galoperine (Paris: Bibliothèque de la Pléiade, Gallimard, 1965).

Œuvres poétique, eds. S. Fumet & J. Petit (Paris: Bibliothèque de la Pléiade, Gallimard, 1967).

———, Paul Claudel interroge le 'Cantique des cantiques', *Œuvres complètes*, Vol. XXIII (Paris: Gallimard, 1967).

Descartes, René, *Les Passions de l'âme*, in *Œuvres choisis de Descartes* (Paris: Garnier, 1916).

Duras, Marguerite, *Les Petits chevaux de Tarquinia* (Paris: Folio, Gallimard, 1953).

———, *L'Amant* (Paris: Minuit, 1984).

Flaubert, Gustave, *Œuvres*, eds. A Thibaudet & R. Dumesnil, 2 vols (Paris: Bibliothèque de la Pléiade, Gallimard, 1951–52).

Irigaray, Luce, *Speculum de l'autre femme* (Paris: Minuit, 1974).

———, 'The Poverty of Psychoanalysis', *Critique*, 365 (Oct. 1977).

Laclos, Ch. de, *Les Liaisons dangereueses* (Paris: Garnier, 1961).

La Fayette, Mme de, *La Princesse de Clèves* (Paris: Imprimerie Nationale, 1980).

Lamartine, *Œuvres poétiques complètes*, ed. M.-F. Guyard (Paris: Bibliothèque de la Pléiade, Gallimard, 1963).

Mallarmé, Stéphane, *Correspondance*, ed. H. Mondor, Vol. I (Paris: Gallimard, 1959).

Mauriac, François, *Mémoires intérieures* (Paris: Flammarion, 1959).

Nerval, Gérard de, *Sylvie* (Paris: SEDES, 1970).

Péret, Benjamin, *Anthologie de l'amour sublime* (Paris: A. Michel, 1956).

Plato, *The Republic*, trans. D. Lee (London: Penguin, 1974).

Ronsard, *Les Amours*, eds. H. Weber & C. Weber (Paris: Garnier, 1963).

Rousseau, Jean-Jacques, *Julie ou La Nouvelle Héloïse*, ed. R. Pomeau (Paris: Garnier, 1974).

Sade, Marquis de, *Œuvres complètes*, 16 vols (Paris: Cercle du livre précieux, 1966–70).

Stendhal, *De l'Amour*, eds. D. Muller & P. Jourda (Paris: Champion, 1926).

Teilhard de Chardin, Pierre, *Le Milieu divin, essai de vie intérieure* (Paris: Seuil, 1957).

Tournier, Michel, *Vendredi ou les limbes du Pacifique* (Paris: Folio, Gallimard 1972).

Valéry, Paul, *Œuvres*, ed. J. Hytier, 2 vols (Paris: Bibliothèque de la Pléiade, Gallimard 1957, 1961).

———, *Cahiers*, 29 vols (Paris: CNRS, 1957–61).

Weil, Simone, *Œuvres*, ed. F. de Lusssy (Paris: Quarto, Gallimard, 1999).

Zola, Émile, *Nana*, ed. H. Mitterrand (Paris: Folio, Gallimard, 1977).

Works of criticism

Adler, Laure, *Marguerite Duras* (Paris: Gallimard, 1998).

Alquié, Ferdinand, *Philosophie du Surréalisme* (Paris: Flammarion, 1955).

Autrand, Michel, *'Le Soulier de Satin': Étude dramaturgique* (Paris: Champion, 1987).

Bastet, Ned, 'Ulysse et la sirène. Le quatrième acte de "Lust"', in *Cahiers Paul Valéry 2, 'Mes théâtres'* (Paris: NRF, Gallimard, 1977).

Beaumont, Ernest, *Le Sens de l'amour dans le théâtre de Claudel. Le thème de Beatrice* (Paris: Les Lettres Modernes, 1958).

Blanchet, André, *La Littérature et le spirituel*, 2 vols (Paris: Aubier, 1959–61).

Bowie, Malcolm, *Freud, Proust, Lacan* (Cambridge: Cambridge University Press, 1987).

————, *Proust Among the Stars* (London: HarperCollins, 1998).

Burke, Carolyn, Schor, Naomi & Whitford, Margaret (eds.), *Engaging with Irigaray* (New York: Columbia University Press, 1994).

Campbell, John, *Questions of Interpretation in 'La Princesse de Clèves'* (Amsterdam: Rodopi, 1996).

Deleuze, Gilles, *Proust et les signes* (Paris: Presses universitaires de France, 2e édn aug., 1970).

Duras, M., Lacan, J., Blanchot, M., Mascolo, D. & Gauthier J.-P. (eds.), *Marguerite Duras* (Paris: Albatros, 1975).

Emmanuel, Pierre, *Baudelaire, la femme et Dieu* (Paris: Points, Seuil, 1982).

Febvre, Lucien, *Amour sacré, amour profane: Autour de l'Heptameron* (Paris: NRF, Idées, Gallimard, 1971).

Florival, Ghislain, *Le Désir chez Proust* (Louvain & Paris: Nauwelaerts, 1971).

Foucault, Michel, *Histoire de la folie à lâge classique* (Paris: Plon, 1961).

Fourny, Jean-François, *Introduction à la lecture de Bataille* (New York: Peter Lang, 1988).

Fox, Michael V., *The Song of Songs and the Ancient Egyptian Love Song* (Madison, WI: University of Wisconsin Press, 1985).

Frappier, Bernard, *Vues sur les conceptions courtoises dans les littératures d'Oc et d'Oil au XIIe siècle*, in *Cahiers de Civilisation médievale*, IIe année, no. 2, avril–juin 1959.

Gascoigne, David, *Michel Tournier* (Oxford: Berg, 1996).

Griffiths, Richard, *Claudel: A Re-appraisal* (London: Rapp and Whiting, 1968).

Hill, Leslie, *Marguerite Duras: Apocalyptic Desires* (London & New York: Routledge, 1993).

Jaspers, Karl, *Nietzsche* (Paris: Gallimard, 1950).

————, *Nietzsche et le christianisme* (Paris: Minuit, 1949).

Lazar, Moshé, *Amour courtois et Fin'amors dans la litterature du XIIe siecle* (Paris: Klincksieck, 1964).

Madaule, Jacques, *Le Drame de Paul Claudel* (Paris: Desclée de Bouwer, nouv. édn aug., 1947).

Marchal, Bertrand, *La Religion de Mallarmé* (Paris: Corti, 1988).

Marini, Marcelle, 'La Mort d'une érotique' in *Duras, Beckett, Cahiers Renaud Barrault*, 106 (1983).

Mercier-Campiche, Marianne, *Le Théâre de Claudel, ou la puissance du grief et de la passion* (Paris: Pauvert, 1954).

Moriarty, Michael, *Roland Barthes* (Cambridge: Polity Press, 1991).

Owen, D. D. R., *Noble Lovers* (London: Phaedon, 1975).

Pastoreau, Henri, 'André Breton, les femmes et l'amour', *Europe*, March 1991.

Petit, Jacques, *Pour une explication du 'Soulier de Satin'* (Paris: Archives des Lettres modernes, Minard, 1965).

Plouvier, Paule, *Poétique de l'amour chez André Breton* (Paris: Corti, 1983).

Pluchart-Simon, Bernard, *Proust – L'Amour comme vérité humaine et romanesque* (Paris: Larousse, 1975).

Raimond, Michel, *Proust romancier* (Paris: SEDES, 1984).

Richardson, Michael, *Georges Bataille* (London: Routledge, 1994).

Rivers, J. E., *Proust and the Art of Love: The Aesthetics of Sexuality in the Life and Art of Marcel Proust* (New York: Columbia University Press, 1980).

Surya, Michel, *Georges Bataille: An Intellectual Biography*, trans. K. Fijalkowski & M. Richardson (London & New York: Verso, 2002).

Varillon, François, *Claudel* (Paris: Les Écrivains devant Dieu, Desclée de Brouwer, 1967).

Vircondolet, Alain (ed.), *Duras, Dieu et l'écrit* (Paris: Édns du Rocher, 1998).

Whitford, Maragaret, *Luce Irigaray: Philosophy in the Feminine* (London: Routledge, 1991).

———— (ed.), *The Irigaray Reader* (London: Routledge, 1991).

The Hermeneutics of Love, Desire and Transcendence

Alexandrian, Sarane, *Les Libérateurs de l'amour* (Paris: Seuil, 1977).

Andreae, Simon, *Anatomy of Desire: The Science and Psychology of Sex. Love and Marriage* (London: Little, Brown, 1998).

Aries, Philippe & Béjin, André, *Sexualités occidentales*, Communications, 35 (Paris: Points, Seuil, 1982).

Aubert, J.-M., *La Femme, anti-féminisme et christianisme* (Paris: Aubier, 1975).

Augustine, Saint, *Confessions*, trans. H. Chadwick (Oxford & New York: Oxford University Press, 1998).

————, *De Civitatis Dei*, vol. 35 of *Œuvres de saint Augustin* (Paris: Société des études augustiniennes, 1947).

Baruzi, Jean, *Saint Jean de la Croix et le problème de l'expérience mystique* (Paris: Alcan, 1925, 2nd edn 1931).

Benayoun, *Érotique du Surréalisme* (Paris: Pauvert, 1965).

Blondel, Éric (ed.), *L'Amour* (Paris: Corpus, Garnier Flammarion, 1995).

Bristow, Joseph, *Sexuality* (London: The New Critical Idiom, Routledge, 1997).

Brown, Peter, *The Making of Late Antiquity* (Cambridge, MA: Harvard University Press, 1978).

Buber, Martin, *I and Thou*, trans. Walter Kaufmann (New York: Charles Scribner's Sons, 1970).

Burney, *L'Amour* (Paris: Que sais-je?, Presses Universitaires de France, 3e éd. revue et corr., 1984).

Buttrick, G. (ed.), *The Interpreters' Bible*, 12 vols (New York: Abingdon Press, 1952–57).

Citron, Suzanne, *Le Mythe national: L'Histoire de France en question* (Paris: Édns. Ouvrières, 1991).

Copplestone, F., *History of Philosophy*, Vol. 1 *Greece and Rome* (New York: Doubleday, 1948).

Daniel-Rops, Henri, *De l'Amour humain dans la Bible* (Paris: Tallone, 1949).

D'Arcy, Martin, *The Heart and Mind of Love. Lion and Unicorn: A Study in Eros and Agape* (London: Faber and Faber, 1945; revised edn 1954).

Dodd, Charles. H., *The Founder of Christianity* (London: Collins-Fontana, 1971).

——, *The Interpretation of the Fourth Gospel* (Cambridge, Cambridge University Press, 1960).

Emmanuel, Pierre, *Baudelaire, La Femme et Dieu* (Paris: Points, Seuil, 1982).

Etiemble, *L'Érotisme et l'amour* (Paris: Biblio essais, Le Livre de poche, Arlea, 1987).

Finkielkraut, Alain, *La Sagesse de l'amour* (Paris: Folio, Gallimard, 1984).

Freud, S., *The Standard Edition of the Complete Psychological Works of Sigmund Freud*, eds. J. Strachey & A. Freud (London: Hogarth Press and the Institute of Psycho-Analysis, 1953–66).

Fuchs, Eric, *Le Désir et la tendresse* (Geneva: Labor et Fides, 4e éd., 1982).

Gifford, P., *Valéry: Le Dialogue des choses divines* (Paris: Corti, 1989).

——, 'Les Pas de l'Écriture dans *La Jeune Parque*', in P. Gifford & A. Goulet (eds.), *Voix, traces, avènement: L'Écriture et son sujet. Actes du colloque de Cerisy* (Caen: Presses Universitaires de Caen, 1999).

—— & Gratton, J. (eds.), *Subject Matters: Subject and Self in French literature from Descartes to the Present* (Amsterdam: Rodopi, 2000).

——, Hart, Trevor, Archard, David & Rapport, Nigel (eds.), *2000 Years and Beyond: Faith, Identity and the 'Common Era'* (London: Routledge, 2002).

Girard, René, *Mensonge romantique et vérité romanesque* (Paris: Grasset, 1961).

——, *La Violence et le sacré* (Paris: Grasset, 1972).

——, *Des Choses cachées depuis la fondation du monde* (Paris: Grasset, 1978).

——, *Colloque de Cerisy 'Violence et Vérité', Autour de René Girard*, ed. Paul Dumouchel (Paris: Grasset, 1985).

——, *La Voix méconnue du réel: Une Théorie des mythes archïques et modernes* (Paris: Grasset, 2002).

——, *Les Origines de la culture* (Paris: Grasset, 2004).

Gordis, R., *The Song of Songs and Lamentations: A Study, Modern Translation and Commentary* (New York: Jewish Theological Seminary KATAV, 1954, 3rd edn 1974).

Granier, J., 'La Critique nietzschéenne du Dieu de la métaphysique' in *Procès de l'objectivité de Dieu* (Paris: Édns. du Cerf, 1969).

Guillebaud, Jean-Claude, *La Tyrannie du plaisir* (Paris: Seuil, 1998).

Guitton, Jean, *L'Amour humain* (Paris: Aubier, 1946).

Jean, Raymond, *Lectures du Désir: Nerval, Lautréamont, Apollinaire, Éluard* (Paris: Points, Seuil, 1977).

Jeannière, A., *Anthropologie sexuelle* (Paris: Recherches économiques et sociales, Aubier, 1964).

Kierkegaard, Søren, *Works of Love*, trans. Howard Hong & Edna Hong (London: Collins, 1962).

Lacan, Jacques, *Écrits 1* (Paris: Points, Seuil, 1966).

————, *Écrits II* (Paris: Points, Seuil, 1971).

Lecercle, Jean-Louis, *L'Amour* (Paris: Les Thèmes littéraires, Bordas, 1991).

Levinas, Emmanuel, *Entre nous: Essais sur le penser à l'autre* (Paris: Biblio essais, Grasset, 1991).

Lewis, C. S., *The Four Loves (Affection, Friendship, Eros, Charity)* (London: Collins, 1960; Collins Fount, 1977).

Lilar, S., *Le Couple* (Paris: Grasset, 1966).

————, *Le Malentendu du deuxième sexe* (Paris: Gonthier, 1966).

————, *A Propos de Sartre et de l'amour* (Paris: Grasset, 1967).

Knight, George & Golka, Friedemann, *The Song of Songs and Jonah: Revelation of God* (Edinburgh & Grand Rapids: Erdemans, 1988).

Lacoque, André & Ricœur, Paul, *Penser la Bible* (Paris: Seuil, 1998).

Marion, Jean-Luc, *Le Phénomène érotique: Six meditations* (Paris: Grasset, 2003).

Mead, Maragaret, *L'Autre sexe* (Paris: Gonthier, 1966).

Moltmann, Jürgen, 'Progress and Abyss: Remembering the Future of the Modern World', in P. Giffford et al. (eds.), *2000 Years and Beyond: Essays in Faith, Identity and the 'Common Era'* (London: Routledge, 2002).

————, *The Coming of God: Christian Eschatology*, trans. M. Kohl (London: SCM, 1996).

Murdoch, Iris, *Metaphysics as a Guide to Morals* (London: Penguin, 1993).

Natanson, J., *La Mort de Die: Essai sur l'athéisme moderne* (Paris: Presses Universitaires de France, 1975).

Nédoncelle, Maurice, *Vers une philosophie de l'amour* (Paris: Aubier, 1957).

Nietzsche, Friedrich, *L'Antéchrist* (Paris: J.-J. Pauvert, 1967).

————, *Ecce Homo. Comment on devient ce qu'on est.* Trans. G. Colli and M. Montinari (Paris: Idees NRF, Gallimard, 1969).

————, *Par delà le bien et le mal*, trans. G. Bianquis (Paris: Union générale des éditeurs, 1962).

————, *La Volonté de Puissance* 2 vols. (Paris: Gallimard, 1995).

————, *Le Crépuscule des idoles* (Paris: Gallimard, 1988).

Nora, Pierre (ed.), *Les Lieux de mémoire*, 3 vols (Paris: Gallimard Vol. 1, *La République*, 1982; Vol. 2, *La Nation*, 1986; Vol. 3, *Les France*, 1992).

Nygren, Anders, *Eros et Agape: La Notion chrétienne de l'Amour et ses transformations*, trans. P. Jundt (Aubier, 1943; 4e édn 1962).

Onfray, Michel, *Théorie du corps amoureux Pour une érotique solaire* (Paris: Grasset, 2000).

Pauvert, Jean-Jacques, *La Littérature érotique* (Paris: Flammarion, 2000).

Rabouin, David (ed.), *Le Désir* (Paris: Corpus, Garnier Flammarion, 1997).

Raimond, Marcel, *Marsile Ficin: Commentaire sur le Banquet de Platon* (Paris: Les Belles Lettres, 1978).

Ricœur, Paul, *De l'Interprétation: Essai sur Freud* (Paris: Seuil, 1965). Trans D. Savage, *Freud and Philosophy: An Essay on Interpretation* (New Haven & London: Yale University Press, 1970).

————, *Le Conflit des interprétations: Essais d'herméneutique* (Paris: Seuil, 1969).

Trans. Don Ihde, *The Conflict of Interpretations: Essays in Hermeneutics* (Evanston: Northwestern University Press, 1974).

——, *La Métaphore vive* (Paris: Seuil, 1975). Trans. Robert Czeray, *The Rule of Metaphor: Multidisciplinary Studies of the Creation of Meaning in Language* (Toronto & Buffalo: University of Toronto Press, 1977).

——, 'The Hermeneutics of Revelation', in L. S. Mudge (ed.), *Essays on Biblical Interpretation* (London: SPCK, 1981).

——, *Soi-même comme un autre* (Paris: Seuil, 1990). Trans. Kathleen Blaney, *Oneself as Another* (Chicago & London: University of Chicago Press, 1992).

Rougemont, Denis de, *L'Amour et l'Occident* (Paris: Plon 1938; éd. definitive, 10/18, Minuit, 1972). Trans. *Love in the Western World* (New York: Pantheon Books, 1956).

——, *Les Mythes de l'amour* (Paris: Albin Michel, 1961).

Russell, B., *History of Western Philosophy* (London: Allen and Unwin, 1979).

Scott, W. (ed.), *The Song of Songs: A Symposium* (Philadelphia: The Commercial Museum, 1924).

Singer, Irving, *The Nature of love*, 3 vols (Vol. 1, *Plato to Luther*, New York: Random House, 1966; Vol. 2, *Courtly and Romantic*, Chicago: University of Chicago Press, 1984; Vol. 3, *The Modern World*, Chicago: University of Chicago Press, 1987).

Steiner, George, *Real Presences: Is There Anything in What We Say?* (London: Faber, 1989).

Taylor, Charles, *Sources of the Self: The Making of Modern Identity* (Cambridge: Cambridge University Press, 1989).

Thérèse d'Avila, *Œuvres complètes*, trans. M. Auclair (Paris: Desclée de Brouwer, 1964).

Tournay R. J., *Word of God, Song of Love: A Commentary on the Song of Songs*, trans. J. Edward Crowley (New York: Paulist Press, 1988).

Vasse, Denis, *Le Temps du désir* (Paris: Seuil, 1969).

Wagoner, Robert, *The Meanings of Love: An Introduction to the Philosophy of Love* (Westport, CT & London: Praeger, 1997).

Index